Popular Resistance in Palestine

POPULAR RESISTANCE IN PALESTINE

A History of Hope and Empowerment

Mazin B. Qumsiyeh

PlutoPress
www.plutobooks.com

First published 2011 by Pluto Press
345 Archway Road, London N6 5AA

www.plutobooks.com

Distributed in the United States of America exclusively by
Palgrave Macmillan, a division of St. Martin's Press LLC,
175 Fifth Avenue, New York, NY 10010

British Library Cataloguing in Publication Data
A catalogue record for this book is available from the British Library

ISBN   978 0 7453 3070 9   Hardback
ISBN   978 0 7453 3069 3   Paperback

Library of Congress Cataloging in Publication Data applied for

10 9 8 7 6 5 4 3

Designed and produced for Pluto Press by
Chase Publishing Services Ltd
Typeset from disk by Stanford DTP Services, Northampton, England
Simultaneously printed digitally by CPI Antony Rowe, Chippenham, UK
and Edwards Bros in the United States of America

To friends of Palestine around the world.
To all those who suffer in the causes of justice.

Contents

Preface and Acknowledgments

The subject of popular resistance is raised frequently in discussions with Palestinians and internationals of various political persuasions. Many ask about resistance because of the media's distorted emphasis on violence. Their questions indicate a lack of information in this area. Even activists may not know that their actions constitute forms of civil resistance. One young man, for instance, who was producing documentaries on Palestine and helping other young people, declared that he would 'like to do nonviolent resistance' and was rather bemused when I told him he was already doing it. Stories like this are why it is so important for us to tell others these stories in order to advance peace and freedom in Palestine.

This book is not intended as a comprehensive catalogue of civic actions for Palestine – an impossible project that would fill many volumes. Instead, we cite notable examples that focus on lessons learnt, relate them to each other and look to future actions. To the many hundreds and thousands of actions and people not included here, I hope they will write to us for inclusion on a website we plan to build.

This book is organized in 14 chapters. Chapter 1 is an introduction to the book and generally explores issues of the structure and definition of civil resistance. Chapter 2 explains that Palestinian civil resistance from its inception has overwhelmingly been about the creation of a democratic society which respects and affords equality to all. In Chapter 3, we delve deeper into the what, why and how civil resistance is practiced. The local context of civil resistance presented in Chapter 4 explains how civil resistance in Palestine relied on a wealth of Palestinian religious traditions of tolerance, respect and drawing boundaries around what is and is not permissible in conflicts. These four opening chapters are followed by chapters which detail popular resistance in different periods of history.

In Chapter 5 we look at popular resistance during Ottoman Imperial rule from the first hints of political Zionism in the 1840s to 1917. Chapter 6 chronicles the increased resistance following the qualitative leap forward in the Zionist project from the Balfour and Jules Declarations leading to Hibbet Al-Buraq in 1929 and what followed to 1935. The uprising of 1936–39 is investigated in

Chapter 7, as systemic violence entered the equation and armed and popular resistance became a staple of the Palestinian discourse for the following decades. Political paralysis ensued with the destruction of political leadership and World War II; nevertheless, acts of civil resistance continued and are described in Chapter 8. Chapter 9 cites examples of civil resistance in the period from the *nakba* of 1948 to the *naksa* of 1967. As Israel occupied the rest of Palestine in 1967, an era of one-state oppression emerged, as did resistance throughout Palestine (Chapter 10). We devote Chapter 11 to the intifada (uprising) which became known as *Intifadet Al-Hijara* (1987–91). The historical analysis closes with the Oslo years and Al-Aqsa Intifada in Chapter 12. Finally, we discuss boycotts, divestments and sanctions strategies in Chapter 13 and the book concludes with a chapter summarizing lessons learned from the 130 and more years of struggle and looks to the future.

Books, resources and other materials were supplied by Anna Baltzer, the Palestinian Academic Society for the Study of International Affairs (PASSIA), Union of Palestinian Medical Relief Committees, the Holy Land Trust, the Palestinian Center for Rapprochement between People, the Applied Research Institute of Jerusalem, Wi'am Center, Bethlehem University Turathuna Center, Badil, Holy Land Trust, among others. I am especially grateful to Sara Newton and Ruth Willats for editing the English version, and to Mary Elizabeth King for constructive input to the final version. I am also grateful to Manal Safi, Reem Helal, Sahar Qumsiyeh, George Nimr Rishmawi, Ghassan Andoni, Jad Isaac, Mubarak Awad, Jessie Chang, Lubna Masarwa, Ridgely P. Fuller and many others. I am indebted to all those and to hundreds of others who provided information and technical assistance. This book could not have been completed without much help and support, but the errors of commission and omission remain mine.

1
Introduction

Cowardice asks the question – is it safe? Expediency asks the question – is it politic? Vanity asks the question – is it popular? But conscience asks the question – is it right? And there comes a time when one must take a position that is neither safe, nor politic, nor popular; but one must take it because it is right.

Martin Luther King, Jr.[1]

Even those with good intentions misunderstand what happened in Palestine with regard to popular resistance. Jesse Jackson, Sr. once wrote an open letter to Yasser Arafat urging a strategy of nonviolence to achieve 'statehood'.[2] Similarly, in an address to the Muslim world in Cairo, President Barak Obama asked Palestinians to 'struggle for a state' by nonviolent means.[3] As well meaning as these two men are, they fail to understand the true nature of the struggle by reducing the message to a statement about the undesirability of violence on the part of an oppressed people. Both ignore the rich history of precisely such nonviolent struggle while failing to appreciate what Palestinians really want: freedom and the right of return, not a flag over a canton called a state. Though Jackson and Obama are more understanding than others in the West, right-wing individuals like Dick Cheney and Tony Blair, and neoliberals with Zionist leanings like Thomas Friedman, deliver far harsher Orientalist lectures. We also see a minimization or total ignorance among those in the West of the far more deadly violence required and exerted to achieve a Jewish state in a land that, before 1917, had a Jewish population of less than 7 percent. Is it logical that foreigners who have not experienced what we experience should ask us to adopt nonviolence in our struggle against an apartheid colonial system? Is this not more problematic when such Westerners ignore the great work accomplished by Palestinians and internationals to effect real change over the decades and without the use of arms?

As we report in this book, the reality is that popular resistance in Palestine developed indigenously, organically, naturally and beautifully. And it has accelerated in the past two decades. An internet search of 'Palestinian popular resistance' now gives over

1

8.5 million hits. This resistance was and continues to be against the Zionist goal of transforming a central part of the Arab world from a multi-ethnic and multi-religious society into a Jewish state; a goal that required: 1) support from world powers; 2) convincing, organizing and mobilizing Jews for Zionism; and 3) crushing any and all resistance from the native population. Securing international support proved to be an achievable task due to the number of Zionists in key positions in Western countries; but crushing local resistance was more difficult than anticipated. The Palestinians' refusal to be dispossessed quietly was met with increasingly harsh oppression throughout the decades. The Palestinian people rose from the ashes of each onslaught to engage in novel forms of civil resistance. After nearly 130 years of political Zionism, it is hard now to think of Palestinians without thinking of resistance. It is difficult to think of the conflict in the Holy Land without an opinion on the forms and nature of this resistance. Because of the media's conditioning in Western societies, many automatically think of armed (violent) resistance whenever the word 'resistance' is mentioned.

There has been no shortage of discussion of the conflict's history at the political level, the violence that accompanied the struggle, the accusations and counter-accusations, and so on. Many books are written in the West supporting the Zionist version of history.[4] Fewer report the Palestinian version of the same events.[5] Occasionally, new historians challenge mythologies sometimes decades after key events; we have seen this with the Israeli new historians Avi Shlaim, Ilan Pappé, Tom Segev, Simha Flapan and Hillel Cohen, who deconstructed the myths around the mass exodus of native Palestinians before, during and after the founding of Israel.

Western books portraying a positive image of Palestinian history have been appreciated, but lack the full understanding that a local Palestinian author has. Critiques of a few Western historical perspectives include: Johan Galtung's *Nonviolence and Israel/Palestine*,[6] which does a fair job showing some aspects of the period 1987–89, but suffers from ignoring the political forces at work and not analyzing the reasons behind the events he describes. The period of the 1987 intifada is included in Peter Ackerman and Jack Duvall, *A Force More Powerful: A century of nonviolent resistance* and its accompanying TV program, but again in an essentially descriptive way.[7] Another example is Mary Elizabeth King, *A Quiet Revolution: The first Palestinian intifada and nonviolent resistance*,[8] and is based on interviews with individuals who identify themselves as leaders of the Palestinian popular struggle. The book emphasizes the period of Palestinian resistance to Zionist colonization after 1987 and sets out an excellent framework for discussion. However, it was not well received in the *Journal of Palestine Studies*:

> She [King] overstates her case by allowing her methodology and convictions to color a complex reality. Steered by her convictions and her sources inside the East Jerusalem bubble, King attempts, ex post facto, to force a popular uprising characterized by a powerful blend of civil disobedience and stone throwing into the ideological straitjacket of nonviolence. It doesn't fit. This is a lamentable drawback to a book that otherwise is highly readable and admirably rich in detail.[9]

I think this is exaggerated. The work by King is very good compared to treatments like those found in Herbert Adam and Kogila Moodley.[10] More distorted accounts are found in Zionist-centric logic which assumes that actions by Palestinians, armed or unarmed, are not resistance but are illegal and that Israel reacts in order to defend its legitimate goals (albeit with its army sometime not fully 'prepared' and even 'over-reacting').[11] Yet, other Western historians go in the opposite direction and romanticize and oversimplify the Palestinians' struggle and history.[12] These books further suffer from the flaw that the authors do not read Arabic and thus cannot refer to the original data on a subject that is a struggle of an indigenous, Arabic-speaking people.

While having differing takes on history, most books document actions by governments and powerful leaders in conflicts. Fewer consider peace based on justice, human rights and international law or tell the stories of ordinary people living, adapting and struggling in extraordinary circumstances. We find little acknowledgment of the rich history and phenomenal achievements of popular resistance in Palestine. Some books written by Westerners, unfamiliar with the local language and dependent on published sources or interviews with elite Palestinians, have failed to do justice to this subject.

In addition to the wealth of academic literature, there is a torrent of negative and rather depressing news coming out of Palestine: murders, economic deprivation, torture, walls, imprisonment, home demolitions, land confiscation, corruption, denial of basic rights, lack of freedom of movement and denial of the right of return, etc. It is hard to mobilize people who are bombarded with these issues. In this book, we document and analyze the struggle by ordinary

Palestinians forced to live in unusual times since the inception of the political ideology called Zionism. Such a story changes the tone of the conversation. Stories of successes and positive achievements provide incentives for further activism. We Palestinians have no shortage of inspirational, unsung heroes.

A respected Palestinian stated about just one period in our history:

> Nonviolent resistance demands strong leaders. In the first days of the occupation in 1967, the Palestinian nonviolence movement had a surplus. A dynamic voluntary work movement sprang up under the guidance of democratically elected municipal councils. This movement created jobs, built schools, established youth clubs, and created public libraries ...[13]

Mohammed Omar Hamadeh's *A'lam Falastine: From the first to the 15th century Hijra, from the 7th to twentieth century AD* (1985) lists hundreds of inspirational Palestinian leaders, authors, intellectuals and many others. But it is hard for people to read what essentially amounts to a Palestinian *Who's Who*.[14] In this book, we summarize and analyze the rich history of popular resistance in Palestine. The book is essentially about the power of individuals working together to transform themselves and their societies, while living in exceptional and extremely difficult circumstances.

VIOLENCE AND NONVIOLENCE

The twentieth century was perhaps the bloodiest in human history, but was also a century replete with examples of popular resistance that shaped the future without resorting to violence.[15] Yet, school history books in most countries seem to give no more than cursory attention to nonviolence. Few are written about common people's struggles. And any such books are not used as school texts.[16] Violence seems ubiquitous. Laws and institutions in most countries focus on dealing with state-monopolized violence. Even some of our vocabulary evolved from wars and conflicts; many common English expressions have military origins, including 'the whole nine yards', 'clean bill of health', 'rummage sale' and 'show your true colors'. Thus, to appreciate popular resistance, we need to know something about the culture of violence in our societies.

Violence consists of actions intended to harm others on the assumption that this will help achieve a concrete result or goal. However, perceptions of what constitutes violence are highly varied.

Many individuals when confronted with examples of behaviors that hurt others will not associate them with 'violent behavior'. In societies that condone capital punishment, some individuals would not describe the act of executing a condemned person as an act of violence. Even when a society chooses to use extreme force against an opponent, its history texts do not describe the society as engaging in violence, let alone terrorism.[17] The dropping of atomic bombs on Hiroshima and Nagasaki, which killed hundreds of thousands of civilians, is justified as a 'necessary action' to bring World War II to an end.

There are two schools of thought. One proposes that violence is encoded in our genetic make-up, the other that it is a learned behavior and so can be unlearned.[18] As an evolutionary biologist and geneticist, and having examined the issue in some detail, I would contend that the answer lies somewhere between the two: that our evolutionary history gave us a blueprint for violence, altruism and collaboration, while giving us the intellectual ability to educate for or against violence in meaningful ways.

Popular resistance is far more coherent philosophically than violent resistance. Societal violence has traditionally been legitimized and legalized, while violence by non-state actors has been denounced and made illegal, giving the state a monopoly on its use. Avelar explained how strong states, like the US and Israel, have engaged in acts of war (without calling it war) in the name of law enforcement.[19] Those who engage in violent action legitimize what they do according to what they consider are 'good' means to a legitimate end. The cause of opponents is not considered legitimate and their use of violence is not justified. No party aims to establish a violent society, and those who justify the use of violence, base their argument on the justice of the ends; the ends justify the means. Whether one accepts the violent means criterion or not, it is a useful means to help achieve the ends sought. That is where the discussion mostly focuses – the issue of utility – and thus opens up violent logic to self-contradictions.

Rulers and occupiers maintain a power structure to dictate their agendas. As such, resistance typically focuses on changing the power structure. Historians can only offer examples of a mix of violent and nonviolent actions to varying degrees. Some may argue that the Algerian revolution against the French occupation resorted more to violent resistance while the Indian revolution against British colonial rule relied more on nonviolent resistance. It is impossible to come up with quantitative measures to say a revolution was 60 percent or 80 percent nonviolent. The closest we can come is, presumably, to compare the number of people killed while resisting violently with those who were killed resisting nonviolently. However, this is a subjective and highly fluid judgment; colonizers often claim they shot protesters because soldiers' or police officers' lives were at risk. We also know that, in some cases, Israeli undercover agents have thrown rocks or opened fire in demonstrations to create the pretext for shooting.[20]

The false dichotomy sometimes argued is that societies can choose to use moral methods that are ineffective, such as nonviolent resistance, or amoral methods that are effective, such as violent insurrection; but this is essentially a misleading and defeatist attitude, which ignores both the history and possibilities of humanity, while overlooking the reality that it is individuals, not societies, who make choices.[21]

In reflecting on apartheid South Africa, people in the West tend to forget that the African National Congress, led by Nelson Mandela, was a guerrilla movement fighting violently for liberation, as well as using various forms of popular resistance. Individuals who believe in violence tend to minimize the role of people like Desmond Tutu, Mahatma Gandhi and Martin Luther King, Jr., while others tend to consider them key elements of change in society. Ironically, in both situations, some argue that liberation would not have been won without violent resistance, while others argue that it could not have been won without nonviolent resistance. This is a moot point because its foundation is a hypothetical situation that has never existed. All struggles to date have used both violent and nonviolent resistance. Can we really know exactly what the tipping point was in each situation? Can we truly say what would have happened to the civil rights movement without the 'good cop' Martin Luther King, Jr. and the 'bad cop' Malcolm X? History is usually written by the victors; thus the leaders of the Algerian revolution consider that violence was the key to ending the French colonial occupation. In the transformation of the US in the 1960s, historians typically emphasize popular resistance over the influence of the Black Panthers and Malcolm X and so we find no national holidays commemorating the life and sacrifices of Malcolm X, Crazy Horse or Geronimo.

What would have happened in South Africa without Tutu's popular resistance or Mandela's more violent struggle? For that matter, can we imagine what would have happened without diversity within the oppressor population? Was President Johnson or King, or Malcolm X for that matter, critical in securing popular rights in the US? Do Israeli groups, like the Israeli Committee against Home Demolitions or B'Tselem, make a vital difference? I think the answers given by advocates in favor of the dichotomy are not that simple. But as an individual, I can make a judgment as to what I can and should do, without cursing or condemning alternative judgments. The Stanford Prison experiment shows that humans are highly influenced by circumstances. In this experiment, students were randomly assigned to play the role of prisoner or prison guard. The experiment had to be halted in a matter of days because nearly a third of the 'prison guards' started exhibiting abusive behaviors and many of the 'prisoners' began to show signs of psychological disturbance.[22]

William J. Thomson suggests a hierarchy of violence from lower (personal) to higher (societal) and suggests some trends:[23]

a) The lower in the hierarchy (e.g., physical), the more widely available is the form of violence. That is, physical violence is potentially available to almost everyone, and from numerous studies (e.g., Stanley Milgram's obedience-to-authority work) we must reluctantly conclude that almost everyone is capable of physical violence under appropriate circumstances.

b) Higher forms of violence (e.g., economic) are reserved for those with the resources to implement them.

c) In general, higher forms of violence are more likely to be successful over lower forms of violence.

d) In general, people will use the highest form of violence available to them, because it is less physically (and otherwise) dangerous, the power differentials (and likelihood of success) are greater and it is more likely to be legal.

e) This is a key point: Violence of any kind tends to elicit a violent response.

Violent tactics are often defended as unpleasant means to a 'good' end. This argument is presented by both strong and weak parties. The justness of the end justifying the means is referred to as the 'natural law' argument. Others try to justify violence in terms of the legality of the means, irrespective of the justness of the end. In such a logic, the person committing the violence must do it under a legal guise accepted by society (e.g., a soldier participating in a defensive action or a prison warden executing a prisoner sentenced to death). Their actions are judged separately from what they aim to achieve. The third option is to reject violence altogether and consider the possibility of a nonviolent response to any violence. Weaknesses and strengths can be found in each of these positions. While recognizing the appeal and necessity of popular resistance, understanding human nature does not allow us to condemn or condone those who engage in violence, especially when a community is subject to a ruthless colonial power. Yet we should be free to criticize acts of violence, or nonviolence for that matter, for it is a very different issue from criticizing its perpetrators.

In our case, violent resistance by Palestinians was used as a justification to brutalize the population, further uproot us and destroy our homes and lands both at the time of the British Mandate and after 1948. This policy took advantage of a natural reaction to colonial domination by intensifying colonial activity. Traditionally, the 'Zionist response' to injury or attacks on settlers has been to remove more Palestinians and build more settlements. Israel monopolizes the use of state power, leaving Palestinians little hope of containing the cancerous growth of colonial settlements on their land by violent methods. The exceptions are few and do not nullify that generalization. Some Palestinians state that Israel's evacuation of the Gaza Strip was due to armed resistance. This is only partly true because Israel, like any power, calculates the risks and rewards of any action. It calculated that the public relations, diplomatic and economic benefits of withdrawing settlers and soldiers from Gaza, while maintaining the occupation of Gaza by siege, far outweighed the small disadvantage of empowering those who support violent resistance. We must all be cognizant of the usual imbalance of power between the two and the fact that colonization never happens peacefully. Colonizers always use violence because it is the only way to remove people from the land, while those being colonized can choose to resist by other means. The development of state power results in wars being waged without calling them wars and dispensing violence with declaring war.[24]

There are arguments to be made on all sides. Did the scalping of European settlers by Native Americans terrorize them into leaving the land? Or did it inflame passions and enforce stereotypes of savagery which resulted in accelerated colonization? Psychological studies done on suicide bombers show that perpetrators are driven, not by nationalistic ideologies, but largely by a desire for revenge (after their homes have been demolished, relatives injured, land or jobs confiscated).[25] Ideologies such as imperialism, Zionism or Nazism held by those in positions of power obviously provided a far greater incentive to resort to violence. We do recognize that nonviolence is a possibility and it does happen that people who engage in violence later decide to abandon it. This is true both for violence that is considered legitimate in international law (resistance to colonialism and occupation) and violence considered illegitimate (occupation, ethnic cleansing, etc.).

Armed resistance by the occupied must be carried out in clandestine operations under constant threat of infiltration and liquidation by the colonizers. Thus, such resistance requires strong leaders with executive power and limited circles of consultation. Leadership cannot reasonably be assigned by popular vote and democratic structures in guerrilla institutions because of safety/security issues. The skills of managing such operations are very different from those required to manage governmental institutions by democratic means. Leadership of popular resistance can evolve organically in different directions. It can be elected democratically and its leaders generally cannot resist effectively without the widest consultation possible of those involved. This also discourages the cult of leadership. The biologically limited lifespan of a leader is insignificant compared to the more meaningful lifespan of a people and its struggle.[26]

Resistance by violent means has far more constraints and is more likely to fail than popular resistance because it requires much more logistical support (arms, etc.), secrecy, killing of armed combatants, difficulty in establishing geographic areas for armed control, and much more. This is particularly true when armed resistance has to contend with leaders from among its own people who are collaborating with the occupiers.

Another point to consider is that when resistance fails, nonviolent forms leave far less devastation (social, economic, lives lost, etc.) than armed resistance.[27] That is not to say that this form of resistance is safe. On the contrary, popular resistance can in many situations be more dangerous than armed resistance (after all, we have only our bodies and willingness to suffer). In fact, in many ways, it is reliant on willingness to suffer by people. All leaders of popular resistance when articulating thoughts on this explained how willful subjugation to suffering can itself be an empowering event and also confuses and confounds the opponents. Bishop Munib

Younan explains the concept of willingness to suffer for the cause of resistance:

> The church needs a theology of martyria. It's a concept misunderstood, misused and even missing from the vocabulary of many Christians. What does it mean to be a martyr? In a simple sense, it means no more than to be a witness. That is how it is translated [from Greek]. It means a life of witnessing in word, and also in deed. The third component is suffering. Martyria is expressed when one's faith makes one vulnerable to the suffering in this world. It means exposing yourself, risking one's life for the other.[28]

ON TERMINOLOGY

People who participate in revolutions against oppression are always diverse: some support armed resistance, some support popular resistance, some support both. There is no clear division between the three groups due to extensive overlap and subdivisions. Among those who support armed resistance, there are always arguments about what kind of violence is justified in defense of a just cause. Among those who support nonviolent resistance there are arguments about what defines it. Popular resistance can be active or passive. In the active forms there are also questions about the popular forms that do not cross the line into violent resistance. Is damaging infrastructure used for oppression violent?

Mahatma Gandhi used the Urdu word *Satyagraha* because he had a problem of vocabulary similar to that faced by Khalid Kishtainy:

> 'Nonviolence' (la 'unf' in Arabic) is not the best translation of Gandhi's 'ahimsa' in Urdu. To avoid this negative hint, we agreed on 'civilian resistance' or 'civilian struggle', but I advocate 'civilian jihad' to give it a Muslim coloring. Other writers are now using this term, and the Sudanese leader and former Prime Minister al-Sadiq al-Mahdi adopted it for his concept of nonviolence. The term was inspired by a hadith that the Prophet pronounced whenever he came back from battle: 'We return from the minor jihad to the major jihad,' meaning from military action to civilian work. The abused and misunderstood term 'jihad' does not mean 'holy war' but 'the exertion of effort'.[29]

Muqawama sha'biya, the term commonly used in Palestine, is roughly translated as popular resistance. The word *sha'biya* has its roots in *sha'b* (people) and is understood by many Palestinians to refer to the kinds of resistance practiced by large numbers of the population, as opposed to more narrow armed resistance (*muqawama musallaha*). On the other hand, we do have in common use *thawra sha'biya*, or people's revolution. When I asked 20 Palestinians on the streets of Bethlehem what they understood the difference was between *thawra sha'biya* and *muqawama sha'biya*, 14 suggested that violence is more characteristic of the former than of the latter. In English, it is more accurate to use nonviolent resistance to differentiate it from violent resistance; but the term translated literally into Arabic would be a very poor (and rather negative) description of the complex and empowering acts of popular resistance practiced in Palestine that cannot count as armed resistance. But because of the limitations of language, we shall use the term 'popular resistance' in this book.

Popular resistance is as old as humanity but key people are frequently cited as inspirational in their shedding of violence and embarking on the path of popular resistance. Mohandas Gandhi, also known by the honorific title 'Mahatma' meaning 'great soul', successfully developed and used many strategies of nonviolent resistance. He developed the concept of '*satyagraha*', a word that is derived from the Sanskrit word '*satya*' (truth) and '*graha*' (steadfastness) ('*sumud*' in Arabic). This concept involves far more than persistence in telling the truth, and is considered an active form of willingness to sacrifice oneself in order to achieve justice. *Sumud* also conjures up many images that reflect steadfastness, persistence and success in the face of difficult obstacles. It is not mere passive patience in the face of adversity, but rather an active form of popular resistance. Gandhi's other concept, '*ahimsa*', is also hard to translate (it is wrong to translate it to 'nonviolence' in the negative). In Sanskrit the concept includes a mix of love, honesty, non-aggression and peace. Gandhi recognized that there are no enemies, but only those we should challenge because of their actions that harm the people. Change of the self-proclaimed 'enemy' is the ultimate triumph of humanity and truth.

2
What We Want:
Plurality, Justice, Human Rights

I believe that wounded justice, lying prostrate on the blood-flowing streets of our nations, can be lifted from this dust of shame to reign supreme among the children of men. I have the audacity to believe that peoples everywhere can have three meals a day for their bodies, education and culture for their minds, and dignity, equality and freedom for their spirits.

Martin Luther King, Jr. [1]

The evolution of the methods and strategies of resistance in Palestine has been no different from other struggles by people facing a colonial settler population. There are many comparative studies of the struggles of the people in Palestine, Native Americans, South Africans under apartheid, Algerians under French rule, Vietnamese, and others.[2] While each historical situation is unique, we can point to similarities pertinent to our discussion of resistance. First and foremost, when history is written objectively about all these struggles, there is never any question of the right of the people being colonized to defend themselves and mount a vigorous resistance to those oppressing them.

Internationally recognized leaders of popular resistance have expressed opinions on Palestine. Martin Luther King, Jr. stated in a letter about the tripartite (France/Britain/Israel) attack on Egypt:

I have been keeping up with the situation in Egypt, and as you know this is one of the most important issues in the world today. It will determine whether we live in peace or whether we will die in war. Naturally my sympathies are with Egypt, rather than with the Western Colonial and imperial powers.[3]

King's support of oppressed people in his own country could not be separated from support of oppressed people in other places. While some tried to convince him to not push for an end to the war on Vietnam, he explicitly rejected those calls. This is the nature of activist work and the essence of thinking as a human being not in terms of narrow national, religious or other contexts. It is thus not surprising that Mohandas (Mahatma) Gandhi had a strong opinion on Palestine:

My sympathies are all with the Jews. I have known them intimately in South Africa. Some of them became life-long companions. Through these friends I came to learn much of their age-long persecution. They have been the untouchables of Christianity. The parallel between their treatment by Christians and the treatment of untouchables by Hindus is very close. Religious sanction has been invoked in both cases for the justification of the inhuman treatment meted out to them. Apart from the friendships, therefore, there is the more common universal reason for my sympathy for the Jews. But my sympathy does not blind me to the requirements of justice. The cry for the national home for the Jews does not make much appeal to me. The sanction for it is sought in the Bible and the tenacity with which the Jews have hankered after return to Palestine. Why should they not, like other peoples of the earth, make that country their home where they are born and where they earn their livelihood? Palestine belongs to the Arabs in the same sense that England belongs to the English or France to the French. It is wrong and in-human to impose the Jews on the Arabs. What is going on in Palestine today cannot be justified by any moral code of conduct. The mandates have no sanction but that of the last war. Surely it would be a crime against humanity to reduce the proud Arabs so that Palestine can be restored to the Jews partly or wholly as their national home. The nobler course would be to insist on a just treatment of the Jews wherever they are born and bred. The Jews born in France are French in precisely the same sense that Christians born in France are French. If the Jews have no home but Palestine, will they relish the idea of being forced to leave the other parts of the world in which they are settled? Or do they want a double home where they can remain at will? This cry for the national home affords a colorable justification for the German expulsion of the Jews ... And now a word to the Jews in Palestine. I have no doubt that they are going about it the wrong way. The Palestine of the Biblical conception is not a geographical tract. It is in their hearts. *But if they must look to the Palestine of geography as their national home, it is wrong to enter it under the shadow of the British gun. A religious act cannot be performed with the aid of the bayonet or the bomb. They can settle in Palestine only by*

the goodwill of the Arabs. They should seek to convert the Arab
heart. (emphasis added)[4]

This may have been true in 1938. But we have now had 70 years
of very painful history and new realities. We must project a future
where Palestine/Israel belongs to all its current inhabitants (Jews,
Christians, Muslims) in full equality. Such a resolution would not
necessarily entail full restorative justice in the sense of getting all
Palestinian properties, but must include at least partial restorative
justice, for example with generous compensation paid to those who
volunteer to relinquish some of their rights. Of the eleven million
Palestinians in the world, seven million are refugees or displaced
people. Today, the remaining Palestinians live either as tenth-class
citizens or under occupation with no citizenship on the still shrinking
reservations (less than 10 percent of historic Palestine).

The underlying cause, or what we in the medical field call the
etiology, of the conflict is not complicated as many gatekeepers in
the media and politics want us to think it is. It can be summarized in
a few sentences. The indigenous Palestinians adopted monotheistic
religions at different periods, but continued to live in a multi-
religious and multicultural milieu for over 4,000 years. Jews were
discriminated against, especially in nineteenth-century Europe when
ethnocentric nation-states were created. A minority of Western
European Jews, supported by the governments of the Great Powers
(primarily France and England, and later the US), created its own
ethnocentric nationalistic paradigm called Zionism. Other Jews
responded to discrimination by promoting humanism, assimilation
and coexistence. Zionists planned and executed a strategy to bring
those who happen to be Jewish (regardless of their ethnicity and
background) to establish a Jewish state. In a tortuous history over
many decades, the area was transformed from majority Muslim
and Christian Palestinians to having millions of Jews gathered from
around the world in a militarized and economically advanced, yet
highly unstable state. The well-organized and well-financed process
led to many wars and the creation of the largest current refugee
population in the world: two-thirds of the eleven million Palestinians
today are thus refugees or displaced people. This is the essence of
what transpired. While the details are contested, the net result of
transformation in Palestine and displacement of the natives is now
more or less uniformly agreed.

The Jewish population of Israel/Palestine grew from about
60,000 in 1917, on the eve of the Balfour Declaration, to about

5.5 million today. Landownership in the past 60 years has changed from being 93 percent Christian and Muslim to the majority currently controlled by a supranational Jewish National Fund and Israel Lands Authority, both of which service the interests of 'Jewish people everywhere'. Thus, 530 villages and towns were completely depopulated between 1947 and 1950; and in the next six decades most of the remaining Palestinian land was taken over. While native Jews have lived in Palestine for the past 2,000 years, thousands of European and Russians came to live in Palestine during the nineteenth century, either fleeing persecution or for religious reasons. This migration was not unique to non-native Jews or non-native Christians, Muslims and others. Ethiopian Christians, Persian Baha'is, Druze and others had migrated from nearby areas. A large wave of Armenian migrants also came to Palestine during the massacres and atrocities of the early twentieth century. All were welcome. But the political Zionist program aspired to establish a Jewish nation-state in Palestine that was different from the goals of other immigrants of various faiths. Its political ideas originated in the mid-nineteenth century and found fertile ground in England, materializing in 1878 with the establishment of Petah Tikveh, the first European Ashkenazi colony in Palestine. As Zionist leaders anticipated from the beginning, Palestinians were unhappy about the direction of this political movement and attempted to resist it. Yet Palestinian resistance to Zionism, from its inception in the 1880s, was not resistance to Judaism or immigrants who were non-Zionist; after all, Jews have always been part of the fabric of Palestinian society.

Israeli General and Army Chief of Staff Rafael Eitan once stated: 'When we have settled the land, all the Arabs will be able to do about it will be to scurry around like drugged cockroaches in a bottle.'[5] But the 'cockroaches' have proved themselves to be amazingly resilient. Here we are more than 130 years later and 50 percent of Palestinians still live between the River Jordan and the Mediterranean (i.e., their historic homeland). We have a solid majority of people in what was designated as Eretz Yisrael (the same geographic area) rejecting Zionism. Anti-Zionism and post-Zionism are now common themes, and not only among the 1.5 million Palestinian-Israeli citizens and the 3.5 million living under the brutal Israeli occupation. They are widespread in segments of Israeli Jewish society (the 5.5 million who are identified by the state as privileged Israeli Jews). Further, nearly half a million Israelis have voted with their feet by choosing to live in the West.

The problem thus remains: Zionism requires maximum geography for a Jewish state with minimum demography of Palestinian Christians and Muslims living in the coveted land. The solution of a Palestinian statelet in the West Bank and Gaza is increasingly recognized as a mirage promoted to defer the inevitable day of reckoning while Israel continues to create facts on the ground in the form of colonial settlements on Palestinian land. Some in Israel are engaging positively in this discussion and question the national anthem about Jewish yearning or the national symbols of being Jewish in the modern state. The schism today remains as it has for decades: not a schism between states or between people, but between ideologies (separatism vs. integration, apartheid Zionism vs. pan-Islamic nationalism vs. pluralistic democracy).

From narrow individual interest to putting the community's interest first is a big leap. Historical experimentation, from ethnic nationalism to empires, obviously failed to prevent suffering and war. My prediction is that the twenty-first century is likely to witness the most intense struggle between local democracy combined with a humanistic globalization and globalized military-industrial hegemony combined with ethnocentric nationalist tendencies. I believe the former will ultimately win; if the latter wins, there will be no one left to celebrate the victory.

In Palestine peace could be achieved based on international law and the basic tenets of human rights. Some would argue that the 2002 'road map to peace', the two-state solution, needs to be implemented and Palestinians and Israelis should be forced to comply. The road map has some good elements (e.g., requiring Israel to freeze all settlement building, including natural growth in all the occupied territories); but remarkably, in 2,218 words, it fails to mention or address international law and human rights. Further, Israel has the fifth strongest military in the world with hundreds of nuclear, chemical and biological weapons, etc., while Palestinians are occupied, colonized people with few resources at their disposal. 'Negotiations' in such a situation are predicted to yield few fair resolutions. A real 'road map to peace' would be based on the Universal Declaration of Human Rights.

Amnesty International has articulated ten principles for a lasting peace based on human rights:[6]

1. Everybody has the right to life, liberty and security of person ...
2. No one should be subjected to torture or to cruel, inhuman or degrading treatment or punishment ...

3. No one should be subjected to arbitrary arrest and detention …
4. Everyone has the right to a fair trial …
5. All persons are free and equal in dignity and rights …
6. Everyone has the right to freedom of movement …
7. Everyone has the right to return to his or her country …
8. Everyone has the right to freedom of thought, opinion and expression …
9. Women have the right to full equality …
10. There should be no impunity for human rights abuses.

The African National Congress Charter provides a good model with universal appeal, which can be adopted in dealing with the question of Palestine/Israel.[7] Combining human rights with a struggle against apartheid offers a better road map to peace.[8]

Palestinian Civil Society Calls for Boycott, Divestment and Sanctions against Israel until it Complies with International Law and the Universal Principles of Human Rights

July 9, 2005
One year after the historic Advisory Opinion of the International Court of Justice (ICJ) which found Israel's Wall built on occupied Palestinian territory to be illegal, Israel continues its construction of the colonial Wall with total disregard of the Court's decision. Thirty-eight years into Israel's occupation of the Palestinian West Bank (including East Jerusalem), Gaza Strip and the Syrian Golan Heights, Israel continues to expand Jewish colonies. It has unilaterally annexed occupied East Jerusalem and the Golan Heights and is now *de facto* annexing large parts of the West Bank by means of the Wall. Israel is also preparing – in the shadow of its planned redeployment from the Gaza Strip – to build and expand colonies in the West Bank. Fifty-seven years after the state of Israel was built mainly on land ethnically cleansed of its Palestinian owners, a majority of Palestinians are refugees, most of whom are stateless. Moreover, Israel's entrenched system of racial discrimination against its own Arab-Palestinian citizens remains intact.
   In light of Israel's persistent violations of international law, and
   Given that, since 1948, hundreds of UN resolutions have condemned Israel's colonial and discriminatory policies as illegal and called for immediate, adequate and effective remedies, and

▶

Given that all forms of international intervention and peace-making have until now failed to convince or force Israel to comply with humanitarian law, to respect fundamental human rights and to end its occupation and oppression of the people of Palestine, and

In view of the fact that people of conscience in the international community have historically shouldered the moral responsibility to fight injustice, as exemplified in the struggle to abolish apartheid in South Africa through diverse forms of boycott, divestment and sanctions;

Inspired by the struggle of South Africans against apartheid and in the spirit of international solidarity, moral consistency and resistance to injustice and oppression,

We, representatives of Palestinian civil society, call upon international civil society organizations and people of conscience all over the world to impose broad boycotts and implement divestment initiatives against Israel similar to those applied to South Africa in the apartheid era. We appeal to you to pressure your respective states to impose embargoes and sanctions against Israel. We also invite conscientious Israelis to support this Call, for the sake of justice and genuine peace.

These nonviolent punitive measures should be maintained until Israel meets its obligation to recognize the Palestinian people's inalienable right to self-determination and fully complies with the precepts of international law by:

1. Ending its occupation and colonization of all Arab lands and dismantling the Wall;
2. Recognizing the fundamental rights of the Arab-Palestinian citizens of Israel to full equality; and
3. Respecting, protecting and promoting the rights of Palestinian refugees to return to their homes and properties as stipulated in UN resolution 194.

Endorsed by:

The Palestinian political parties, unions, associations, coalitions and organizations below represent the three integral parts of the people of Palestine: Palestinian refugees, Palestinians under occupation and Palestinian citizens of Israel.

It is in fact impossible to envisage a peace that would work without human rights.[9] Such a malformed structure was sadly attempted via the agreements signed between Israel and the PLO in Oslo, Geneva and beyond. These agreements disregard basic human rights, including those enshrined in the Fourth Geneva Conventions (refugee rights, illegal settlement activities, collective punishment). It is essential for success in future peace agreements to ensure respect for human rights and international law. As we shall see, most popular resistance efforts in Palestine in the past 130+ years have had similar goals of achieving justice, peace and full democracy for people regardless of their religion. Some have occasionally strayed from these paths and conflicts generate oddities and hatred on all sides; it is notable that Palestinians who engage in popular resistance have called for a representative democracy in all of Palestine from the late nineteenth century to the present day.

More limited and clearer goals have been now articulated in the Palestinian Civil Society Call to Action, issued on July 9, 2005. This should be a signpost for all those who want to engage in popular resistance, whether in Palestine or elsewhere.

3
The Logic of Popular Resistance

Whereas it is essential, if man is not to be compelled to have recourse, as a last resort, to rebellion against tyranny and oppression, that human rights should be protected by the rule of law.

Preamble to the Universal Declaration of Human Rights[1]

Anyone objectively examining the Palestine situation, and others like it, will recognize that there are no examples of completely nonviolent struggle for freedom from colonial occupation. The struggles against the communist regimes in Eastern Europe came very close, but obviously that was merely an internal struggle over political control between those loyal to the Soviet Union and the larger number of people opposed at a time the Soviet Union was disintegrating. Neither Mahatma Gandhi's India nor Martin Luther King, Jr.'s United States was free of violent resistance. Violent and nonviolent resistance coexisted in Algeria under French rule and in South Africa under apartheid. Furthermore, the right of resistance is internationally recognized and supported by binding instruments of international law.[2] Article 3 of the 1949 Geneva Convention states that the occupying army must equally treat those who engage in rebellion and those who do not as protected under the Convention. Other articles recognize the right of resistance to an occupying army. According to Foda:

> The occupying country cannot take actions against ... protected person simply for engaging in resistance. The rules stem from the fact that International law recognizes occupation authorities as *de facto* authorities not *de jure* authorities and as such the occupied people do not have to obey rules and laws instituted by the occupation authorities.[3]

The Israeli author Hans Lebrecht wrote and translated from Hebrew the following passage from his book *The Palestinians – Past and Present*:

According to international law, the people of a country, occupied by a foreign power, has the full right to fight for their liberation ... This right is based, among other reasons, also upon the guiding lines set for the International Tribunal in Nuremberg, which, after World War II, had been established to judge the main Nazi criminals ... The statutory argument in article 2 of the indictments (concerning transgressions against the laws on conducts of war) at the Nuremberg Tribunal was based upon the Hague International Convention of 1907. Article 6(b) of the Tribunal's rules relies upon articles 1 and 2 of the accompanying letters of the said Hague Convention, which particularly lay down the right to popular resistance against military occupation, within the occupied territories themselves, as well as outside them ... This determination was, at the time, important to forestall any claim by the Nazis that the partisans, ghetto fighters, and other underground resistance forces in the territories occupied by them had allegedly been bandits and terrorists.[4]

Mahatma Gandhi stated:

Where there is only a choice between cowardice and violence, I would advise violence ... but I believe that nonviolence is infinitely superior to violence.[5]

Of course, one must realize that while international law does sanction violent resistance, nonviolent resistance can be and is practiced in all struggles. In fact, I cannot think of a single historical precedent where the struggle for rights was waged solely by violent means or solely by nonviolent means. It seems that the history of human struggle is a mix of both to varying degrees. In retrospect, societies that change will naturally choose to emphasize the positive elements. In retrospect, we find that there are more successes among societies that use predominantly nonviolent and popular struggle than those that use predominantly armed struggle. And after the victory, the predominant form is celebrated. Thus, in the US, Martin Luther King, Jr. and others who struggled nonviolently were far more positively regarded than Malcolm X and the Black Panthers. The occupied people do have choices and do make them individually and collectively in the manner, timing and logic of their resistance. Faisal Al-Husseini told Mary Elizabeth King in 1989:

When there is an occupation, people have the right to fight it by any means when they can, including the armed struggle. But it is not a must. If it is necessary, it can be used at a certain period, but it is not an end in itself. I believe that at this stage, other means will work better. I am not saying we should renounce the armed struggle, but now we are not using it. The armed struggle is only part of the political struggle.[6]

Many believe that nonviolent resistance and solidarity explain in part the much less violent post-revolutionary success in South Africa as compared to Algeria. But we must also recognize that the world is more complex than our wishes and desires; ultimately, it is what we choose to emphasize that shapes our actions as well as our inactions. Just as saying there is only one way to cure a disease, so statements such as 'violence is the only way' or 'nonviolence is the only way' are too absolutist to be true. Overall, there is more tolerance among those who promote popular resistance because those who engage in it believe it is possible to change the behavior of their (violent) opponents by peaceful means. Nonviolent advocates thus understand better those who engage in violence than those who engage in violence understand those in nonviolent struggle. This does not mean there is little diversity in the two camps. Among those who back violence, there are always arguments about what kinds of violence are justified and among those who support nonviolence there are arguments about what exactly qualifies as nonviolence. For those of us in the nonviolence camp, it is always encouraging to note rare deserters from the popular resistance camp while more and more combatants lay down their arms to join popular nonviolent resistance.[7]

Popular resistance can challenge colonial occupation and unjust leaders. If these leaders come from the same group, they are usually interested in maintaining their power so their policies are a little more flexible than under colonial occupation. There are many examples of dictatorial leaders adapting their policies in the face of popular pressure, and the leeway of change has been used frequently. Gandhi was inspired by the mass demonstrations against the Russian Tsar in 1905. In 1999, while the PLO leader Yasser Arafat was engaged in negotiations with Israeli leaders, a mass movement mobilized to put pressure on the Palestinian negotiators not to cede the right of refugees to return. I was involved in a movement that collected, over a period of ten months, more than 800,000 signatures (the majority Palestinian) in affirmation of the rights of refugees. Arafat did not agree at the Camp David negotiations in 2000 to renounce that right. Several of his confidants stated publicly that they were aware of how significant this issue is to Palestinians in general. The basic assumption of this kind of grassroots activism is that it is possible for individuals to effect social change. In an influential essay titled 'Civil disobedience', the American Henry David Thoreau argued convincingly why one should engage in active civil disobedience to abolish slavery and end wars. The essay, like Gandhi's examples, should be read by anyone interested in understanding the duty of one human to another in any situation of injustice.[8] One of the main leaders of the civil rights movement in the US, Martin Luther King, Jr., highlighted the importance of Thoreau's essay in his autobiography:

> During my student days I read Henry David Thoreau's essay 'On Civil Disobedience' for the first time. Here, in this courageous New Englander's refusal to pay his taxes and his choice of jail rather than support a war that would spread slavery's territory into Mexico, I made my first contact with the theory of nonviolent resistance. Fascinated by the idea of refusing to cooperate with an evil system, I was so deeply moved that I reread the work several times.[9]

In Oriental martial arts, the first lesson in self-defense is not to meet the power of your opponent with power, but to deflect that power and make it meaningless. Nonviolence in many ways attempts to do just that. Power only works when the population accepts it as a means of control. Acts of non-cooperation, civil disobedience and deflecting power can make the opponent lose balance, just as the act of engaging in nonviolent resistance immediately reveals that the power structure has failed. Beyond that, it can accomplish a great deal, including but not limited to the following:[10]

- It can reduce the human resources that the rulers call on.
- It can deny knowledge and expertise.
- It can deny material resources (taxes, etc.).
- It can increase the costs (in terms of material and people) to the rulers of maintaining the system of oppression.

I believe that civil resistance's greatest advantage is its ability to recruit and transform a large pool of people, thereby making a significant impact on society. Popular resistance can even recruit large segments of the international community (as we shall see later with the International Solidarity Movement). As Jonathan Kuttab and Mubarak Awad wrote:

> Those who support occupation and its crimes must be shamed and challenged everywhere. This creates a worldwide arena for a nonviolent struggle based on morality and international law. South Africa's apartheid regime faced such a fight and ultimately collapsed. Israel is far more vulnerable because it is highly dependent on the rest of the world, particularly Europe and the United States, and cannot afford to ignore these voices.[11]

Persuading others to become active in popular resistance begins by convincing them that activists do make a difference. History is full of examples of unjust practices giving way to grassroots efforts. The use of strikes is a very successful example of nonviolent resistance that spread across Europe during the industrial revolution in the nineteenth century and is still practiced today. As people moved from working on family farms and in individual skilled labor to working in factories, organization of the labor force became natural. Workers could strike and shut down factories until the owners or government agreed to improve their working conditions or pay them more. Use of nonviolence historically has been the more dominant force of both individuals and society, but unfortunately most people are unaware of the extent of its use or what it has achieved. Even at the individual level, from birth to death, we see the use of nonviolent methods. Individually, this ranges from a baby crying for attention and food, to adults complaining, pleading or requesting change to redress small injustices in rights or privileges. At the social level we find examples, as when the citizens of Rome left the city in 494 BC and stayed in the mountains until the nobles and senators agreed to negotiate their just demands.[12] German forces admitted after the World War II that nonviolent resistance in occupied areas had a significantly greater impact on their operations than violent resistance.[13]

Here are six more examples, among hundreds, where grassroots work made a difference:

- Against British occupation of India (Mahatma Gandhi and others in the 1930s and 1940s).
- Against racial discrimination in the US (the civil rights movement).

- Against the war in Vietnam in the 1960s in the US.
- Against apartheid in South Africa (both within South Africa and outside, e.g., in the US especially in the 1980s with boycott campaigns).
- Against preparations for nuclear war (in Europe and the US in the 1970s and 1980s).
- Against the continued division of Germany and Soviet control of East Germany resulting in the collapse of the Berlin Wall.

INDIVIDUAL AND SOCIAL FORCES OF POPULAR RESISTANCE

Several years ago a prominent person in the Palestinian right to return movement repeatedly criticized Edward Said (then at Columbia University) for 'self-interest'. While some are tempted to dismiss such comments, self-interest, self-sacrifice and collective work are worth examining when looking at what makes activists 'tick'. A better understanding of what makes us do things could help us involve more people in the movement for peace and justice and remain active, even after setbacks and challenges. Said was a brilliant professor of literature, a prominent music critic and a noted commentator on human conditions. My background is in evolutionary biology, including genetics and behavioral biology; I thought it worthwhile to comment on motivations for popular resistance, especially in light of so-called self-interest. It is unnecessary, for the sake of this discussion, to review the exhaustive literature on the evolution of social behavior. We do know that every individual has basic needs that are easily recognized: water, food, shelter, safety, social interaction and sex. In many parts of the world with limited technological development, people still have to focus on their day-to-day survival needs (scavenging for food, finding shelter, etc.). In technologically advanced societies, we still find such people in our ranks – among the homeless in towns and cities around Europe and North America. But even when basic survival needs are met, we recognize that it is very hard to live without social interaction; hence, solitary confinement is a much feared punishment. Lack of social interaction is known to depress the immune system, cause extreme behavioral change and lead to premature death.

Humans have concepts of self-sacrifice, collective work and the common good. Other animal societies (e.g., ants, bees, elephants) exhibit many of these features, but *Homo sapiens* has complex communication systems, ponders its existence, reflects on life after death and has evolved a set of moral standards unparalleled in the animal kingdom. Why have human societies developed such amazing individual forms of complex behaviors that involve such acts as standing in front of a bulldozer attempting to demolish a house of someone totally unrelated to you (as Rachel Corrie did)? Such behaviors call for deeper explanations that, as a result of their personal nature, are very hard to analyze objectively or rationally.

Could one argue that Mother Teresa or Mahatma Gandhi were driven by a pure form of self-sacrifice and altruism or by what we may term as enlightened self-interest? Are these distinguishable? Mother Teresa's diaries, which she did not want published, upset many of her supporters, who were shocked to learn that throughout a life of doing good for others, she had doubts about many things (even the existence of God). Yet, this simple woman epitomizes love of the poor more than we can imagine. Such love should be our starting point when discussing sacrifice and enlightened self-interest. Love between a child and a parent involves significant sacrifice and may be the easiest to understand in linking biology (genetic relationship), learned behaviors and perhaps much more. In ancient China, children would sometimes even cut off their own flesh to feed an ailing or starving parent. Caring for immediate family members is biologically ingrained for the obvious reason that they share our genes. But human intellectual and social development produces other traits that sometimes overcome biological 'hardwiring'. Examples such as love and sacrifice for adopted children or people who donate to the point of impoverishing themselves to help children in distant countries are not easily explained by biology. The love of couples for each other also cannot be reduced to biological or even social needs. Caring for each other by people living on communal farms far exceeds their needs or desires; it is something much more profound and much less readily analyzed than mere language or logic can describe.

Nonviolence not only throws the opponent off-balance and undermines his authority, but it gives him the opportunity to leave the oppressive behavior in a dignified manner. The goal of gaining maximum participation is important; so rulers and occupiers who see the number of people who admire them shrinking re-evaluate their position, due to a natural biological need to be admired and respected. No one is immune. No one is so callous as to be totally unaffected by the behavior of others. We know that even the cruelest Nazi soldiers sometimes modified their behavior. We know that soldiers who witness or participate in atrocities are left psychologically scarred. The tens of thousands of US veterans of the war in Vietnam provide an excellent case study, as do the Israeli soldiers involved in the atrocities of 1948 or in the invasion and atrocities in Lebanon in 1982.[14]

Religion is sometimes a motivating or call-up factor as well. The American Clarence Jordan was raised as a privileged white man in the segregated South in the 1940s and 1950s. His study of ancient languages and the teachings of Jesus transformed him. His faith led him to challenge the clergy in the South and to establish Koinonia farms in Georgia, where blacks and whites lived and worked together. They were frequently firebombed and attacked, but they never gave up. When I listen to tapes of his sermons and speeches, I am impressed by his optimism and belief in goodness. His vision was validated while he lived and after he died; Habitats for Humanity was founded at Koinonia farms.

Thinking about future generations and working on behalf of them is not restricted to religious people seeking to secure a place in heaven; it is also found among atheists, agnostics, communists and others. It is an innate human characteristic. Who would see a child fall and not step in to help? The Arab proverb 'They planted and we eat, we plant so that they eat' explains our responsibility to future generations.

This reflection also makes me think of Dorothy Day ('my job is to comfort the afflicted and make the comfortable less comfortable'), Martin Luther King, Jr. (his vehement rejection of war is forgotten by a government that names streets after him), Desmond Tutu, Mahatma Gandhi, Sheikh Mohammad Hussein, Father Naim Ateek, Abouna Hanna Atallah, Father Elias Chacour and countless others. A while back I started compiling a list of names of people we honor on my website,[15] but that is an endless task since there are literally millions of people, most of whom we have never heard of. Yet even that task would be quite simple compared to the task of understanding what inspired them. When Rosa Parks, a black woman, refused to give up her bus seat to a white man in Montgomery, Alabama in 1955 and was arrested for violating a racist ordinance, she set in motion a chain of events that led to a total boycott of the public bus system there. The civil rights movement, which escalated in the 1950s and 1960s, led to dramatic change in the structure of American society.

Human societies evolved in spite of sometimes incredible odds precisely because of such thoughtful, committed, loving people. Howard Zinn's *A People's History of the United States* gives many examples from the history of just one country.[16] This history, and others like it, shows that pure, individual altruism is hard to come by, but enlightened self-interest (ESI) was critical in key developments. ESI drove abolitionists to save thousands of slaves before the American civil war. Reconciliation after the civil war is another example. ESI was also responsible for gaining women's right to vote in the 1920s. ESI got us the 40-hour week and other workers' rights. ESI is what ended the war in Vietnam and 30 years of US support for apartheid South Africa. None of this was done by people who claimed their actions were exclusively altruistic.

We can explain ESI in terms of a nagging conscience, morality, religion, logic, psychological hedonism or any combination of these, but we cannot deny its existence or widespread impact on human history. I have spoken with people who believe that Jesus was the Son of God, those who think of him as a prophet of God and those who don't believe in God. All agree that Jesus lived and gave of himself for humanity even as they differ on what his message was or the extent of his impact on human history. We can cite religious reasons for doing good even at the expense of our material wellbeing (this is also enlightened self-interest if we think of ourselves as vessels and tools of God). We can cite moral or other reasons, such as a livable and humane society for helping others even if we are not religious. But we can also cite genetic and behavioral studies to show that self-sacrifice for the group is a trait that exists and evolves in mammalian societies. My son did a computer simulation with random mutations and noted that group behaviors evolved that, surprisingly, included altruism and self-sacrifice. There are many ways of looking at these issues, but something deeply personal and at the core of our humanity urges us not to harm others but to help them, even when there is a direct cost to ourselves.

We do not need to look beyond our own experiences to confirm this. We can think of individuals we most admire and reflect on their qualities, especially in terms of positive motivation for social activism. For me it was an uncle, the first zoologist in Palestine and who was killed in 1970 just after he completed his PhD (after he had already made significant scientific and other contributions to humanity). His letters and motivation to help, not just his relatives, but humanity as a whole made a difference in my own life. I am sure each of us knows someone like that.

Engaging in nonviolent resistance is just as risky (sometimes more risky) than engaging in violent resistance. Countless Palestinians were killed while engaging in nonviolent resistance. Even an

American student, Rachel Corrie, was killed standing in front of a bulldozer (this is an unusual case; Palestinians are killed frequently). Under colonial occupation, people are killed, injured and jailed who are not resisting, other than by being on the coveted land; this can be considered a form of nonviolent resistance. Thousands of Palestinian civilians have been killed and tens of thousands injured over the past few decades for simply being Palestinian in Palestine. Over 650,000 Palestinians – 40 percent of the male population in the occupied territories – have experienced Israeli detention at some point. Every Palestinian has a story of oppression to tell beyond the issue of killing, injuring and unjust imprisonment. For example, over 5,000 homes were demolished in the past seven years alone and hundreds of Palestinians died as a result of being denied healthcare. What is surprising is not the extent of the violent resistance, but the extent of steadfastness and nonviolent resistance among Palestinians. After all, the first suicide bombing was in April 1994, over 100 years after the start of the Zionist colonization program. Further, that suicide bombing occurred 40 days after an Israeli colonial settler (an American) entered a mosque in Hebron and killed 29 Palestinians, including children, and injured many others. The Israeli government responded by punishing not the racist settler movement, but the Palestinians in Hebron, which resulted in further ethnic cleansing and economic devastation to make life more comfortable for the racist Jewish settlers. Yahya Ayyash, a leading Hamas bomb-maker killed in 1996, was quoted as saying that 'martyrdom bombings' were adopted to 'make the Israeli occupation that much more expensive in human lives, that much more unbearable'.[17] Popular resistance in Palestine, though effective, also faces a brutal response.[18]

To those who believe in it, popular resistance is superior on both moral and utilitarian grounds. We believe violence is not easily defensible on utilitarian grounds because it breeds more violence and is usually counterproductive. Violence to defeat the opponent is a zero-sum game and generates opposition and, even if 'successful', can create traumatic post-conflict situations that are very difficult to overcome (compare Algeria after liberation from French colonialism). But also in terms of morality, violence creates the kind of society that we all think of as amoral. Popular resistance, as we shall see from the hundreds of examples cited in the following chapters, gives those who engage in it a level of humanity that inspires and mobilizes others to act.

4
The Local Context of Popular Resistance

We are accustomed to believing, outside Israel, that the Arabs are all desert savages, people like donkeys, and that they neither see nor understand what is happening around them. But that is a great mistake.

Asher Ginsberg (Ahad Ha'Am), 1893[1]

Popular resistance in Palestine is a movement of direct action intended to accomplish what other similar movements have done before:

1. Pressuring opponents to understand the injustice that they engage in.
2. Weakening the grip of opponents on power.
3. Strengthening the community, including forms of empowerment and steadfastness (*sumud* in Arabic).
4. Bolstering the ability to withstand injustice and do something about it (a positive, can-do attitude is challenging with any other technique).
5. Building self-sufficiency and improving standards of living.
6. Achieving justice, including the right to return and self-determination.

In Palestine, resistance is made up of popular resistance (strikes, demonstrations, etc.), organized resistance in the form of committees and political movements for self-determination, and building economic and social self-sufficiency and independence in all spheres of life.[2] These forms of popular resistance are supported by local religious and philosophical traditions that go back hundreds of years. It could be argued that the most renowned and earliest philosopher of popular resistance in Palestine was Jesus. He was born in Palestine and spoke Aramaic, a Semitic language that gave rise to the Arabic alphabet and most modern Arabic. He articulated a vision that was different from the Old Testament notion of an 'eye for an eye'. He was executed for engaging in nonviolent resistance to a colonial power. He spoke very clearly, telling all who would listen:

> Blessed are the meek, for they shall inherit the earth. Blessed are those who hunger and thirst for righteousness, for they shall be satisfied. Blessed are the merciful, for they shall receive mercy. Blessed are the pure in heart, for they shall see God. Blessed are the peacemakers, for they shall be called sons of God. Blessed are those who have been persecuted for the sake of righteousness, for theirs is the kingdom of heaven. (Matthew 5:5–10)

> You have heard it said, 'an eye for an eye and a tooth for a tooth'. But I say to you, do not resist him who is evil; but whoever slaps you on your right cheek, turn to him the other also. (Matthew 5:38–9)

> You have heard it said, 'love your neighbor and hate your enemy'. But I say to you, love your enemies, bless those who curse you, do good to those who hate you, and pray for those who spitefully use you and persecute you, that you may be sons of your Father in heaven. (Matthew 5:44–5)

When Jesus was crucified he was not being passive or submitting to injustice. He could have avoided his fate, but chose to show a better way to resist and reach out. Self-sacrifice is the key for the ideas to win. His nonviolent resistance was far more successful than anyone in his period ever dreamt of. Now nearly two billion people call Christianity their religion, and a further 1.5 billion follow Islam, a derivative religion that venerates Jesus. Thus, a message believed by over half the world's population started with sermons like the Sermon on the Mount, where we were told to love those who do us harm and that the meek shall inherit the earth.

Islam emerged in the seventh century as an Abrahamic religion of justice. The Prophet Muhammad traveled a number of times to Bilad Al-Sham (Greater Syria, which includes Palestine) and was very familiar with the religious traditions that preceded him. The Qur'an makes a number of references to events in the Holy Land and venerates all previous prophets, giving Jesus the greatest importance. It is a religion that completes rather than competes with other monotheistic traditions. It demands of its followers action to repair the state of the world (essentially mirroring the Tikkun Olam concept of Judaism or Jesus' concept of active involvement for justice and mercy). Muslims looked to Jerusalem as the first direction of prayer and consider the Haram Al-Sharif (the Al-Aqsa mosque) in Jerusalem to be the third holiest site in Islam (after those in Mecca and Medina). The first regions to join the fold of Islam did so not after armed conquest but through nonviolent, direct persuasion and discussion. There was no compulsion to adopt the new religion but many did because they found it fitted their worldview and was more unifying than their previous beliefs. Nearly half of the Canaanite inhabitants of Palestine adopted Islam

---

Palestinian Bishop Munib Younan: The Church Views Occupation as Violence[3]

The church views the occupation itself as violence against the Palestinian people, violence that takes many forms. There is daily physical violence inflicted by Israeli soldiers 'to keep order', as they say: the shelling, the shootings, the beatings.

There is emotional violence when soldiers daily humiliate grown men and women at checkpoints, forcing them to their knees, abusing them with words of hatred and stripping away their human dignity. There is violence in the denial of basic human rights like water, homes and healthcare.

There is the violence of terror. When Israeli helicopters shelled the town of Beit Jala, the children were left with psychological problems: 'Mommy, will they shell us again tonight? If I go to sleep, will I wake up again?' Every time these children hear the sound of a helicopter, they tremble because of the possibility that shelling may resume.

There is economic violence as closures prevent people from going to work and force them to live on an average of two dollars a day in poverty. UNRWA [United Nations Relief and Works Agency] estimates 60 percent current unemployment and two-thirds of the population living on less than two dollars a day. They do not have the income of their land. They are forbidden to harvest their crops, and their lifelong investments of property are destroyed.

And there is violence of the word. Every day, the media portray the Palestinian people as a violent people who only want to cause trouble. They are described as parents who send their children purposely into the line of fire. To the world, Palestinians are seen as terrorists. They are not portrayed as real human beings. Those who misuse words also must be held accountable for this violence.

not as a new religion, but as an extension of their existing religions (Judaism and Christianity). But a significant number remained true to their traditions. The notion of civilian struggle was strengthened in our area by the philosophies and religious practices of the natives. Christians, Muslims and Jews lived in relative harmony for centuries until the crusaders came and later Zionism.

Islam is consistent with the principles of human rights and universal justice, and with popular resistance to tyranny.[4] The true Muslim seeks peace with God and fellow men, with God by total submission to His will because He is the source of all goodness and purity and with man by doing good and spreading good deeds. The Muslim greeting (like that of other monotheistic religions) is *asalamu alaykum* (peace be upon you), from the Qur'an 10:10: 'Wa Tahiyatuhum fiha salam' (their greetings contain peace). Heaven is described as a place where no ill is spoken, only the word of peace (Qur'an 19:62). We are reminded again that 'Allah calls you to the abode of peace' (Qur'an 10:25). And the faithful are enjoined to use peace: 'The worshippers of the merciful [God] who walk the earth lightly if addressed by the ignorant will say peace' (25:63). God himself dislikes those who start wars and conflicts: 'Every time they light a fire for war, Allah puts it out and they spread corruption in the land and Allah does not like the corrupt [people]' (Qur'an 5:64). But Islam is not passive:

> O you who believe! Stand out firmly for justice, as witnesses to Allah [God], even as against yourselves, or your parents, or your kin, and whether it be [against] rich or poor: for Allah can best protect both. Follow not the lusts [of your hearts], lest you swerve, and if you distort [justice] or decline to do justice, verily Allah is well acquainted with all that you do. (Qur'an 4:135)

These and other verses emphasize the need for action to achieve justice and that violence is to be used only in self-defense.[5] And in the *Hadith* (sayings and doings of the Prophet Muhammad, peace be upon him) we find:

> Whoever among you sees something abominable should rectify it with his hand; and if he is not able to do so; then he should do it with his tongue; and if is not able to do so, then he should [abhor it] from his heart, and that is the least of faith.[6]

As in Christianity, Islam does not encourage us to hate those who do evil but to hate their evil deeds. Love your enemies does not mean loving their acts of injustice. The believers are those who dislike evil deeds (*yakrah al-munker*) and not evil-doers (*al-munkireen*). In other religions (Buddhism, Judaism, etc.) you find similar sayings. The tradition of Mahatma Gandhi and other active pacifists states the same: challenge wrong deeds but leave the option and the door open for those who do wrong. As Awad and Said write: 'In the *Hadith* it is said, "a true Muslim is one whose tongue and hands bear no violence and a perfect Mujahid is he who has given up those that are prohibited by God". Jihad is an effort; a striving for justice and truth that need not be violent.'[7]

The Qur'an is quite explicit on when violence can be used: 'And fight in the way of Allah those who fight you and do not transgress for Allah does not like those who transgress' (190:2). Violence is to be used only in self-defense in godly ways and it has its limits: justice without hurting non-combatants, especially women, children and older men, and extends to not even damaging trees or crops in the land of the enemy. It is also enjoined to seek peace if the opponent agrees to seek peace: 'If they lean to peace so you lean to peace and rely on Allah for He is the all-hearing and the all-knowing' (8:61).[8] Advocacy for nonviolence in Islam finds backing in the statements of the Prophet in the first ten years of spreading Islam strictly by conversations and discussions, resorting to force only when attacked.[9] Mohammed Abu-Nimr further explains:

There is a complete compatibility between such methods of nonviolence and Islamic values and beliefs which instruct the faithful to resist injustice, oppression, pursue justice and *sabr* (patience), protect the sacredness of human dignity, and be willing to sacrifice their lives for this cause. To fulfill and follow these values, the Islamic approach to nonviolence can only be based on active rejection and resistance of '*zulm*' (aggression) and injustice ... There are many examples in which we can illustrate the use of nonviolent methods in Islamic history and context. Probably the best known example is the 13 years of nonviolent struggle and resistance of the Prophet (PBUH) in the Meccan context. No single violent act or expression was used or even legitimized by the Prophet or his early followers. Muslims were not passive and they did not surrender to their fate, on the contrary they preached their message and faith and confronted non-believers on a daily basis.[10]

In the Islamic and Arabic world, popular resistance has thus become well established. One of Gandhi's colleagues in the Indian subcontinent was a Muslim named Abdel Ghaffar Khan. In the 1920s and 1930s, Khan established his army of nonviolent resisters among the Muslims of Peshawar. They had a unique uniform, discipline and totally nonviolent methods. Yet in one demonstration alone, the British forces opened fire, killing hundreds of them.[11]

In Egypt on November 11, 1918, Saad Zaghloul and other grassroots leaders asked the new British occupation forces to permit the development of an Egyptian leadership with a view to independence. When this was rejected, these leaders collected over two million signatures which endorsed a new leadership anyway. The British responded by arresting the leaders and this led to general strikes and demonstrations. The disturbances accelerated in 1919 and continued until 1922 when the British allowed the formation of an Egyptian government, albeit ruled by a monarch subservient to British interests.[12]

In Iraq in 1948, behind-the-scenes British deals with a quisling Iraqi leadership for permanent military bases were leaked and mass demonstrations ensued. In one day (January 26, 1948) over 100 peaceful demonstrators were gunned down in Baghdad. The demonstrations succeeded in scuttling the agreements, but the government compensated by instituting more dictatorial powers to prevent the recurrence of popular unrest.[13]

As we shall see, Palestinian Christians and Muslims drew heavily on these traditions of active popular resistance. For example, in the 1987–91 uprising, mosques, as well as churches, were centers for organizing activism and mobilizing people for popular struggle.[14] A good example came after the massacre of 17 Palestinian laborers in Rishon Lezion by an Israeli soldier when the unified leadership called for a day of fasting. In one town (Beit Sahour), the local imam sat to the left of the pulpit in the mosque while the local priest sat to the right. All around them, people sat in silence observing the fast. At the end of the day, they all walked to the nearby Greek Orthodox church.[15]

5
Popular Resistance during Ottoman Rule

Jews lived as fellow Ottomans loved by all Ottoman sections ... they lived in the same neighborhoods and all children of the society went to the same schools but the Zionists put an end to all that and prohibited any mixing between Jews and local residents. And they boycotted the Arabic language and the Arab merchants and announced their intention to wrest the country from the hands of its residents.[1]

Except for very brief periods, the Ottoman Empire ruled Palestine from 1517 to the end of World War I. In 1831, the Egyptian armies of Muhammad Ali occupied Palestine, appointing Muhammad Ali's son Ibrahim as ruler. A Palestinian peasant uprising against Egyptian rule echoed earlier revolts in 1808 and 1826 against the Ottomans. On May 19, 1834, notables of the towns, villagers and Bedouins told Egyptian officials in Nablus, Jerusalem and Hebron that they would not supply the quotas of conscripts. This act of civil resistance was followed by riots in the Hebron region in which villagers of Sa'ir killed 25 Egyptian soldiers and Palestinians overran the garrison and detained the governor. The revolt spread throughout the countryside. The price was heavy: thousands of Palestinians were transported to Egypt in forced conscriptions, hundreds were killed, others jailed and the Muslim district of Bethlehem was demolished.[2] The success of the uprising came slowly as Egyptian rule was weakened and the provinces were restored to Ottoman rule in 1840. Perhaps more importantly, the uprising ignited a sense of nationalism and provided a model of endogenous political activism and resistance that was to be repeated in the decades to come.

Sultan Abdul Majid was only 16 years old when he came to power in 1839 and his reign was marked by further decay in the Empire to the benefit of the European powers. They have always coveted a return to Palestine since the Crusades. Britain and France in particular started looking to use the idea of a 'Jewish homeland' in Palestine to plant themselves firmly in this strategic region, which links three continents. Zionism as a tool serving the interests of the imperial powers had strong precedence, starting with Napoleon

Bonaparte. But Britain had more practical plans and some wealthy British aristocrats advanced the notion that it might be wise to create a Jewish colony as a 'buffer zone' at this critical junction of Asia and Africa.[3]

A DECAYING OTTOMAN EMPIRE AND DEVELOPING EUROPEAN INTEREST

Coincidentally with the revival of European interests in Palestine in the mid-nineteenth century was an obscure Jewish movement that viewed the discrimination faced by Jews in Europe not as a problem of integration, but one whose only solution was Jewish sovereignty. A minority of European Jews supported cultural or religious forms of migration to Palestine, but even most of them, and certainly the vast majority of Jews in the nineteenth century, did not endorse political Zionism. Proto-Zionist ideas were articulated in the writings of Moses Hess (1812–75), Judah Leib (Leon) Pinsker (1821–91), Moses Lilienblum and Nathan Birnbaum (Mathias Ascher) who coined the term Zionism based on the ideas of Hess and Pinsker. Hess, for example, argued in his influential book *Rome and Jerusalem* (1862) that the solution to the 'Jewish problem' lay in finding a homeland. The practical form of these intellectual exercises commenced when wealthy Jewish capitalists pledged financial backing and received practical support from European governments.

Under nineteenth-century Ottoman rule, Palestine had over 672 villages and towns with a population of over 460,000 (not including the Bedouins) of whom 15 percent were Christian and less than 3 percent were Jewish.[4] Palestinians were mostly peasants, but also included many Bedouins and city dwellers. A Palestinian from Jerusalem, Yusif Dia Pasha Al-Khalidi, was president of the council of the first House of Representatives in the Ottoman Empire after the reforms of 1876. Local representatives had little power; this was held by Turkish military officers who encouraged native Palestinians to develop a feudal system, dependency and patriarchal authority. (This was the case not only in Palestine but also in most of the so-called Third World under colonial rule.)

Between 1850 and 1874, there were conflicts pitting coalitions of Qais and Yemen clans in different cities and towns throughout Palestine. The Ottomans encouraged such divisions (the classic divide-and-rule strategy) and intervened militarily only when the conflicts got out of hand or directly threatened their authority. Unlike other countries under colonial rule, Palestine had the added and incredible weight of the Zionist program to settle the area and turn it into a Jewish state. The feudal society rose to the challenge slowly at first. Even as early as the first settlements in Palestine by the Zionist movement at the end of the nineteenth century, two classes of Palestinians shared a distrust and antagonism towards this movement and tried to unite the ranks to fight it as Palestinians. These were the intellectuals and included the representatives elected to the Ottoman parliament and the peasants, known as the *fellahin*.

The stirrings of Arab nationalism and resistance to Zionism started as early as 1868 with the establishment of the secret organization *Al-Jam'iya Al-Surriya* (the Syrian Association) based in Damascus but with members throughout Bilad Al-Sham (Greater Syria, including Palestine). Their slogan was *Tanabahu wa Istaiquthu Ya Arab* (Wake and be alert ye Arabs).[5] The decades to follow brought an influx of Zionists pushing such organizations to strengthen both their Arab nationalist and anti-Zionist directions. The relationship between the natives, Zionists and Ottoman rulers became more fractious.

Starting in 1849, the Ottoman rulers relaxed the landownership laws permitting Western Jewish purchases. The same year, the British Jewish millionaire Moses Montefiori (1784–1885) visited Palestine accompanied by Lt. Col. George Gawler, Governor of Southern Australia. Gawler had completed a study for the British government, published in 1845, on the feasibility of establishing Jewish colonies in Palestine.[6] Montefiori used his privileged position in British society (he was the second Jewish mayor of London and the first Jew given a knighthood). Taking advantage of the weakening Ottoman Empire during the Crimean War, he visited the Sultan en route to Palestine and secured a permit to purchase land there. His acquisitions enabled the first Jewish settlements to be built in Jerusalem and Jaffa between the 1850s and the early 1870s (among them Gan Montefiore, Yemin Moshe, Mahaneh Yisrael and Mea Shearim). It is notable that these early efforts happened long before what modern Zionists consider the first Zionist immigration.

Officially, the first political Zionist colony in Palestine was Petah Tikva ('Opening of Hope', named after a biblical passage) near Jaffa, which was established as a colonial settlement in 1878. The purchase and development was helped by generous funds from Baron Edmond de Rothschild. These were the beginnings of what later became recognized as the first wave of Zionist immigrants (the first *'aliya'*).

From its inception in the mid-nineteenth century, the Zionist project was a collaborative venture between Jewish political Zionists and British elites interested in advancing imperial interests. In 1864, the British authorities set up the Palestine Exploration Fund whose charter was to undertake studies on Palestine establishing the link between ancient history and modern locations and paving the way for 'reconstituting' Palestine as a Jewish state.[7] Not to be outdone, the American Society for the Exploration of Palestine was established in 1870. Such Western 'exploration' societies have always been used as a tool to study a targeted area for colonization and exploitation. After Britain conquered Egypt in 1882, the Empire's interest in Zionism waned because their colonial ambition to control part of the Middle East had been achieved. But oppression of Jews in other parts of Europe (especially in Russia) led to a wave of migration to Palestine, which is now known as the first wave of Zionist migration. Colonial interests revived in 1907 when European governments convened a committee to look at protecting their interests and ensuring that their colonial power lasted longer than previous empires. The committee included experts from England, France, Belgium, Holland, Spain, Portugal and Italy. Its conclusion was that it was critical to create a foreign body that split the African wing of the Arab world from the Asian wing.[8]

LAND LAWS AND 'PIONEER' SETTLEMENTS

The Ottoman land laws introduced in 1858 had a significant impact in transferring ownership from communally owned land to private ownership available for sale. Many farmers had to assign names to areas that traditionally were owned by a clan or village. Productive farms were 'registered' in the names of wealthy individuals who could pay taxes and meet their obligations to the Ottoman government. This meant that many farmers became essentially tenants on land that was now registered in the names of government officials, tribal leaders or elites who were free to sell it to the Zionist movement. Some of those who became wealthy landowners also acquired titles to previously allocated *waqf* lands (which were supposed to remain a holding for the particular religious sect). In this way, wealthy families, like the Nashashibi and Al-Husseini in Jerusalem and Tamimi in Hebron, were made pre prominent.[9]

The land law of 1858 was followed by the registration law in 1861 (Tabu) and in 1867 a law that made foreign landownership easier. These changes and enforcement of taxation laws bankrupted many villagers and enabled the state to confiscate their lands and sell them in public auction. By the end of the nineteenth century, 250 large landowners (local and absentee) owned 4.14 million dunums (1 dunum = 100 m^2) or close to 45 percent of the cultivated lands in Palestine.[10] The Zionist movement was well placed to take advantage of the laws, but only slowly under the Ottoman Empire (far faster under British rule later, as we shall see in Chapter 6). The Alliance Israélite Universelle was founded in France in 1860 as a non-Zionist organization with financial support from Baron Maurice de Hirsch and Baron Edmond de Rothschild with the aim of helping distressed Jewish communities. One of its founders, Charles Netter (1826–82), and other Zionist Jews failed over many years in convincing the board to encourage settlement in Palestine. Netter finally founded an agricultural school near Jaffa in 1869 and this was opened in 1870 with permission from the Ottoman rulers.[11]

The rather ambitious goal of Zionist 'pioneers' was clear from the beginning. As history shows, Palestinian natives' fears of what was to come were justified. This had nothing to do with xenophobia. From Sharkas to Druze to Armenians, Palestine has been a magnet for persecuted people and other refugees, who have found a welcome here. The same was true of Jews who did not come under the banner of Zionist colonization but to flee persecution (e.g., during the nineteenth-century pogroms in Russia). Migrants, including non-Zionist Jews, integrated successfully in Palestinian society and thus became Palestinians in all aspects. The Zionist program from its inception had different plans and emphasized 'reclaiming' the land as 'Jewish' land, 'Jewish' labor and 'Jewish "defense" forces'. No attempt was made to integrate into Palestinian life.

The impact of the landownership laws on the life of the local peasants came only after British occupation and its implementation of a far more efficient centralized system of tax collection.[12] Between 1850 and 1914 only 418,100 dunums of land were acquired by Jewish Europeans in Palestine, of which 58 percent was purchased by Zionists from absentee non-Palestinians landlords, 36 percent from absentee Palestinian landlords and the remainder from local landlords and *fellahin*.[13] By 1891, only about 10,000 Jews had relocated to the 'pioneering' Zionist settlements in Palestine. That same year, the Jewish Colonization Association was founded in London by a German, Baron Maurice de Hirsch.

The sale of the richest agricultural area in Palestine was a harbinger of what was to come. The Marj Ibn Amer village lands (including Afula, Maloul and Bethlehem) were considered state land even though villagers had farmed there for hundreds of years. After the land laws of 1858 and 1967, the land was privatized and then sold in 1869 to wealthy Lebanese moneychangers and lenders: Habib Bastras, Nicola Sarsaq, Tuwaini and Matta Farah. Nicola Sarsaq (also known as Sursuq) subsequently bought out the others, so he owned most of the valley. In 1872, the government sold other village lands, including Al-Majdal. Sarsaq ended up with 70 square miles of the best agricultural land in Palestine.[14] The Sarsaq family sold the Afula area to Zionists in 1910. Villagers were allowed to continue to farm their lands as long as they paid part of their income to the Sarsaq and other wealthy landowners. Villagers were forcibly removed from lands sold to the Zionists by the Sarsaq family in 1901 under Ottoman law and again removed when Sarsaq sold more land (see pp. 57 and 60).

The *fellahin*'s resentment soon turned to anger and frustration. These first displaced Palestinians of the late nineteenth and early twentieth centuries were followed by refugees of the *nakba* in 1948. They are the central issue for the Palestinian civil struggle and subsequently the armed resistance. In fact, the famed martyr Sheikh Izz al-Eddin Al-Qassam lived among these first displaced *fellahin* for years in the slums of Haifa where he understood their pain and initially tried in vain to help their cause through the existing Ottoman system.[15]

Decades before armed resistance started, Palestinians attempted to influence the course of the history by other methods. In 1886 villagers of Al-Khdaira and Malbas protested against the expansion of the settlement of Petah Tikva, causing the government to restrict settlement of those who entered the country as tourists and overstayed their three-month entry visa.[16] Verbal protests in 1890 were followed by a petition from Muslim and Christian notables in Jerusalem on June 24, 1891 to the Grand Vizier to prevent foreign Jews from purchasing Palestinian lands.[17] The response was a decree that prevented European Jewish migration, but this was short-lived and was rescinded following pressure on the Sultan from the British government.

There were very few successes for the Zionist movement the year that Theodore Herzl convened the first Zionist congress in Basel in 1897. After nearly three decades of colonization, they had 19 tiny settlements inhabited by a few thousand Zionist Jews. Far more Jews were natives and they lived and worked among Palestinians in Safad and Jerusalem (Jerusalem alone had 28,000 native Jews in 1897). But the small, disciplined, militarized settlements, together with voluminous Zionist writings, were a signal to the native Palestinians of the imminent transformation of Palestine. The Zionist conference merely emphasized their naked and ambitious plans. Because of this, native Palestinians, especially those educated and mobile enough to see what was going on, raised the alarm. The Ottoman parliament debates of 1897 show how Palestinian notables like Yussef Diauddin Al-Khalidi expressed such concerns.[18] Al-Khalidi had been speaker of the Ottoman parliament (from 1876) and had held a number of important posts in the Ottoman government (including as governor of a Kurdish province). He compiled the first Kurdish-Arabic dictionary and served as mayor of Jerusalem in 1899 when he wrote a letter to a French rabbi objecting to Zionism.

In 1897, the Mufti of Jerusalem, Muhammad Taher Al-Husseini (1842–1908, father of Amin Al-Husseini), convened a commission, with governmental authority, to study and prevent Jewish Zionist immigration and land purchases. This effectively stopped all such purchases for the next five years.[19] In 1898 Sheikh Mohammad Rashid Rida wrote in *Almanar* about the dangers of Zionism and its potential impact on the native Palestinians. He argued that Zionist goals went way beyond providing safety for Jews from Europe to building a Jewish political domination in Palestine.[20] In 1899, Reverend Henri Lamanse wrote an article in the magazine *Al-Mashraq* (published in Beirut) detailing Zionist settlements, active groups and future plans, and warning of the impending catastrophe for native Palestinians.[21] In 1902, villagers from Al-Shara, Misha and Melhamiyya held protests to resist the attempt to remove them from 70,000 dunums of their lands which had been sold to the Jewish National Fund. Supporting them on nationalist grounds was the Arab Qaimmaqam Amir Amin Arsalan.[22]

In his book *The Awaking of the Arab Nation* (1905), Najib Azouri warned of the danger of the Zionist project in Palestine:

Two important phenomena, of the same nature but opposed ... are emerging at this moment in Asiatic Turkey. They are the awakening of the Arab nation and the latent effort of the Jews to reconstitute on a very large scale the ancient kingdom of Israel. Both these movements are destined to fight each other continually until one of them wins. And the result of this struggle between two people representing two opposing principles lies the future of the world.[23]

Other writers and intellectuals also spoke out. Of those we recall the Jerusalemite Bandali Al-Jouzi who was later exiled by the British for exposing the dangers of Zionism and the petty divisions in Palestinian society.[24]

In 1881, France took over Tunisia and Morocco and in 1882 Britain gained control of Egypt and in 1883 of Sudan.[25] When Italy conquered Libya in 1911, all of North Africa was, for the first time in 1,400 years, without direct Islamic rule. Palestine became a footnote in this complex history. 'Missionaries' were sent and powerful consulates set up as 'protectors of minorities' in exchange for easing pressure on Abd Al-Hamid elsewhere. Yet, as we saw above, this first period of Palestinian popular resistance directed at Ottoman rulers was to prevent further concessions of Palestine to Zionist aspirations and was successful. In 1902, having been refused by the Ottoman Empire, Herzl and the World Zionist Congress turned to the British Empire for support.[26] The Ottoman government suspended all land transfers to Jews in both the *sanjak* (administrative district) of Jerusalem and the *wilayat* (province) of Beirut to the dismay of the Zionist Congress of 1905.

THE CHANGES AFTER 1908

The Young Turks' *coup d'état* of 1908 forced Abd Al-Hamid II to revive the constitution in 1876. The reinstatement of the constitution nominally guaranteed freedom of press and the right of assembly. Palestinians and other 'subjects' of the Empire were jubilant because they hoped for more freedom, equality and prosperity in a decentralized Ottoman administration. However, while newspapers did flourish, repression soon returned. Groups that called for Turkish-Arab brotherhood lost momentum and locals were forced to develop popular resistance struggles against Ottoman rule. This involved mostly developing nongovernmental institutions which were covertly or overtly Arab nationalists. Khalil Sakakini, a giant of Palestinian education and literature, founded a school, *Al-Madrasa Al-Dusturiya* (Constitution School) that used the Arabic language. Arab national consciousness grew and materialized in the form of secret organizations such as *Al-Qahtaniyah*, founded in 1909 by a group of Arab military officers and civilians led by 'Aziz 'Ali Al-Masri,

> which advocated a dual Arab-Turkish empire not unlike the Austro-Hungarian system; [and also groups like] Al-Jami'yah

Al-'Arabiya Al-Fatat (the Young Arab Society, founded in Paris in 1911 by Arab students and moved to Beirut in 1913 and Damascus in 1914), which called for Arab independence from any foreign domination.[27]

Al-Fatat was founded by Awni Abd Al-Hadi, Jamil Mardam, Rafiq Tamimi and others. After infiltration and torture of one of its member, a derivative secret organization was formed, called *Al-'Ahd*.[28] The first Arab Brotherhood Society was founded in Istanbul in 1908 and included Palestinians like Shukri Al-Husseini, and locally in the Jerusalem branch run by Ismail Al-Husseini. The next year, the Literate Forum (*Al-Muntada Al-Adabi*) was founded and called for decentralization.[29]

The five Palestinian representatives in the Ottoman parliament of 1908 were vocal in their challenge to Zionist plans. Ruhi Al-Khalidi and Said Al-Husseini (who spoke Hebrew) in particular spoke out vociferously against the Zionist project, as did the other three: Hafez Al Saeed, representing Jaffa; Al Sheikh Ahmad Al Khamash, representing Nablus; and Al-Sheikh Assad Al-Shukeiri, representing Acre.[30] Ruhi Al-Khalidi was born in Jerusalem in 1864, studied Islamic sciences and philosophy in Paris, and lectured at the Sorbonne and Institute for Foreign Languages in Paris. He was appointed Consul General of the Ottoman Empire in Bordeaux from 1898 to 1908, and then elected in Jerusalem to the Ottoman parliament in 1908 and again in 1912, serving as vice-president of the parliament in 1911. He was the first Arab to research and write a monograph on Zionism. He died on August 6, 1913 in Istanbul. His friend and contemporary Ragheb Al-Nashashibi was a representative in the Ottoman parliament during the World War I and was a co-founder (with Aref Al-Dajani of Jerusalem and Sheikh Suleiman Taji Al-Farouki of Jaffa) of the Palestinian Arab National Party in 1923 and later the National Defense Party in 1934. He became its representative to the Arab Higher Committee in 1936. The party called for good relations among all sectors of society in Palestine – Jews, Christians and Muslims – and for cooperation with the British authorities to achieve the goals of freedom and equality.

The struggle at the popular level intensified in 1908. In December, villagers of Kafr Kama (near Tiberias) tried to reclaim land taken by the Jewish Colonization Association.[31] Shafir concludes that in this period:

popular opposition and political opposition were united and generated a distinctly anti-Zionist Palestinian nationalism [but] it was precisely the inability of Palestinian Arabs to combine in the long run these two levels of opposition to Zionism that undermined effective Palestinian efforts.[32]

The indigenous media also began to develop as forms of popular resistance after laws permitted publication, and between 1908 and 1914, over 19 publications were launched in Jaffa, Haifa and Jerusalem. The four most notable papers challenging Zionist plans for Palestine and calling for Arab awakening were:[33] *Al-Asma'i*: founded in 1908 by Hanna Abdullah Alissa in Jerusalem; *Al-Karmel*: founded in 1909 by Najib Alkhoury Nassar in Haifa; *Filastin*: founded in Jaffa in 1911 by Issa Al-Issa and edited by Yousif Al-Issa; and *Al-Munadi*: founded in 1912 by Sa'id Jadallah.

Filastin was forcibly closed on a number of occasions for its leading role in opposing Zionism (including in January 1914 following Zionist complaints); it was also issued in English and distributed free to British parliamentarians to great effect locally and abroad.[34] Unlike the editors of *Filastin*, Najib Nassar supported an alliance with England, which he believed (at least up to the 1920s) to be capable of honoring its promise of independence for the Arabs.[35] His work with the Jewish Colonization Association made him aware of Zionist goals and he was radical in exposing them, thereby gaining him the nickname Majnoon Al-Sahyuniya.[36] This resulted in restrictions on distribution and the outright banning of the newspaper on several occasions.[37] Overall, the articles published in these papers showed a significant degree of political sophistication and understanding of reality (e.g., distinguishing between Judaism and Zionism).[38]

In 1910, the Lebanese capitalist Elias Sarsaq agreed to sell the lands of Afula to the Jewish National Fund and the agreement was certified by the *wali* in Beirut, but opposed by the local Arab *qaimmaqam* Shukri Al-'Asali, who went as far as publishing articles in widely read papers of the time.[39] The case of dispossession of the villagers became a rallying call for Arab nationalism. Rashid Khalidi pointed out that land sales and transfers to Zionist collectives instigated a number of peasant-led rebellions, including those in Afula in 1910–11 and in the Tiberias region in 1901–2.[40]

1911 saw a qualitative and quantitative intensification of a mini-uprising against Ottoman rule and Zionist migration. Popular resistance began to manifest itself in the form of political parties and formal organizations. In Jaffa, the first modern political party in Palestine, *Al-Hizb Al-Watani* (the National Party), was formed.[41] Secret groups like *Al-Arabiya Al-Fatat* were founded in 1911 and called for independence from Ottoman Turkey.[42] In the same year, Arab representatives in the Ottoman parliament formed *Al-Hizb Al-Watani Al-Othmani* (the National Ottoman Party) to try to bring pressure on the government to stem the flood of Zionist immigrants.[43]

An Ottoman movement led by Jamal Basha and Talia Basha started in 1912 to emphasize Ottoman unity, promote the Turkish language and suppress autonomy for the provinces (including the Arabs). This led to increased alienation among Arabs, who had originally called for Arab-Turkish unity and equality within the Ottoman Empire. The sense of alienation and need for change intensified among many Arabs (including Palestinian Arabs) on the eve of World War I. Those same activists also understood the danger of Zionism in Palestine. The Palestinian newspapers *Al-Karmel* and *Filastin* issued statements criticizing the Arab activist summit in Paris for not giving due regard to the Zionist problem in Palestine (the conference focused mostly on Arab nationalist aspirations for independence from the Ottoman Empire). In 1913 a society was founded in Nablus to challenge Zionism, and in 1914, a circular titled 'General Summons to Palestinians: Beware of Zionist Danger' signed by 'a Palestinian' warned of 'The Zionist desire to settle in our country and expel us from it'.[44]

Khalidi cites an editorial of May 1914 published in *Filastin* in which the editors of this fiercely nationalistic paper defended their position. They attacked the central Ottoman government for its attempts to shut down the newspaper for portraying Zionism as a threat to the Palestinian nation (*Al-Umma Al-Falastinia*).[45] Unfortunately, these small pro-Palestinian stirrings were no match for Great Power plays which would completely redraw the Middle East map. Palestinians also resisted Ottoman rules by developing their own educational systems:

> Palestinian recognition of the value of education and the importance of being able to shape what is learnt goes back to the British mandate and beyond ... Under the Ottoman Empire (1517–1917) Arab students formed in mosques as an indigenous response to Turkish control.[46]

When Turkey entered the Great War on November 29, 1914, the government tried to suppress any potential dissent in the Arab provinces. The failure of the Ottoman attack on British forces in the Suez area and British successes in Iraq in 1915 led to a severe crackdown. After forced 'confessions' from scores of Arab national activists, they were publicly hanged in the streets of Jerusalem, Damascus and Syria. The Ottomans also confiscated food supplies and means of livelihood, and drafted men into the army, thereby depriving families of their breadwinners. Draft evasion was punished severely. The conscription of my great-grandfather led to my grandfather becoming orphaned for he lost not only his father, but also his mother, brother and two sisters. The Ottomans also confiscated working animals, destroyed fruit trees to use as fuel and to build railroads and moved populations in a manner that destroyed the social fabric created and stabilized for hundreds of years. Population statistics before and after the war show a decline of nearly 30 percent. This was the most devastating demographic change to occur in Palestine up to that point. Added to this destruction and destabilization was the systematic Zionist colonization program. The cited examples of resistance in these last few decades of Ottoman rule seem remarkable and inspiring in light of these conditions.

Meanwhile, the fate of Palestine was being drawn elsewhere by politicians who had scant regard for the local inhabitants. The British schemed to divide up the Arab world with France under the Sykes–Picot agreement of 1916. In areas of British influence, British rulers established petty kingdoms subservient to their imperial interests. The Al-Saud family was put in charge of the area of Hijaz (which was to become Saudi Arabia) at the expense of the Hashemites, who were compensated by being promised northern Arabia (Bilad Al-Sham, or Greater Syria). They were happy to do what Great Britain asked them with regard to Palestine. Abd Al-Aziz Al-Saud responded in 1915 to British requests by writing in his own hand:

> I the Sultan Abd Al-Aziz Bin Abd Al-Rahman Al-Faysal Al-Saud decide and acknowledge a thousand times to Sir Percy Cox the representative of Great Britain that I have no objection to give Palestine to the poor Jews or to others as seen [fit] by Great Britain that I would not go outside [disobey] its opinion until the hour of calling [end of the world].[47]

6
Balfour, Al-Buraq and the Zionist Build-up, 1917–35

For in Palestine we do not propose to go through the form of consulting the wishes of the present inhabitants ... The four great powers are committed to Zionism and Zionism, be it right or wrong, good or bad, is rooted in age-long tradition, in present needs, in future hopes, of far profounder import than the desires and prejudices of the 700,000 Arabs who now inhabit that ancient land.

Lord Balfour, private memorandum to Lord Curzon, his successor (who initially opposed Zionism), August 11, 1919[1]

The energetic and charismatic Zionist leader Chaim Weizmann relocated to London in 1904 after failing to get Ottoman support. The Zionists had a slow start securing British backing, but a breakthrough came during World War I. Germany had offered generous peace terms to an exhausted England and France as the war appeared to be approaching stalemate with a slight advantage to Germany. Precisely at this opportune time, the Zionist movement offered to get the US to join the allies in exchange for a public commitment of support on the part of France and England to a Jewish homeland in Palestine.[2] The promise from France came via a letter sent from Jules Cambon, Secretary General of the French Foreign Ministry, to Nahum Sokolow, an official of the World Zionist Organization:

You were kind enough to inform me of your project regarding the expansion of the Jewish colonization of Palestine. You expressed to me that, if the circumstances were allowing for that, and if on another hand, the independency of the holy sites was guaranteed, it would then be a work of justice and retribution for the allied forces to help the renaissance of the Jewish nationality on the land from which the Jewish people was exiled so many centuries ago. The French Government, which entered this present war to defend a people wrongly attacked, and which continues the struggle to assure victory of right over might, cannot but feel sympathy for your cause, the triumph of which is bound up with that of the Allies. I am happy to give you herewith such assurance.[3]

Five months later, on November 2, 1917, the British Foreign Secretary, Arthur James Balfour, sent Lord Rothschild a similar declaration of sympathy for Zionist aspirations; this later became known as the Balfour Declaration. These promises to European Jews of a 'national home' were issued when Britain and France had no jurisdiction over the area, against the wishes of the inhabitants of the land and when the Allies were receiving significant support from the Arabs who had revolted against the Ottoman Turks. Three years earlier, Britain had promised the Arabs (in the McMahon-Hussein correspondence) independence and self-government.

Another complicating factor was that Emir (later King) Faisal of Hejaz had also corresponded with Weizmann and they agreed to support the Balfour Declaration in return for the Zionist movement helping establish independence for the Arab areas. Treacherous as it was, this agreement contained a clause stating that unless a unified Arab country were established throughout the area (present-day Syria, Jordan, Iraq, Saudi Arabia and other countries), the whole agreement would be null and void.[4] However, the Faisal–Weizmann agreement established the precedent of Arab leaders making deals with the Zionists behind closed doors without consulting the native Palestinians who were directly impacted.

EARLY YEARS OF THE BRITISH OCCUPATION

Palestinians supported the Allies because they had been under Ottoman rule for so long. But those familiar with European colonial history were justifiably suspicious that the Europeans would prove to be far worse than the Ottomans. European colonizers traditionally ruled people by dividing them, while the Ottomans kept the Arab areas unified. The 1916 Sykes–Picot secret agreement to divide the area between Britain and France illustrated the future. T. E. Lawrence ('Lawrence of Arabia') later explained how the British government betrayed Faisal despite earlier assurances. It is now believed that Faisal later lost his throne because of his refusal to part with Palestine, a lesson not lost on his brother Abdullah, who became King of Jordan. The subjugation of the Arab and Islamic world and its dismemberment via such deals were common.[5]

Strengthened by these machinations, Zionists made a huge practical leap forward one cold winter day, December 9, 1917, when British forces marched into Jerusalem. The Ottoman ruler decided to spare the city from British bombardment and surrendered it without a fight. Headed by General Allenby, commander-in-chief of the Egyptian Expeditionary Force, the British entered two days later (December 11) to be received by Palestinian elites and religious leaders, including the mayor, Hussein Sakeem Al-Husseini. Allenby pledged support for religious freedom and protection of the communities and the holy places. But immediately, the doors to increased Jewish immigration from Europe opened in fulfillment of the Balfour Declaration.

The Zionist movement won concessions that would have been unimaginable under Ottoman rule (as we shall see). Jews in Palestine in 1917 represented less than 7 percent of the population, most of them were not Zionists and they owned less than 2 percent of the privately owned land. By the end of British rule, they represented nearly a third of the population and owned nearly 7 percent of the land. The success must be credited not only to the Zionist movement but to the British elite's interests. Many British officers were far more comfortable working with English-speaking European Jews than trying to understand and deal with the local inhabitants. Palestinians who first saw the British as allies against the Ottomans now began to see them as invaders. Tellingly, when Allenby delivered his first speech in Jerusalem, he mentioned completion of the cycle of the Crusades.

While Ottomans still had armies in northern Palestine, the first Jewish Zionist delegation from Europe after the British occupation arrived and met General Ronald Storrs, Governor of Jerusalem, on April 27, 1918. Immediately, voices of protest began to be heard. Palestinian-organized protests led to the founding of Muslim-Christian societies which showed not only opposition to colonialism but also local solidarity and camaraderie. The symbol for each of these societies was a cross within a crescent. They operated efficiently and methodically to challenge British and Zionist attempts to create sectarian rifts based on religion. It is no surprise, then, that these societies made a point of distinguishing native Arab Jews from the Zionist Jewish colonizers.[6] In the second half of May 1918, the Arab flag and the Arab national anthem of revolt were adopted by the Palestinian national movement despite objections by the British.[7] This was followed in the first week of June by the establishment of a number of nationalist organizations, notably in Jaffa and Jerusalem.

In 1918, two youth organizations (Christian and Muslim mixed) were formed in Jerusalem representing clan alignments: *Al-Nadi*

Al-Arabi (the Arab Club) and *Al-Montana Al-Adabi* (the Culture Forum). Founders of the former included members of the Al-Husseini family, and of the latter Fakhri Al-Nashashibi and Hassan Sudki Al-Dajani.[8] This was the first hint of familiar sectarian division in politics of Palestine.

Arab mistrust and anger grew, especially when the Zionist movement held loud and boisterous commemorations on the first anniversary of the Balfour Declaration (November 2, 1918). That same day, the Jaffa Muslim-Christian Society sent a letter of protest to General Clayton. The increased activities of the Palestinian nationalist forces alarmed both the British rulers and leaders of the Zionist movement. Weizmann wrote reports and letters detailing and sometimes exaggerating the build-up of local native resistance, insisting that 'Palestine is for the Palestinians'.[9] An organizational leap forward was achieved when the local Muslim-Christian societies collaborated to form a more centralized society with by-laws approved in Jerusalem in January 1919 calling for education of the youth and encouraging national development in different areas, while protecting individual and national rights. This paved the way for the first Palestinian Arab Congress held in Jerusalem, January 27–February 4, 1919 with 27 delegates attending from throughout Palestine.[10]

The British authorities allowed the conference to go ahead because they were hoping that the eleven delegates who were supportive of Britain would be able to sway the conference. Instead, on the first day, the conference decided to send a letter to the 1919 Peace Conference in Paris, which stated:

> The people of Palestine ... met and chose their delegate who attended and held a meeting in Jerusalem to discuss the form of government suitable for their country. They decided as a first priority to send your esteemed conference their strong complaint for what they have heard that the Zionists received a promise to make our country a national home for them and that they aim to migrate to this country and colonize it ... We urge your esteemed conference not to take any decisions about this country until after you know what our desires and wishes are ...[11]

A statement to the 1919 Peace Conference was also sent by prominent American Jews (including one congressman):

We raise our voices in warning and protest against the demand of the Zionists for the reorganization of the Jews as a national unit, to whom, now or in the future, territorial sovereignty in Palestine shall be committed ... We ask that Palestine be constituted as a free and independent state, to be governed under a democratic form of government recognizing no distinctions of creed or race or ethnic descent, and with adequate power to protect the country against oppression of any kind. We do not wish to see Palestine, either now or at any time in the future, organized as a Jewish state.[12]

Fifteen of the 27 delegates to the first Palestinian Arab Congress also attended the Syrian Congress in Damascus on July 3, 1919. The conference emphasized Arab unity. While the Zionists were at the Paris Conference rallying for implementation of the Balfour Declaration, the British forces prevented the departure of Palestinian leaders who merely wanted delegates to know the wishes of the locals. There was a symbolic act of resistance when Palestinians tried to sail from the port of Jaffa and were prevented by the British. Elite non-Palestinian Arab interests were represented, including the British-backed King Faisal.

The US administration was initially reluctant to support British policy in Palestine. President Wilson had stated as early as 1918:

The settlement of every question, whether of territory, of sovereignty, of economic arrangement, or political relationship, rests upon the basis of the free acceptance of that settlement by the people immediately concerned, and not upon the basis of the material interest or advantage of any other nation or people which may desire a different settlement for the sake of its own exterior influence or mastery. If that principle is to rule, and so the wishes of Palestine's population are to be decisive as to what is to be done with Palestine, then it is to be remembered that the non-Jewish population of Palestine – nearly nine-tenths of the whole – are emphatically against the entire Zionist program. The tables show that there was no one thing upon which the population of Palestine more agreed upon than this. To subject a people so minded to unlimited Jewish immigration, and to steady financial and social pressure to surrender the land, would be a gross violation of the principle just quoted, and of the People's rights, though it is kept within the forms of law.[13]

Accordingly, Wilson's delegates to the 1919 conference were instructed to propose self-determination for the Palestinians, but they were willing to compromise and make an exception by setting up a commission of inquiry formed of two delegates from each interested country 'to study the situation'. Only the US proceeded to send its two delegates (Henry C. King and Charles R. Crane) on a fact-finding trip to Palestine. Two months before the King–Crane commission was to visit Palestine, the Muslim-Christian Society held a meeting to plan to submit demands for the US administration to follow Wilson's stated goal of Palestinian self-determination. They declared their opposition to Zionism, but affirmed their kinship with Jews: 'Local Jews are nationals who will have what we have and endure what we endure.'[14]

The declaration was published and Palestinians who met the King–Crane commission expressed the same opinion. The commission concluded that local Palestinians (representing 90 percent of the population) were unanimous in their desires and aspirations. So while they were initially sympathetic to Zionism, King and Crane showed their objectivity in explaining why the Balfour Declaration was wrong and contradicted the notion of self-determination. This commission issued a lengthy report but this was suppressed and only excerpts of it were published in 1922, with the full report published only in 1947. The British proceeded with their plan to rule the areas based on the Sykes–Picot and the Balfour–Cambon agreements.

In Egypt, a revolution between 1919 and 1922 showed that Arabs wanted independence. In 1919 several new publications appeared expressing this desire: *Surya Al-Janubiya* (*Southern Syria*, edited by 'Aref Al-Aref and Amin Al-Husseini); *Mir'at Al-Sharq* (*Mirror of the East*, edited by Bulus Shihadah); and *Bayt al-Maqdis* (*Jerusalem*, edited by Bandali Mushahwar).[15] When Faisal returned to Damascus from Paris in 1919, the atmosphere was revolutionary and delegates from *Hizb Al-Istiqlal Al-Arabi* proposed to elect a national assembly and declare Arab independence in a united Syria (i.e., including Palestine, Transjordan, Iraq and an autonomous Lebanon). Clashes occurred with French troops and this escalated after the General Syrian Congress proclaimed Faisal King of Greater Syria on March 8, 1920. Rowdy demonstrations in Jerusalem unsettled the Allies. This was followed by the Iraqi people crowning Faisal's brother King of Iraq. The news prompted the Allies to convene a conference in San Remo on April 25, 1920 to confront these early signs of independence and reaffirm the commitment of France and Britain to the treacherous Sykes–Picot and Balfour–Cambon deals.[16]

On February 20, 1920, British officials gathered notables in Jerusalem to tell them that Britain was seeking a mandate over Palestine which would include the Balfour Declaration; in other words, Palestinians should resign themselves to the reality. Seven days later, an official proclamation was issued to the same effect. That day, February 27, 1920, two events signaled what was to come in response. First, the second Palestine Arab Congress was held in Damascus and again emphasized the need for Arab unity, for resistance to the British occupation and the Balfour Declaration, and for self-determination; and secondly, a demonstration was held in Jerusalem demanding the same. The demonstrations spread on March 11, 1920 to all major Palestinian cities.[17] In Haifa, thousands signed a petition against making Palestine a Jewish national homeland and was delivered to the military ruler there, Colonel Stanton.[18] The 1920 Al-Quds uprising spread quickly, with mass resignations, protests, strikes and other forms of popular resistance.

On April 4, 1920 the annual religious festival known as *Mawsam Al-Nabi Musa* was transformed into a mass nationalist demonstration. The crowds heard from Aref Al-Aref, mayor of Jerusalem Musa Kadhem Al-Husseini and Amin Al-Husseini. Al-Husseini had served with the British and Sharif Faisal in recruiting support for the Allies to bring an end to Ottoman rule, but was then disliked by the British. Despite his vacillation, he emerged to become a strong and commanding leader of Palestinian Arab nationalism and a spiritual leader of the resistance.[19] As the crowds entered Jerusalem through the Jaffa Gate, they were harassed by Zionists led by Zeev Jabotinsky, who exploited conflicts to increase the ranks of his underground forces. They got what they asked for as communal violence erupted and five Jews and four Palestinians were killed. The British administration sentenced Aref Al-Aref and Amin Al-Husseini *in absentia* to ten years' imprisonment each, but they had both fled to Syria. They also sentenced Jabotinsky to 15 years but released him within three months, making him instantly a known entity among the Zionists. Here it is worth noting that Aref Al-Aref was born in Jerusalem in 1891 and had studied in Turkey. He advocated aggressive but nonviolent resistance. He spent three years in exile in Siberia, escaping after the Russian Revolution and then returning to Palestine. He edited the newspaper *Surya Al-Janubiyya* published in Jerusalem from 1919. He was an intellectual who didn't live in an ivory tower, but with his people. He was just as comfortable having tea with West Jerusalem elite Palestinian families as with Bedouins in simple tents in the Negev. After a tumultuous career in British-occupied Palestine he became mayor of Jerusalem in 1950 and died on July 30, 1973 in Ramallah.

Musa Kadhem Al-Husseini resigned as mayor of Jerusalem rather than agreeing to implement occupation diktats. He was born in 1853, spoke fluent Turkish and served as an Ottoman administrator before becoming mayor in 1918. He was elected representative of Jerusalem to the third (December 1920, Haifa), fifth (August 1922, Nablus), sixth (June 1923, Jaffa) and seventh (June 1928) Congress of the Arab Executive Committee and was its president from December 1920. He led a nonviolent demonstration in Jaffa on October 27, 1933 protesting against Zionist mass immigration where he was injured, and this hastened his death on March 27, 1934. The British found a willing replacement in the form of the more compliant Ragheb Al-Nashashibi. Al-Husseini's removal from office in 1920 deepened an existing fissure between the two factions in Palestine led by the Nashashibis and the Al-Husseinis. On policy issues, the Nashashibi faction believed in *khuth wataleb bilbaaki* (take and then ask for what remains), a compromise position of give and take with the Mandate. The Al-Husseini faction believed in resistance and rejection.

THE SAMUEL ERA AND THE GROWTH OF RESISTANCE

The British authorities prevented another Palestinian congress taking place in May 1920 which had intended to discuss the San Remo Conference. But the authorities appointed a secret investigative committee whose findings were not declassified until 1946 due to Zionist pressure. They concluded that the cause of the 1920 disturbances was the aggressive nature of the Zionist leadership in pushing for the transformation of Palestine into a Jewish state. The report detailed the extent of the Zionist build-up of parallel institutions, including an intelligence service that knew more about secret British documents than the British knew about the Zionist movement.[20] Ignoring the report, the British government replaced its military rule with a civil administration on June 30, 1920. The chosen face for this occupation was an ambitious man who liked to wear white suits. Herbert Louis Samuel was a prominent Jewish Zionist who proved his mettle by silencing critics of the Balfour Declaration and by being on the official Zionist delegation to the 1919 Paris Peace Conference. Samuel states that he was appointed not only with known Zionist sympathies, but largely *because* of those sympathies.[21]

Samuel's appointment was met with objection by British officers such as Lord Curzon, who warned of the ramification of choosing, as the first civil administrator in Palestine, a Zionist Jew. Upon his appointment, Samuel toured Palestine and visited ten Jewish colonial settlements. He then claimed that the British military has exaggerated Arab enmity and that things were far more hopeful for fulfilling the Balfour Declaration.[22] His appointment sparked immediate protests and boycotts. Many Palestinians responded by mass resignation from government jobs (a notable example was Khalil Sakakini) strikes, protests, petitions and pleas for change. Letters of protests poured in from the Muslim-Christian Society in Jaffa on June 23, 1920 and from women in north Palestine, among others.[23] Despite a call to boycott him, many leaders attended a meeting with Samuel in Jerusalem on July 7, 1920, and in Haifa the next day. This emboldened him and the British government into believing they could isolate the people from the elite leaders of Palestine.[24]

Parallel with Samuel's machinations, on July 14, 1920 France demanded that King Faisal in Damascus end conscription and surrender his garrisons to French troops. He was forced to concede against the wishes of his people, but the French still betrayed him and forced him out of Damascus. This blow to Arab independence had negative repercussions on Palestinians, who were left with little or no outside Arab support. The Allies then forced an agreement with defeated Turkey on August 10, 1920, which ensured Turkey had no claim over the 'liberated' Ottoman provinces. President Mustafa Kemal Atatürk initially rejected this agreement but was forced to accept an even stronger version in Lausanne on September 28, 1923. With the removal of this technical legal hurdle, the Zionist project could now advance rapidly.

The actions and policies that followed signaled the first hints of a nascent apartheid system. The Zionist viceroy Samuel had unprecedented executive, legislative and military authority, and at one point was likened to a new Jewish King of Palestine. He did not hesitate in segregating communities, in giving economic concessions to Zionists and in allowing the *Yishuv* (Jewish community) to establish an independent Jewish police force, Jewish schools, Jewish colonies, Jewish industries, and so on. Samuel also appointed a number of leading Jewish Zionists to sensitive government positions, including immigration, finance, and trade and industry. While Jews constituted less than 10 percent of the population at the time, they filled 60 percent of government positions. The few Arabs in government tended to be chosen for their loyalty and acquiescence. In September and October 1920, Samuel issued a series of regulations on landownership that made it far easier for the Zionist movement to acquire vast tracts of land, thereby making it difficult for locals to keep control of their land. He even appointed another Zionist, Norman Bentwitch, to administer land registration.[25] He allowed the formation of the Haganah (the forerunner of Israel's army) as a 'defense force' for the expanding Zionist colonies. This added to local fears that Zionist Jews intended to take over Palestine, a fear validated by direct statements from the leaders of the Zionist movement and from the Zionist High Commissioner himself.[26] Samuel accepted the Jewish Agency and the leadership of the *Yishuv* as self-designated leaders of the Jews in Palestine, but refused to accept that the Palestinian Arab Congress represented Palestinians.[27]

Increased Jewish immigration and unfair land laws instituted by Samuel squeezed the Palestinian peasants. For hundreds of years, most cultivated land in Palestine was *amiriya*, lands whose farmers paid a tax known as *'ushur*. For all practical purposes these were lands traditionally owned communally by the villagers. Samuel used his wide authority to reassign such lands to the private ownership of Zionists or wealthy owners and people connected to the government, who in turn could sell it to the Zionist movement. When villagers were notified they could no longer use lands that their ancestors had farmed for hundreds of years, it came as a great shock. Samuel had also instituted laws that stated that absentee landowners could not profit from use of their lands, but could sell it. This prompted wealthy families like the Sarsaq to sell large tracts in Marj Ibn Amer and elsewhere to the Zionist leadership. Samuel also instituted laws that allowed the transfer of large tracts of 'public lands', though much of it was used by Palestinians, to the exclusive use of the Zionist movement, claiming that 'public good' resulted. Thousands of Palestinians were forcibly evicted. These unfair laws were thus instituted by an occupying power to benefit a foreign Zionist movement at the expense of the native Christians and Muslims who represented some 90 percent of the population and without consulting them. It was predictable that resistance would increase.

The third Palestinian Arab Congress was held in Haifa on December 14, 1920 and repeated calls to repudiate the Balfour

Declaration and promote self-determination. This placed Haifa on the map of cities of resistance and organization.[28] But this congress faced new challenges. The exile of Faisal from Syria and the events in Iraq showed that the British and French occupiers had succeeded in bringing an end to the idea of a pan-Arab state (or even a united Bilad Al-Sham). This set the stage for Palestinians to re-evaluate and refocus on a narrower form of Palestinian nationalism.[29] The congress elected an executive committee headed by Musa Kadhem Al-Husseini. When Samuel showed no interest in responding to their demands, the executive committee traveled to Cairo to meet Winston Churchill, then British Colonial Secretary, but the latter merely agreed to hear their views when he visited Jerusalem. They met in Jerusalem on March 8, 1921, where their demands included: no national home for Jews in Palestine; the end of immigration and land transfers; a national government to represent all the people of Palestine; and no separation of Palestine from its neighboring areas. Churchill rejected these demands and told those gathered that self-determination would only come after 'our children's children' had died.[30]

While Churchill was delivering his insulting speech on March 18, 1921 in which he glorified the crusaders and the Maccabees, a day of general strikes and protests was called for throughout Palestine and one demonstration was met with a hail of British bullets killing several people at the funerals of Edward Mansour and Mustafa Al-'Ajouz.[31] In the demonstration in Tulkarem, thousands gathered and marched from the southern edge of town towards the government building. The march was led by students followed by religious leaders (Christian and Muslim), tribal and political leaders, merchants and ordinary people, all carrying black flags.[32] In Haifa, a Christian child and a Muslim man were killed in a demonstration held in defiance of a ban.[33]

When the British ambassador was giving a speech on April 14, 1921, a young Palestinian named Jibran Kazna got to his feet and demanded that the British government stop transforming Palestine into a Jewish homeland and implement article 22 of the League of Nations on self-determination.[34] On April 29, 1921, a British officer, Colonel Cox, arrived in the Galilee to put down the unrest. He questioned one of the accused 'troublemakers', Habib Wahbeh, charging him with fomenting mutiny, objecting to Zionism, joining the Arab Conference and being a member of a nationalist society. Wahbeh replied that all the allegations were true, except starting a mutiny: 'As for being against the Zionist government, this is something I do not deny for I believe Zionism would destroy hopes and aspirations of all Palestinians.'[35]

As the nonviolent demonstrations were met with violence, the situation deteriorated. Conservative estimates suggested that 48 Arabs and 47 Jews were killed in April 1921. More realistic estimates give over 100 Arabs killed, mostly on April 5 in Jaffa. At that time Jaffa was in the sights of the British authorities as the hub of resistance. Only after the April violence did the British government appoint yet another commission of inquiry.[36]

In early May 1921, a number of demonstrations were held to coincide with Churchill's arrival in Palestine. Churchill had just made a deal with Emir Abdullah to let him rule Transjordan in exchange for acquiescence to British plans in mandated Palestine (including the Zionist 'national home'). This was to be added to the Faisal–Weizmann agreement as yet another Hashemite family concession to the Zionist movement. In Gaza 20,000 people flocked to meet Churchill's train, and angry demonstrations took place in Beisan and Haifa (where 20 Palestinian casualties were reported after British troops opened fire). The authorities removed the Palestinian governor of Beisan after that demonstration called for ending the Balfour Declaration.[37] In the same issue of *Al-Karmel*, a picture is reproduced of the telegram sent by the Islamic Society of Haifa, signed by its head, the Mufti of Haifa Muhammad Murad, to the British government and to the *Sun* and *Morning Post* newspapers in London all warning of things getting out of hand if the government tried to force through the Balfour Declaration against the wishes of the inhabitants.

Later that month, the fourth Palestinian Arab Congress was held in Jerusalem and elected a group led by Musa Kadhem Al-Husseini. They traveled to London in July 1921 to try to persuade the British government to reverse its policy of support for the Zionist movement.[38] *Al-Karmel* published the decision by the Congress that objected to the government's banning of peaceful demonstrations, which 'led to the unfortunate incident in Haifa in which the blood of innocents was shed'.[39] At the same time, the Muslim-Christian Society in Nablus issued a statement denouncing the decision to arm the Jewish colonies.[40]

In September 1921 one group of Palestinians went to give testimony to the British government in London and another group traveled to attend the Syrian-Palestinian conference in Geneva. Disagreement ensued when those attending the Geneva conference supported the call against the British Mandate while those in London merely wanted the British Mandate to abandon its support of the Balfour Declaration and allow self-governance.[41]

The British issued a White Paper in October 1921 which reiterated some of the conclusions of the military (to the chagrin of Samuel and the Zionist movement) stating the main cause of the disturbances was the fear of transforming Palestine into a Jewish homeland. The report emphasized that there was no problem with Jewish and non-Jewish relations in Palestine under Ottoman rule without Zionism. It added that the Zionist idea of Jewish empowerment in politics to rule over Palestine was the cause of the friction. To undermine the White Paper, Samuel moved briskly to increase the pace of transformation in Palestine. In December 1921, he revised the 1920 landownership law to remove limits on the number of sales and to allow sales by people living outside the country (enabling collaborators and other wealthy landowners ample latitude to sell to the Jewish Agency). He also imposed taxes on uncultivated lands to encourage their sale, as many Palestinians could not afford the taxes. Through unfair laws, the fertile lands of seven villages in the valley of Marj Ibn Amer were sold in 1921 by the wealthy Lebanese Sarsaq family to the Zionists. Even though they were promised that they would receive equivalent land and homes elsewhere, the villagers were given nothing and were forcibly expelled. In all, 400,000 dunums of land belonging to 22 villages of this fertile valley were taken between 1921 and 1925 and 1,764 families comprising 8,730 individuals were expelled.[42] A similar expulsion of 1,500 villagers from Wadi Al-Hawareth was accomplished by force (killing some of the peasants in the process). The villagers' anger led to the creation of acts of vigilante resistance in the area, the most famous of which are the two 'Robin Hoods' of Palestine: Ahmed Al-Mahmoud ('Abu Jildah') from Al-Tamoon and Saleh Ahmed Al-Mustafa ('Al-Armeet') from Beita. Their exploits became famous throughout Palestine in the early 1930s. The slogan echoed across the villages of northern Palestine: '*Abu Jilda and Al-Armeet, yama kassaro batraneet*' (Abu Jildah and Al-Armeet, oh how they broke [British] helmets).[43]

In the years following Samuel's new land laws and policies, hundreds of thousands of dunums were acquired by the Zionists at knock-down prices (averaging £3.6 per dunum), and in some cases land was granted free via government allocation. The people living and farming these lands for hundreds of years were expelled. In total in the five years of Samuel's rule, the Zionists increased their landholdings by 64 percent (from 650,000 to 1,095,740 dunums).

Samuel moved briskly in the direction of empowering Jewish Zionists and disempowering native Palestinians. In desperation, Musa Kadhem Al-Husseini led a delegation to London bypassing Samuel to present their case directly to the House of Lords. The delegation's meeting with Churchill on August 15, 1921 was unsuccessful; he simply asked them to meet Weizmann. Weizmann in turn merely intensified their fears by clarifying that indeed the aim was to transform Palestine into a Jewish state. They held a second meeting with Churchill on August 22, 1922. In the meantime, Arab collaborative members of the committee appointed by Samuel sent a telegram claiming that the elected executive committee of the Palestinian Arab Congress did not represent Palestinian interests.[44] Division between collaborationists' interests and true nationalists has been repeated in Palestinian politics since then.

Samuel's biased administration had an impact on another British White Paper, issued on June 3, 1922, which reiterated the same failed and destructive policies. Churchill went further than the Balfour Declaration in asserting that Jewish immigrants would become Palestinian by right and not by privilege, even though he emphasized this did not mean a Jewish Palestine or a Jewish state in Palestine. The White Paper also rejected the idea of a democratic representative body in Palestine. The role of the Zionist movement, thanks to Samuel, in getting this unconditional support was spelled out in Weizmann's autobiography.[45]

THE YEARS LEADING TO THE UPRISING OF AL-BURAQ

After the Zionist movement secured US backing in the form of a congressional vote on June 30, 1922, the League of Nations voted on July 24, 1922 to approve the British Mandate of Palestine. The resolution reiterated the language of Balfour. The rather lengthy resolution did not deal with the people of Palestine as an indigenous population with rights to their country, nor did it take into consideration that they were the majority in possession of political and national rights. They were simply residents in a country that was to be transformed into a national home for Jews from around the world. With this resolution and Samuel's Zionist administration in Palestine, the Great Powers had given legitimacy to the project of separating Palestine from its native people.[46] Much had already changed before June 24, 1922. At this point, most Palestinians came to realize that the Zionist project and the British Mandate were inseparable; resistance to one meant resistance to the other. Thus, the Arab Executive decided on June 23–27 that, when the Mandate was finalized, people should engage in mass demonstrations and strikes and other forms of popular resistance against the occupation. Religious leaders discouraged adherents from selling land to Zionists or agents of the Jewish Agency. A general strike on July 13–14, 1922 brought commerce across the country to a standstill. Nationalist Palestinian leaders traveled to Mecca to muster Muslim support. The British admitted in private correspondence that the Arab leadership was pushing for popular resistance and resisting calls for armed rebellion.[47]

A decree from the High Commissioner on August 14, 1922 called for a 'legislative body' that would have no authority to legislate anything that the High Commissioner did not approve. This was roundly rejected in the fifth Palestine Conference held in Nablus on August 22–25, 1922. Palestinians refused to participate in the sham elections in 1923, which consequently failed.[48] The High Commissioner decided to create a 'consultancy committee' in May 1923 but, less than a month later, nine Arab members of the committee resigned under public pressure even before the committee held its inaugural session.[49] These nine members (Ismail Al-Husseini, Aref Al-Dajani, Ragheb Al-Nashashibi, Mahmoud Abu Khadra, Sulaiman Tuqan, Abdel Fattah Al-Sa'di, Sulaiman Nasif, Habib Salem and Fraih Abu Mdein) were known to be supporters of the British government, but they found their position untenable in light of public fury.[50]

The failures of the British authorities between February 1922 and May 1923 caused them to return to the tried-and-tested colonial practice of divide and rule. Between 1921 and 1935, Amin Al-Husseini and members of the Executive Committee of the Palestinian Arab Congress became prime targets. Unfortunately, Al-Husseini did not set up institutions of governance or a democratic structure, but kept the reins of power in his own hands. This cult of personality was to have a significant detrimental effect, not only during this period, for it set a precedent that infected Palestinian polity for years to come, finding its most vivid expression in the 40-year leadership of Yasser Arafat.[51] Yet, it must be said that Al-Husseini and the leadership of the Executive Committee, insular as they were, did manage to isolate the collaborationist elements of Palestinian society, kept the cause alive and ensured that the cause was not isolated from its Arab and Islamic dimension.

The British supported opposition to the leadership of Al-Husseini and the patriotic forces from a group led by Asaad Shuqairi, Aref

Al-Dajani and Ragheb Al-Nashashibi. With help from the British authorities, they set up the Arab National Party on November 8, 1923. This party included wealthy landowners, merchants and Western-educated intellectuals; prominent leaders included Suleiman Taji Farouqi and Ragherb Nashashibi. The Agriculture Party was also formed in 1923, with a similar agenda of division and support for British policies and in their case the hope to divide rural from urban Palestinians. There is now ample evidence of the British-Zionist connection to these groups. Eventually, those who bet on the British authorities moved on, some finally abandoned their collaborative efforts, while others actually strengthened their commitment to the British and, by extension, the Zionist agenda, thus undermining the Palestinian cause.[52]

On June 5, 1923, an agreement signed between the British government and the Hashemite family which ruled Hejaz and Trans-Jordan recognized the British Mandate. The head of the Arab Executive Committee, Musa Kadhem Al-Husseini, sent a letter of inquiry to King Abdullah and was told that the agreement was not yet completed. The Palestinian Arab Congress held in Jaffa on June 16, 1923 objected to any such agreement. When King Hussein of Hejaz rejected it under popular pressure, he received a letter of thanks from the Palestine Executive Committee. Unfortunately, he then lost British support which was transferred to the Saud family, which still rules the kingdom now called Saudi Arabia. The same month as this shameful deal was being worked out (June 1923), the Executive Committee met in Jaffa, with Khalil Sakakini as secretary. This giant of Palestinian literature represents an unbroken trend of patriots challenging Western machinations.

During the 1920s, new movements flourished in Palestine despite the obstacles. While Christian-Muslim cooperation was the norm, the Jewish community remained largely isolated, albeit with a few exceptions. Zionism was an anti-assimilation idea and it distanced itself from local Palestinians and emphasized 'Jewish labor', 'redeeming Jewish land', etc. Such attitudes became prevalent among the small community of Jews in Palestine as early as the 1880s and accelerated after the establishment of the world Zionist programs in the early 1900s. David Ben-Gurion managed to convince otherwise liberal socialists contemplating inclusion of Arab workers that it was better to set up separate unions because:

This would allow the Jewish workers in mixed workplaces to improve their position through cooperation with their Arab

co-workers while preserving the exclusively Jewish character of
the Histadrut and its trade unions, which would thus remain free
to carry out their Zionist ('national') tasks, including the struggle
for removal of the Arab workers by Hebrew labor.[53]

In response, the Palestine Communist Party was founded in 1923
and took on the task of organizing Arab and Jewish workers.[54]
It was the first political party that admitted Zionists and native
Palestinians. But the alliance was fragile and in 1943 the party broke
up into two spin-offs: the National Liberation League, which called
for Palestinian independence, and the Educational Communist
Union, which supported Zionism.

On October 11, 1923, the British authorities asked if the Arab
Executive Committee was willing to form an 'Arab Agency',
analogous to the Jewish Agency. The letter of rejection of
November 9, 1923, signed by Musa Kadhem Al-Husseini, stated
clearly that it would reduce the Arab natives to parity with
Zionist outsiders, 'trying to influence [the government]'; a more
rational solution would be to fulfill the British obligation to grant
self-determination, including the right to vote, to all residents
of Palestine. The underlying assumption of the British scheme
was acceptance of the illegal British occupation and the Balfour
Declaration.[55] In retrospect, while rejecting British attempts at
creating a quisling leadership, the Palestinian Arab Congress could
have taken proactive steps to have democratic representation for
all sectors of the Palestinian society.

The British acted brutally to suppress the 1920–22 uprising, but
it took them many years and two more uprisings (in 1929 and
1936) to set up yet another commission, this time headed by Lord
Peel, to look into the causes of Palestinian unrest and how to quell
it. The Peel Commission concluded in July 1937 that the events
of 1920, as well as 1936, had taken place because the locals were
disaffected at British refusal to honor the promise of independence,
the Balfour Declaration and fears of transforming their homeland
into a Jewish state.[56] That is certainly closer to the truth than the
usual Zionist myth that people like Amin Al-Husseini incited and
controlled Palestinian anger.[57]

When Balfour made his one and only trip to Palestine in March
1925 to help inaugurate the Hebrew University, he was met with
black flags on shuttered windows, a strike, a period of mourning
and noisy demonstrations. Only the discredited mayor Ragheb
Al-Nashashibi, three municipal employees and a handful of Arab

sheikhs attended the event in defiance of the boycott. The protests forced the authorities to quickly transfer him to Damascus (then under French mandate), but there he was met by similar demonstrations which forced him to cut the trip short and head for Beirut, before returning to Paris.[58] In 1925, there was a revolt in Syria against French rule. Palestinian Arabs established the Central Committee to Aid Syria's Afflicted, which raised funds to support the resistance in Syria, an act of solidarity appreciated and reciprocated eleven years later during the Palestinian revolt of 1936.[59]

The period 1923–28 saw a significant retrenchment and weakening of the Palestinian national movement. The Executive Committee of the Arab Palestinian Congress scaled down its demands on the British and lowered its expectations. Instead of independence, it called now for representation. Instead of rejecting new European Jewish immigration, they called for proportional representation. The nadir of the Palestinian situation was evident in the seventh Palestinian Arab Congress, held in Jerusalem on June 20–27, 1928. The 250 delegates represented family and clan interests, both nationalist and collaborationist forces, colonizing resisters and those who were selling land. The Executive Committee was enlarged to 48 (36 Muslims, 12 Christians) in order to satisfy different regions, factions and trends. The leadership emerged fragmented and weakened.[60] Demands no longer included the end of British occupation or rescinding the Balfour Declaration, but focused on more 'moderate' requests, including changing British rules to employ Palestinians and objections to the British granting concessions to Zionist companies.[61] Participants in an economic conference in 1923 in Jerusalem also asked for lower taxes and aimed to support farmers.[62] The weakness continued to be self-inflicted as Palestinian divisions were exploited by the British to support their own policies. It seemed even nature was antagonistic: Palestine was shaken by a powerful earthquake in 1927 in which 272 people were killed, 833 injured and thousands of homes and other buildings damaged.

The era of petitions, complaints, demonstrations and limited boycotts seemed to be reaching its limits. Prior to 1929, the few notable successes using these civil tactics were only able to inconvenience the implementation of the Zionist project. The machinations of power were such that the British government was able to frustrate resistance efforts, exacerbate divisions among the locals and push forward. The strong Zionist lobby in London and from right-wing conservatives ensured no rational solutions.[63]

Frustration mounted and the ground was ripe for another uprising. As before and later, the fuse was lit by the Zionists themselves.

1929: THE AL-BURAQ UPRISING

Controversy arose at a section of the Haram Al-Sharif (Temple Mount), called the Western Wall by Jews and Al-Buraq by Muslims. Some Jews believe it is part of an old temple, some Muslims believe it is where the Prophet Muhammad tethered his horse on his night journey to Jerusalem. Historians have shown it is not related to the Temple period. The wall and small area adjacent to it are part of the Muslim *waqf* but Muslims have allowed Jews to pray there by custom. Instigated by the Jewish Agency, some Jews violated both tradition and British policy by erecting a partition and a table at the site, suggesting a beginning of the establishment of a synagogue. This provocation occurred on September 24, 1928, a day that many Jews consider marks the destruction of the Temple in Jerusalem, adding fears of an attempt to 'rebuild' a temple at the Holy Islamic site. As the days passed and the Jews refused to take down the barrier despite agreements, Muslim anger mounted and moved on from letters and protests in November 1928. The British ruled on August 15, 1929 that Jews must remove any permanent structures at the wall and reiterated that the site belongs to the Islamic *waqf*, while Jews are permitted to pray there by tradition.

The Jewish Zionist leadership rejected the ruling and instead held a noisy rally that marched (surprisingly unmolested) through the Muslim quarter to the wall where they raised the Zionist flag and sang the Zionist anthem (Ha' Tikva). Another Zionist demonstration demanding ownership and control of the Western Wall was held in Tel Aviv on August 14, 1929. Muslims marched to the wall in response on August 16, 1929, the day marking the birth of the Prophet Mohammed, and following the Friday prayers. They demanded implementation of the British ruling and respect for historical arrangements, and denounced the Zionist provocations. As the British could not or would not implement their own rulings, demonstrations and riots were held after the next Friday prayers (August 23, 1929) in Jerusalem. The police opened fire on demonstrators, some of whom were carrying sticks, swords and even guns. Enraged Palestinians descended from other cities spreading information and rumors about a Jewish takeover of holy sites and the British killing of Palestinians.

A political conflict took on a religious character because the Zionists thought that it was the way to mobilize more Jewish support for their cause. Indeed, the wall dominated the World Zionist conference held in Zurich that year. Sigmund Freud captured the essence of it when he explained his refusal to sign a petition condemning Arab riots in Palestine and supporting the Zionist project:

> I cannot do as you wish. I am unable to overcome my aversion to burdening the public with my name, and even the present critical time does not seem to me to warrant it. Whoever wants to influence the masses must give them something rousing and inflammatory and my sober judgment of Zionism does not permit this. I certainly sympathize with its goals, am proud of our University in Jerusalem and am delighted with our settlement's prosperity. But, on the other hand, I do not think that Palestine could ever become a Jewish state, nor that the Christian and Islamic worlds would ever be prepared to have their holy places under Jewish care. It would have seemed more sensible to me to establish a Jewish homeland on a less historically-burdened land. But I know that such a rational viewpoint would never have gained the enthusiasm of the masses and the financial support of the wealthy. *I concede with sorrow that the baseless fanaticism of our people is in part to be blamed for the awakening of Arab distrust. I can raise no sympathy at all for the misdirected piety which transforms a piece of a Herodian wall into a national relic, thereby offending the feelings of the natives.* Now judge for yourself whether I, with such a critical point of view, am the right person to come forward as the solace of a people deluded by unjustified hope. (emphasis added)[64]

This uprising, both armed and nonviolent, came to be known as Hibbet Al-Buraq. When things calmed down, it left in its wake 116 Arabs and 133 Jews dead. Over 1,000 were brought to trial.[65] The original provocation to fan hatred and garner support for Zionism seemed to have worked, resulting in arming and militarizing the Jewish colonies.[66] The troubles were also fanned by British officers with Zionist leanings who wanted to see Arabs react violently; in Hebron, for example, two British officers fanned the flames of Arab hatred by spreading rumors that resulted in Arab attacks while other Arabs shielded and protected their Jewish neighbors.[67] Hibbet Al-Buraq made it clear to Palestinians the extent of British bias in favor of the Zionist project. One Jewish police officer who had executed an Arab family was sentenced to death, but his sentence was reduced to seven years' imprisonment. On the other hand, three leading Palestinians (Fuad Hijazi from Safad, Ata Alzeer and Mohammed Jamjoum from Hebron) charged with killing Jews were publicly hanged on June 27, 1930.[68] The Arab High Commission held a meeting on August 8, 1930 objecting to the reduced sentence on the Jewish terrorist Joseph Mizrahi Elorufli while hanging three Palestinians on weak evidence.[69] The busy market of Tulkarem sacrificed lucrative business days to join a national strike on August 26, 1930.[70]

Hibbet Al-Buraq inspired the grassroots popular resistance movement to mobilize the Arab streets, realizing that change must come. Popular Palestinian mass struggle had always involved all sectors of the society.

It is always instructive to note that even in such a traditional and patriarchal society, women have held their own and pushed for representation and impact. This push was not just on issues concerning women's rights, discrimination, forced marriages and family planning, but also on colonization and occupation. Groups like the Arab Ladies Association pushed for independence and self-determination. The Arab Palestinian Women's Union (*Al-Ittihad Al-Nissai Al-Arabi Al-Filastini*) was founded in Jerusalem in 1921. There were many others, including *Zahr Al-Ukhuwan* (The Lily Flower society), founded in Jaffa 1936, and the Women Solidarity Society, founded in 1942.

The first Arab Women's Congress of Palestine was held on October 26, 1929 in Jerusalem and was attended by about 200 women. The demands were those of the Palestinian people against: the Balfour Declaration and the establishment of Jewish colonies, and for self-determination. They elected a 14-member executive committee headed by Matiel E. T. Mogannam.[71] Mogannam later wrote a book titled *The Arab Women and the Palestinian Problem*, which detailed the activities of the movement.[72] The women who participated were diverse. Some were fully veiled and some very liberal, some Christian and some Muslim. In their meeting with the British High Commissioner, the women 'threw back their veils' and presented their demands in strong language.[73] The High Commissioner was impressed, but stated plainly that his 'authority is limited and some things must be decided by the Ministry of Colonization ... [however,] I am pleased with the progress of the women's movement in Palestine ... and will do my best to help in the educational areas of the Palestinian woman so that she can reach her appropriate place in society'.[74]

Energized by this meeting, the Congress concluded with a 120-car motorcade through the old city of Jerusalem and sent a telegram to Queen Mary, which opened with these words:

> Two hundred Palestine Arab Muslim and Christian women representatives met in twenty-sixth instant in Congress Jerusalem, unanimously decided to demand and exert every effort to effect abolition Balfour Declaration and establish National Democratic Government deriving power from Parliament representing all Palestinian Communities in proportion to their numbers; we beseech assistance in our just demands.[75]

The group was active for many years, developing novel forms of Palestinian resistance such as silent protests, publishing letters in foreign newspapers, direct support of those suffering from the occupation and prisoner support groups. They 'sent hundreds of letters to the British government, newspapers, and news media outlets, Arab leaders, and other women's organizations'.[76] It was not without an impact; for example, their persistent letters about political prisoners in British jails resulted in three prisoners being pardoned.[77]

On the other hand, a new guerrilla movement was created in the Galilee during the autumn of 1929 called *Al-Kaf Al-Akhdar* (the Green Palm), led by Ahmed Tafesh. Its military actions against the British occupation forces lasted only a short while before the movement was crushed and its participants killed or captured. The main form of resistance remained demonstrations, protests, civil disobedience and other forms of popular struggle. And there was, of course, still the same group of elites who thought the best way was to work within the system to get whatever the British and the Zionists would willingly give as this was the 'pragmatic approach'. The gap between the different Palestinian streams widened during Hibbet Al-Buraq. The increased pressure forced the British and the Zionist movement to seek alternative solutions to mollify the growing Arab anger. Ben-Gurion, for example, gave the green light to Judas Magnus, president of the Hebrew University and a bi-nationalist, to explore some form of accommodation. Magnus consulted many Palestinian Arab leaders and came up with an idea of shared representation in government with protection for minorities. But Ben-Gurion rejected the idea outright and insisted that the goal remain a Jewish majority state. However, to appease critics, he offered the formation of a nine-member ministerial council, consisting of three British (Justice, Finance and Transportation), three Jewish (Settlement, Labor, Immigration) and three Arab (Education, Health and Commerce) members. This was a biased solution but was still rejected by the Zionist leadership.[78]

Separately, Palestinians traveled to Britain two months before the investigative committee under the leadership of Sir Walter Shaw issued its report. They pressed the authorities to recognize Arab rights, but stopped short of calling for an end to the Mandate and the Balfour Declaration. The response was still negative and the government insisted on its 'obligations' under the Mandate to the Jewish Agency without regard to the rights of the indigenous people. The Shaw Commission concluded about the events of 1929 that the Palestinians had a right to reject the changes at Al-Buraq and that Al-Husseini did not incite the violence, but that other elements, especially Jewish demonstrations at the Western Wall and prevailing political conditions, precipitated acts of resistance. The report also alluded to 'problems' that were created following such events as the removal of 15,500 villagers from Wadi Al-Hawareth after the transfer of ownership of 30,000 dunums.[79] One of the recommendations of the Shaw Commission was implemented when the British government commissioned an expert to study landownership and use in Palestine. Sir John Hope Simpson, an internationally renowned expert, toured Palestine in July and August 1930 and concluded that, of the 6,544,000 dunums of cultivable land, Zionists already owned nearly one million, or 14 percent, and that the remaining land was barely enough to sustain the local people. Thus increased Jewish immigration did not make sense.[80]

The British Prime Minister Ramsay Macdonald allayed the fears of the Zionist movement days after the release of the report in a letter to Weizmann stating that there would be no change in the commitments under the Mandate, including the Balfour Declaration. His letter of assurance became known as the black letter (as it was in response to the White Paper). What little hope there was among the native Palestinians thus quickly dissipated.[81] Officials directed administrative authorities to help 'rebuild' Jewish economic power and interests. Jewish militias were authorized to arm themselves and 'defend' the colonial settlements. The Hagannah (Jewish paramilitary organization) was recognized and accepted and more Jews enrolled in British police forces to gain fighting skills.

Yet popular resistance continued. An Arab village conference was held in Jaffa on November 5–6, 1929. A letter sent from the conference asked for the removal of taxes like *ushr* and *wirco* and to replace them with simple customs taxes. Other suggestions included opening an agricultural credit union and measures that could reduce the increasing bankruptcy of farmers.[82] A student conference was held in Akka in 1930 and, in early 1931, a national fund (*Sandook Al-Umma*) was established relying mostly on donations from Palestinians and other Arabs in and outside Palestine. Its aim was to help farmers threatened with loss of their land to the Zionist project. The British authorities had closed the bank that lent to the farmers in March 1920 and refused repeated requests to reopen it. The national meeting in Nablus on September 18, 1931 endorsed the fund project officially and June 16, 1932 was agreed as a national day of fundraising to protect threatened lands. However, with very limited funds it made little impact during its eight years of operation, saving only some lands in Beit Hannoun and Jules. This was no match for the magnitude of the British-Zionist conspiracy to strip farmers of their lands.[83]

THE UPRISING DIES AND THE ECONOMIC DEPRESSION GATHERS PACE

Small projects, petitions and protests were all far too little to stem the Zionist-British onslaught that was overwhelming Palestine in a period of international economic depression. The Zionist movement had grown strong and aggressive and started making more demands on their British benefactors. The High Commissioner was replaced in November 1931 under pressure and direction from Weizmann. Local Palestinian leadership became even more disillusioned about the effectiveness of using only popular resistance. Anger and calls for violent resistance grew. In a meeting in July 1931 in Nablus, delegates called for armed resistance against the British and Zionists and even set up a committee to procure weapons, but the committee did nothing. Though few practical steps were taken in that direction, the meeting modeled the rhetoric for a Palestinian armed revolt. It would take time to change from 50 years of popular resistance to a mixed form of resistance. Amin Al-Husseini and his supporters kept to the diplomatic track. They organized a general Islamic conference on December 7–17, 1931, attended by 145 key Islamic scholars and leaders from 22 countries. The proposals presented at the conference included setting up an Islamic university (the

Hebrew University) in Jerusalem and an agricultural company to help Palestinians struggling in the depressed economy to stay on their lands. The conference was largely symbolic and while strengthening the personal status of Amin Al-Husseini, no practical steps to help Palestine materialized.[84] But leaders of the previous organization *Al-Arabiya Al-Fatat* and supporters of independence were mobilized, 50 of whom met on December 13, 1931 in the home of Awni Abd Al-Hadi and drafted an Arab nationalist covenant. This document re-emphasized the regional Arab context for the struggle for Palestine as a joint effort against imperialism and evolved later to form *Hizb Al-Istiqlal* in 1933. The Arab nationalists' split from pan-Islamic nationalists would become a feature of the Palestinian struggle to the present day. The problems for pan-Arab nationalists, then as now, were interference from outside and quarrels between Arab leaders (e.g. the Hashemite-Saud family rivalry). The strength was in the principled demands that people like Amin Al-Husseini were unwilling to adopt because of their close connection to the British authorities at the time.[85]

Awni Abd Al-Hadi founded *Hizb Al-Istiqlal* in 1932 as a successor to the earlier nationalist party by the same name founded under Ottoman rule. The party demanded changes in the Arab Executive Committee to recruit new and younger generations of leaders who would support Arab unity and independence.[86] In assemblies on February 24, 1933 and March 26, 1933 attended by over 500 delegates, plans and ideas were explored for ending any cooperation and using nonviolence and non-cooperation to achieve the goals of independence.

In 1929, the number of Jewish immigrants was about 5,000; by 1933 this had risen to over 30,000 annually.[87] Palestinians expressed their feelings against dumping Europe's problems on them in mass demonstrations. An Arab Women's march to demand an end to the Zionist program on April 15, 1933 heard speeches delivered by such notable Arab feminists as Tarab Abd Al-Hadi. A large demonstration on September 13, 1933 in Jerusalem led by Palestinian religious and civic leaders spilled over to other cities.[88]

On October 13, 1933, 7,000 angry demonstrators filled the streets of Jaffa. The British forces opened fire, killing twelve and wounding 78 Palestinians. One policeman was also killed. Two weeks later, on October 27, 1933 in Jaffa, 24 peaceful demonstrators were killed and 204 injured. The indiscriminate and brutal attack on unarmed civilians incensed an already seething population. Musa Kadhem Al-Husseini was in the demonstration and was beaten; later, he and the Arab High Committee met the British High Commissioner, Sir Arthur Wauchope, and the old Palestinian broke down, explaining that civilized troops do not fire on unarmed civilians.[89]

Petitions and objections from natives halted plans for further Zionist expansion, but that was when protests were directed at Arabs. For example, local *Hizb Al-Istiqlal* people wrote to Syrians about plans to sell land near Al-Hula and objected successfully to King Abdullah's agreement to grant a 99-year lease on land in the Jordan valley to the Zionists in early 1933.[90] The demonstrations and protests against the British continued. Musa Kadhem Al-Husseini, aged 83, headed a large, 'unauthorized' protest in Jerusalem on October 13, 1933. The success of this demonstration led to another one in Jaffa on October 27, which representatives from as far away as Syria and Jordan attended. That demonstration was met with a hail of British bullets which killed 26 and injured 60.[91]

The High Commissioner's abrupt decision to hold municipal elections in 1934 was probably due to his hope that the divisions in the Arab leadership and increasing Jewish numbers could change the make-up of the municipal councils in ways that would serve his interests. But nationalist forces won and in some towns, the High Commissioner appointed mayors from the opposition even though the elected majority were nationalists.[92] In that same year, on May 12, a conference was held on the tax situation in Palestine to try to get the government to reduce the unfair tax burden at a time when increased Jewish migration had bankrupted many Palestinians and forced large numbers of farmers off their lands.[93]

The government ignored the unrest and continued with its policies of encouraging Jewish immigration and land purchases, supporting the *Yishuv* as a state-in-the-making and simultaneously pulling the rug from under the feet of the Palestinian farmers. Sami Al-Sarraj, writing in *Al-Difa'* on January 15, 1935, praised the escalation:

> Come oh Arabs let us disobey the laws one time. Come ye writers let us disobey the laws without worry about what the legal system will do to us ... and ye Arab, there is nothing that forces you to buy products of foreigners and certainly not products of your enemies ...[94]

A conference of Islamic scholars and judges was held on January 25, 1935 under the leadership of Amin Al-Husseini and issued statements banning the sale of land to immigrant Jews.[95]

The High Commissioner proposed a legislative council in 1935 to include 25 members: five government officials, eight Muslims, seven Jews, three Christians and two representing commercial interests. The Arab High Committee accepted after some deliberations, but the Zionist movement rejected it. The British retracted the scheme following debates in the House of Commons where the Zionists had a strong lobby.[96] That failure set the stage for more instability. By the beginning of 1936, the political scene in Palestine was ripe for revolt and had a number of political parties that could indeed lead it.[97]

Hizb Al-Istiqlal

This began on the sidelines of the Islamic conference of 1931 and represented an Arab nationalist strand that rejected imperialism and Zionism. It called for the end of both the British Mandate and the Balfour Declaration. Prominent leaders included Awni Abd Al-Hadi, Subhi Al-Khadhra, Akram Zueiter, Salim Salameh and Fahmi Al-Aboushi.

Hizb Al-Difa'

Hizb Al-Difa' called for general nationalist trend, but avoided calling for Arab unity. Its leaders believed more in negotiations, compromise and working out arrangements between them and the British and Zionist leaders. They also had a close relationship with King Abdullah of Jordan. Prominent figures included Ragheb Al-Nashashibi, Fakhri Al-Nashashibi, Sheikh Asaad Al-Shuqairi, Sulaiman Toukqan, Adel Al-Shawa and others.

Al-Hizb Al-Arabi

Founded in 1935 by Jamal Al-Husseini to call for independence of Palestinian and Arab unity and essentially a successor to Hizb Al-Istiqlal, this party gained broad popularity and drew significant support from highly respected leaders, including Sheikh Hasan Abu Als'ood, Farid Al-Anabtawi, Sheikh Muhammad Al-Khatib, Yosef Sahyoun, Dhaher Farhan, Aldellah Samara, Kamel Dajani and Yosef Al-Alami among others.

Mu'tamar Al-Shabab

Originally established as a youth movement in Jaffa in 1932, it later transformed essentially into a political party with all ages represented. It developed practical popular resistance methods, including a fund to aid in development, a group of lookouts along the coast to prevent the entry of illegal Zionist immigrants and established the scout movement in Palestine. Its second general conference in May 1935 had 1,000 delegates. Its most prominent leader was Yacoub Al-Ghosein.

Hizb Al-Islah

Formed on June 18, 1935, this party had similar principles and in many ways was a successor to *Al-Hizb Al-Arabi*. It had no president but three co-equal secretaries: Hussein Fakhri Al-Khalidi (elected mayor of Jerusalem in the 1934 elections), Mahmoud Abu Khadra and Shibli Al-Jamal.

Hizb Al-Kutal Al-Wataniya

Formed in Nablus on October 4, 1935 it staked a position between *Hizb Al-Difa'* and *Al-Hizb Al-Arabi* and called for unity among the various parties.

Hizb Al-Shuyuii Al-Falastini

The Communist Party of Palestine traces its roots to 1919 in partnership with Jewish communists (who believed in Zionism). In 1923, it moved away from Zionism and more towards a true communist (Marxist) agenda.

Jamiyyet Al-'Omal Al-Arab

Starting in 1923, Arab laborers began organizing as unions under the Arab Railway Workers' Club, but their efforts were met viciously by the Histadrut (Jewish Labor Federation) and the British authorities. The latter allowed Jewish workers to organize but not Arab workers. They finally applied to set up a society for Arab workers. The most recognized labor leader of the period was Michel Mitri, who led a number of actions to challenge the hegemony of the Histadrut and was assassinated in December 1936 for his popular resistance activities.

These parties were all represented in the Arab Higher Committee and wrote to the British authorities asking for democratic government representation according to the Charter of the League of Nations and to section 2 of the Mandate declaration. The response came on January 12, 1936 and reiterated British rejection of those demands.[98] The failure of British efforts in 1935 to form a legislative council that included Arabs and Jews added to the natives' frustration. The combination of factors led to massive pressure on the natives and it was in this period of civil engagement and civilian resistance met by stonewalling and rejection and after over 15 years of British occupation that the first major organized violence occurred.

These trends were coupled with the failure of early attempts in 1931–34 to develop economic self-sufficiency. This failure was due to lack of capital as compared to vast sums available to the Zionists, the British propensity to give economic interests and franchises to Zionists, and the lack of knowledge of modern economic structures. The economic and political empowerment of the Zionist movement was thus accompanied by an erosion of economic and political power, creating even more resentment and setting the stage for further resistance.

7
The Great Revolt of 1936–39

Those who make peaceful revolution impossible, make violent revolution inevitable.

John F. Kennedy[1]

We saw in Chapter 6 how the British authorities advanced Zionism at the expense of the native people, who resisted with limited but some notable successes. Yet, the transformation of Palestine was accelerating by the mid-1930s. The Zionist movement acquired nearly one million dunums of the best land, mostly through direct transfer from the British authorities or through purchases from absentee owners, who had unfairly acquired large tracts and were now urged by the British authorities to sell them to the Jewish Agency. British policies to promote European Jewish colonial migration also tripled the percentage of Jews in Palestine. The Palestinian middle and lower classes' economic hardships were due to actions by the Palestinian elite, Jewish settlers and British occupiers. Tens of thousands of Palestinian peasants were made homeless and destitute by the land policies. Zionist labor policies also ensured that even displaced peasants had few job opportunities. The policy of 'Jewish labor only' in Zionist enterprises, combined with the British policy of essentially giving all industrial concessions to Jewish Zionist capitalists, meant that more than 90 percent of the industrial base in Palestine (capital and labor) came into Jewish Zionist hands by 1937. This aggravated the disparity in the availability of jobs and was even more pronounced in the wage structure.[2] The worsening economic situation worldwide in the early 1930s and clear signs of Zionist intentions to take over the country by force made this an extremely volatile situation.

The local political scene included nascent Palestinian parties, trade unions and vibrant media. Yet, Palestinian society was still inexperienced in Western ways and unable to cope with the onslaught of the well-organized *Yishuv* movement. Palestinians were frustrated by the lack of response from the British to their demands. Flare-ups with the British forces in 1934 and 1935 were small and contained, but beneath the surface there was seething anger. The

situation thus was ripe for an uprising, though how it would start
was unclear.

On October 16, 1935, a barrel marked 'cement' was dropped and
burst open as it was being unloaded from a ship in Jaffa, spilling
out guns, grenades and ammunition. This shattered the illusion
of those who mistakenly thought that Zionists were interested in
migration only and were not intent on taking over the country.
Publicity about the secret shipments to the underground Zionist
terrorist militias was the spur to mobilization. The British authority
did not mount a serious challenge to arms smuggling and instead
continued to give great leeway to the Zionist institutions to build
a state within the Mandate.[3] Palestinian media exposed this secret
arming and publicized Zionist intentions, so adding to Palestinians'
sense of anger and betrayal.

What triggered the chain of events leading to the full-fledged
uprising of 1936–39 is debated. Some credit the event in Jaffa;
others credit the suppression of a demonstration held on November
2, 1935 on the anniversary of the Balfour Declaration; while the
appropriation of land from Tulkarem Agricultural School for Jewish
use is cited by others as a pivotal event.[4] Akram Zueiter, former
editor of *Mir'at Al-Sharq* in Jerusalem and later co-founder of *Hizb
Al-Istiqlal*, cites November 17, 1935 because that is when the Royal
Commissioner returned from England with further support for
Zionists and the demonstrations that followed were suppressed by
excessive violence.[5] Zueiter had left his teaching post in Acre at the
age of 20 to become editor and an activist. He was arrested and
imprisoned for three months, then 'deported' to Nablus, where he
stepped up his work against the British occupation.[6] He co-founded
Hizb Al-Istiqlal and was arrested in the uprising of 1936. Later,
he headed an Arab delegation to Latin America and wrote a book
about that experience.

The historian George Antonius, who had been a British civil
servant but who resigned in 1930 in protest over British policies
in Palestine, described the revolt in his seminal work *The Arab
Awakening:*[7]

> The rebellion today is, to a greater extent than ever before,
> a revolt of villagers, and its immediate cause is the proposed
> scheme of Partition and, more particularly, that aspect of it which
> envisages the eventual displacement of a large Arab peasantry
> to make room for the immigrant citizens of the proposed Jewish
> state. The moving spirits in the revolt are not the nationalist

leaders, most of whom are now in exile, but men of the working and agricultural classes who are risking their lives in what they believe to be the only way left to them of saving their homes and their villages. It is a delusion to regard it as the work of agitators, Arab or foreign. Political incitement can do much to fan the flames of discontent, but it cannot keep a revolt active, month after month, in conditions of such violence and hardship. Far from its being engineered by the leaders, the revolt is in a very marked way a challenge to their authority and an indictment of their methods. The rebel chiefs lay the blame for the present plight of the peasantry on those Arab landowners who have sold their land, and they accuse the leaders of culpable neglect for failing to prevent the sales.[8]

Grassroots activists in Nablus issued a call on November 13, 1935 for a strike throughout the country, even though the leadership of most political factions were opposed to such a move. On December 9, 1935, strategy meetings and popular gatherings were held to commemorate the anniversary of the British occupation of Jerusalem. The revolt intensified. A massive demonstration was held in Haifa on January 5, 1936, 40 days after the deaths of the Palestinian guerrilla leader Sheikh Qassam and his comrades. On April 17, 1936, two farmers, Hassan Aburas and Salem Al-Masri, were killed by Zionists in an orange grove near Al-Aujah river. Two days later, the authorities faced an angry demonstration in the streets of Jaffa which turned into a riot during which Zionists were killed.

A meeting of key Palestinian organizers on April 20, 1936 called for a general, open-ended strike inspired by the successful 45-day strike in Syria which led the French to cede to their demands. After grassroots pressure, on April 21, 1936 the political factions reluctantly declared their support for the strike and agreed to a policy of non-cooperation, including some forms of civil resistance, until Palestinian demands were met. Grassroots pressure continued. When these same political leaders convened in Jerusalem on April 25, 1936, headed by Amin Al-Husseini, young activists surrounded the building demanding that the mayor of Jerusalem, Hussein Fakhri Al-Khalidi, come out and respond practically and publicly to the mayor of Tel Aviv. Al-Khalidi did not come out initially, but Nashashibi did. The youths were not satisfied with what he had to say. After standing their ground, Al-Khalidi finally came out to repudiate the Tel Aviv mayor's racist comments.[9] Public pressure on these parties resulted in the formation of the Arab

Higher Committee that same day. This brought rivals from the Arab Party (*Al-Hizb Al-Arabi*) (Jamal Al-Husseini and Alfred Rock), the Defense Party (*Hizb Al-Difa'*) (Ragheb Al-Nashashibi and Yacoub Faraj), the Independence Party (*Hizb Al-Istiqlal*) (Awni Abd Al-Hadi and Ahmed Hilmi), the Nationalist Coalition (*Al-Kutla*) (Hussein Fakhri Al-Khalidi), the Reform Party (*Al-Islah*) (Abdel Latif Salah) and the Youth Congress (*Mu'tamar Al-Shabab*) (Yacoub Al-Ghosein) under one umbrella.[10]

In response to the growing call for popular resistance, the Arab Car Owners and Drivers Committee, which represented hundreds, issued a call in late April 1936 encouraging citizens to withhold their taxes.[11] The tax revolt spread and the Arab High Committee (AHC) took up the call. On May 5, 1936, the British High Commissioner met the AHC and warned them of legal and other consequences if they pursued the tax strike and other popular resistance actions. On May 7, 1936, a contentious meeting of 150 delegates representing all sectors of the population was held in Kulliyat Rawdat Alma'aref in Jerusalem and the overwhelming majority voted to continue with the strikes and demonstration until their demands were met. These included a halt to Zionist immigration and colonization, a ban on the transfer of Palestinian lands to European Zionists and the establishment of a democratically elected government. Their program included the first use in Palestine of the slogan 'No Taxation without Representation'.[12]

A conference of the national committees met in Jerusalem the following day and declared that, from May 15, onwards, people should stop paying taxes unless their demands were met. National committees were formed in many cities to promote the strike and develop other types of nonviolent resistance and service committees for the needy.[13] The local support committees treated the sick, cared for those in need and supported the families of those arrested, injured or killed. That people helped each other makes the 1936 uprising a genuinely grassroots community effort which even the British acknowledged was extremely efficient and successful.[14]

Demonstrations were held throughout Palestine after Friday prayers on the deadline, May 15, 1936. In one large demonstration in Jaffa, British forces opened fire, killing and injuring many protesters. When complaints about the brutality of the British response went unheeded, the young opted to organize their own protection and the residents of Jaffa elected 15 young men who were dubbed the National Guard.

The Controversial Amin Al-Husseini

Amin Al-Husseini was born in Jerusalem in 1895 and studied religious law at Al-Azhar University, Cairo and at the Istanbul School of Administration, but never completed his studies. After pilgrimage to Mecca in 1913, he became known as Haj Amin. Like many Palestinians of his age, he was conscripted into the Ottoman army during World War I. The British accused him of participating and leading the demonstrations of 1920 and sentenced him *in absentia*. This propelled him onto the national scene. He was pardoned by the High Commissioner and returned to Jerusalem in August 1920. The High Commissioner appointed him to the newly created position of Grand Mufti of Jerusalem on May 8, 1921 to further create divisions in Palestinian society. He headed the first Palestinian delegation to London in 1921 and was appointed president of the first Supreme Muslim Council in March 1922. He headed the Palestinian delegation to London in 1930 and was elected president of the Arab High Committee, which was established in April 25, 1936. He was a prudent diplomat and managed to straddle different interests as long as the strings of power led to him. Thus, it was not difficult to find statements by him against 'agitation' and violence while also finding strong nationalist speeches in response to grassroots pressure. The British considered him an important ally for some years. He really had little to do with the uprising, which was a spontaneous popular movement.[15]

He had a daring escape to Lebanon after being sought by the authorities, then moved on to Iraq, Italy and finally Germany. In keeping with his tradition of seeking allies to maintain his power base, he sought support from Britain's enemy: Germany. Hitler wanted Al-Husseini to help in propaganda efforts for the Axis Powers among Bosnian Muslims. Al-Husseini wanted Hitler to help him regain political power if Germany won the war. Contrary to Al-Husseini's expectations, Nazi Germany did not come to the support of Palestine and instead made deals with the Zionist leadership based on a shared vision of Jews not belonging in Europe.[16] The diminished Al-Husseini was nevertheless elected president of the Arab Higher Executive (Fourth Higher Committee of the Arab League). He was later named president of the National Assembly, set up by the Arab High Committee Congress on October 1, 1948, in Gaza. The short-lived experiment in Palestinian independent leadership was snuffed out by Jordan and Egypt and Al-Husseini remained marginalized, although many Palestinians continued to back him.

He died on July 5, 1974 in Beirut.[17]

The authorities responded to the growing resistance by declaring a state of emergency, with general curfews and drastic measures against any disturbances. Villages and towns were fined for refusing to pay taxes. Personal property was confiscated and homes demolished. Hundreds of strike organizers were imprisoned. On May 17, 1936, prisoners in Nur Shams declared a strike and confronted the prison guards who ordered soldiers to open fire. One inmate was killed and several wounded as prisoners shouted in defiance: 'Martyrdom is better than jail'.[18] On May 23, 1936, Awni Abd Al-Hadi, secretary general of the Arab High Committee, was arrested.

The authorities continued to ignore the demands of the growing movement. The British authorities approved the entry of thousands of new immigrants and opened a port in Tel Aviv operated by Zionist workers to replace the striking Jaffa port. Locals accelerated their resistance. On May 18, thousands of Palestinians from dozens of towns and villages attended a large rally at Abu Ghosh in Jerusalem. At the Friday demonstrations in Nablus on May 23, 1936, the authorities used live ammunition against nonviolent demonstrators killing four (Husni Hammad, Bakra Issa, Fawzi Al-Taher and an unidentified person).[19] The mayor of Jaffa, Asem Bek Al-Sae'ed, called for a meeting of the mayors of many cities. Held in Ramallah on May 30, 1936, the mayors resolved to endorse and support the strikes, the first time in Palestinian history where municipalities engaged in collective action. Students went on strike, as did all the religious leadership and the 1,500 sailors and dockworkers in Jaffa, paralyzing business, commerce and other aspects of normal life.[20]

ARMED RESISTANCE IN THE 1930s

Since arriving in Haifa on February 5, 1922, the charismatic leader Sheikh Izz Al-Din Al-Qassam had been working among the poor and marginalized members of society, especially farmers displaced by land laws that favored Zionism. This work convinced him that Zionists did indeed intend to take over and that armed resistance should be combined with political and media work. Amin Al-Husseini rejected Al-Qassam's call for armed revolt. Al-Qassam and a few friends formed *Al-Kaf Al-Aswad* (the Black Hand) to resist the occupation and declared their existence on the anniversary of the Balfour Declaration (November 2, 1935). Nearly 400 British and Arab forces surrounded a small band of fighters in the forests of Y'bed, near Jenin on November 20, 1935 and ordered them to surrender. The sheikh and his comrades chose to fight and die instead. He and four others (Sheikh Yousef Abdullah, Mustafa Al-Zeibawi, Hanafi Atiya Ahmed and Hamad Aby Kassem Khalaf) were killed. Others were injured or captured (including Sheikh Nimr Al-Sa'di) and a third group (led by Sheikh Farhan Al-Sa'di) escaped to resume fighting later.[21] At the mass funeral over 5,000 people attended and stood in front of British soldiers, who opened fire on the crowd. The wave of popular grief at Al-Qassem's martyrdom embarrassed traditional leaders, including Al-Husseini, who had spurned him in life but now claimed him as one of their own and even held a memorial service for him in Haifa on January 5, 1936. A rival memorial drew twice as many attendees and was organized by Qassam's own group, the Young Men's Muslim Association of Haifa.[22] The historian Emil Tuma believes that this movement transformed the Palestinian struggle from an era of demonstrations and acts of disobedience and protests to one that included armed resistance as a key strategy.[23]

Musa Kadhem Al-Husseini spent half his life under British occupation and died in nonviolent resistance to that occupation. Frustrated by the slow pace of change, his 24-year-old son, Abd Al-Qader, co-founded *Al-Jihad Al-Muqaddas* (Holy Jihad) in 1931 to fight the British, using a mix of violence and nonviolence. He organized a congress of educated Muslim to demand equality and justice. In parallel, a small band of guerrilla fighters started operating in a corridor from Jaffa to Nablus. Battles were fought between these rebels and the British authorities in the Nablus area on April 25, 1936 and elsewhere. Abd Al-Qader became Jerusalem district commander and was exiled in 1938, but returned under cover and was killed in a Zionist attack at Al-Qastel (Jerusalem District) on April 8, 1948.

In September 1936 various groups advocating armed resistance unified under the leadership of Fawz Ed Din Qawuqji. It was estimated that the armed resistance at its peak had 5,000–8,000 Palestinian participants.[24] The militant resistance and the strike both ended with calls from the leaders of Arab countries in November 1936, who declared their trust and hope that the British authorities would act fairly. This was supported on November 12, 1936 by the AHC leaders of the civil resistance and Qawuqji, who was leading the armed resistance.[25] An uprising is not a tap that can be turned on and off by declarations. Thus, sporadic resistance continued. An upsurge occurred after the failure of the British government to do anything meaningful to protect indigenous rights and especially after the partition plans of 1937.

Acts of resistance escalated between October 1937 and early 1939. On September 9, 1939, fighters took over Beersheba government facilities and released political prisoners from the central jail. On October 4, 1938 they took on Tiberias. A few days later, the rebels seized control of the old city of Jerusalem.[26] According to official statistics, 4,969 rebel operations were carried out in 1938. The tactics the British used to try to quell the unrest varied and centered on extensive use of collective punishment, banned by international law. For example, on July 28, 1937, all 93 homes of the village of Baqa Al-Gharbiya were demolished and lands and crops destroyed.[27] Before April 1936 there were about 2,000 British soldiers in Palestine, but by 1938 there were 25,000. Curfews became increasingly frequent and lengthy. Cities and towns were fined and made to pay compensation. The British used Palestinians as human shields and sent in saboteurs for operations that were blamed on the rebels. All these tactics were to be adopted by Israeli forces decades later.

BUT THE POPULAR RESISTANCE CONTINUES

Forms of nonviolent resistance included demonstrations, boycotts, tax revolts and other forms of civil disobedience. There were also hundreds of acts of economic sabotage, from attacks on rail track to the destruction of settler and government buildings and other infrastructure. Both the Zionist and British leadership described the acts as 'criminal', 'lawless', 'thuggery', 'sabotage', and so on. The Zionist movement profited by getting the British to train and pay for Zionist militias to 'defend' the Jewish settlements. The British authorities took drastic steps to put down both the violent and nonviolent revolt. The worst of these measures for many Palestinians was the collective punishment of demolishing hundreds of homes in Nablus, Bethlehem, Hebron, Lod, Safad, Al-Majdal and Qalqilia. On June 18, 1936 the authorities demolished large sections of the old city of Jaffa, leaving 6,000 homeless.[28] One of the Palestinians affected sued and the British Chief Justice, Sir Michael McDonnell, ruled that the demolitions were indeed excessive and illegal. Palestinian activists printed the ruling and handed out thousands of copies to British soldiers.[29]

On June 10, 1936, a Palestinian delegation, which included Jamal Al-Husseini, Shibli Jamal, Emile Ghori and Izzat Tannous, traveled to London to discuss the disturbances with British officials. Although the delegation failed to get the British to end the Zionist project, they helped establish a parliamentary group that supported the Palestinian cause and opened an Arab Center in London.[30]

On the ground in Palestine, the repression continued. The authorities fired Palestinian employees who were deemed to be nationalist supporters. After nearly four years as head of the Arabic section of the Voice of Palestine radio station, Ibrahim Touqan was fired for broadcasting programs that supported self-determination.

Britain then advanced the idea of partition as a possible 'solution' to the problem they had created. Most Palestinian political parties and figures were adamantly opposed to it, a notable exception being the National Defense Party led by Raghib Al-Nashashibi (mayor of Jerusalem 1920–34). However, when the Peel Commission came up with its recommendation in July 1937, which included the most productive lands, as well as Haifa and Acre, to be given to a Jewish state, even the NDP opposed it.[31] This episode, and others like it, illustrate the shifting of power politics when confronted with a popular uprising.

By September 27, 1937, when the authorities declared the AHC and all Arab national committees to be 'unlawful associations', the uprising began to subside. The Mandate authorities arrested many, executed some and exiled a number of the leaders to the Seychelles.[32] By 1938, daily life had 'normalized', in terms of routine British occupation and Zionist colonization. Occasional spurts of activity continued, for example when a huge Arab Women's conference in support of the Palestinian struggle was held in Egypt on October 28, 1938 with a prominent Palestinian presence led by Tarab Abd Al-Hadi.[33]

The Palestinians paid a heavy price for the uprising of 1935–39 in material and human losses. In the first year of the uprising, about 1,000 Palestinians were killed, more than half of them unarmed; by the time the uprising ended over 5,000 Palestinians were dead and thousands more injured (per capita these casualties were higher than the intifadas of 1987 and 2000). As collective punishment, whole sections of Jaffa and many other places were demolished and the local economy devastated. Approximately 10 percent of adult males were imprisoned. Hundreds were executed and hundreds more exiled. On the social and political level, the impact was also devastating. The AHC was now more divided than ever and the Mufti increased its power at the expense of the progressive and grassroots organizations. The British were able to divide the Palestinians further into factions squabbling over everything from remaining and dwindling resources to tactics to philosophy.[34] The diplomatic struggle and the confusion created by pressure from British collaborators who headed puppet Arab governments kept the lid on any major activities for nearly a year. This was a devastating loss of momentum for the Palestinian cause and gave time to build Zionist strength in Palestine. The Jewish Haganah forces and *Yishuv* leadership were strengthened in some cases by the British directly and in others indirectly as they benefited from the British suppression of the Palestinian revolt.

Abd Al-Jawad Saleh (Palestinian leader from Al-Bireh) stated about the six-month strike of 1936:

> It is true that the 1936 strike was one of the instruments to promote the emerging Palestinian identity. It is true that it was an unmistakable signal of rejection. It is also true that it gave the appearance to the nation's enemies of being united with a real coherence. But it is equally true that this long strike weakened the Palestinian economy, and also eased the position of the Jews against the Palestinians and enhanced their self-reliance. For example, the strike of sailors and Arab workers in the port of Jaffa led to establishing the Port of Tel Aviv ... The negative effects of the strike factored strongly into the weakening of Palestinian society and its ability to deal with the confrontation that erupted 10 years later leading to the catastrophe of 1948.[35]

There were some successes as a spontaneous revolt spread across the country forcing the British to bring in reinforcements from Britain, Egypt and Cyprus. Violent and nonviolent resistance was a potent mix, making the country almost ungovernable. With a population of nearly 1.5 million, the authorities had to contend with ten disturbances or more (some violent, some nonviolent) every day for months, even though they had over 25,000 heavily armed troops trying to put down the insurgency. Psychologically, the uprising also influenced people around the Middle East who were inspired that Britain, with a well-equipped army, could not put down a peasant uprising of a few thousand. The uprising also shattered any illusion about the utility of collaboration with a British policy that had long been hijacked by the Zionist movement.

The British underestimated the resentment their policy created and attempted to undercut the growing revolt with statements that were inconsistent with their actions on the ground, in the form of severe repression and increased support for the Zionist program between 1922 and the late 1930s. At one point, the British proposed dividing the country into a small Jewish state and a larger Palestine to be incorporated under Britain's puppet government of Jordan. This proposal touched off more demonstrations and continued unrest, which the British were not able to quell until 1939. The British also brought in Nuri Al-Sa'id, Foreign Minister of Iraq, as a 'mediator' and succeeded in creating confusion among elite leaders of the uprising as to what to do with initiatives to mediate between them and the British. While the usual collaborative elites agreed to his formulation of vague promises to 'look into' their demands, most people did not concede.[36] At the request of the British government, King Abd Al-Aziz Al-Saud called on Arab rulers to issue a statement calling on the Palestinians to end the revolt. The public declaration, issued on November 11, 1936, stated:

> We were pained by the current situation in Palestine. We in agreement with the Kings of the Arabs and Amir Abdullah [Hashemite family of Hejaz who were put by the British as ruler of Jordan] call on you to adopt quietness and stop the strike to prevent the spilling of blood relying on God and on the good will of our friend The British government and her declared desire to achieve justice. And trust that we will continue to strive towards helping you.[37]

This was an easy way out for the AHC, which was not convinced of the strength of the Palestinian people and had only reluctantly joined the revolt.

The British issued two White Papers (on November 9, 1938 and May 17, 1939) offering a sliver of carrot while simultaneously deploying a heavy stick (literally and metaphorically). The 1939 White Paper was intended to calm the situation so that Britain could focus on war with Germany; it conceded that the Mandate and Balfour Declaration never intended to create a Jewish state against the wishes of the Palestinian Arabs. But the Palestinian and Zionist leadership both verbally rejected this.[38] Only the Palestinian leadership offered the cessation of unrest the British wanted. The White Paper, as Jonathan Dimbleby points out, was a 'pious and belated assertion of principle, a last lunge towards common sense, [and] did not even gather dust before it was trampled underfoot by the irresistible force of Zionism which had been unleashed by the British themselves'.[39] The Zionist militias, nurtured by the British, intensified their military activities, including the use of terror tactics against both the Palestinians and their British benefactors.

THE UPRISING SUBSIDES

As we shall see later in the uprising of 1987, the grassroots movement was co-opted by self-serving elite leaders. In the second half of British rule, new leaders from the traditional political families jockeyed for power and, like their predecessors, paid little attention to the grassroots movement. The Iraqi diplomat Mohammed Jamali wrote:

> One of the basic factors which led to the Palestine tragedy was the problem of leadership and the lack of democratic organization on the part of the Palestinians. The Leadership of the people was attained by arousing popular sentiment. Personalities might rise to leadership by personal charm, family background and a dose of nationalism. Once a leader was in the saddle, he was usually not removable or changeable by democratic procedure. Authoritarianism on the part of a leader might lead to dissensions and conflict of personalities, which might weaken the whole national body. This was true of most of the Arab world and the Palestinians were no exception ... The charisma, popularity and control of Haj Amin left no room for another person. When Haj Amin returned after the War he was not popular either in Iraq or with the victorious Allies. This perpetuated the crisis of leadership.[40]

Amin Al-Husseini asked for a meeting in Cairo with Jamali because he did not like the idea of the nascent Palestinian media office led by Musa Al-Alami, funded by Iraq and supported by the Arab League. Al-Alami, born in Jerusalem in 1897, studied law at Cambridge and represented Palestinian political parties at meetings preparing for the establishment of the Arab League. He founded communications offices to serve the Palestinian cause in Jerusalem, Beirut, London and Washington.

It is hard now to measure accurately what violence vs. nonviolence accomplished. King suggests that:

> Palestinians utilized predominantly nonviolent strategies to preserve their way of life, which resulted in little if any effect on British policies or Zionist goals. The specific instances in which the Palestinians actually influenced British policy involved wild bloody riots and paramilitary operations.[41]

I believe the results were mixed for both. Palestinians remained subject to British rule and whims, and no indigenous Palestinian leadership was able to rise above pettiness and clan interests to build the institutions of self-governance.[42] Taken together, history shows that the failure of the Palestinian national movement to achieve its goals in this period was due to a number of factors: Palestinian social weakness, international collaboration with the Zionist movement, British brutality which destroyed much of the Palestinian society, leadership vacuums, a lack of logistics and support, Arab countries' weakness and collaboration, and divisions among Palestinians. These factors were to persist over the following decades. But, as noted above, this does not detract from the heroic efforts at popular resistance that gave meaning, direction and lessons for the even more difficult periods to come. To cite just one example, it was during this uprising that the traditional head covering (the *hatta* worn with the *'iqal*, also termed *kufiya*) of the peasants became a symbol of the link with the land and defense of peasant rights. The resistance fighters made special efforts to spread the culture of returning to Arab roots by wearing native clothes and a few even went to the extreme of attacking the use of the *tarbush* (the headdress associated with Ottoman Turks and Western-leaning officials like some of the Nashashibi notables).[43]

8
Devastation to *Nakba*, 1939–48

There is no denying that the Mandate (which incorporated the Balfour Declaration) contained contradictory promises. In the first place, it promised the Jews a National Home and in the second place, it declared the rights and position of the Arabs must be protected. Therefore, it provided what was virtually an invasion of the country by thousands of immigrants and at the same time said that this was not to disturb the people in possession.

UK Foreign Secretary Ernest Bevin, statement to
the House of Commons, February 23, 1947[1]

The confusion about the 1939 White Paper and its impact coincided with the confusion among the Palestinians about the potential impact of the outbreak of the World War II on Palestine. But many were also worried about supporting an imperial power that occupied Palestine and nurtured the Zionist program. However, more than 19,000 Palestinian Arabs and 28,000 Jews enlisted in British forces. Few Palestinian and Jewish leaders were willing to end their cooperation with the British and even fewer were willing to cooperate with the Axis Powers (Germany, Italy and Japan). The fact that the resistance ended in Palestine in 1939 and crucially was to remain dormant throughout the war was a huge gift to the Allies. By contrast, attacks by the Lehi (Fighters for the Freedom of Israel, an underground military group also known as the Stern Gang, after its founder, Avraham Stern) continued against both Palestinians and British citizens. The Arab countries as a group generally supported the Allies, hoping that after the war the British would be more receptive to their aspirations than the Axis.

When the British government felt more confident in 1942–43 about the prospects of winning the war, it released some Palestinian political prisoners and allowed others to return from exile. Attempts to revive political activity during this period were nugatory. Awni Abd Al-Hadi returned from exile in 1943 and revived *Hizb Al-Istiqlal*, with help from Rashid Alhaj Ibrahim and Ahmed Hilmi Abdel Baqi, and even started a national fund.[2] The Arab Party was revived in 1944 and Palestinian Arab mayors held a conference and issued a report reminding the British that the population had kept quiet in support of the war efforts and asked the government to implement the White Paper.[3]

The Zionist movement continued to consolidate and expand its gains while Palestinians heard feeble declarations from feudal Arab rulers, like those made at the 1946 inaugural meeting of the Arab League. All were unelected kings or rulers dependent on Britain and France for staying in power. International maneuverings continued. At a meeting in London in May 1946, Arab delegates presented a proposal to the British government and the world community which called for elections to a partially governing body whose decisions could be vetoed by the British authorities. They also called for implementation of the 1939 White Paper recommendations to limit Jewish immigration consistent with the country's capacity and to avoid worsening local conditions. The British rejected the proposals and instead proposed a five-year extension of the British Mandate in the hope that the situation would somehow improve. When the sides could not agree, the British threatened to pull out and let the United Nations decide the future of Palestine, and in fact ended up doing exactly that not long after.[4]

Amin Al-Husseini had made his way to Cairo after the war, but was prevented from entering Palestine. He thus reconstituted an Arab High Committee (AHC) in 1946, not to be inclusive of different political parties, but as a family affair. All seven key positions were from the Al-Husseini family; others – Hussein Al-Khalidi, Mu'een Al-Maadi, Rafiq Al-Tamimi, Izzat Darwaza, Ishaak Darweesh and Sheikh Hasan Abu Saud – were sympathetic.[5] Clearly, this was not a group that could influence the rapidly changing situation on the ground because they were outside and disconnected.[6] An alternative leadership was already emerging inside Palestine. On November 22, 1945, a twelve-member Arab National Committee (ANC) was formed representing different parties and allegiances. It included Abdul-Hamid Shoman, Yousef Haikal, Faris Serhan, Ahmad Al-Shuqairi, Emile Ghori, Kamel Abdul-Rahman, Henry Cattan, Sami Taha, Fuad Saba, Kamel Dajani, Izzat Tannous and Muhammad Abd Al-Baqi. Here it might be worth noting the eclectic and highly diverse backgrounds of those mentioned. Some were discussed earlier. To take an example: Fuad Saba was born in Acre and graduated from the American University of Beirut practicing as an accountant in 1920 in Haifa. He helped set up the Palestinian National Fund in 1930. He was appointed secretary of the Arab Higher Committee in June 1936 before being deported to the

Seychelles by the British in 1937 for his political activities. In the 1940s he was managing director of the Palestine-based Al-Mashriq Financial Investment Company and a consultant to the Arab Bank.[7]

Grassroots popular resistance continued locally without real political leadership. As education spread in newly semi-independent Arab states, students became a vanguard of political activism in the 1940s. Palestinian students in Egyptian universities organized in 1944 mainly around political issues, forming the Association of Palestinian Students (*Rabitat Al-Tulab Al-Falastiniyeen*). After the 1952 revolution in Egypt, the student movement grew and its leaders developed skills they would later use in forming and leading various Palestinian liberation organizations.[8] Trade unions played a similar role. In 1945, the 17 branches of the Arab Workers Union had 15,000 dues-paying members.[9] This left-leaning union made alliances with the People's Party (*Hizb Asha'ab*, led by Musa Al-Alami) against the Arab Party (*Al-Hizb Al-Arabi*, the Mufti group), which was led on the ground by Jamal Al-Husseini (their newspaper was *Al-Wahda – Unity*). A key supporter of the leftist factions was Sami Taha who was assassinated on September 11, 1947, presumably by Mufti supporters.[10] The day after his assassination, the third conference of the Arab Workers Union was held in Jaffa as scheduled, but the movement was now facing the imminent break-up of Palestine.[11]

AFTER WORLD WAR II

Inside Palestine, the postwar period saw a crystallization of political trends that are still prevalent today. Arab nationalists, some veterans of the 1936–39 uprising, held a meeting on June 25, 1946 and then issued a new newspaper, *Al-Sha'b*, that would carry the message of liberation and Arab unity. The Muslim Brotherhood, originating in Egypt, established a small following among disenfranchised Palestinians. And when the Soviet Union joined the Allies, the British government allowed communist parties in Palestine more leeway and they became a significant force. The Palestine Communist Party split in 1943 into a Jewish group that had become more Zionist and was in favor of partition and an Arab party, led by Radwan Al-Hel, called the League for National Liberation. The Arab Party had its headquarters in Haifa from where they issued the publications *Al-Ittihad* and *Al-Ghad*.[12] Only after Israel was founded did the Arab and Jewish communist parties unite to form the Israel Communist Party. In late 1945, a lawyer named Mohammed Nimr Al-Huwari established *Al-Najadeh* and declared support for the exiled Mufti. Unlike the 1930s, there was little that could bind these disparate factions because their platforms and outlooks were so divergent.[13]

It is not surprising then that, given the lack of unified policies or leadership, few popular resistance events are recorded in this period and those few were too minor and came too late to effect a change in the circumstances after the war. A general strike on May 3, 1946 and further boycotts of international commissions came in response to the Anglo-American Commission recommendation of April 20, 1946 to admit 100,000 Jewish immigrants.[14] In August 1946, Tannous was tasked by the Arab Higher Committee to set up and administer a national fund, *Beitl-Maal Al-Arabi* (Arab national treasury), for Palestine, a monumental task that came too late, as he himself admitted.[15] Abd Al-Hamid Shoman (who founded the Arab Bank) contributed the first 4,000 Palestinian pounds. Between April 1, 1947, and March 31, 1948, its total receipts were 220,000 Palestinian pounds, the equivalent of US$400,000, compared to the millions spent by the Jewish Agency. The money was used to relieve villagers, promote economic development, help prisoners and detainees, and for media work. But its activities were small and the partition resolution and the onset of the Zionist program of ethnic cleansing brought an end to it.

The British authorities which had created the massive militarized Zionist presence in Palestine were now reeling from attacks by these same Zionists and less so by natives. Some British officers showed great support for the Zionist project on the ground (e.g., when General Stockwell helped in the ethnic cleansing of Haifa's 50,000 Palestinians on April 21–22, 1948);[16] some British officials were more sympathetic to the Palestinian position; and some merely made apologetic declarations.

The major power after the war was the US, where the Zionist movement had been mobilizing support for decades. When the pragmatic and even-handed President Roosevelt died in office, an opportunity arose with the ambitious Vice President, Harry Truman, who now became acting president until the next election. At the UN, the US administration advanced the formation of the UN Special Committee on Palestine (UNSCOP) to investigate the situation and present a program of potential solutions. The AHC boycotted UNSCOP because it was clearly biased, as it was composed of countries pressured by the US to support partition. UNSCOP predictably submitted a report in favor of partition on September 3, 1947. The newly established Arab League held a meeting at prime ministerial level on October 7, 1947 to which the AHC was not invited because the rulers of Jordan and Iraq disagreed with Amin Al-Husseini. However, the latter made an uninvited appearance and none of the attendees dared eject him. Al-Husseini proposed the formation of a Palestinian government-in-exile to replace the AHC, but this was rejected, again by the delegates representing Iraq and Jordan. From that point onwards, the Palestine question was handled by Arab countries, the UN and the powerful Jewish Agency.

The UN General Assembly dutifully voted on November 27, 1947 to recommend partition of Palestine to give the Zionist movement control over 55 percent of Palestine and leave the Palestinians, with more than two-thirds of the population, with the other 45 percent. In the proposed Jewish state, there would be almost as many Christian and Muslim Palestinians as Jews. The vote was passed because of significant pressure from Truman's administration due to his need for Jewish backing in the election. James Forestall, US Secretary of Defense at the time, recorded in his diaries: 'the method that has been used to bring coercion and duress on other nations in the General Assembly bordered on to scandal'.[17]

The power politics machinations that led to this infamous resolution and violated the UN Charter were summed up by an Arab diplomat at the time:

> The Arab delegations had tried actively to convince other delegations to vote against partition by appealing to logic, justice and law. Their efforts were successful with delegations with a conscience and independent judgment. But some delegations were compelled to change their stand when they saw power and the material interests of their countries on the other side. We remember how the Haitian delegate shed tears when he was forced to change his country's vote to one in favor of partition. We recall how General Romulo of the Philippines left the USA, because of Zionist threats. Dr Arce of the Argentine, who had stood against partition, came to me and said that he was sorry that he had to abstain rather than to vote against partition, but this was the result of pressure on his government. These are a few of the several delegates who were forced to vote against their convictions. Sometime before the vote was taken I was talking with Lester Pearson, then Minister of Foreign Affairs of Canada and later Prime Minister. I said, 'Mr Pearson, do you believe that the act of partitioning Palestine against the will of its inhabitants is an act dictated by conscience and law?' He answered me frankly,

'Dr Jamali, politics doesn't know conscience or law unless they are supported by power.'[18]

The AHC responded to the partition vote by calling for a three-day general strike to be held on December 2–4, 1947.[19] Before that though, clashes between Arabs and Jews erupted on December 1, 1947 on the road between Jaffa and Tel Aviv (no one was reported killed). On December 2, six Arabs and eight Jews were killed. Some Jews burned down the Arab-owned Rex Cinema in Jerusalem and Arabs retaliated by setting fire to shops near the Jaffa Gate. The Zionists had mobilized nearly 50,000 well-armed men by December 1947, exceeding both in quantity and quality any potential alliance of adversaries. Disturbances and clashes were used as a pretext to extend the process of the ethnic cleansing of Palestine. Starting in December 21, 1947, the Haganah and other underground Zionist forces attacked villages on the coastal plain north of Tel Aviv and, on December 31, massacred 60 villagers in Balad Al-Sheikh (Haifa district), which unleashed dozens more massacres that emptied nearly 200 villages and towns of their Palestinian population even before May 15, 1948.[20]

The Arabs inside and outside of Palestine tried to mobilize to face the impending military takeover by Zionist forces too late. Two competing groups of volunteers were created: *Jaish Al-Inkaath* (the Army of Rescue) by the Arab countries and *Al-Jihad Al-Muqaddas* (Holy Jihad) by the AHC. Both were poorly armed and barely trained and no match for the professional and experienced units of the Zionist militias, 15,000 of whom had trained and worked with the British army. But the AHC also tried other avenues to halt the onslaught on Palestine, sending a delegation to the Vatican where the pope met them for 25 minutes, but did not speak out against partition.[21] However, the language of violence started on December 21 by the Zionist forces became the language of communication and more Arabs than Jewish Zionists were always killed. Sporadic attempts to call for reason fell on deaf ears. For example, a statement released on March 3, 1948 by the Christian Union of Palestine, addressed to all world religious and political leaders, was signed by all the Christian denominations in Palestine. The statement strongly denounced partition and 'in solidarity with their Muslim brethren' in resistance to the schemes, called for self-determination as envisaged by the founding Charter of the United Nations.[22]

The 33 massacres committed by Zionist forces included a pivotal one, Deir Yassin, on April 9, 1947, which helped the cause of creating a Jewish state tremendously. Even here, acts of heroism in popular resistance are recorded. For example, Haya Al-Balbisi, a 19-year-old teacher from Jerusalem who was not in Deir Yassin at the time, rushed back to help the villagers. She was shot while treating an injured villager.[23]

Arab disunity and infighting, together with Zionist military superiority at every stage of the war, were instrumental in ensuring a Zionist victory.[24] Zionists had twice as many armed men, who were far better trained and equipped. They were energized and ready, while the Palestinians were disheartened because their society and their leadership had been decimated during the 1936–39 revolt. Between December 1947 and the end of the last ceasefire agreement in 1949, Palestinian society was devastated and reduced to communities of refugees, displaced people, isolated behind the borders of Jordan and Egypt.

From December 1947 until the armistice was signed in 1949, over 800,000 Palestinian were driven from their lands, creating the largest population displacement after the war and still the largest refugee population in the world, when 530 towns and villages were wiped off the map. A new militarized colonial state called Israel rose from the ashes of what remained. The resistance, first by villagers and later by the Arab irregular militia, was futile and ineffective. The treachery of the Arab Army (led by Lt-Gen. John Bagot Glubb, also known as Glubb Pasha) and the collaboration of King Abdullah and the Zionist movement to divide Palestine played a significant role in this catastrophe.[25]

The UN appointed Count Folke Bernadotte as a mediator for Palestine by a Security Council decision of May 29, 1948. As head of the Swedish Red Cross, he had saved many Jews during the war. This highly respected man delivered his report to the UN on September 16, 1948. He was killed by the Zionists the next day, together with one of his aides, Colonel André Serot. Instead of honoring him by implementing his recommendations, including allowing the return of refugees, the UN allowed Israel to consolidate its gains and thus extend hegemony over 78 percent of the land of Palestine (50 percent more than the partition recommendation had called for). Stories of attempted resistance by simply refusing to leave are commonplace among Palestinians. Several books have been published telling the stories of the *nakba* and a website is available where oral and documentary history of this period can be found.[26] Let me quote just one of millions of stories, that of

Umm Ibrahim Shawabkeh, a refugee from Beit Jibrain, which was attacked by Israeli troops in October 1948:

> I was twelve in 1948 when the Jews drove us out. We fled from the village when the soldiers came and started shooting people. My grandparents did not want to leave their home; they hid in a cave near the village and the soldiers found them and shot them.[27]

The AHC convened a congress in Gaza and elected a government on October 1, 1948. A constitution was drafted and the delegates elected a cabinet led by Ahmed Hilmi Abd Al-Baqi as prime minister and Amin Al-Husseini as first president of Palestine. The nascent government was recognized by many countries, including all Arab countries with the exception of Trans-Jordan. This act of popular resistance did not last long – it was put down first by the Jordanian government, which wanted to thwart Palestinian nationalism and bring the remaining areas of Palestine under its control, and later by the Egyptian government, which moved the provisional government from Gaza to Cairo and relegated it to obscurity. The King of Jordan convened a conference in Jericho on December 1, 1948 of unelected Palestinian elites who were to profit from agreeing to his annexation of what became known as the West Bank of Jordan. Later, the Jordanian monarch and his British Army commander turned the Negev and the Galilee over to Israel to allow the further expansion of the nascent state.[28] The ancient name of Palestine was thus erased on both sides of what was to be called the Green Line (the armistice line) and a new political geography was created. The Palestinians, more than half made refugees, called this period of nearly two years of ethnic cleansing *al-nakba* (the catastrophe). The *nakba* defined and shaped Palestine; history before the *nakba* and after the *nakba* became like the difference between history before and after World War II for Europe: acute, unmistakable and with fundamental implications for every aspect of daily life. The decades to come would prove that it was a catastrophe for the whole region, and perhaps the world, because it ushered in a volatile period that was to include many wars, acts of violence on all sides, but still more outstanding acts of popular resistance.

9
From *Nakba* to *Naksa*, 1948–67

The new political geography codified in the armistice of 1949 in Rhodes meant that Palestine as a coherent society and united geographical unit ceased to exist and the new state of Israel controlling 78 percent of the land of Palestine was created. Palestinians were divided into discrete groups:

- Those who became refugees in Lebanon, Syria, Jordan and Gaza. These included Palestinians who were scattered around the world and denied the right to return.
- Those who managed against the odds to remain in the new state of Israel.
- Residents of the West Bank, which came under Jordanian rule.
- Residents of Gaza, which came under Egyptian rule.

The emerging state of Israel, having rid itself of most non-Jewish natives via ethnic cleansing,[1] instituted laws to prevent the return of natives: laws to take over their lands, businesses, bank accounts and other property were many. In acts of nonviolent resistance, many Palestinians tried to return despite these laws. Few succeeded and many were shot in the attempt. Glubb observed:

> Some deep psychological urge, which impels a peasant to cling to and die on his land. A great many of these wretched people are killed now, picking their own oranges and olives just beyond the [armistice] line. The value of the fruit is often negligible. If the Jewish patrols see him he is shot on the spot, without any questions. But, they will persist in returning to their farms and gardens.[2]

Palestinians who tried to return to their homes and lands after the fighting ended were simply shot on sight.[3] Thus, 'between 1949 and 1956 between 3,000 and 5,000 infiltrators were killed, the vast majority unarmed. The vast majority of those who infiltrated were peasants trying to slip home, either to return, or to see relatives or to harvest crops either on account of acute hunger or out of deep attachment'.[4] But many did succeed and this itself was a major act of popular resistance during and after the *nakba*.

Dispossession, dislocation and separation were a devastating blow that added to the humiliations and a series of other catastrophic events between 1936 and 1948.[5] Many Palestinians died in refugee camps from health-related problems. It took nearly a generation to recover and re-establish a strong resistance (both violent and nonviolent). The period 1949–67 did see acts of resistance that slowly gained in strength and saw its fruition in the formation of Palestinian organizations with sophisticated political structures beginning in the 1950s and maturing by the mid-1960s.

THE ARABS ON THE INSIDE

The Palestinians who remained inside what became the state of Israel faced a unique situation: natives who found themselves treated as foreigners in their own land. Of the 1.4 million Palestinians of 1947, some 160,000 managed to stay in the 78 percent of Palestine that was transformed into a Jewish state in 1949. Most of their support structures and political leadership, and indeed most of their land, wealth and previous sources of power, were decimated. Israel prefers to call them 'Arab Israelis' or merely 'Arabs in Israel'. The Zionist program which had acquired lands thanks to Ottoman and British rulers now had become the sovereign rulers and had no restraints.

With lightning speed and ruthless efficiency, the new immigrant masters now disinherited and disempowered the few Palestinians who remained, ensured that those who had left would never return and empowered immigrants to settle on stolen Palestinian lands – acts that were 'legalized' by laws passed quickly by the Zionist Knesset. Those who fled or were forced to leave in the ethnic cleansing of 1947–49 were denied the right to return through explicit laws. Their property was taken over under other racist laws (as 'absentee property') that turned them over to the Jewish state. Natives who did remain were not immune from these laws and many were removed, with the state seizing their homes, lands and businesses for new Jewish immigrants.[6] The state thus destroyed the remaining Palestinian communities in the major cities of Haifa, Tiberias, Ramle, Lod and Jaffa, and destroyed dozens of villages between Tel Aviv and Jerusalem, in the western and eastern parts of the Galilee, and those near the ceasefire borders. The latter provided some cruel examples of postwar ethnic cleansing: Iqrith on November 5, 1948, Kufr Bar'am on February 4, 1949 and 700 refugees who took shelter in Kufr Yassif after their own villages were destroyed.[7]

Twelve villages in the Galilee were declared closed military zones. The all-Catholic Palestinian village of Iqrith was occupied on October 31, 1948 without any resistance and five days later the residents were told to vacate it 'temporarily for two weeks'. When the two weeks turned into months, the villagers petitioned the Israeli High Court of Justice, which, surprisingly, ordered on July 31, 1951 that they be allowed to return. This is perhaps one of the earliest acts of resistance using the Israeli legal system. Yet, the military authorities ordered full evacuation on September 10, 1951 and the village was completely destroyed on Christmas Day 1951 – a doubly painful act for the Christian villagers.[8] Kufr Bar'am residents were similarly ordered to evacuate so they too decided to go the High Court, which ordered, in early September 1953, that they be allowed to return. Instead, the Israeli army attacked the village by air and land; the bombardments completely destroyed it.[9]

The result was to concentrate the Palestinians into three easily controlled areas: Central Galilee, the Triangle and the Negev. Later, these would be further squeezed into even smaller areas so that the Palestinians who owned 93 percent of the land before 1948 would end up on less than 3.5 percent of it. The Israeli regime was not satisfied and first attempted to drive out those who remained and subjected them to a cruel military rule that continued from 1948 to 1966. To aid this process, Israel amended, expanded and intensified laws from the emergency regulations used by the British in the 1930s. Only non-Jews were subject to these rules and three military commanders were assigned to oversee the three areas in which the remaining Palestinians were concentrated. Palestinians were denied economic development, work, the right to move even to nearby villages (they had to get special permits) and any semblance of social or cultural freedom. The goals of the military rule were to: 1) facilitate the work of land transfer and confiscation; 2) control and manipulate any potential Palestinian votes in the Knesset; and 3) prevent the formation of independent political movements that would protect Palestinian rights.[10]

Palestinians focused popular resistance initially on steadfastness (*sumud*). Those who could hold on to their lands did so against the odds. A quarter of the Palestinians who remained lost their lands and became under Israeli law 'present absentees': present because they are within the borders of the state, but with their lands confiscated and turned over to the Jewish Agency for the settlement of Jews. In international law, they are called 'displaced persons' and they do have a right, as refugees do, to return to their homes and lands. Yet, Israel refused to recognize this right. To control them even in their shrinking ghettos, the state created mechanisms to encourage segregation and division, and re-education to make them compliant to the policies of the Jewish state.[11] The Zionist authorities had studied the divisions that were of benefit to the British, like the Al-Husseini and Nashashibi divisions in the 1920s and 1930s. They proceeded to encourage and emphasize divisions by designating Palestinians into 'nationalities' and pitting their interests against each other to keep them weak, while focusing on building a 'Jewish nation' that oversees them. Palestinians were divided into Bedouins, Druze, Circasians, Christian Arabs, Sunni Arabs and Baha'is. Resistance to this division was later dubbed by Israeli authorities 'Palestinization' as if this was a dirty word.[12] The Israeli authorities were able to find willing collaborators in every community, but the majority opted to support the 'rejectionist' trend, which was to become organized in the next few years.[13] After the *nakba*, it took a few years for Palestinians to recover from the shock and start mobilizing, for example by forming a *rabita* (committee) for poets in 1952.[14] Popular resistance of this nature during military rule until 1966 remained largely unrecognized until Ghassan Kanafani published *Literature of Resistance in Palestine* in 1968.

The first political party for which Palestinians inside the state of Israel cast votes and joined was the Communist Party because it demanded that Israel give equality to Arabs and become a state of all its citizens. The party was not revolutionary since it supported many aspects of the state of Israel as constituted and even expelled members who espoused revolutionary principles.[15] The Arab and Jewish Communist Parties had separated in the early 1940s over precisely this neoliberal and rather un-Marxist support of Zionism. The Arab party was called *Usbat Al-Taharrur Al-Watani* (the National Liberation League). The decision by many Arabs to join the reunited Jewish-Arab Communist Party (*Rakah*) after 1948 was due to lack of an alternative. *Rakah* became a defender of Arab rights, and Arab members of the party like Hanna Naqara and the Arab language newspaper *Al-Ittihad* became well known. In the first Israeli elections, Arab and Jewish voters gave the party four seats in the Knesset. The party's cultural and social programs helped support growth in nationalist feelings and give voice to poets and writers (Mahmoud Darwish, Samih Al-Qasem, Tawfeeq Ziad, Salem Jubran, Hanna Abu Hanna and others).[16] In 1959, the authorities removed 13 Arab communists from their communities for trying to organize committees to defend lands threatened with confiscation.

The second organized movement to appear within the Green Line was pan-Arab nationalist in nature. A meeting held on February 11, 1956 took inspiration from the pan-Arab national movement led by Egyptian President Jamal Abdel-Nasser and pushed for unity, struggle and self-determination.[17] Israel's invasion of Egypt with the help of Britain and France in 1956 created an opportunity to put pressure on the remaining Palestinians to flee across the borders. The Israeli authorities issued orders to place villages near the Green Line under curfew and shoot on sight any violators (a form of terror to force people to leave). In one incident, 49 civilians of Kufr Qassem were shot in just two hours on October 29, 1956. Villagers have tried to hold commemorations every year at Kufr Qassem but these were banned.[18]

The massacre gave impetus for activists to work to defend themselves from the onslaught. Two conferences were held simultaneously on July 6, 1958 in Nazareth and Akka and were attended by about 120 Palestinians (40 others were placed under house arrest, preventing their participation). They agreed to create the Arab Front (Al-Jabha Al-Arabiya), elect an executive committee and issue a list of demands which included the return of refugees and displaced people, ending land confiscations, military rule and discrimination, and permitting the use of the Arabic language.[19] When it tried to register, the name was refused, on the pretext that it was racist to include the word 'Arab', even though there were hundreds of organizations with 'Jewish' in their name. It had to rename itself Al-Jabha Al-Sha'biya (Popular Front, commonly referred to as the Arab Popular Front and later the Popular Democratic Front). The Popular Front split after disagreements between the communists and pan-Arab nationalists in the short-lived United Arab state (Egypt and Syria).[20] The terror in this and other villages was part of the program of completing the ethnic cleansing of 1948, but the persistence and resistance of the people ensured that the program was not completed so the Israeli authorities devised alternative strategies to deal with the remaining Palestinians other than outright transfer.[21]

A faction from the Popular Front developed into Harakat Al-Ard (the Land Movement), which began with a meeting in April 1959 called for by Mansour Kardoush (Nazareth) and Habib Qahwaji (Haifa) which agreed to publish a weekly magazine, Al-Ard (The

Land). The magazine was closed by the authorities in January 1960, but the activists attempted alternate ways to keep the movement alive despite prohibition and infringement on freedom of speech and assembly under the brutal 'emergency military regime'.[22] The main difference with the Communist Party was that *Al-Ard* did not believe in normalizing the Israeli state and merely asking for equality, but had a pan-Arab and rights-based approach.[23] On June 23, 1964, the movement sent a 13-page memorandum to the United Nations on the status of Palestinians inside the state of Israel. The authorities responded by disbanding the movement in November 1964, expelled two key members (Sabri Jiryis and Habib Qahwaji) to Lebanon and sentenced one member (Saleh Baransi) to ten years' imprisonment. After his release, Baransi founded a cultural center in Nazareth and Kardoush established a cooperative press and organized a society in support of prisoners.[24]

The popular resistance movement was not intimidated by brutal Israeli tactics but instead proliferated. In 1961, three Palestinian Christians decided to defy the military order and attempted to travel to Egypt for work and study. They were killed near Gaza and thousands gathered to mourn and show solidarity with the families despite Israeli insistence that the funerals be discreet and small.[25]

A meeting attended by progressive elements in the society including Arab students at the Hebrew University was convened on December 2, 1961 and established the Arab Jewish Committee 'to end the military rule'.[26] In April 1962, the military authorities closed the roads to Al-Ba'na in the Galilee to prevent a meeting about land confiscations and in August 1963 a similar planned meeting was met with a closure order on Al-Tayba in the Triangle; 18 were arrested.[27] Arab students enrolled at the Hebrew University attempted to organize a meeting in 1964 to plan the establishment of an Arab club in Kufr Qare' in the Upper Triangle, but the night before, five of them were arrested and when the others tried to hold the meeting, the authorities declared the area a closed military zone and arrested 40 who attempted to enter the village.[28] Arab student activism in Israeli universities mushroomed in the decades to come.[29]

Military rule ended in 1966 aided by the economic imperative of the state which wanted to use Arab labor in its economic growth, funded by German war reparations. Other state initiatives moved Mizrahi and Sephardic Jewish low-skilled labor into skilled labor so that Arabs were needed to fill the menial jobs left vacant.[30] The Emergency Land Regulation Law of 1949 allowed the Israeli authorities to steal the lands of the native Arabs, both those who fled during the war and those who remained, for 'the defense of the state, public security, the maintenance of essential supplies and essential public service, the absorption of [Jewish] immigrants or the rehabilitation of ex-soldiers'. The remaining Arab villages lost on average half their lands and, by the 1970s, two-thirds. The percentage of Arabs working in food production (agriculture, fishing, etc.) decreased from 57 percent in 1931 to 38 percent in 1963 and to 19.9 percent in 1972.[31]

BEYOND THE GREEN LINE

While the 12 percent of Palestinians within 'Israel' struggled to survive and resist, essentially by civil methods, their brethren beyond the Green Line did the same. Nearly a million refugees dispersed in the West Bank (under Jordanian occupation), Gaza (under Egyptian occupation) and in other Arab countries (primarily Lebanon, Syria, Jordan and Egypt). The most pressing activism needed and which started immediately was humanitarian. Bethlehem district alone housed nearly 50,000 refugees, stretching its absorption capacity. My family and others, with aid from Quakers and people of good will around the world, fed and clothed refugees until the United Nations Relief and Work Agency (UNRWA) was created. Once the shock of the catastrophe was absorbed and the Palestinians beyond the Green Line adjusted to the new reality, they began to reorganize and build their institutions. Initially, these were merely family- and clan-based. Refugee camps were even divided spatially along clan and village boundaries and traditional leaders tried to restore a structured society to function in exile.

As the traditional ways of making a living disappeared, exiled Palestinians emphasized the need for education to rebuild their lives. The youth in Arab universities were especially politicized and ready for action when their parents were still licking their wounds and mourning their dead. In the early 1950s, a group of young Palestinian students in Egypt and in Egypt-controlled Gaza started organizing and training in a context of re-emergent nationalism. The first Palestinian student league was set up in Cairo, in 1954. These students would become the leaders who would inherit the mantle of the aging and dead leaders of the 1930s and 1940s. For example, Yasser Arafat studied engineering at King Fuad I University (later the University of Cairo), where he met Salah Khalaf and Khalil Al-Wazir in 1951 (children of grocers from Jaffa and Ramallah). Al-Wazir was already undertaking guerrilla operations from the

Sinai. They ran for election to student councils, winning seats by having a very broad platform and creating lists that included rival political ideologies. With Khaled Al-Hasan (from Haifa) and Farouk Al-Qaddumi, they later founded the Palestinian Liberation Movement (known as Fatah or Fateh). Strengthening Palestinian national identity was their main initial focus.

Just as inside the Green Line, activist Palestinians on the outside were mostly left-leaning. Most of the organized movements were even communist, bringing significant pressure from governments like Jordan which cracked down on leftists in the mid-1950s. The Israeli attack on Gaza on February 28, 1955 was met with sizeable demonstrations in Gaza and by Palestinians in Egypt, especially students. This led to a meeting with President Nasser and included four leaders: Abdel-Hamid Al-Tasye' (Ba'athist), Izzat 'Odeh (Communist), Fuad Ahmed (Arab Nationalist Movement) and Salah Khalaf (Palestinian Nationalist, later Fatah leader).[32]

During the 1956 tripartite occupation of Gaza and the Sinai, students developed skills of resistance and became empowered as leaders-in-the-making by the withdrawal of Israeli, British, and French forces under pressure from US President Eisenhower. Many of those leaders moved to the Gulf States where jobs were plentiful and where many educated people were critical in building the emergent economies of the Gulf States (Qatar, Kuwait, Saudi Arabia, etc.). The Kuwait group included Arafat and Al-Wazir and Farouk Kaddoumi and was critical in the formation of the burgeoning movement called *Harakat Tahrir Falastiniya* (an acronym in reverse is pronounced Fatah in Arabic, which also means conquering). This movement was officially launched in 1957. One of its charismatic co-founders, Arafat, wanted to begin armed struggle in early January 1965. A compromise was reached to launch such a struggle under the name of *Al-Asifa* (the Storm) so that if it succeeded, it would be adopted by Fatah and if it failed it would not be recognized as part of Fatah.

Elsewhere in the Arab world, the budding student movements faced similar challenges and succeeded in organizing small local groups for Palestine. The General Union of Palestinian Students (GUPS) convened on November 11, 1959, the twelfth anniversary of the UN partition resolution.[33] Unfortunately, GUPS was not allowed to operate openly in Jordan or the West Bank and had to use surrogate entities. The differences between the Ba'athists and Arab nationalists hampered GUPS activities and a split was formalized in 1963, paralleling the split between Egypt and Syria, reflecting the impact of inter-Arab politics on Palestinian movements.[34] The splinter group in Damascus was smaller and withered away. The main group headquartered in Egypt maintained the Arab nationalist line and supported the Arab League-initiated PLO in 1965. But the defeat of the Arab armies in 1967 moved many Palestinians to the narrower Palestinian nationalist brand, led by Fatah, which took control of GUPS in 1969. Unfortunately, internal Arab divisions and external factors led to the union holding its last meeting in 1990 in Baghdad.

The situation of Palestinians in Jordan between 1949 and 1967 deserves special mention. The Hashemite ruling family in Jordan was put in power by the British after World War I. It clearly served British interests, which were themselves allied with Zionist aims. King Abdullah had made an agreement with the *Yishuv* leadership during the partition discussions to thwart Palestinian nationalism and divide Palestine between an expanded Jordanian kingdom and a Jewish state.[35] Two carefully staged conferences in October and December 1948 declared allegiance to the king and began a process that culminated in annexing the parts of Palestine under his control in 1950. Abdullah also thwarted the Arab League's efforts to recognize and support a Palestinian government in 1948. For these actions, King Abdullah was assassinated by a Palestinian nationalist in 1950. But the control of the Hashemite family over the West Bank continued and included transferring administrative controls trying to reduce the centrality of Jerusalem in Palestinian life by demanding the transfer of economic and political centrality to Amman. Palestinians resisted these moves. Plascov explains:

> The thrust of the regime's policy can be seen clearly in the gradual transfer of key administrative offices from Jerusalem to Amman. The significance of these moves was highlighted by the Mayor of Jerusalem in his correspondence with the Minister of the Interior, in which he reminded the Minister that 'Jerusalem is the first town in the West Bank and the center of all religious sects, the next in importance to Amman'. Palestinian appeals 'to turn the city into the Kingdom's second capital' were expressed a number of times up to the mid-1950s. However, such calls excited little attention among the bulk of the Palestinians and the regime refused to grant the city such a status. The term *in'ash*, which in essence meant the revival and restoration of Jerusalem, was prominent in all these demands. Jerusalemites nevertheless wanted the government to regard the city as a frontline settlement and to do its utmost to

strengthen it. Instead, they faced a consistent policy aimed at exactly the opposite. Vehement protests were made by West Bankers in general and Jerusalemites in particular, against the actions of the Jordanian government seeking to weaken the city's administrative and economic position. The transfer of all important offices to Amman was a source of grievance to the West Bank's population which constantly protested against the government's refusal to allow even UNRWA's Jordanian headquarters to be situated in Jerusalem, the center of the West Bank – where 75 percent of the refugees were living ... The government's purpose in all this was two-fold, first, it wanted tight control of all UNRWA affairs, and, second, it sought to develop the center of the Kingdom. In economic terms, UNRWA's offices in Amman meant a substantial contribution to a country intent on improving its poorer areas. As a result of this policy and of the absence of a prominent and united local leadership, Jerusalem lost its seniority. In order to weaken the city's position further, the authorities even considered moving part of the Muslim law courts to Amman, once again over the futile protests of the City Council. Such treatment was a great insult to the Palestinians and served as further proof of their lowly status. Even so, protests against the regime's discrimina-tory policy, as expressed by West Bankers throughout the 1950s, never went so far as to call for the separation of the West Bank but only for a change in government policy.[36]

There was a period of non-cooperation and direct resistance in between which intensified and culminated in a crackdown on Palestinian resistance in 1956. This was led primarily by leftists. The National Liberation League, a splinter group of the Palestine Communist Party of the early 1930s, had been quite moderate in its goals of liberation and peace; it even accepted the two-state solution. After Jordan gained *de facto* rule over the West Bank, the League sprouted the Jordanian Communist Party whose members were many but its sympathizers even more numerous. There were demonstrations against Jordanian rule in 1955–56 which were put down brutally by the army of the young King Hussein. My uncle was one of over 1,000 suspected leftists of that era jailed in Al-Jafr prison in east Jordan. With prodding and support from Britain and the US, King Hussein especially targeted socialists and communists. Most had only been engaged in speaking out for labor rights or for the return of refugees. King Hussein's going along with Nasser on issues of Pan-Arabism is attributed by many researchers as an attempt to mollify this resistance.

THE BIRTH OF THE PALESTINE LIBERATION ORGANIZATION

Arab dictators held a meeting with the Arab League to design what were rather ineffective and minimal strategies but mostly to issue declarations that were sufficient to maintain their subjects' support and the backing of Western powers, themselves under Zionist influence. The Arab League convened a meeting in Jerusalem between May 28 and June 2, 1964 which included 396 Palestinian delegates from around the world to found the Palestine Liberation Organization (PLO). This included a Palestine National Fund and the Palestine Liberation Army. This was partly a response to the burgeoning popularity of nascent Palestinian movements like Fatah and partly popular pressure to do something. The well-intentioned Ahmed Shuqairi was leader of the PLO from its founding until he resigned following the June 1967 defeat (the *naksa*). Shuqairi first became politically active in his early twenties as a member of the Al-Istiqlal Party in north Palestine in 1930s and had been head of a Palestinian public relations office in the USA in 1945 and served as an assistant to the secretary general of the Arab League on the issue of Palestine from 1951 to 1957.[37] The PLO under Shuqairi could accomplish little for several reasons: it had sidestepped the traditional Palestinian leadership (e.g., the Al-Husseini and Al-Nashashibi families), it had been overtly and covertly controlled by powerful Arab states that did not want to see direct confrontations with the Israelis, and it did not have popular grassroots support. The PLO was ignored or critiqued by the Arab High Committee on Palestine, still led by Amin Al-Husseini, and by Fatah, led by Al-Wazir and Arafat, and other major Palestinian factions. The defeat of Arab forces in 1967 and the success of Fatah and other factions in the battle of Al-Karameh in 1968 changed the landscape; Fatah and other factions led the PLO in 1969. Thanks to excellent organizational capacity, the PLO (Fatah being now the dominant force) expanded into all sectors of Palestinian life in exile. The Palestinians under the umbrella of the PLO soon forced a supine and reluctant world not only to recognize their existence but also to recognize that they had a national liberation struggle with political goals that were to be respected.

10
One State of Oppression, 1967–86

In the occupied territories today, the resistance against the occupation does not generally reflect violent methods. School and commercial strikes, petitions, protest telegrams, advertisements and condemnations in the daily papers, and the attempts to boycott Israeli goods are, in fact, manifestations of nonviolent struggle.

Mubarak E. Awad, 1984[1]

THE *NAKSA*

I was ten years old when Israeli tanks rolled into the West Bank in 1967 in the *Blitzkrieg* that came to be known as the Six-day War in which it captured what remained of Palestine (the West Bank and Gaza, which represent 22 percent of historic Palestine). I recall my mother giving civilian clothes to some Jordanian soldiers who were fleeing east through our home town of Beit Sahour, and the shelling of these men – shelling that killed one civilian in Beit Sahour, a teacher by the name of Elias Salem Rishmawi. I also remember the funeral and the white flags hung from houses. I enrolled at a private school for two months until the public schools reopened after a dispute with the Israeli authorities on revising the curriculum.

The war created a new political geography. Israel's military dominance gave its leaders the arrogant notion that they could dictate terms to a submissive population. The transformation resulted in the removal of another 250,000–300,000 Palestinians, some of them made refugees for a second time. Israel demolished a few neighborhoods, including Hai Al-Magharba in Jerusalem, to create a huge plaza in front of Al-Buraq/Wailing Wall. Three Palestinian villages to the north-west of Jerusalem were bulldozed and about 9,000 residents driven out of their homes and forced to march for days over rocky hillsides to safety. The site was later turned into 'Canada Park', funded by Jewish Canadians.[2]

Israel added vast new territories under its direct rule while destroying the Arab armies. It did not want to annex these areas immediately, except for East Jerusalem, because of the large Palestinian population there, including those in over 22 refugee camps. In fact, Palestinians chose to remain, having learned in the *nakba* that if you leave during warfare you will not be allowed to return – a significant act of civil resistance (*sumud*). Soon, Israel would begin building settlements to drive out Palestinians little by little from the newly occupied areas economically or physically, and control the rest in shrinking enclaves. Israel's tactics after 1967 served its primary political goals: keeping and profiting from its illegal acquisitions.[3] The building of settlements in the occupied areas has been the most visible facet of this aggressive colonization policy and has created its own class of violent behavior. The Israeli peace activist David Shulman explains:

> Make no mistake about it: Israel like any society has violent, sociopathic elements in it. What is unusual about the last four decades in Israel is that many destructive individuals have found a haven, complete with ideological legitimation [*sic*], within the settlement enterprise. Here in places like Chavat Maon, Itamar, Tapuach, and Hebron they have, in effect, unfettered freedom to terrorize the local Palestinian population [and] to attack, shoot, injure, sometimes kill – all in the name of the alleged sanctity of the land and of the Jews' exclusive right to it.[4]

The Six-day War became known as the *naksa* (defeat), but in reality it had redrawn the political geography and promoted civil resistance. Palestinians and other Arabs engaged in nonviolent grassroots action learned 'on the job' on both sides of the now transparent Green Line (the 1949 armistice line).

PALESTINIANS INSIDE THE GREEN LINE

Palestinians inside the Green Line struggled in silence and bravely for 19 years under the brutal Zionist regime. These *Arab Al-Dakhel* (Arabs of the Inside) could now share their experiences with their Palestinian compatriots beyond the Green Line, and vice versa. In 1950, Israel instituted the absentee property law which took land away from Palestinians (both refugees and displaced individuals within the state), who were dubbed 'present absentees'. That is how the majority of the lands were turned over to the Jewish Agency and the Israel Land Administration. In 1965, Israeli authorities promulgated the Planning and Building Law, which listed communities and their available areas of development. Palestinian communities were restricted to small, shrinking areas and dozens of other Palestinian communities became 'unrecognized'.

Unrecognized villages and towns were considered illegal and home demolitions were common in these areas and on the outskirts of the small, 'recognized' communities. Even when left standing, the unrecognized communities received no government or other public services (schools, roads, clinics, electricity, water, sewage or other infrastructure). The struggle of these 1948 Palestinians, whom Israelis call 'Israel's Arabs', remained out of the public eye in the West and even in the Arab world.

The 1967 *naksa* showed the depth of divisions, treachery and incompetence of the Arab regimes. This brought more Palestinians with nominal Israeli citizenship to become better connected with their Palestinian identity, thereby strengthening nationalism.[5] Most rejected the definition of being merely 'Arabs' living in the state of Israel. The main split between the Communist Party, which supported equality within the state of Israel, and the pan-Arab movements continued. The Communist Party supported UN resolution 242 and called for Israel to withdraw from the newly acquired territories, but also adopted statements and policies that challenged the right of Palestinians to self-determination and supported a 'right' of establishment and maintenance of a Zionist state in Palestine. *Rakah* also opposed the Palestinian armed struggle which developed after 1965 in the form of guerrilla movements.

Another trend among Palestinians on the inside was their refusal to accept the legitimacy of the Israeli state or participate in the Knesset elections. An organizational framework was developed in 1969 at Umm Al-Fahm on the initiative of Hassan Jabarin, Ghassan Fouzi and Muhammad Salamah, and was formalized in 1972 as *Al-Haraka Al-Wataniya Al-Takadumiya – Abna' Al-Balad* (National Progressive Movement – Sons of the Land). This movement had a significant impact on the popular resistance to follow from the early 1970s until today.[6] More recently, Palestinians in Israel have formed a third faction, *Al-Rabita Al-Islamiya* (the Islamic Association), paralleling the growth in Islamic movements throughout the Middle East in the past 20 years (see below).

After the October 1973 war, Palestinian morale was raised, and renewed energy and mobilization was found in all these movements. The mass mobilization also forced changes in existing structures. International recognition of the PLO in 1974 was followed by the Israeli Communist Party supporting the notion that the PLO did represent the Palestinian people. It also stopped emphasizing UN resolution 242 and instead emphasized basic Palestinian rights to the land. These changes allowed the party to gain support, winning the municipal elections in Nazareth.[7] The change in direction helped the Communist Party gain support and it capitalized on this by forming the Democratic Front for Peace and Equality (*Al-Jabha Al-Dimoqratiya Lil-Salam wal-Musawa*, a front of Arabs and Jews) in March 1977, which did well first in the Nazareth municipal elections in 1975 and then in the Knesset elections of 1977. After this the front lost momentum and started to backslide in relation to the issue of how much control the Communist Party had over the decision-making process.[8] In 1981, a splinter movement, *Al-Haraka Al-Taqadumiya Lil-Salam*, was formed, attracting significant support in the Nazareth municipal elections in 1983. But it won only one seat in the Knesset, which it lost in later elections.[9] In parallel, Abna' Al-Balad developed strategies to reach out to university students, forming the National Progressive Movement (*Al-Haraka Al-Wataniya Al-Taqqadumiya*). The movement had to wait until the late 1980s to gain support from its moral stand on the intifada. In the 1990s it helped form political parties and supported candidates for the Knesset.

A small band from the Islamic movement which originated with Muslim Brotherhood attempted to organize armed resistance in 1979, but its members were captured and it had ended by 1981. After 1983, a Muslim Shabab movement was formed and began establishing institutions that serve the community and later entered municipal council elections in 1989. After 1996, a split appeared in the Islamic movement between those that support participation in the Knesset elections and those that don't.[10]

Away from politics, grassroots efforts were functioning. The increased mobilization among Palestinians inside the Green Line took a dramatic and bold step forward with a large meeting in August 1975 in Nazareth attended by 110 individuals to defend the land. At this meeting, a committee was selected, headed by Anees Kardoush, to prepare for an even larger meeting. This meeting, held in October 1975, included about 5,000 activists from many factions and created the Committee for Defense of the Land (*Lajnat Al-Difa' 'An Al-Aradi*) with 100 members and an eleven-member secretariat. It began by protesting against the confiscation of 22,000 dunums in the Galilee and the declaration of an even larger parcel of land belonging to three villages (in the Al-Mil area) as closed military zones, with the intention of building nine Jewish settlements in this closed zone. A meeting was held in Nazareth on March 6, 1976. This included 48 heads of municipalities and local village councils and called for a day of protests and strikes on March 30,

1976 should Israel go ahead with its land confiscation policies. When it appeared the strike would take place, many areas outside of the Galilee joined it, including in the West Bank.[11] This became known as 'Land Day' throughout Palestine. The events actually started on March 29, with a demonstration against the Israeli army's provocative mobilizations in the village of Deir Hanna. Later that evening, the village of Araba Al-Batoof demonstrated in solidarity and a young man, Khair Muhammad Yassin, was killed by Israeli soldiers. He was the first martyr of the 1976 Land Day. More martyrs fell over the next 24 hours. The events were well organized and participation was high. The Israeli authorities reacted violently. Many were injured, six nonviolent protesters killed and hundreds arrested. The events coincided with the secret Koening Memorandum which laid out plans for further discrimination and ethnic cleansing to 'make the Galilee more Jewish'. The Israeli government condemned the leaking of the memorandum, but no government official repudiated its racist content.[12] After this successful popular event, differences arose that weakened the organizing committee and yet, the movement continues strongly to this day.[13]

In parallel, we saw the formation of the regional committee for heads of the local Arab authorities (*Al-Lajna Al-Qutriya Li-Ru'asa' Al-Sulutat Al-Mahaliya Al-Arabiya*). Activists had begun planning for this in 1973, but the official launch date with a press conference was in February 1975; the committee did not support the call for the Land Day in 1976 and was challenged by grassroots activists on this and other instances of standing with the Israeli authorities because of the presence of some members who belong to Zionist parties. Yet, the committee did accomplish some things, like slightly reducing the ratio of government spending on Jewish vs. Arab towns from over 20– to 4–5-fold.[14]

Many Druze religious and traditional elders collaborated with the Zionist movement before the state of Israel was founded. Some even joined the forces that fought against Palestinian and other Arab militia. But many rebelled against the traditional leaders and joined the Palestinian resistance; some lost their lives defending the village of Al-Barwa in 1948. In 1956, when the formalized drafting of the Druze was initiated as a result of an agreement between the government and the Druze collaborative religious and political figures, 1,100 Druze young men (out of what was then a total population of 16,000) signed a petition rejecting the call.[15]

Despite repeated verbal declarations from the Zionist regime of the 'equality between Druze and Jews', the collaboration did not save Druze villages from the fate of other Palestinian villages in terms of land confiscation, discrimination and economic deprivation. The Israeli army even mistreated Druze soldiers, asking them to do the most morally repugnant acts that it engaged in *vis-à-vis* other Palestinians and put them in the line of fire. For these reasons, the strength of the factions within the Druze community resisting Zionist ideas and racism grew. It found organizational expression in 1972 with the formation of Committee of Druze Initiative (*Lajnat Al-Mubadara Al-Durziyya*), led by Sheikh Farhoud Farhoud from Al-Rama village. Thousands of Druze were jailed for refusing to serve in the Israeli army and nonviolent activists were attacked by Israeli soldiers on numerous occasions (e.g., in Beit Jan on April 13, 1987).[16]

The first Palestinian student organizational structure inside Israel was the Arab Student Committee at the Hebrew University in 1958. This was followed in other universities and then coalesced in 1974–75 to form the Regional Union of Arab Students (*Al-Ittihad Al-Qutri Lil-Talaba Al-'Arab*). Within these structures, the student movement reflected divisions within society at large.[17]

In the 1984 elections, Uri Avnery and General Matti Peled established the Progressive List for Peace (PLP) with a program of helping establish a Palestinian state in the West Bank and Gaza and calling for equality of all people in Israel regardless of their background. The insistence that an Arab lead the party was credited with poor reception among Israeli Jews (it gained 20 percent of the Arab vote in the election).[18] *Rakah* and the PLP gained the votes of Palestinians who sought to accommodate the reality of the Israeli state. Other Palestinians chose not to participate but focused their energies on movements and groups that rejected partition and even the notion of a state of Israel in historic Palestine. The presence of Arab and Jewish progressives in the Knesset could be useful to the large political parties as proof of Israeli democracy or for bargaining and gaining a few extra votes (e.g. Shlomo Hillel was elected as speaker of the Knesset thanks to the votes of Mohammed Miari and Matti Peled in exchange for recognizing Umm Al-Fahm as a municipality).[19]

On July 31, 1985, the Knesset amended the Basic Law on elections by adding:

A list of candidates shall not participate in Knesset elections if any of the following is expressed or implied in its purpose or deeds: 1) Denial of the existence of the State of Israel as the state of the Jewish people, 2) Denial of the democratic character of the State, 3) Incitement to racism.

What this meant is that any candidate calling for turning the state into a secular democratic state of all its citizens, instead of the apartheid state it is, would be barred from running for elections.

In the 1992 elections, PLP did not reach the threshold for the Knesset, the Jabha was headed for the first time by an Arab and the Islamic movement now decided to support the election, lending its weight to the Arab Democratic Party (ADP). The ADP called for equality within the state and for the establishment of a Palestinian state in the West Bank and Gaza (the Oslo two-state solution). The Labor Party's tenuous foothold in the Knesset was rescued only with the backing of the Arab parties. In return, some achievements were possible, including equal family allowances, development in Nazareth, construction in Arab towns and halting destruction of Palestinian homes in those towns.[20] While none of these on its own can be considered significant, collectively they showed the power of engagement in society to effect change even within a hostile system and vindicated the political direction of the ADP.

Al-Tajamu' Al-Watani Al-Dimocrati (the National Democratic Assembly) did not agree with the ADP on politics, nor did it support Oslo's two-state solution, but instead believed in turning Israel into a state of its citizens. Led by Azmi Bishara until recently, *Tajamu'* made significant inroads in educating the public about the racist nature of the Israeli political system and the difficulty of achieving rights within a Zionist racist government structure. *Tajamu'* entered into partnership with *Hadash* in the 1996 elections including five seats, including one for Bishara.[21] Bishara began his political career in 1974 by organizing regional committees for Arab high school students. He represented the Union of Arab University Students, which he co-founded in a central committee that organized the March 30, 1976 Land Day events.[22]

To understand the nonviolent struggle inside the Green Line, I recommend the book by Hatim Kanaaneh. In the preface we find this poignant statement:

Throughout my professional years of service, whether in medicine, in public health or in development, and especially in my proactive role in the NGO movement, I had one overarching goal: to introduce my community to the world, to transcend the wall of seclusion and concealment behind which our state had isolated us. That had been my strategy for fighting the racial discrimination practiced against my community. And it all was right there, on audiotapes. Here was my chance for a last attempt at exposing our secret existence, suffering and promise to the world.[23]

Occasionally, brave Israelis venture to live among the marginalized Palestinian communities and write equally poignant descriptions of the harsh reality there.[24]

OUTSIDE THE GREEN LINE

In the first seven years in Jerusalem and other occupied areas, Palestinians tried to fill the vacuum created by the departing Jordanian authorities by strengthening existing Arab institutions and showing *sumud* (steadfastness) in the face of the occupation while hoping for liberation from outside. The Israeli authorities proceeded with large-scale settlement activities in East Jerusalem and within a few years, they had confiscated nearly a third of the private lands of East Jerusalemites. Determined local resistance was able to maintain significant Palestinian presence against difficult odds:

If Israeli leaders had their way, most of the Arab population of east Jerusalem would have left long ago. This is a harsh statement but is the truth. Policy decision after policy decision on east Jerusalem showed that Israel was doing everything possible to encourage, and at times force, east Jerusalem Arabs to leave the city. This was particularly true with regards to housing and land policy.[25]

The first priority for the Israeli occupation was to take over and integrate Jerusalem into the 'Jewish state'. For this, Palestinian resistance was critical to frustrate, or at least significantly delay, the inroads being made by the occupiers. Immediately upon occupying Jerusalem, the Israeli Ministry of Religious Affairs tried to take over Muslim affairs but, in a meeting on July 24, 1967 presided over by Sheikh Abdel-Hamid As-Sayeh, a Muslim religion committee was constituted that put Israel under the *de facto* independence of the Muslim religious leadership.[26] In similar spirit, the Arab Chamber of Commerce refused to be integrated with Israeli Chambers of

Commerce and instead encouraged merchants not to pay taxes in 1967.[27]

The case of the Jerusalem Electric Corporation (JEC) is an inspiring example of popular resistance in the occupied areas. Since 1957, six municipalities in the West Bank and nearly 2,000 shareholders have held the publicly owned company. Repeated attempts to take over the company or derail its efforts to continue to supply service to its customers after 1967 are detailed by Michael Dumper.[28] At one point, the mayor of Arab Jerusalem, Rohi Al-Khatib (also chairman of the JEC), contested the Israeli plan to take over as a 'successor' municipality after the occupation; although he won the case in the Israeli courts, he himself was deported. Unfortunately, Israel denied the JEC the right to buy new generators and the company was forced instead to buy electricity from the Israel Electric Company. The Israeli authorities also tried to take over Al-Makassed hospital in Jerusalem and bring it under the control of the Israeli Ministry of Health, but the plans were thwarted thanks to the popular resistance of the managing committee (led by Ibrahim Dakkak) and the help of the international community.[29]

Women Take the Lead

From the 1920s and 1930s women took the initiative at the most critical times when even the will of the strongest men was tested.[30] Thus it was not surprising that women also took the lead in the early years of the post-1967 era while the national will was debilitated. The first demonstration in Jerusalem held in Spring 1968 was led by women and was dispersed by force.[31] In February 1968, over 300 women demonstrated in Gaza about the policies of the occupation, including the expulsions and land confiscations.[32] Kuttab and Awwad explained that 'Women's political associations connected with the different Palestinian political parties are considered the core of the Palestinian women's movement. These include organizations such as the Union of Palestinian Women's Work Committees (UPWC) and the Federation of Women's Action Committees. The General Union of Palestinian Women (GUPW), founded as a body within the Palestine Liberation Organization (PLO) in 1965, is an umbrella institution of the different women's committees and charitable societies.'[33]

▶

In 1965, the Society for the Rejuvenation of the Family (*In'ash Al-Usra*) was founded by Samiha Khalil. She was born in Anabta, Tulkarem in 1923 and lived in the 1940s in Asqalan (Ashkalon). She became a refugee in 1948 in the Gaza Strip and in 1952 traveled via Beirut to the West Bank, becoming a member of the Palestinian National Council in 1965. She served as president of the Women's Federation Society (*Al-Bireh*), of the Union for Voluntary Women's Societies and the General Union of Palestinian Women (GUPW), also founded in Jerusalem in July 15, 1965.[34] Such women's groups mushroomed in the 1970s and played a significant role in the uprising of 1987. In February 1968, 300 women demonstrated against the policies of deportation and land expropriation.[35] On March 8, 1978, the Women's Work Committee was established and by 1989, had more than 5,000 members.[36] The growth of Palestinian women's movements since then has been strong, though many challenges remain.[37]

Resistance to the occupation slowly expanded in response to Israeli repression and due to external factors.

The school year was due to begin in August, but the Israeli authorities wanted to revise the curriculum. Educators protested in very strong language and refused. Public schooling was consequently delayed until November when a compromise was reached thanks to the stiff resistance from teachers and school administrators.[38] On October 4, 1967, 129 notables from the West Bank issued a statement that challenged the Israeli invasion and emphasized Arab unity.[39] But as the second school year under occupation commenced in August 1968, the Palestinians declared strikes and engaged in protests across the occupied areas. The demonstrations in 1968 and 1969 were met with force.

In 1970, large demonstrations erupted in Gaza which scared the Israeli army due to the number of people participating. General Ariel Sharon was sent in to suppress the resistance – both violent and nonviolent. He became known as the 'Bulldozer' because of the manner in which he got his way: strongly and aggressively. Home demolitions, massive shelling and killing civilians became his hallmark. Palestinians responded to these atrocities in different ways. Some did so by demonstrations and appeals to the international community; for example, on the sixth anniversary of the 1967 occupation, an appeal by 107 notable Palestinians from various political affiliations to the UN demanding an end to the occupation and the right to self-determination.[40] Others, frustrated by decades of the indifference and silence of the world community, went to the other extreme, engaging in violence, even extreme violence, in response to Israeli violence and ethnic cleansing. Palestinian violence in the 1960s and early 1970s mimicked actions taken by the Zionists in the 1930s to the1950s (bombings, hijacking, kidnapping, etc.). These tactics succeeded in attracting world attention to the issues, but sometimes generated far more negative publicity (e.g., the plane hijackings, the kidnapping of Olympic athletes).

The 1967 war had a significant impact in making many Palestinians realize that the Arab world which 'managed' the crisis with Israel was not really up to the job and that the cause must be Palestinian. These Palestinians joined Fatah. Others believed in pan-Arab unity and joined the leftist groups like PFLP and DFLP. These groups moved to take control of the PLO, originally created in 1964 by the Arab League, but by 1968 fully managed by independent-minded Palestinians. The PLO's main factions had their center of activities in Jordan in the 1960s. Their military successes included a decisive battle with Israeli forces which invaded Jordan in 1968 at Al-Karameh. Emboldened by this victory, Palestinian guerrilla forces courageously engaged in operations against Israeli forces on many fronts, resulting in armed insurrection in Gaza in 1968–69. A group led by Mahmoud Al-Aswad was so effective that he became known as Gaza Gifara. This also led to asserting far more authority and even setting up checkpoints in Jordan, excesses that formed a direct challenge to the ruling Jordanian royal family. King Hussein finally sent his forces and routed the factions from Jordan. In the process, Jordanian troops committed atrocities in some of the Palestinian refugee camps.

The Gaza armed resistance was also crushed ruthlessly by Sharon's infamous unit 101. Lebanon was available and had no strong central government that could challenge the Palestinian armed presence. Yet, there were already signs of moderation that first came only from the socialist and communist Left. Nayef Hawatmeh became the first major Palestinian leader of an armed guerrilla group (DFLP) to suggest a Palestinian state alongside Israel in 1970 and in seeking more diplomatic approaches than other parties like Fatah (led by Arafat) or the Popular Front for the Liberation of Palestine (led by George Habash). More Palestinians began to re-evaluate the situation between 1970 and 1974. The years of re-evaluation of the military and political struggle were very important in shaping the agendas of many political factions as well as the ideas of people on the street. This altered dramatically the political landscape that existed up to the tragic events of the conflict in Jordan in September 1970 when the PLO forces were expelled to Lebanon. The Israeli authorities designated the PLO and all associated factions as targeted terrorist groups and, in the early 1970s, sent Mossad death squads to murder Palestinian leaders or potential leaders. Those who engaged in popular resistance were also targeted. Thus, the novelist Ghassan Kanafani was murdered by a car bomb in Beirut on July 8, 1972. He was from Acre, was editor of *Al-Hadaf*, a member of the Political Bureau of PFLP and author of many books.[41] Hundreds of activists were killed, jailed or exiled from Palestine between 1967 and 1973.

CHANGE FOLLOWING THE 1973 WAR

On the day the October 1973 war broke out, an estimated 70,000 Palestinian workers employed in Israeli businesses went on strike. The only one initiated by Arab countries, the October 1973 war showed that the Israeli military was not invincible when the Arab masses worked in concert with their leaders. It was also the first and only time Arab countries used the 'oil weapon', cutting off supplies to the US and other countries that supported Israel – a form of nonviolent resistance. Israel was saved from defeat and from having to give up the Sinai and the Golan Heights, occupied illegally in 1967, by a massive infusion of military aid from the US under the auspices of Zionist Secretary of State Henry Kissinger. The Soviet Union backed away from supporting Arab countries under direct threat from the US, showing that the US was emerging as an uncontested superpower. Like other pivotal moments, this changed the landscape once again, giving impetus to both political change and grassroots movements for change.

Two months later, the higher Muslim council in Jerusalem defied Israel by declaring its support for the PLO. With the realization that resistance pays, a small uprising (*Al-Wathba*) began with a student-led movement in Ramallah and Al-Bireh holding demonstrations on November 11, 1974. Within a few days, these spread to other parts of the West Bank and later (November 21–26, 1974) to Gaza. The main centers of activism in Palestinian society after 1973 were the student movements at the sprawling colleges and universities established around the same time. The Palestinian universities of Bethlehem and Birzeit (both established by 1973 and later Hebron,

Al-Najah, Al-Azhar, Al-Islamiya, etc.) became hotbeds of activism. The main organizational structures at the universities mimicked the factionalism of the larger society. Hence, student bodies included groups affiliated with Fatah, PFLP, DFLP, communists and Islamic forces. Israeli forces tried many means to quell all student political activities regardless of their nature and direction.[42]

Meron Benvenisti explains why the pressure was building on these emerging universities:

> the military government view of the universities as hotbeds of subversion in academic guise. The Israeli view of political expression as subversive activity aimed at the destruction of Israel, and the Palestinian view of Israel as an occupying power and illegitimate ruler, made the clash inevitable.[43]

The immediate initiating events of *Al-Wathba* of 1974 were Israeli economic and political measures which made life more difficult for the Palestinians in the occupied areas. This included their colonial settlement policies which were contrary to the Fourth Geneva Convention. The Israeli authorities escalated their economic warfare by blocking exports, curtailing travel and freezing the remittance of tax revenue to the municipalities in response to the PLO gains in the diplomatic arena mentioned above.[44] The genies of resistance and self-confidence that were liberated in October 1973 were hard to put back in the bottle. The PLO capitalized on the changing world climate by moderating its position and the world community responded with wide diplomatic recognition. In February 1974, the Islamic summit in Pakistan with 38 Muslim countries represented declared support for Palestinian rights. The Arab summit in Morocco in September 1974 recognized the PLO as the sole legitimate representative of the Palestinian people. This was followed on October 14, 1974 by a vote in the UN General Assembly recognizing the PLO as the representative of the Palestinian people; 105 countries voted in favor to four against (US, Israel, Bolivia and the Dominican Republic). The PLO's acceptance of UNGA 181 and UNSC 242 and 338 allowed it into the UN. In November, by a vote of 95 to 17, the PLO was granted UN observer status and Arafat gave a speech in Geneva in November 1974 declaring that he was holding both a gun and an olive branch and that the world community should not let the olive branch drop from his hand.

The PLO's shift towards moderation (led by Arafat) and concomitant international support for the PLO was met by a shrug of the shoulders by the ruling elites in Israel and the US. In fact, the Israeli grip on the occupied territories intensified. The occupation authorities moved ahead with their plans, focusing on three areas: crushing resistance locally and outside, using the Israel-first lobby in the US to ensure pressure continued on other countries to support Israel, and divide and rule. Palestinians were divided from each other and from the Arab and Islamic hinterland. Israel also started to interfere in Arab affairs to divide Arab countries from each other; in Lebanon, by propping up proxy forces, and in Egypt, by a deal with the Egyptian dictator Anwar Sadat. Simultaneously, Israel experimented by various means to crush any resistance locally. This included extending so-called 'administrative detention' (detention without trial) for up to six months, resulting in a strike among Palestinian political prisoners that lasted from July 11, to August 6, 1975.[45]

Israeli authorities tried to deepen their collaboration with King Hussein of Jordan to move the public towards accepting 'autonomy' in the form of a 'local civil administration', in lieu of self-determination.

Israel accelerated colonial settlement and intensified its oppression of Palestinians in the West Bank and Gaza. The resistance thus grew and expanded in proportion to political marginalization, economic deprivation, harsh occupation measures and attempts to impose a local pliant leadership on the Palestinians. In Gaza, the Israeli authorities appointed an Israel-friendly mayor, but he was soon forced to resign under public pressure. Gaza residents had to obtain a 'Shawwa permit' to travel to Jordan for several years. The Palestinian National Council decided to create a popular local entity, *Al-Jabhja Al-Wataniya Al-Falastinya* (Palestinian National Front or PNF), in the occupied areas in January 1973. This is the group that fielded candidates in the municipal elections of 1976 and won 18 of the 24 seats. It was declared illegal by Israel in October 1978 and almost immediately, a successor network, *Al-Lajna Al-Wataniya* (the National Guidance Committee or NGC), was formed.[46] Mayors like Bassam Al-Shak'a and Khalaf were recognized as leaders of the NGC and were not on good terms with the PLO. Israel later disbanded the committee and imprisoned or exiled its main leaders in the early 1980s.

Demonstrations, vigils, letters of protest and strikes grew and especially intensified in late 1975. Particularly vicious Israeli attacks on demonstrators (e.g., in the Al-Qassaba area of Nablus in early December 1975) were enforced. When an Israeli court issued a ruling that would allow Jews to perform rituals in the Al-Aqsa mosque; demonstrations were held the next day at the site, followed by a number of other demonstrations in other cities. These events culminated in an extended strike in early March 1976 despite a brutal crackdown in the preceding weeks. Public pressure resulted in the Israeli Supreme Court issuing a ruling on March 24, 1976 that, while upholding the rights of Jews to enter the area of the *Haram Al-Sharif*, said that this could not be done blatantly or in ways that disrupted public order or offended the Muslim sensibilities.[47]

The small uprisings of 1974–76 established in the minds of both Palestinians and the Israeli authorities that the local Palestinians could not be expected to remain quiescent. Popular resistance succeeded in forcing the Israeli authorities to back down (e.g., on the issue of Jews entering the Al-Aqsa and, temporarily, on the settlements near Nablus). The locals who collaborated with Israel and with the Jordanian regime lost significant power. From then on, the PLO's primacy over the Palestinian was unchallenged. But a counterforce was the removal of Egypt as a center of Arab governmental support for Palestine following a deal made by President Sadat. That deal ignored the rights of Palestinian self-determination and bypassed the PLO to call for a limited form of autonomy negotiated by the governments of Jordan, Israel and Egypt. Having secured its southern borders with Egypt, Israel tried to liquidate once and for all 'the Palestinian problem' by focusing on two areas: destroying the PLO in Lebanon and crushing unrest in the occupied areas. This led to its incursion into Lebanon and the atrocities committed by its forces and its proxies against Lebanese and Palestinian civilians, but also to the rise of the indigenous resistance force Hezbollah.[48]

The invasion of Lebanon came as a blow and the PLO leadership was shown to be incapable of defending its bases outside the country, let alone the people inside and help liberate them from outside. Arafat's drift to establish a pact with King Hussein was not well received by many of the cadres and remaining leadership of the NGC inside. They were relieved when that arrangement was finally dissolved. This led to a closer working relationship between King Hussein and Israel (e.g., in the appointment of new mayors, in opening branches of Jordanian banks in the occupied areas and attempts to gain support locally by improving some aspects of the Palestinian economy). This coincided with the Unity Government under Shimon Peres, which took a carrot-and-stick approach in the territories. The 'stick' seemed to gain strength in 1986 with home demolitions, expulsions, torture, detention without charge, and more.[49] But the war in Lebanon in 1982 caused the Israeli economy a significant setback which peaked in 1985 and 1986, leaving many Israeli construction and industrial sectors devastated. This also had a detrimental effect on the Palestinians who were the first to lose their jobs in Israeli businesses. Economic friction added to the political tension.

The struggle continued in the 1970s and 1980s and centered on saving land from being taken to build settlements in the occupied West Bank and Gaza. The settlement movement had accelerated especially after 1978 when Israel was emboldened by international acceptance following the peace agreement with Egypt. In 1978, plans and proposals for settlements throughout the occupied areas were put into place. Palestinians were left to defend themselves against these tactics alone, but did get a little financial assistance after the Arab summit of 1979. The money was channeled through the Jordanian-Palestinian committee. The funds went to housing, religious issues and some infrastructure, all intended to strengthen *sumud* (steadfastness) in the land. Religious organizations also tried to help their communities. In all these cases, the projects were hindered or stalled by the refusal of the Israeli authorities to issue housing permits or allow other developments. In 1976 and after years of unrest, Israel decided to try a new strategy: to allow municipal elections and push for collaborators to run. The strategy backfired as Palestinians overwhelmingly elected people who were highly respected and who spoke out forcibly against the occupation. Bassam Al-Shak'a, elected mayor of Nablus in 1976, was dismissed from office by the Israeli authorities a short while later and lost his legs in an Israeli bomb attack in 1980 and was banned from traveling in 1981. In June 1979, he led a 1,500-strong march to the military government offices to object to the building of the colony of Elon Moreh.[50] Later, the Israeli army attempted to deport him and other activists; in response, in an amazing act of solidarity, 21 mayors tendered their resignation.[51] Demonstrations followed and the disturbances forced the Israeli army to rescind the order and release Al-Shak'a on December 5, 1979.[52]

Volunteer work committees, created soon after the 1967 occupation, played a significant role in these acts of popular resistance in the 1970s. Abd Al-Jawad Saleh, an academic at Birzeit and mayor of Al-Bireh, told me that these activities were directly connected to their academic programs. This included volunteer work in refugee camps and remote villages: cleaning, plowing, literacy programs, etc. I recall how more than 40 students in my class were 'drafted' by such committees for street cleaning. These were forms of civil and national resistance that instilled a sense of community which would mushroom in the late 1980s during the 'Intifada of the Stones'. Organizers were targeted and severely punished by the Israeli occupation authorities with imprisonment and even deportation. Saleh himself was exiled for ten years.

One retired school principal, Yaqoub Al-Atrash of Beit Sahour, relates in his memoir an illustrative story that happened in the mid-1970s in Beit Sahour. It seems a military convoy arrived during a particularly sensitive period. One commander noticed some youngsters throwing stones, and one of them wearing a green shirt later ran into the school. The commander went to the school and demanded to see the principal. He ordered the principal to hand over the boy in the green shirt. The principal stated that his job was as an educator and nothing else. The commander stated that he would give him half an hour to produce the child. Time went by and the commander grew angry; he called the mayor and then the superintendent of schools. But the principal stood his ground. Both the principal and the superintendent were summoned to the military commander's office later that night. The commander threatened that consequences would follow. Days went by and no action was taken. A sympathetic Yemenite Israeli soldier later told the principal that meetings were held to take a stance on this, but that an educated military commander overruled any potential reprisal.[53]

In another incident, a military command ordered all students to stay in their school until 7 pm (i.e., five hours past the usual end of the school day) because, allegedly, some youngsters had earlier thrown stones at a military jeep. The school was surrounded to prevent the students leaving. Instead they performed political dances, recited poetry, held competitions, political theater and more, loudly and clearly within sight and earshot of the army. Later, the soldiers were distracted while students crept out for food. One student fainted and was taken by car to a clinic. The same car was then used to smuggle in food. When 7 pm came, the principal demanded all military leave the area before the students were allowed to return home. The students were happy that this act of nonviolent resistance was a success.[54]

Emboldened by neutralizing the largest Arab country and by the change in US administration (Ronald Reagan succeeded Jimmy Carter) the Israeli government felt free to launch a number of 'initiatives', ranging from annexing the Golan to intensified settlement activities to increased repression in the occupied areas and adventures in Lebanon. The common people moved on, undertaking more interesting and certainly more inspiring actions. As Israel cracked down on political activities, Palestinians established social and health service institutions. For example, leftist forces established the Union of Palestinian Medical Relief Committees which started with ten volunteer professionals and now employs hundreds of people working in over 400 communities that serve hundreds of thousands of Palestinians.[55] The lawyers Jonathan Kuttab and Raja Shehadeh founded *Al-Haq*, a Palestinian center for human rights.

THE EARLY 1980s: PRELUDE TO THE UPRISING

Israel issued military order 854 in 1980 to force educators to sign an agreement to have no contacts with the PLO and other conditions that violate freedom of education and association. Locals resisted pressure from Jordan and some PLO leaders, and they won over Abu Jihad, who later managed to take the pressure off. Educators, represented by the Council of Higher Education, led an international campaign that forced the occupying authorities to suspend the order in 1982.[56] Palestinian educators were ingenious in finding ways around many other obstacles placed in their way by the occupying authorities.[57] As Israel cracked down on foreign reporters, Palestinians founded alternate information media and reached out to foreign journalists via new forms of communication (e.g., fax).

When the Israeli government, claiming the restoration of an old Jewish neighborhood, decided on March 23, 1980 to build a colony in the heart of Hebron, Mayor Al-Qawasmah issued a statement challenging the decision and the people pledged popular resistance, including a boycott of the occupation.[58] When Zionist extremists tried to assassinate Palestinian mayors in June 1980 injuring three of them (Bassam Al-Shak'a, who lost both legs, Ibrahim Tawil and Kareem Khalaf), a wave of protests ensued which was described as a small uprising. It made a significant impact locally and abroad.[59] The mayors formed the National Guidance Committee (NGC) and emphasized that the PLO represented all the Palestinian people. But there were differences between the NGC and the PLO on tactics. For example, when Israel expelled some mayors in 1979 others decided to resign and went ahead even though the PLO leadership under Arafat was opposed to it. Fatah was ambivalent about the NGC and Jordan was outright hostile. There is evidence that the joint PLO-Jordanian committee set up after 1978 tried to starve the NGC of funds.[60]

Israeli authorities then issued military order 752 establishing 'Village Leagues', a network of collaborators to administer and entrench the occupation on its behalf.[61] Residents were forced to go to the appointed League collaborators for permits to leave the country, electricity and water supplies, land arbitration, etc. League members were armed and trained by Israel and did not hesitate to kill, maim or beat those who opposed them. Palestinians showed incredible resilience and resistance (*sumud*) in actions ranging from boycotts, public statements and religious leaders shunning these people; in some cases priests excommunicated church members who collaborated or committed other crimes.

A story related by Said Aburish illustrates popular resistance during this era. Sabri Garib and his family, who lived in the small village of Beit Iqza near Ramallah, owned 30 acres of excellent land. They had a well-appointed house and had farmed the land for over five generations. In 1978, Israel built the settlement of Givon Hadashah near his land. From 1978 to 1981, they tried to buy his land and when it became clear that he would not accept any offer, they issued confiscation and seizure orders. Garib began a long journey in Israel's (biased) courts that lasted from 1982 to 1990. His troubles included regular attacks by settlers and soldiers, vandalism of his home by settlers, imprisonment and more. His Israeli lawyers withdrew after they came under threat. Jonathan Kuttab took up his case and succeeded in delaying eviction of the family from their home. Ultimately, though, facing the might of a colonial racist system, it was difficult to win. Aburish also relates the stories of the Bedouin tribe of Al-Rashaidah (south of Bethlehem), who were forced off their ancestral lands to make way for settlements. He mentions a Palestinian (withholding his identity to avoid reprisals against him) who, like Jonathan Kuttab, was trying to help the tribe resist.[62]

The persistent resistance was supported by intellectuals and students in schools, colleges and universities in the West Bank in the early 1980s. Right-wing politicians in Israel insisted that the army crack down harder. In 1982, 140 teachers were dismissed by the military authorities for joining a strike to help organize a teachers union to get basic rights, such as an increase in salary and more funding for the schools.[63] A number of demonstrations and other acts of popular resistance proliferated in the West Bank and Gaza in response to Israeli atrocities in the occupied areas. The activities of students and teachers prompted the occupation authorities to close Birzeit University on July 8, 1982 for three months.[64] Loud protests led by municipalities in the West Bank and Gaza also encouraged Palestinians inside the Green Line to rise up and demand an end to Israeli atrocities in Lebanon and in the occupied areas.

Emboldened by the lack of any meaningful international criticism of Likud's policies and continued Arab disunity, the Israeli government invaded Lebanon, with the intention of wanting to crush the PLO 'terrorists' who were meddling in the West Bank. In reality, the PLO external factions were not involved in active resistance on the ground in the occupied areas because they had far more pressing issues abroad. The most visible PLO leader to stay in touch with local events was Al-Wazir (Abu Jihad), who was in many ways more popular among the younger generations than Arafat. The work he did in the 1970s and 1980s was critical in expanding Fatah's base and led eventually to his assassination in Tunisia by an Israeli death squad.[65] Locally, the factions concentrated more on attracting loyalists by providing healthcare and other social services.

Israel occupied nearly half of Lebanon and surrounded, starved and shelled Beirut. Finally, under pressure from some in his administration, Reagan got involved and a deal was brokered to withdraw Israeli forces in exchange for Arafat and his forces relocating to Tunisia.

The spiraling events forced Reagan to propose a plan on September 1, 1982 to give Palestinians autonomy in the framework included in the 1978 Camp David accords signed by Egypt and Israel on March 26, 1979. The 'autonomy' was to morph into a confederation with Jordan. Palestinians were told they could not be represented by the PLO and would have to renounce the right of return and self-determination. A week later, the Arab summit submitted its own peace plan in Fez (Morocco), which basically endorsed a two-state solution along the 1967 borders. Israel rejected both plans and responded by giving the green light to the massacres at Sabra and Shatila.[66] These and other Israeli atrocities in Lebanon mobilized resistance to Israel among Palestinians outside and inside Palestine. But resistance also took root in Lebanon (Hezbollah was born in this period) and abroad. Many of the key activists of my generation today, including tens of thousands of internationals of various religions, trace the beginning of their activist careers to this period. In retrospect, the beginning of the decline of the fear of the might of Israel started precisely when the state showed its most brutal face.

MOVING TOWARDS THE INTIFADA

Settlers took their cue from their government on how to deal with the unwanted natives. For example, on November 27, 1983 Kiryat Arba settlers attacked Al-Khalil University with weapons and bombs and sent threats to Birzeit and Bethlehem Universities.[67] During this period, the Israeli authorities used torture as a routine means of extracting information from detainees. On May 2, 1984, *Al-Haq*, led by Raja Shehadeh, addressed the president of the Israel Medical Association (IMA) about 'several disturbing reports of alleged participation of Israeli physicians and other medical personnel in the interrogation of detainees in West Bank prisons'. Instead of resolving the problem, the IMA issued a press release on June 7, 1984, accusing *Al-Haq* of making malicious and libelous accusations against the medical profession in Israel.[68]

The stresses locally generated interesting political trends. In January 1984, the Israeli Mapam Party held meetings with some Palestinian leaders from the occupied territories, including Sari Nusseibeh, Hanna Seniora, Faisal Al-Husseini and Sa'id Kenan.[69] These Palestinians gave strong signals of breaking away from PLO positions that were seen as divorced from reality on the ground. They claimed that the PLO was dominated by Fatah, and Fatah itself dominated by Arafat, who seemed to go in any direction in an attempt to please everyone. This meant Arafat made a deal with King Hussein in 1986 and abandoned it a year later under pressure from the public. But the PLO retained its standing as the representative for Palestinians inside and outside of Palestine. For 14 months in 1984 and 1985, the Palestinian academic scene was characterized by demonstrations and activities to protest against the Israeli insistence that foreign academics working at Palestinian institutions sign a document agreeing not to deal with the PLO. The protests led the army to relent in November 1983.[70]

The four major factions of the PLO competing for support on the ground were the PFLP, DFLP, Fatah and the Communist Party (PPP). Prior to April 1987, it seemed most of their energy went into the NGOs that were providing services to the public. NGOs were proliferating in this period. On the positive side, they built an infrastructure of self-sustenance. Some of the active groups were critical in ensuring Palestinians stayed on their land and survived the persistent Israeli attacks and attempts to clear them from the land through economic and other pressures. For example, the Palestine Agricultural Relief Committees (PARC) worked with farmers to teach them up-to-date agriculture and pest control techniques. To this day, the services they provide have not been matched by any government agency or agriculture support group anywhere in the world.

The negative aspect of the proliferation of NGOs was that competition between the groups resulted in redundant services and petty differences that sapped energy (e.g., in the clinics). Most of these institutions were run by older Palestinians who saw no reason for a more systematic popular struggle; later they joined the intifada of 1987. There were also few Palestinian intellectuals who understood the potential for educating for mass mobilization.

In 1985, Israel attempted to take over 500 dunums of land from Sur Baher to expand the colony of Talpiot. This was met with massive resistance and a compromise was struck whereby Palestinians were able to continue farming the land.[71] Mubarak Awad and others attempted to educate and supply information on the power of such resistance in the mid-1980s.[72] Awad's father had been killed by a sniper in 1948 and his mother was forced to hand him over to an orphanage. His background and education led him to advocate popular resistance. On March 16 and 17, 1983 a meeting was convened at the Jerusalem Fund in Washington, DC and attended by Awad and a number of Palestinians, including Hisham Sharabi, Jonathan Kuttab, Kamal Boulata and others (Eqbal Ahmed, Jim Fine, Gene Sharp, Beth Heisy Kuttab, R. Scott Kennedy). While some disagreement over how best to use nonviolence at this stage of the struggle evolved, the meeting did result in concrete initial steps to raise money for Awad to open a Palestinian Center for the Study of Nonviolence in Jerusalem, which opened at the end of that month.[73] In its first year, the Center engaged in education and outreach, including translation of works of and about Mahatma Gandhi, Martin Luther King, Jr., Gene Sharp and Abdul Ghaffar Khan. Workshops such as 'How to Get Your Rights without Firing a Single Shot' were held. Arabic pamphlets titled 'Nonviolence in the Occupied Territories' were distributed in 1983.[74]

One of the Center's first calls to action was to Palestinians urging them to visit their ancestral homes and explain to current residents the history of the house they were occupying. These reconciliation and outreach visits were to be made in sorrow and love, not in hate or anger.[75] Another direct action in January 1986 in the village of Qattana near Bethlehem came in response to the settlers erecting a fence and destroying an agricultural area belonging to villagers who asked Awad for help. Hundreds gathered and peacefully started to dismantle the fence. The settlers shot and injured seven of them but the work continued until the military arrived. Within a few days, the land was reclaimed by the owners when the military and settlers backed down temporarily.[76] The trees they planted were unfortunately uprooted despite promises to the contrary.[77]

During the same period, Awad and his nonviolent Center tried to help shopkeepers in Hebron whose areas were coveted by settlers and where Israeli soldiers erected barbed wires along the street, searching and harassing those who tried to reach the impacted shops. Some of the actions were filmed by the BBC and others covered by Israeli media, especially when Israeli volunteers joined to help the besieged Palestinians.[78] Soon after the PCNV organized a protest on June 14, 1987, they met with local and international officials to ask for the right of family reunification.[79]

Awad was criticized in various quarters: from the Israelis, who had an agenda to vilify Palestinians, from Palestinian militants, from skeptics on many sides, from those who believed he was not arguing for nonviolence on moral grounds and from those who believed he was too idealistic. But he also received support and protection from notable figures like Faisal Hussaini.[80] Israel denied Awad his Jerusalem residency on the grounds that he had US citizenship and had been out of the country for too long – something they do not do to Israeli Jewish citizens and something that is against international law. Renewal of his tourist visa was rejected and he was arrested on May 5, 1988 and ordered to be deported the next day. Appeals from a US Senator and Coretta Scott King were rejected by Prime Minister Shamir. He remained in solitary confinement for 40 days while his case went to appeal in the Supreme Court. He went on hunger strike and was joined by others, including Edward Kaufman, a Jewish professor at the Hebrew University, who held vigils outside the prison. The court's decision validated Israeli annexation and illegal measures that affected Jerusalem residents because 'they had the option of becoming Israeli citizens'.[81] In an unusual move, US Secretary of State George Shultz and the US Ambassador to Israel Thomas Pickering spoke out against the deportation order. Israel's ambassador to the US felt it important to explain the deportation in an op-ed in the *New York Times* on June 17, 1988.[82] The actual deportation on June 13, 1988 elevated Awad's stature and gave his ideas significant publicity.[83]

In March 1986, tens of thousands attended the funeral of the mayor of Nablus, Thafer Al-Masri, and chanted nationalistic slogans, including support for the PLO.[84] The demonstrations and activities in 1986 were again most visible in the universities. For example, the authorities had set up checkpoints on the road to Birzeit University effectively closing down education; the students demonstrated loudly. In one such demonstration in December 1986, soldiers chased students inside the university and used live ammunition, killing two and injuring twelve.[85] After the right-wing Israeli government exonerated its soldiers, demonstrations intensified throughout Palestine. Arab and Jewish students protested at the Hebrew University in Jerusalem against the decision by the administration to bring six students before a disciplinary tribunal after they participated in a demonstration on December 7, 1986 in solidarity with Birzeit University.[86]

Elsewhere in Palestine and the occupied Golan, there were further acts of popular resistance. The Negev Bedouins of Al-Khawaled, who were displaced from their homes, planned a demonstration with support from Arab members of the Knesset on January 6, 1987.[87]

Palestinians denied family reunification took part in a demonstration in front of buildings where Anatoly Sharansky (a Russian Jewish refusenik, recently released from Soviet detention after an international campaign) was to speak. They asked why Jews from around the world could settle in Palestine with automatic citizenship while the owners of the land and native people were denied the same right.[88] Even though most of the original residents had been ethnically cleansed in 1967 and prevented from returning, the remaining residents of the Golan intensified their resistance, especially after Israel decided to formally annex the Syrian territory in 1981. Israel responded with arrests and extended curfews. The villagers developed methods of survival and persistence:

When one village ran short of food, the villagers walked en masse to the neighboring village, overwhelming by sheer numbers the IDF soldiers positioned there to prevent it ... the elderly and young violated curfew in order to harvest crops. Arrest of the elders created greater resolve among the villagers ... groups of women surrounded Israeli soldiers, wrested at least sixteen weapons from their hands, and handed the guns over to army officers, suggesting the forces be removed. Guns sometimes were swapped in exchange for release of Druze in jail ... a diversion resulted in several soldiers being locked inside a stable. Villagers took the keys to the commanding officer, told him where they were locked up, and suggested he let them out and send them home; one village took advantage of being home on strike to complete a major sewer project. They had been refused funds and permits for years by Israeli authorities. A 'strike-in-reverse' resulted in trenches being dug and pipeline installed; and villagers began developing cooperative economic structures, such as sending the entire community out to spray trees with the understanding that the crops would be shared by all. They also began to set up their own schools.[89]

On March 30, 1987 on the anniversary of Land Day, strikes and demonstrations were held throughout the West Bank, Gaza and Palestine 1948 areas. Israeli authorities broke locks and forced open shops in many cities and attacked brutally but failed to quell large demonstrations held in Beit Hanun, Beit Lahia, Deir Al-Balah, Khan Younis (Gaza), Tira, Rahit (Negev) and Balata refugee camp (Nablus).[90]

This period in Palestinian history ended on a sad note with the loss of an icon of popular resistance in Palestine. On August 29, 1987 the renowned Palestinian cartoonist Naji Al-Ali died of injuries sustained a month earlier in an assassination attempt in London. Al-Ali was born in the village of Skajara in northern Palestine in 1938 and became a refugee at the age of ten, spending his early years in Ein Al-Hilwe refugee camp in Lebanon. He published his first drawings in the early 1970s in Lebanon, then moved to Kuwait and finally London. His famous cartoons always featured a diminutive Palestinian refugee boy, bare-footed and with torn clothes, named Hanthala whose face is not shown. Hanthala is looking back 'to Palestine', at the absurdity of the scenarios that Naji drew as a form of resistance – a way of reclaiming the dignity of our humanity. The topics covered varied and in some cases did not spare Arab and Palestinian leaders from criticism. Most of his work dealt with putting the image and reality of exile in a symbolic way that captured our hearts. Popular resistance activists wore T-shirts, pendants or bracelets depicting Hanthala. In the next period of Palestinian popular resistance, the symbolism of Naji Al-Ali and Hanthala continued.

11
Intifadet Al-Hijara, 1987–91

People do not find the courage to fight continually against as powerful an army as Israel's without some reservoir, some deeply and already present fund of bravery and revolutionary self-sacrifice.

Edward Said[1]

LIGHTING THE FUSE: OCTOBER–DECEMBER 1987

As we noted in Chapter 10, the landscape in the five years after the Israeli invasion of Lebanon played a significant role in preparing the ground for the uprising that became known as the 'Uprising of the Stones' (*Intifadet Al-Hijara*). The Israeli invasion of Lebanon and subsequent relocation of the PLO to Tunisia in 1982 helped end the myth that liberation could come from outside and led to early forms of self-reliance among Palestinians in the occupied areas.[2] Between 1982 and 1987, the Arab political scene seemed impotent as Israel intensified its colonial repression. Israeli forces committed atrocities, ranging from shooting civilians in cold blood to home demolitions, deportations, collective punishment and beatings. New quasi-legalistic structures were created to hide what were clear violations of international law in many cases amounting to war crimes and crimes against humanity. For example, in May 1987, a commission headed by Judge Moshe Landau approved torture in coded terms:

> the means of pressure should principally take the form of nonviolent psychological pressure via a vigorous and lengthy interrogation with the use of stratagems, including acts of deception. However, when these do not attain their purpose the exertion of a moderate measure of physical pressure is not to be avoided.[3]

The uprising of 1987–91 is perhaps the most studied of all the Palestinian uprisings.[4] We shall not try here to write another monograph on this period but cite just a few examples from thousands of inspirational and innovative actions. Forms of popular resistance matured significantly in response to the intensified pressures even before 1987. On November 15–18, 1986, a summit was held in Jordan on the use of nonviolence. Most of the participants were Palestinian.[5] A statistical analysis of monthly events that could be classified as popular resistance (demonstrations, strikes, petitions, flying flags, etc.) jumped from 933 in 1985 to 1,358 in 1986 to 2,882 in 1987 and novel forms of resistance were created.[6]

By the autumn of 1987, a number of events could be construed as initiating the uprising. On October 3, 1987, Palestinians demonstrated and engaged in a strike involving schools and colleges in the Gaza Strip to protest at the killing of three citizens near Al-Bureij refugee camp.[7] These demonstrations were brutally attacked by Israeli soldiers and this led to more anger and demonstrations. On October 8, 1987, a number of demonstrations were held in cities, villages and refugee camps in the Gaza Strip after another four Palestinians were killed by the occupation forces.[8] The marginalization of Palestine, the PLO and Arafat at the Arab summit in Amman on November 8–11, 1987 added to popular unrest. From these, other, more intense demonstrations spilled over and spread throughout both the occupied areas of 1967 and the 1948 areas. The characteristic pattern of these demonstrations soon became evident: youths (8–20 year olds) responded to Israeli brutality by throwing stones. This triggered massive reprisals – youths were killed and collective punishment was imposed. I am not sure why some authors try to date the start to when demonstrations were held after some Palestinian laborers were run over and killed by a truck driven by an Israeli (see below) – perhaps because this may have been an accident and the Israeli-influenced media could score a PR point by stating that Palestinians overreacted to a 'traffic accident'. Clearly, the events of October and November 1987 were pivotal.

On October 10, 1987, demonstrations were held in many locations accompanied by strikes; 25 Palestinians were shot.[9] These demonstrations and strikes spread to the West Bank when a woman was killed and four injured in a peaceful demonstration in Al-Manara Square, Ramallah on October 12, 1987.[10] Her murder prompted more demonstrations in the days that followed. Refugee camps in the Gaza Strip, Bethlehem, Nablus and East Jerusalem (the Shufat refugee camp) played a leading role in these demonstrations.[11] During the visit of US Secretary of State Shultz to Jerusalem, a general strike was declared and demonstrations were held in Jerusalem and Nablus, with one youth killed by the Israeli forces.[12]

In one bloody incident the army attacked demonstrators at Bethlehem University on the morning of October 28, 1987, injuring three students. One (Ishaq Abusrour from Aida refugee camp) died two days later from his injuries.[13] Subsequently, the occupying army ordered Bethlehem University to be closed for three months.[14] Ishaq's death sparked more demonstrations in the Bethlehem area and the cycle of demonstrations, Israeli killings of Palestinians and more demonstrations continued. Demonstrators and graffiti denounced the occupation, spoke of Palestinian rights, supported the PLO and honored the martyrs. Israel intensified the use of curfews, deportations, forced closures of schools and universities and forced opening of shops during the strikes. What was surprising was the Palestinians' restraint. From 1982 to 1987, there were few armed attacks. While the Israeli forces used torture, targeted assassinations, home demolitions and other brutal tactics, few Palestinians resorted to arms.

On November 29, 1987, on the fortieth anniversary of the partition resolution and the international day of solidarity with the Palestinian people, demonstrations were held throughout the occupied areas. Five youths were shot in Rafah and Balata refugee camp.[15] Scattered demonstrations throughout Palestine occurred on December 1, 1987 and several youths were shot in Khan Younis.[16] On December 8, 1987, in Gaza, when an Israeli truck plowed through two cars carrying Palestinian laborers four were killed and five (some say nine) were injured. Rumors spread that the Israeli settler was related to an Israeli who had stabbed a Palestinian. On December 9, 1987 word went round to meet for a morning demonstration in the middle of Jabalya refugee camp in Gaza. The location is known as *Birket Abu Rashid* (Abu Rashid pool, not a freshwater pool but a fetid mix of rain, dirt, sometimes sewage and lots of garbage). One 17 year old, Hatem Asisi, was killed instantly.[17]

Patrick White reported on an example of one of the milder confrontations between students at Bethlehem University and the Israeli military:

> The beginning of a demonstration was always attended by the fear of the unexpected and a sense of hysteria. Young freshmen student were frightened and fearful wondering what was going to happen next. Groups of girls, often from the campus and sometimes wearing kiffiyeh [*sic*] to disguise themselves, ran around the campus placing buckets of water in strategic places ... the bangs that were associated with the tear gas firing would commence.

The canisters would arch their way into the grounds. Screams and shouts would accompany the stampede for cover and safety away from the appalling gases. Canisters would fall near doorways, and the gases would float down corridors. Occasionally some canisters actually went into buildings. Those students actively engaged in the confrontation would try to put the canister, before they exploded, into buckets of water. Others who had gloves on throw them back at the troops. I saw one young man, he would have won 'the throw the cricket ball' competition at an English garden party, pick up a canister and launch it skywards in a parabola almost certainly sending it into the group of soldiers down Frers Street. At the end of the day he proudly showed me his hand. The heat of the canister had made his hand one huge blister.[18]

Defense Minister Yitzhak Rabin first ignored the unrest but, as it escalated, gave the go-ahead for increased repression, stating at one point that 'the first priority is to prevent violent demonstrations with force, power, and blows'.[19] Schools, universities and civil organizations were forcibly closed by the occupation army. Demonstrations became more frequent in response to the growing repression. Israeli soldiers also continued to use lethal weapons. Yet, the first year of the Palestinian uprising remained essentially nonviolent and no Israeli soldiers were killed while 204 Palestinians died during the same period, nearly half of them children.[20]

Other Israeli actions added fuel to the raging fire. Ariel Sharon moved to a house in Arab East Jerusalem (in the old city, Hay Al-Wad), which led to a demonstration on December 15, 1987 that was suppressed brutally.[21] By January, demonstrations were being held every day in various parts of Palestine and were met by Israeli fire that killed on average between two and five youths every day. Arrests soared – for example, on December 31, 1987 alone 177 were taken.[22] The Israeli paper *Maariv* discussed the use of water cannon in addition to expanding use of administrative detentions and expulsions in the attempt to control the increasing demonstration.[23]

Inklings of growing solidarity in the West Bank and a call by Palestinians inside the Green Line to hold a general strike on December 21, 1987 in solidarity with their compatriots in Gaza raised fears in Zionist circles.[24] Indeed, demonstrations started taking place in the Negev and Galilee in addition to Nablus, Jenin, Bethlehem, etc. Among the Palestinians within the Green Line, committees were formed in every major population center to support the struggle and the steadfastness of the Palestinians outside the Green Line.[25] On January 24, 1988, over 60,000 Palestinian citizens of Israel demonstrated in Nazareth under the collective slogan of ending the occupation and giving the Palestinian people legitimate rights. This signaled the spread of the intifada to areas of Palestine occupied since 1948.[26] Demonstrations, strikes and other activities were held, including a large demonstration in Haifa two weeks later. Walls in towns like Umm Al-Fahm, Kufr Kanna and Shafaamr were covered in graffiti supporting the uprising. These slogans were sometimes signed by specific Palestinian factions or in the name of *Abnaa Al-Intifada* (Children of the Intifada).

In examining hundreds of reports and documents over the period October–December 1987 (only a few examples are cited above), it was clear that the uprising developed spontaneously and beautifully through stages of ad hoc protests, to organized calls, to demonstrations of various forms, to boycotts, to empowerment and establishing a native leadership to replace the occupation authority.[27]

EVOLUTION OF A POPULAR UPRISING

A group of intellectuals centered in Jerusalem and including Sari Nusseibeh and Faisal Husseini was in place to assist the otherwise spontaneous uprising by holding secret meetings and issuing directives.[28] The first declaration and call to action came nearly two months after the initial escalation in demonstrations in October. The call of January 4, 1988 was written by the United National Leadership of the Intifada, but no organizational name was affixed to it. It called for a strike and civil disobedience for January 11–13, 1988. The second leaflet bore the generic name United National Command and the third listed the UNC and PLO.[29]

It is not clear how the first leaflet came about before even the UNC was formed and before the factions of the PLO became formally involved. One story I heard is that it was drafted by Majed Al-Labady of the DFLP. Once the grassroots movement shifted to a more centralized structure, the Palestinian factional leaders became involved. The UNC included key local members of the main secular Palestinian factions (Fatah, PFLP, DFLP). The Palestine Communist Party (PCP, which later became the Palestine People's Party) participated and supported but withheld their endorsement because they found the leaflets were too directive. The latter leaflets contained language suggestive of compromise among committee members to try to get support from all groups. According to Sari Nusseibeh, the initial drafts of these leaflets were written by Izzat

Ghazzawi, Samir Shehadeh and Samir Sbeihat and the draft was then faxed by him to Muhammad Rabaia (Abu Tariq) in Paris for transmission to Tunis, where the PLO leadership (principally Khalil Al-Wazir [Abu-Jihad] until his assassination on April 16, 1988) would give approval with minimal interference; when disagreements with Tunis emerged, the local leadership did not alter the text.

According to many activists I interviewed, a core group met regularly to put forward ideas, suggest actions and plan and put them into effect at the local level in every major town and refugee camp in the occupied Palestinian territories, including Jerusalem. The strands of information led to activists primarily in Jerusalem (many of them also based in Ramallah) but those individuals respected the popular mood of the streets. They included Faisal Al-Husseini, Sari Nusseibeh, Jamil Hamami, Muhammad Jadallah, Mahmoud Aker, Zahira Kamal, Ghassan Khatib, Khalil Mahshi, Riad al-Malki and Hanan Ashrawi, among others.[30] Mahdi Abd al-Hadi told Elizabeth King that while 'Feisal was the face of the intifada; Sari was the brains of the intifada'.[31] But a close reading of events shows that the relationships were much more complicated and there was a more democratic, bottom-up approach in operation. This was the key to the success of the intifada. According to Fatah activist Hatem Abd Al-Qader Eid, activists on the ground provided the main push behind the avoidance of too much reference to armed struggle and an emphasis on nonviolent mass civilian struggle. I confirmed this in interviews with key activists in Beit Sahour, including Hazem Qumsiyeh and Fuad Kokaly, who explained how information was passed on from local activists meeting in secret committees through a hierarchical network to reach Faisal Al-Husseini and his group. The strength of the autonomy of the movement on the ground and its relative independence from 'leaders' 2,000 miles away in Tunis was an important reason for its success. On occasion, the leadership inside made very clear their positions and warned the PLO leadership abroad from moving in a direction contrary to the will of the people (e.g., the PLO's readiness to accommodate Arab regimes, its eagerness to please the US and other Western countries).[32]

But even the directives of the local 'leadership' merely transmitted needs and decisions taken by popular committees. These committees included primarily members of the PLO and at times members of other factions not part of the PLO, and independents. The popular committees were specialized; for example, there were commercial committees made up of business people who decided on hours of operations, how best to boycott Israeli products, etc. Ever since the call by the national leadership on January 18, the Palestinians had boycotted Israeli products. This boycott spread to include boycotting the Israeli court system. Palestinian workers also withheld their labor from Israel. Many Palestinian civil workers and police officers resigned.[33]

There were also education committees that ensured that the educational system continued to function despite Israeli efforts to suppress it. Patrick White reported on the desire for education:

> Some of the university staff who complained about having to get to their lessons at eight in the morning were quite overwhelmed when students of theirs left the Gaza strip at 4:00 am in the morning in order to attend the lesson of two-hours and then return to their camps on another three-hour journey. Another example of student determination was to travel during the strikes to lessons when there was no transportation available. One student walked through the hills from his village of Beit Ummar to Bethlehem to complete a lesson and then returned on foot. When young people make this sort of effort and play down their sacrifices in a very modest manner, present themselves in a gentle and cheerful way, one is quite overwhelmed by their courage and simplicity and feels spurred on to do one's best for them.[34]

Women's committees provided childcare for prisoners. These ensured that the boycotts could continue while maintaining appropriate nutrition. There were provisions committees that made sure food supplies got through, especially to encircled and starved areas or areas that had been targeted by the occupation forces. There were healthcare committees, transportation committees, donor committees, intellectual committees, agricultural committees and more. The youth committees became known by the abbreviation *Al-Shabab* (Young People) and they trace their origin to a pilot project headed by Adnan Milhelm in Anabta refugee camp.[35]

Political prisoners in Israeli jails also organized themselves into effective committees which carried out collective strikes, which were especially effective in the 1980s and early 1990s.[36] King interviewed Qaddourah Faris (from Fatah) who was a key leader of the prisoner movement. He talked about a successful hunger strike for humane treatment that involved 15,000 prisoners throughout Israeli jails.[37] In 1990, Israel held over 14,000 Palestinian prisoners in more than 100 jails and detention centers at one time according to Human

Rights Watch.[38] Even Israeli supporters like Anthony Lewis became outraged enough to write:

> The Israeli Government has taken thousands of Palestinians from the occupied West Bank and Gaza into what it calls 'administrative detention.' That means they are held as prisoners, for up to six months at a stretch, without trial. At least 2,500 of the detainees are imprisoned in Ketziot, a tent camp in the burning heat of the Negev desert. On Aug. 16 Israeli soldiers shot and killed two of the detainees there ... The story had further grim details that I shall omit because they cannot be confirmed ... The prisoners at Ketziot, it must be emphasized, have not been convicted of doing anything. They have had not a semblance of due process. They are there because someone in the Israeli Army suspects them – or wants to punish them. Mr. Posner went to Ketziot to see two Palestinian lawyers being held there and four field investigators for a West Bank human rights group, Al Haq. He concluded that they had been detained because of 'their work on human rights and as lawyers'.[39]

One of the mistakes that had significant repercussions came from the PLO leadership outside, which thwarted the formation of networks in the occupied territories as they considered such moves as threatening its monopoly of Palestinian organization.[40] Despite these and other difficulties, the actions in the first six months were outstanding, well coordinated, used a variety of popular resistance actions and involved wide public participation so that they were hard to ignore by the Israeli and international media. These actions included strikes, the erection of memorials to commemorate victims of the occupation, refusal to pay taxes, developing self-sufficiency through farming and other methods, mass resignations (from the police, municipal councils and other authorities), refusal to pay swingeing civil and criminal fines, holding public prayers, refusal to obey military orders to close universities and schools (classes were held in people's homes, mosques and churches, and even cellars and caves), refusal to adhere to military orders to close shops and other private institutions, flying the Palestinian flag (this was forbidden by military order) and many others. Here, we can only list a few examples to illustrate the range of techniques used.

On January 4, 1988, in Qalqilia, a women's demonstration involving hundreds was dispersed violently, followed by arrests. A curfew was then imposed on the whole city.[41]

On January 14, 1988, Palestinians from the West Bank and Gaza held a press conference that called for the convening of an international conference for peace to include the PLO. Some of the participants were prevented from attending and two were arrested. The rest presented 14 demands that they said would help the conference succeed.[42] The third leaflet, issued January 18, 1988, called for a boycott of all Israeli products for which local alternatives could be sourced and proposed a tax boycott and other types of popular resistance. The boycott spread with a call to boycott all civil servants and the police force (call 9) leading to mass resignations. It then spread to tax inspectors (call 11) and those working in traffic, planning, housing and identity card issuance (calls 17 and 20).[43]

INNOVATION AND SELF-RELIANCE

In addition to the well-known forms of resistance, there were many other novel forms. As Israel blocked roads to the besieged cities and towns in the West Bank and Gaza, Palestinians reverted to old methods of transport over mountainous tracks on donkeys and mules.[44] Sales of sparklers and other fireworks were banned, so local people improvised with kitchen products including wire wool to celebrate Palestinian independence. Flying the Palestinian flag was punishable by up to five years' imprisonment, but one observer noted some interesting and ingenious ways of bypassing this, for example, laundry hung out to dry bore the colors of the flag: red, white, green and black.[45] The banned Palestinian flag also 'flew over local council buildings in many of the 530 Arab municipalities, towns and villages in the West Bank'.[46]

Gardening, teaching children in clandestine classrooms when schools were closed by the military and countless other methods of self-sufficiency were developed and expanded. My friend and fellow biologist Jad Isaac was jailed for teaching gardening skills to our people. As summarized by Frankel:

[Isaac], ever the practical man, quickly saw a connection between politics and food. One Sunday that month [January 1988], he and civil engineer Issa Tawil, a childhood friend, drove to Jericho, a West Bank Agricultural center, and came back with seeds and 500 seedlings to distribute to neighbors and relatives. Word spread quickly, and by the next day the seedlings were gone. Isaac [sic] went back for 2,000 more, and eventually distributed 40,000 along with bags of seeds, fertilizer, pesticides, rubber hoses and second-hand chicken cages. A friend across the street donated a shed and some land for a small gardening shop. Fourteen people invested a total of about $18,000 to outfit the store. By early March, Isaac, Tawil and Gerasmus Kharoub, a fellow biologist, were doing serious business. They hired three people to work in the shop and even bought a small tractor to rent out for ploughing.[47]

From a note I wrote in Memphis, Tennessee, June 17, 1988

The Israeli military destroyed 18 houses in the West Bank today. The news showed about 10–20 seconds of this and mentioned homeless children. Then they went on to 'more important things'. I keep trying to think that things would eventually get better. A person killed every day on average in the West Bank is not that bad after all, I tell myself. But I cannot help the feelings of anguish. I saw part of a movie yesterday about a black civil rights leader shot in Mississippi in front of his home in 1963. To his wife and children it was an irreplaceable loss. This young freedom fighter never saw any of the changes or freedoms acquired [later] by blacks. I then think that maybe change will come to the West Bank. Maybe change will come to Palestine, South Africa and other places in the world. I get an agonizing thought of my relatives, all my family in such a desperate situation. And then a second worst thought is that the world doesn't care and I am like everyone else: if I did not have family there, if it was not my home country, I may not care so much! This is a most unsettling thought ... I and everybody else should care and grieve for every person dead or suffering *anywhere* in the world.

POPULAR RESISTANCE IN BEIT SAHOUR

In 1988 residents of my hometown of Beit Sahour ceased paying taxes to the Israeli occupation authorities and at one point discarded their Israeli-issued ID cards. The events that followed are worth detailing from published and unpublished sources.[48] The idea for both the tax revolt and throwing away the IDs came from *Lajnet Al-Fasa'el*, a committee of the four main factions (Fuad Kokaly of Fatah, Rifaat Qassis of the PFLP, Walid Al-Hawwash of the DFLP and Lutfi Abu-Hashish of the PPP) and was passed on to the leadership in Jerusalem (Faisal Al-Husseini and others) and subsequently the leadership, then in Tunisia (Abu Jihad). It was subsequently reflected in a United National leadership leaflet. The first major tax raid occurred on July 7, 1988 at 4:30 am when heavily armored Israeli columns rolled into town. People were hauled out of bed and heads of households presented with bills (of an arbitrary amount) and told they had to pay them within a week.

This was met with unexpected defiance. By mid-morning the residents had gathered in front of the town hall to discuss the situation. The idea of discarding the IDs was proposed to the committee of the political factions by Fuad Kokaly, who had spoken with a priest, the late Saba Awad. Awad was the first to toss his ID card on the desk of the deputy mayor, Khalil Khair (the mayor was absent at the time). Israel had developed a system that required all Palestinians who needed to do anything official (from obtaining a birth certificate or a permit to travel outside the country, to getting a marriage or death certificate) first obtain a *Bara'et Thimma* (Document of Innocence). This required many signatures to prove that all duties as a citizen under occupation (no conviction in an Israeli court, no security warnings or issues, no outstanding taxes or utilities bills owed to the Israeli occupation authorities, etc.) had been fulfilled. The ID cards were a vital component of that unjust system.

Nearly 1,000 ID cards were collected by the time the army arrived. At 11 am, the deputy mayor was told to send the people home and that the military governor would negotiate. Residents were told to return at 4 o'clock that afternoon. The deputy mayor led the meeting, where over 2,000 residents were told that the military governor would not negotiate. Then the soldiers ordered the people to return to their homes. 'The soldiers dealt with this disobedience by arresting people and by suddenly opening fire with rubber bullets and tear gas bombs directed at the crowd.'[49] The military governor demanded and held a meeting at midnight with the municipal council and deputy mayor. He threatened to deport 50 notables and punish anyone without an ID card by the morning. The army took the IDs to their owners and threatened to jail anyone who refused to accept them. Many arrests were made.

The town was placed under continuous curfew for ten days. It was finally lifted on July 18, 1988. The day the curfew ended an Israeli soldier dropped a boulder onto the head of one of the residents killing him on the spot. The curfew was reimposed to contain the anger.

On December 15, 1988, The Palestinian Center for Rapprochement between People (PCR) issued an invitation to Israelis of goodwill to come to Beit Sahour. The invitation read in part:

A taste of peace: What will it look like when Israel and Palestine live together in Peace? A town in the West Bank invites you to tour sites in what will some day be the Palestinian state and taste today the peace of tomorrow. Come as a guest, not an occupier.[50]

The day after the invitation was sent, Israeli occupation forces escalated their attacks on Palestinian civilians, killing several and injuring dozens. The day of the visit opened on Sunday, December 18, 1988, with the occupation army declaring Beit Sahour a closed military zone. The residents checked the location of army road blocks into Beit Sahour and found that it was still possible to go by road from Jerusalem to Tequa, which is linked to Beit Sahour by a small back road (this was used by settlers but had no military checkpoints). A convoy of 20 cars carrying 70 Israelis, including Knesset member Ran Cohen, arrived and was warmly welcomed. A gathering was held in a church and opened with the Palestinian national anthem, 'Biladi, Biladi', followed by a speech of welcome from the mayor, Hanna Al-Atrash, who declared that 'force and oppression can never force Palestinians to end their intifada, their struggle for justice, peace, and independence'.[51]

On July 1, 1989, Israeli forces arrested 14 individuals in Beit Sahour whom they considered to be the leaders of the tax revolt and held them in administrative detention (detention without trial). Some of them were involved, most notably Fuad Kokaly, Hazem Al-Mashny Qumsiyeh, and Ghassan Andoni. The second tax raid took place on September 19, 1989. The Palestinian Human Rights Information Center reported:

Since September 19, 1989, Beit Sahour has been besieged by hundreds of Israeli troops. A new military compound has been set up near Shepherds Field for interrogations and rapid enforcement of military orders. What began as a campaign to enforce payment of taxes has become a full-scale military campaign against the residents of Beit Sahour aimed at destroying the city's economy, breaking bones, detaining even children, and pillaging stores, factories and homes. The authorities [were] unable to force any resident to negotiate with them or pay even trivial amounts to regain their property. The campaign moved from shops to homes, where in some cases almost the entire content of homes was carted into trucks and driven away, reportedly for auction in Israel ... Telephone lines were cut off and entry of press and solidarity groups was prohibited ... During the 42 days of siege, hundreds of residents were arrested, many not related to the tax issue. Detainees were used by the authorities as hostages, offering their release in exchange for tax payment. Debtors were arrested in the night and brought to their shops and homes the next day to witness the confiscations. Defense Minister Yitzhak Rabin stated at the time: 'We are going to teach them a lesson there, and no consuls will demonstrate and no Faisal Al-Husseini will hold press conferences. There will not be any attempt to not pay taxes. Even if it has to take a month, in the end they will collapse. We will not let this kind of civil disobedience succeed, and we have to pass through this test. We should tell them: forget it, even if the curfew on Beit Sahour lasts two months.'[52]

Ian Black reported on the tax revolt in the *Guardian* (October 20, 1989):

Hundreds of thousands of pounds worth of goods – including manufacturing equipment, domestic appliances, cash and jewelry – have been carted off by Israeli bailiffs escorted by armed soldiers ... Beit Sahour, a neat and relatively prosperous town of 12,000 in the 'Christian triangle' centering on Bethlehem, has been singled out for economic punishment by the authorities in a controversial operation that now appears to be intensifying ... The confiscations have become routine: the entire town is a closed military area with nightly curfews imposed and telephone lines cut off. Earth ramparts have been bulldozed into position at the entrances and soldiers patrol the streets.[53]

Israel forbade the media, religious leaders and even diplomatic representatives from entering the town to see what was going on (i.e., witnessing the large-scale looting of furniture, etc). A blackout on what was happening was inevitable. Representatives of a number of European countries and church leaders attempted to visit the town while it was under a 42-day siege (during which food, telephone, electricity and other services were cut). They were turned back by the Israeli army, which then encircled the town.[54] Nonviolent resistance cannot succeed with such a blackout so the leaders took it upon itself to break it. In the diplomatic arena, local leaders sent invitations to all foreign diplomats to come to Beit Sahour despite the siege and curfew. They were promised help in getting in. One brave diplomat, the British Consul General from Jerusalem, agreed. He arrived on November 5, 1989 from the north via a back road from Jabal Abu Ghneim in a four-wheel drive with some of his aides. His car was hidden in Yaqoub Al-Atrash's home and he was taken on a tour of the town during the curfew and via back doors and back roads to witness at first hand the devastation of the pillaging that was the tax-raids.[55] He wrote a lengthy report to his government which requested clarification from the Israeli authorities which responded by considering action against the British Consul for violating the 'closed military zone' rules.[56] A resolution was then presented by Arab governments to the UN Security Council calling for the curfew and siege to be lifted. The resolution received near-unanimous support, but was vetoed by Israel's chief benefactor, the US.[57]

Here is part of the letter sent by local leaders on November 11, 1989 to the US president complaining about the veto:

> We the people of Beit Sahour send you this letter to express our deepest sorrow for the unjust position taken by your government through your representative at the United Nations ... for the non-payment of taxes represents a peaceful struggle and is nonviolent and yet it was met with significant violence from the occupation authorities that did not provide any services corresponding with what they collected from direct and indirect taxes from the citizens over 22 years. They have not during this whole period submitted a single budget for the occupied territories. This means that the money that was being collected from the citizens went to the Israeli treasury to build settlements and to be used in suppression of the Palestinian people ... We request that you reassess your positions that are biased against us and to quickly declare an honest and courageous stand to condemn those who violate basic human rights ...[58]

Elias Rishmawi recalled it later in a speech in Spain and it is worth quoting segments from it:

> The agricultural committee had taken care that every piece of land around every house was cultivated to have all the vegetables we need as well as all the meat we need from rabbits, chickens. So while we were under curfew the Israeli soldiers were going

crazy smelling barbecues all around Beit Sahour while people were under curfew ... In September 1989 the longest and the hardest military tax raid started against the little town of Beit Sahour where the town was completely besieged. All entrances were blocked, telephone lines were disconnected and the town was denied access to food and medical supplies. The major confrontation had just begun. It was the time when neighborhood committees, together with popular committees and professional committees, were put in to alert and start functioning day and night 24 hours a day ... In one house, after they started moving, they heard the woman shouting at them to wait. And the smile was on their faces, somebody finally decided to pay. They were enraged when that lady threw the remote control telling them well, you forgot that. In another house they entered, a six-year-old boy was watching cartoons, and the tax collector looked wickedly and figured out that he might play with the emotions of the father, so he told the father: Well you can keep the TV and your son can keep watching television if you pay 100 shekels. The father said:

'No.'

'OK, 50 shekels.'

'No.'

'Well you know something? Pay 1 shekel and you can keep the television.'

You know, the father hesitated for a moment because he was looking at his son watching cartoons and his emotions were moving, but before he could respond, the six year old jumped up, switched off the television and shouted 'No father, let them take it!' It was one of the greatest moments in our history as Palestinians, to show that, to feel that the resistance was so deep in our conscious to the point that all sectors of society, men, women, even children, were all in complete harmony, in civil disobedience, in a nonviolent resistance in the tax boycott. That was so significant and we will tell the story to generations to come.[59]

Economic and military warfare was met with resistance in many other ways, especially developing self-sufficiency. Isaac taught people how to grow food in their back yards. He told me that the uprising gave him the incentive to leave the ivory tower of academia in Bethlehem University and establish the Applied Research Institute of Jerusalem. Patrick White reported on this:

Faced with these new realities, the residents of various neighborhoods in Beit Sahour took action that was not forbidden by any existing laws in the region ... At the same time, doctors of Beit Sahour started a low-cost medical treatment program, merchants announced fixed and lowered prices for various goods, social societies and clubs raised funds to help needy families, and a group of professionals, including agricultural engineers, established an agricultural center to provide the local community with seeds, seedlings, and agricultural equipment ... Doctor Jad was one of five founders of the 'Shed' which I visited one day in April 1988. Jad explained with his usual enthusiasm the early activities setting up 'The Shed'. The group of friends who established the center had, for many years, shared a love of gardening. They decided to provide agriculture supplies and services to neighbors at reasonable prices ... Before the arrest of Doctor Jad it became clear that the effects of these community efforts were amazing. They provided a practical model demonstrating that cooperative social work based on a home economy can provide self-protection through self-help for the people during unstable political situations.[60]

Attempts to develop self-sufficiency were repeatedly challenged by the occupation forces. My cousin Jalal Qumsiyeh related this amusing story about their attempts:

We were sure it would be impossible to get a license for a new cooperative project such as a dairy farm under the martial law of the occupation. Others have applied many times for similar local projects, but in vain. Yet, we took the risk and went to an Israeli kibbutz, bought 18 cows, and brought them to a special place very near town ... The military governor, the Shin Bet people, the civil administration officers, and a lot of soldiers went to the farm, surrounded it, and they took photos of each cow, with identification numbers. Then they gave us a military order to close the farm within 24 hours or else the military governor would order the place bulldozed ... We had no other alternative but to go late at night and move the cows secretly. So when the military governor went the next morning to the farm and didn't find any cows, he got very angry – it seemed like he had lost 18 terrorists ... a wide search campaign was organized. People say hundreds of soldiers participated, even with helicopters, looking for the cows ... but I can tell you something, the cows are still hidden somewhere and they are still providing the children of Beit Sahour with the milk of the intifada.[61]

The siege of Beit Sahour lasted from September 22 to October 31, 1989. During the first five days the curfew lasted round the clock. After that it was imposed from 5 pm to 5 am.[62] At the end of October 1989, Israel ended the tax raids due to the bad press and international outrage.[63]

One of the key participants, a pharmacist, Makram Sa'ad, when asked in 1990 if he had been a leader of the tax revolt answered:

> There were no leaders; everyone participated. If anyone, the religious leaders were the leaders. The Muslim, Catholic, and Orthodox leaders would link arms and march in defiance, and on occasion they prayed together in the main square of the town. We were all Palestinians and there were no leaders; we suffered alike and protested alike.[64]

The story of Beit Sahour was not unique; other towns resisted in diverse ways.

There were hundreds of ways of resisting and surviving. Israel licensed only 40 non-Jewish tour guides compared to thousands of licensed Jewish tour guides in the Holy Land. The aim is to control any messages from Palestinians (Christians and Muslims). Yet many Palestinians, in a form of nonviolent resistance, conducted tours, risking heavy fines, imprisonment and harassment.[65]

To respond to the frequent school closures and curfews that disrupted education, the popular committees 'organized alternate classes in local homes, mosques and churches in order to help the children to continue their schooling'.[66] A student at Balata refugee camp stated:

> They want to make us ignorant. They want to reduce us to being more backward than they are. They know we want to know about the world and especially about our situation. We want to formulate our struggle and to communicate our cause.[67]

THE PAINS AND FRUITS OF THE UPRISING

The strikes and resignations, etc. were expected to evolve into more general civil disobedience and complete separation. There were discussions and disagreement about this and the speed of the escalation required, as well as the length of the strikes, between Fatah and some leftist parties.[68] While this was going on, individuals were left to decide how to proceed with limited support. Towns that boycotted Israel fully were denied services (including electricity and water) and life became difficult for many. Some relented and went back to work. Even some policemen returned to their jobs. Without popular general disobedience, some resistance groups resorted to destroying occupiers' property (including not only military vehicles and infrastructure but also industrial and agricultural property). This phase was short-lived because of Israeli retaliation against Palestinian properties.

The UN Human Rights Commission issued a statement that supported the Palestinians' right to resistance, stating that 'the uprising of the Palestinian people against the Israeli occupation since December 8, 1987 is a legitimate form of resistance'.[69] But the Israeli regime saw things differently: as an assertion of rights that the system was not willing to grant. The Israeli leadership realized 1) that the uprising could or had become a way of life in the occupied territories, and 2) the PLO was the only major Palestinian political power that could end the intifada.[70] As the uprising ground on, even Prime Minister Shamir began to realize that Israel was losing control and needed to regain the initiative. As a result, early in 1989, he authorized his cabinet secretary, Elyakim Rubinstein, and Meridor to work with Defense Minister Rabin on a 'peace' plan. The plan proposed giving Palestinians autonomy in some spheres, while leaving Israel in control of land, security, natural resources and other key areas that are core to true sovereignty. This was to be a five-year interim arrangement while the Israelis negotiated with 'Arabs' (but not the PLO). I believe it was also in keeping with the Israeli practice of buying time while they proceeded to entrench their position and settle more Palestinian lands. The Shamir plan was essentially also a reiteration of what Israel had already agreed to at Camp David in 1978.[71]

Ibrahim Dakkak, chairman of the Engineers Union in the West Bank, was asked about the forms of resistance during the uprising. His answer is revealing:

There seems to be a picture of the intifada outside that it is about throwing stones and Molotov cocktails. The reality is that the intifada has diverse and deep forms. Those who count the dead and injured [Palestinians] observe one side of the intifada. The intifada was an intifada in the underlying construction of the Palestinian people in how people go about their daily lives. The intifada became a way of living and this is not covered in the media. The intifada is moving in the direction of building what might be called a Palestinian independence route. It means independence from Israeli markets, staying as far away as possible from Israeli institutions, and building Palestinian institutions that are as independent as possible ... the intifada evolves in daily confrontation with the occupation and also in reordering the elements of the Palestinian society in light of what fits the situation and what the Palestinian people expect will happen in the future and that is the building of the independent Palestinian state. So the intifada is a civilized and living movement at this time and changing the circumstances in the Palestinian society, a change that is going forward/upward not the other way around.[72]

The uprising was marked by a revival of interest in everything Palestinian: Palestinian flags, Palestinian art, cooking, culture, etc. The symbols of self-determination took on a strong nationalist slant. But simple acts of setting us apart from the occupiers became grounds for punishment. Israeli officials were furious when Palestinians set their clocks to different time and refused to change the time when Israeli time set the clock back one hour on August 26, 1990. On that day, many Palestinians wearing watches with the unadjusted time were punished.[73]

Tactically, the resistance tried to remove the tiers of the Israeli occupation powers gradually. Steps included asking Palestinian policemen to resign by putting pressure on their families. Tactics varied case by case to achieve the desired result. Village councils (councils set up by Israel to facilitate its occupation by managing the local people) were similarly targeted. Most council members resigned voluntarily; others were pressured by various means. The most effective was making people who remained in post social pariahs (no one would talk to them, priests refused to give them communion and they were refused entry to mosques, etc.).

The Israeli army tried desperately to reassert its authority and control life in the occupied territories. It ordered shops to open when they went on strike (forcibly breaking locks on many) and it ordered them closed when Palestinians decided to open them during the curfew and extended closures. Israeli authorities quickly issued orders banning all popular committees with up to ten years' jail for participating.[74] A policy was initiated to break the bones of anyone throwing stones or engaging in other acts of resistance. This policy commenced in early January 1988 but was only officially announced when reporters asked specific questions about it. Within three days of the announcement, over 200 were treated in hospitals and clinics for fractures.[75]

A particularly telling example of this policy in operation occurred on January 21, 1988 in the village of Huwwara near Nablus. Two jeeps drove into the village and seized twelve young men, tied their hands and drove them a distance from the village into a wadi out of earshot of inhabited areas. Upon command, they proceeded to use wooden clubs to break their legs and hands. Some required far too many blows, some clubs broke and the screaming was intense, but the soldiers carried on. The commander ordered that the twelfth man have only his arms broken so that he could walk back to the village to get help.[76] This brutality was to be repeated in other villages and towns under direct orders from Defense Minister Rabin, Chief of Staff Lieutenant General Dan Shomron and West Bank Commander Major General Amram Mitzna.

In the first two years of the uprising, Israeli forces and settlers killed 824 Palestinians, injured over 80,000, deported 58, arrested more than 50,000, imposed 6,163 days of curfews, uprooted 77,689 trees and demolished 1,225 homes or sealed them off. (By contrast, eight Israeli soldiers and three settlers were killed.)[77] In total between 1987 and 1991, 1,100 Palestinian civilians were killed and thousands injured while engaging in nonviolent resistance or not resisting at all (i.e., they were shot in their homes, in schools, etc.). In some cases homes were demolished for such minor infractions as joining a demonstration. But this largely unarmed uprising went on despite the Israeli army brutality.

Young Palestinians were the most affected and formed the backbone of the intifada. In a survey, it was noted that among ninth graders, 80 percent of males and 50 percent of females participated in demonstrations, 68 percent of the males and 34 percent of the females were harassed by Israeli soldiers, 29 percent of males and 2 percent of females were arrested, and 58 percent of males and 13 percent of females were beaten. The numbers among university students were even higher.[78]

A doctor visiting the area reported on the scale of the atrocities:

It was as a physician visiting the Makassed Hospital, one of seven Palestinian hospitals in the West Bank, that the true meaning of 'military occupation' came home to me. This hospital alone admitted 171 patients with gunshot wounds in three months.

More than 700 other severely beaten patients were treated. Of a total of 900 severely injured young people treated, half will be permanently disabled. More than 40 of those were permanently paralyzed. Palestinians, one-third of them children, suffering not only shattered bones, but shattered lives and dreams, filled hospital rooms and corridors. Rubber bullets inflict blindness and broken bones. Tear gas causes convulsions, amnesia, miscarriages, and in the very young and old, death from breathing complications. These grievously wounded Palestinians and their dead compatriots are fellow human beings who should not become just statistics. If it is our American money that buys the rifles, the bullets, and the tear gas that shatters human flesh, lungs, and bones, we must demand media access to the oppressed and accountability of the oppressors. Let us insist that this brutal and pointless occupation be halted before more innocents die.[79]

There were times when one million Palestinians in the West Bank and over 200,000 in Gaza were under total curfew, and when not under curfew, schools were closed for months on end affecting hundreds of thousands of students. All six major universities were closed. Alternative teaching in homes, community centers, churches and mosques continued, despite Israel declaring these gatherings illegal (fining people thousands of dollars and imposing long jail sentences).

Yet, despite the carnage and urge to advocate violent resistance, the uprising showed a remarkable persistence and growth in popular resistance methods. A content analysis of the leaflets distributed show that the vast majority of the first 39 leaflets carried directives for nonviolent methods and a small number for both violent and nonviolent activities, but in these the latter dominated.[80] And the Palestinians of 1948 worked hand in hand to support their brothers and sisters across the Green Line, declaring a day of peace (marked by protests and vigils) on December 19, 1987, marching from Ras En-Naqura to Jerusalem on February 28, 1988, sabotaging Israeli economic interests (e.g. by arson) and sending medical and food supplies to Palestinians under siege.[81]

Palestinian resistance did not forget its solidarity with others facing similar circumstances but called to designate June 25, 1988 a day of solidarity with all resisting racial discrimination, especially in South Africa. The Palestinian uprising was also a turning point in other nonviolent actions within the Green Line. Here is Gila Svirsky, explaining the movements of women inside the Green Line:

Before the intifada began, there were three women's organizations in Israel dedicated to 'peace and coexistence': TANDI (The Movement of Democratic Women in Israel); Gesher; and the Israel branch of WILPF (the Women's International League for Peace and Freedom). A much higher proportion of Israeli-Arab than Israeli-Jewish women participated in these organizations, and the latter were drawn from circles of women who had been highly committed and long-involved politically. Soon after the start of the intifada, the Palestinian uprising against Israeli occupation (in December 1987), an additional seven women's peace organizations suddenly appeared, and they managed to recruit many women who had never previously been politically active. These were Shani (Israeli Women Against the Occupation); the Women's Organization for Women Political Prisoners; the Peace Cloth; Neled (Israeli Women for Coexistence); Reshet (Women's Network for the Advancement of Peace); the Women and Peace Coalition; and Women in Black.[82]

A Glimpse at the Life of Faisal Al-Husseini, 1940-2001[83]

Faisal Al-Husseini was born in Baghdad on July 17, 1940 during his father, Abd Al-Qader Al-Husseini's forced exile from Jerusalem. His father was a leader in the armed struggle in Palestine and died in the battle of Al-Qastal in 1948. In 1958, Faisal Al-Husseini joined the Arab Nationalist Movement (ANM) and was involved in establishing the General Union of Palestinian Students in Cairo in 1959. He was responsible for student affairs in the Palestine government in Cairo, and later worked as an official in the Popular Organization Department of the PLO Jerusalem office in 1965. He joined the Palestinian Liberation Army in 1967 and graduated from Damascus Military College in 1967, but later became a key leader in nonviolent resistance in Jerusalem. Like other leaders, even when he did support violent resistance (in his early career) he hardly did anything violent and most of his activities focused on popular resistance.

After the Israeli occupation of Jerusalem, he became an active member in Fatah. This early phase of his work enabled him to lead the political and nationalist struggle against the illegal Israeli occupation. He was sentenced to one year in prison on October 15, 1967 and

▶

was subsequently harassed and jailed many times. Between 1969 and 1979 he pursued various professions: he was a farmer in Jericho, an oil merchant, a hotel receptionist, a radiology technician and a street vendor. In 1979 Faisal Al-Husseini, along with a small group of Palestinian intellectuals, founded the Arab Studies Society which was threatened by the Israelis and closed several times. In 1981, he led the campaign to end the siege imposed by the Israeli forces on the Golan Heights. The Israeli authorities put him under administrative detention in Jerusalem from 1982 to 1987 which prevented him from furthering his studies as a historian in the Faculty of Arts at The Arab Beirut University in which he had enrolled in 1977.

With an Israeli colleague, Gideon Spiro, he set up a number of ad hoc committees in defense of Palestinian rights. These committees finally evolved in the early 1980s into the Committee Confronting the Iron Fist and held demonstrations calling for an end to deportations, administrative detentions and other Israeli practices that contravened the Fourth Geneva Convention. The committee was one of the first Palestinian-led groups to involve Israelis and implicitly accept the idea of a two-state solution. Al-Husseini, Sari Nusseibeh and others organized a march in Jerusalem on June 14, 1987 attended by hundreds of people and waving 67 large black flags to speak of the occupation of 1967. Some Palestinians believed such moderate demands were a sell-out, but the ranks of such Palestinians expanded and included Hanna Seniora, Sari Nusseibeh, Ziad Abu Zayed and Radwan Abu Ayesh. He was among the most prominent leaders of the 1987 intifada. In 1987 he was jailed for nine months in administrative detention. Released on June 9, 1988, his office and home were raided on July 31, 1988 and documents seized that showed he had been working on a Declaration of Independence for a Palestinian State. The documents reveal a highly developed vision of asserting authority in areas liberated from the occupation via Palestinian self-governance. His key role in the uprising is considered his enduring achievement.

In 1991, Faisal Al-Husseini led the preliminary talks for the Madrid Peace Conference with US Secretary of State James Baker. In 1992 he set up headquarters for the Palestinian Delegation to the peace talks in what later became known as the Orient House. Besides becoming a center for the PLO in Jerusalem, the Orient House also encompassed the Arab Studies Society and became a main center to service the residents of Jerusalem and anchor them in the city.

▶

Al-Husseini penned this poem which best captures the spirit of nonviolent resistance after the massacres by Israeli forces in Al-Aqsa on October 8, 1990.

Oh God, the chest is replete with bitterness ... do not turn that into spite.

Oh God, the heart is replete with pain, do not turn that into vengeance.

Oh God, the soul is replete with fear ... do not turn that into hatred.

Oh God, my body is weak ... do not turn my weakness into despair.

Oh God, I, your servant, am holding the embers ... so, help me maintain my steadfastness.

Oh God, faith is love ... Oh God, faith is forgiveness ... Oh God, faith is conviction ...

Oh God, do not put off the flame of faith in my chest.

Oh God, we wanted for the Intifada to be a white one, so protect it.

Oh God, we wanted freedom for our people; we did not want slavery for others.

Oh God, we wanted a homeland for our people to be gathered; we did not attempt to destroy states of others nor demolish their homes.

Oh God, our people are stripped of all, except for his belief in his right.

Oh God, our people is weak, except in his faith and in his victory.

Oh God, grant us conviction, mercy and tolerance in our ranks and do not make us war against ourselves.

Oh God, turn the blood that was shed into light that will guide us and strengthen our arms and do not turn it into fuel for hatred and vengeance.

Oh God, help us over our enemy so that we could help him reconcile with himself.

Oh God, this is my prayer to you ... my invocation. So listen to it and grant us our supplication and guide us to the Straight Path.

The cost of the uprising to Israel was huge. Even by May 1988, it was estimated that in the first three months of the uprising, government revenues declined by 30 percent compared to the similar period the year before, expenses rose dramatically (for military and security operations), tourism plummeted and Israeli exports tumbled (by 40 percent to the occupied areas and some to other countries).[84]

THE ROAD TO OSLO

After the Gulf War of 1990, the US pressured a rather recalcitrant Prime Minister Shamir (previous head of a terrorist organization and leader of the right-wing racist Likud Party) into attending an international peace conference in Madrid. The Palestinian delegation was combined with the Jordanian delegation and led by Haidar Abd Al-Shafi, a highly respected Gaza physician. The team performed admirably in the negotiations over 22 months and Israel was so stretched by their performance that they decided they could cut a better deal with Arafat behind the scenes in Oslo. Israel also tried to capitalize on the nascent schism between Fatah and Hamas but the two groups signed a 'Charter of Honor' on September 18, 1990 (by Faisal Al-Husseini for Fatah and Sheikh Jamil Hamami for Hamas). The pact did not last long and clashes erupted between the two groups in Gaza in 1991.[85] In mid-December 1992, after five years of uprising Rabin took the unprecedented step of ordering the deportation to Lebanon of 416 Palestinians with Islamist tendencies (an act contrary to international law). This action was taken while he was simultaneously negotiating with so-called PLO moderates (principally Mahmoud Abbas and Ahmed Qurei') in Oslo. A leaflet issued after the deportation co-authored by Sari Nusseibeh of Fatah and Sheikh Jamil Hamami of Hamas called for a strong and unified response.[86]

The almost forgotten idea of 1974 acceptance of UN resolutions (going down the path of two states) received a boost before and at the end of the intifada when things went badly for the PLO as a result of the Gulf War. Bassam Abu-Sharif, an adviser to Arafat, had written a paper that was circulated at the Arab summit held in Algiers on July 7–9, 1988 which called for a compromise and a two-state solution. Arafat handed out the paper himself and let different factions attack it for selling out three-quarters of Palestine. But that notion already existed among many Arafat advisers, including Mahmoud Abbas. Sensing that there was not as much resistance to the idea as anticipated, several Fatah moderates advanced the idea of declaring Palestinian independence based on resolutions such as UNGA 181 and 194 and UNSC 224 and 338 (implicitly accepting Israel's existence). At the nineteenth Palestinian National Council Meeting in Algiers on November 15, 1988, the text of the Declaration of Palestinian Independence was read and approved. (The declaration was initially drafted by the national poet Mahmoud Darwish.)

The hope that this would sway the US position faded, but behind the scenes, Secretary of State Shultz had been working with so-called moderate Palestinians to change more. Schultz denied Arafat the right to come to the US for the UN General Assembly meeting so the meeting voted 154 to 2 (US and Israel) to hold a special meeting in Geneva to address Palestine (the first ever meeting outside the UN headquarters in New York). Arafat addressed the meeting on December 13, 1988 and stated that all parties should live in peace and security, 'including the state of Palestine, Israel, and other neighbors'. With this declaration and his renouncing 'terrorism', the US agreed to talks with the PLO. The first meeting was held in Tunis with Robert Pelletreau (US ambassador to Tunisia) on December 16, 1988. A second meeting was held on March 22, 1989.

In March 1989, Mubarak Awad, Gene Sharp and others met and made presentations to PLO senior officers in Tunisia about civil resistance, but with mixed results. Fatah, as the largest faction, moved much of the events both inside and outside Palestine. Arafat as head was calling most of the shots and, as was his style, he tried to bring people together, thus Fatah's fifth Congress in Tunis in August 1989 verbally supported both armed struggle and 'all forms of struggle'. Yet, money spoke and on the ground Fatah committed itself not to use violence in 1988 and 1989. Salah Khalaf (Abu Iyad) stated as late as 1990 that 'we have been very clear about the need to adhere to a no-arms policy within the context of the intifada'.[87]

Faisal Al-Husseini, Hanan Ashrawi, Radwan Abu Ayyash, Ziyad Abu Zayyad and Ghassan Khatib reached out to Israeli legislatures in January 1990, and some of them agreed to work for peace (and the importance of talking to the PLO). After an Israeli killed seven Palestinian workers and the occupation army killed 15 others, 44 prominent Palestinians engaged in a high-profile hunger strike.[88] However, a bomb that killed one Israeli and an attempt to infiltrate Tel Aviv by a small splinter Palestinian group changed the world's sympathies and the hunger strike was called off.[89] Israel's imprisonment of many of the original nonviolent resistance leaders and deportation of others left a vacuum in the leadership that factions again tried to fill with strident rhetoric about armed resistance. The difficulty of factions both within and outside the PLO to take a unified stance on the ends or means of struggle meant that mixed messages were being sent to the Israeli public, the Palestinian public and the global community.

Some people in Fatah and affiliated with other factions realized the gains from the uprising were due to the restraint (and in most cases outright prohibition) in using weapons. Others saw the sidelining of the Palestinian issue (especially after the start of the Gulf War) and the strain on Palestinian society in the West Bank and Gaza as evidence of the failure of popular struggle and the need to return to armed struggle. The different factions and tendencies caused the splintering of the unified command and many of its members were either in prison or their names leaked, which meant that they lost their influence as anonymous Palestinians. As a result, in 1990, leaflets sending mixed messages to the population became more common. Before the Gulf War, there was a fairly unified local command that had as its main target the Israeli occupation and mass popular resistance as its main tool. During the Gulf War, extensive curfews were imposed and many Palestinians suspended their activities waiting to see the outcome. After the Gulf War, popular resistance returned but unfortunately, interference from Tunisia intensified and violent tendencies also were resurrected. A lack of unified strategy (on means and goals) meant a splintering in the command of the intifada and more individual actions. Discipline broke down. Masked youths took decisions and acted on them, sometimes to the anger of key activists. As the sense of unity dissipated, the uprising fizzled out.

What directly led to the 'Uprising of the Stones' was a complex of internal and external factors – that is, a gradual intensification of Israeli repression responded to by (largely nonviolent) Palestinian resistance. The increase in intensity in these activities was not the result of a single cause or event but was due to an accumulation and intensification of Israeli repressive measures in the occupied areas. The inspiring movement that grew out managed to shed not only the intifada of Palestinian society under occupation but of a political landscape that had become somewhat ossified before 1987 and was not to be the same after 1991. Most of the aims of nonviolent struggle as articulated by the 1983 Mubarak Awad booklet were achieved in the 1987–91 uprising. The only one that was significant and not realized was removing the paranoia and fear in Israeli society, which continued to belittle all the Palestinian nonviolent action or, even worse, described popular resistance as a new kind of threat or simply a cover for violent action. I do not think this can be explained by the sporadic and rare acts of violence between 1987 and 1990. I believe the Zionist education system had implanted from very early childhood the idea that Jews have been persecuted by gentiles (*goyim*) from time immemorial. Children are taught to link the biblical account of slavery in Egypt with the Spanish inquisition, pogroms in Tsarist Russia and the Jewish Holocaust under the Nazi regime. Palestinian resistance to the desire of some Jews to have a national state in Palestine (natural as such resistance is in all colonial situations) is seen as an extension of a 'congenital' hatred of Jews by *goyim*. In this context, violence and nonviolent resistance to the desire of power and privilege are both seen as dangerous.

The outcome from this period in Palestinian history was mixed for the Palestinian cause. On the positive side, the intifada managed to achieve solid gains:

- It strengthened national and group identity among Palestinians, giving them a sense of belonging and empowering them.
- The moral strength and the support received tangibly enhanced the positions of the PLO in many spheres (e.g., in Lebanon by helping break the siege of the camps). This materialized in the fact that dozens of countries accepted the Palestinian Declaration of Statehood on November 15, 1988.
- The Israeli-American project to revive the Jordanian option (i.e., thwarting self-determination) and sidestep the PLO was effectively ended.
- It developed local institutions out of the popular committees, creating a state within a state – the true beginnings of Palestinian independence despite the occupation.
- It developed a local leadership that shifted the weight of activism from areas outside of Palestine to inside.
- It forced society to abandon destructive and regressive cultural habits (including the tradition of wasteful expense on weddings and funerals).
- It resurrected the Palestinian struggle as a central issue in the Arab and Islamic world. After this uprising, it has become significantly clearer that peace in the Middle East is impossible without justice for the Palestinians.
- It cost the Israeli economy over $2 billion (in 1990 US$) and forced many Israelis to re-evaluate whether it is possible to continue to occupy the West Bank and Gaza (this led to pressure on the government to negotiate peace).

That Arafat publicly supported Saddam Hussein in the Gulf War caused significant loss of Arab support and, after the war, many Palestinians were expelled from Kuwait and other Gulf States. The revenues to the PLO from these Palestinians dropped sharply.

Economically, about two-thirds of the PLO's revenues evaporated in one year. This added further stress to the uprising and created more divisions. Thus the uprising effectively died around this period. Acts in 1991 were mostly individual and not well organized; some had elements of violence. On the positive side, George Bush Sr., having promised to address the Israeli-Palestinian conflict after the Gulf War, pushed hard to convene an international conference. While the PLO was not officially invited to Madrid in October 1991, the Palestinian delegation to the talks clearly was coordinating and consulting regularly with the PLO leadership in Tunis. The Bush administration in Washington wanted to move forward and realized the settlements were a major impediment. The issue led to a rare showdown between the US administration and Israeli right-wing coalition government. At a press conference the president was blunt and unscripted, saying that he was

> up against some powerful political forces ... We're up against very strong and effective, sometimes, groups that go up on the hill. I heard today there were something like a thousand lobbyists on the Hill working on the other side of the question. We've got one lonely little guy down here doing it.[90]

The Israeli right-wing leadership was not interested in either a settlement freeze or in moving the peace process forward, but merely in crushing the uprising. The newly elected Labor Party under Yitzhak Rabin saw how the uprising had strengthened the local Palestinian positions (the excellent negotiating team led by Haidar Abd Al-Shafi in Madrid and Washington was really showing Israel to be a recalcitrant rogue state not interested in peace). Israeli leaders thus decided to take the step of reaching out directly to the weakened PLO in Tunis for direct and secret negotiations. The political process and the hope for a peace process ended the 'Uprising of the Stones' and ushered in the Oslo process. Many hoped that the political process would be able to harvest more than token fruits from the rich tree fertilized by the extraordinary sacrifices and struggles of 1987–91.

12
Madrid, Oslo and the Al-Aqsa Intifada

The uprising must move from resistance to achievement. The only way to do this is to diversify the intifada's actions, bring the masses back to the battlefield and directly confront the structures of occupation and control, such as settlements, military bases, and checkpoints, through massive, nonviolent resistance.

Ghassan Andoni[1]

THE OSLO ACCORDS

Internal factors weakened the uprising, including what I call the politicization and commercialization of the resistance. The PLO under Fatah's leadership had started to use money to fund activism. Instead of acting out of patriotic duty, many now believed that payment is due for each sacrifice or action. There were also external factors, including the Gulf War and the promise of a diplomatic breakthrough. There might have been a breakthrough if the Madrid negotiations in 1991 had been administered properly by the US and USSR. The former was influenced by a strong pro-Israel lobby and President Bush's concerns about being re-elected; the latter was struggling with its imminent dissolution.

Israel engaged with a small group from Fatah in secret negotiations in Oslo, because they found local Palestinians hard to defeat and realizing that, above all, Arafat and the PLO wanted international recognition. But the Oslo negotiations were done in haste, with little preparation or consultation, and the end result, the Declaration of Principles, was very biased against long-term Palestinian interests.[2] Azmi Bishara, Edward Said and other intellectuals argued against accepting autonomy as a 'stage' on the road to liberation.[3] According to Baruch Kimmerling, a major reason for the failure of Oslo was its 'skewed incentive structure with its frontloaded benefit for Israelis and its back loaded promises for Palestinians'.[4] As the Israeli professor Tanya Reinhart acknowledged: 'In return for recognizing the PLO and Arafat, Israel expected the Fatah-led PA to contain the frustration of their people and guarantee the safety of settlers, as Israel continued to build new settlements and appropriate more Palestinian lands.'[5]

Oslo had few positives and many negatives. The biggest negative is that it snuffed out resistance in the West Bank and Gaza. It had an opposite effect on the Palestinians who held Israeli citizenship. The agreements had excluded any consideration for the latter group, and they now realized more than ever that they would have to fend for themselves. Similarly, the Israeli Zionist parties realized that the end of the uprising meant they would be able to advance racist agendas inside the Green Line and the occupied areas. Thus, bills were introduced in the Knesset which reflected these two agendas, with the Palestinian members' bills largely failing.[6]

The Oslo process fragmented Palestinians: in exile, in Jerusalem, in the rest of the West Bank, in Gaza and inside the Green Line. It also sharpened divisions among them. Those who accepted Oslo and those who rejected it tried to adjust to the reality of the new landscape. Arafat's administration moved aggressively to build institutions of governance with help primarily from the European Union. Within the same party, some decided to move to positions and authority under Oslo and some remained outside. Fatah co-founder and PLO foreign affairs director Farouk Al-Qaddoumi and others stayed outside. Those who decided to participate found a system that encouraged cronyism and bureaucracy.

Significant changes at the political level reshaped the independent political landscape of the occupied territories into the 'Palestinian Authority'. Elections were held for Oslo's version of autonomy. Many hoped that this would be a prelude to usher in the prescribed five-year interim period of negotiations. It was clear that Arafat would win the presidency of the Palestinian Authority by a landslide, so few candidates were willing to stand against him. By contrast, for the legislative branch there were fierce and highly contested elections in which all parties, with the exception of Hamas and Islamic Jihad, stood. Many older leaders of Fatah and other factions were not successful. Younger activists, veterans of years in Israeli jails, were elected. (By 1996, nearly 10 percent of the adult male Palestinians in the occupied West Bank and Gaza had spent time in an Israeli jail.)

The first democratic elections for Palestinians in the West Bank and Gaza were held on January 20, 1996; there were 672 candidates for the 88 seats. Twenty women ran for parliament and five won seats.[7] Many women became prominent in the liberation movement, among them Matiel Mughannam in the 1920s and 1930s (see pp. 68–69), Intisar Al-Wazir, who headed the social welfare committee of the PLO,[8] and Hanan Ashrawi, who was appointed to the Executive Committee of the PLO. But much more work remains to be done.

The PA leadership under Arafat struggled to live up to the challenges and expectations of the Oslo years. The structure of the Accords left them little room for maneuver. Their authority was highly restricted to small land masses, designated area A, while Israel retained control in areas B and C and also in many aspects of life in area A. The Accords gave Israel the right to protect Israeli citizens in the occupied territories and, under this security guise, Israel transformed the landscape. The settler population doubled from 200,000 to over 400,000 between 1993 and 2000. There were also more restrictions on Palestinians' freedom of movement, increased land confiscation and greater repression. The PA took over the running of mundane, everyday matters in schools, sanitation, medical services, etc. from the occupying authorities.

THE CHALLENGE OF POPULAR RESISTANCE UNDER OSLO

The Oslo Accords created an authority expected to put down resistance and the national struggle became complicated. Armed resistance came from Hamas, which also introduced the first suicide bombing soon after the massacre by a Jewish settler of Muslim worshippers in the Ibrahimi mosque in Hebron. While cracking down on Hamas, Arafat ignored some elements of Fatah who engaged in armed resistance. This left people confused and popular resistance suffered a setback. It became clear that it could now only move if it was willing to confront the PA. Israel and the US insisted that the PA develop autocratic and authoritarian policies, including arrests and censorship of the press, in order to silence all forms of resistance to the occupation. Arafat was put in the untenable position of trying to please external forces while simultaneously maintaining popular support – a difficult feat under normal circumstances, but impossible under colonial rule clearly intent on pursuing its policy of ethnic cleansing. The rather autocratic and authoritarian rule that transpired reflected the traditional operation practices within a secretive patriarchal movement like Fatah. A member of the Fatah revolutionary council admitted to me that corruption was rife, but explained that Fatah, being the largest Palestinian faction, had all Palestinian problems under its umbrella. Another Fatah leader simply said they had to focus on the external threat (Israel) and thus the problems on the inside were ignored as they were not a priority. The other factions were also not democratic or transparent. Yet, thanks to Oslo, the PA was wedged in the untenable position between the people and the Israeli occupying authorities.

Palestinian editors and journalists were detained by Palestinian police on the slightest pretext.[9] On November 1999, a petition was signed by 20 prominent Palestinians criticizing the pattern that materialized after Oslo, including corruption and authoritarian rule. Eleven were arrested, questioned or placed under house arrest, and one was shot in the leg.[10]

Inside the West Bank and Gaza, Palestinians focused on building the institutions of governance and services. Everywhere, one could see signs of development aided by nearly US$1 billion in aid annually. Infrastructure, education, healthcare and other basic services increased. However, the major expenditure was on security; as required by Oslo, the PA was to help crush dissent and resistance. By 2008, security would consume a third of the PA budget. The Oslo structures allowed for tens of thousands of PLO members and nearly 150,000 family members to return from exile, not to their homes and lands, but to the PA-administered areas, especially the 7 percent that is area A. Most of the men were employed in the PA's official structures, including security and administration. When conflict arose it was no longer between Israel and the occupied Palestinians but among Palestinians themselves. The exception was the resistance by the Islamic and other forces who rejected Oslo. It also included splinter factions of Fatah like the Al-Aqsa Martyrs Brigades and Tanzim. The PA engaged in large-scale arrests of anyone engaged in armed resistance. However, the Israeli occupying forces did not even coordinate or request support, but merely went in and killed or arrested fighters.

The large bulk of the general population adopted a 'wait-and-see' position. But their patience was exhausted over the next few years. The five-year interim period should have resulted in a final peace agreement heralding independence, but it ended with Palestinians seeing an even more entrenched occupation than ever. By 1999, Palestinians' freedom of movement was severely restricted. They were not allowed into Jerusalem and hundreds of checkpoints dotted the occupied Palestinian territories. The expansion of the Jewish colonies on Palestinian land was continuing and accelerating. The frustration was bound to heighten and eventually resulted in an explosion in 2000.

As noted, the conditions were such that acts of civil resistance between 1993 and 1999 were small and contained by both the

PA and the Israeli authorities. Yet we can cite a few examples of successful work in this period. Activism by refugees and other Palestinians mushroomed from the mid-1990s and was instrumental in preventing the dangerous slide of the Oslo architects towards sacrificing this basic human right.[11] On December 6, 1998, during President Clinton's visit, over 2,000 political prisoners went on hunger strike demanding to be released. Their message to both the Israeli and Palestinian leadership was not to negotiate issues that do not place their release on the agenda.[12]

RESISTANCE INSIDE THE GREEN LINE

Inside the Green Line more significant political changes were taking place. The number of Arab civil society institutions established in Israel was only 45 between 1948 and 1980, but had jumped to 1,135 by 2004; this was directly attributed to the needs of Palestinians who were now isolated from fellow Palestinians.[13]

The participation of Palestinian parties in Israeli politics had limited results as these parties were not included in any key decision-making positions or committees. When there was a direct election between Ehud Barak and Ariel Sharon for prime minister in February 2001, 82 percent of the Palestinians boycotted it.[14] The percentage of Arabs voting for Jewish-led parties also declined, from 53.3 percent in 1992 to 18.1 percent in 2009; 48 percent of eligible Arab voters boycotted the 2009 elections.[15]

The Palestinians who still voted developed Palestinian-led parties and campaigned to increase the vote for these parties. In 1995, nationalist parties inside the Green Line formed the Patriotic Democratic Alliance (*Al-Tajamu' Al-Watani Al-Dimoqrati*), bringing together groups like *Abna Al-Balad*, the Progressive Socialist Party and *Al-Ansar* group, all agreeing to the idea of transforming Israel into a country of its citizens and maintaining Palestinian national identity. The party first won seats in the Knesset in 1996.[16]

Azmi Bishara was elected to represent the Alliance in 1996. Political differences forced Abna Al-Balad out in 1998, resuming its historic position of boycotting the Knesset. Al-Balad rejected Bishara's call for equal citizenship for Palestinians in Israel, 'converting Israel to a state of all its citizens', because the group believed it critical to not separate issues of Palestinians within the Green Line from all Palestinians, including the right of refugees to return and exercise self-determination.

A parallel split appeared in the Islamic movement inside the Green Line in 1996 between those who supported participation in the Knesset elections, such as Sheikh Abdallah Nimr Darwish and later Sheikh Ibrahim Abdallah, and those who did not, such as Sheikh Raed Saleh and Sheikh Kamal Khatib.[17]

The Oslo Accords also made Israeli and Palestinian politics more intertwined. The idea of declaring a state at the end of the transitional period on May 4, 1999 was contemplated. Israeli elections were to take place two weeks later but, according to the chief Palestinian negotiator, Ahmed Qurei' (Abu Ala'), this was deferred so that a more moderate face to the Israeli government could be presented (Labor, led by Ehud Barak, rather than the more right-wing Benjamin Netanyahu). Qurei' himself admitted that Barak was no better than Netanyahu. Jewish colonial settlement expansion and Palestinian home demolitions continued unchecked and Israel continued to refuse to honor its commitment to withdraw, to serious negotiations and on prisoners, etc. Barak even stepped back from implementing the Wye River Accords, which the right-wing Netanyahu government had signed in 1998 to try to use a provision in leverage to gain more concessions from the Palestinians.[18]

Barak was elected by the Israeli public and promised to advance the peace process. He was an army general who has little interest in compromise or peace. Yet, he thought he could use the opportunity to force an agreement that would create a Palestinian entity that would be called a Palestinian state but be devoid of any element of sovereignty. In other words, autonomy would exist in certain matters, but Israel would control Jerusalem, airspace, natural resources, entry and exit, and more. In July 2000 and as President Clinton was winding up his eight years in office, the Israeli and US governments pushed the Palestinian leadership to a meeting at Camp David to get Arafat to sign a peace deal that renounced basic Palestinian rights. Arafat rejected the deal and the negotiations continued, with Israel withdrawing from the negotiations in January 2001 at Taba.

THE AL-AQSA UPRISING

Israeli policies in the 1990s were to delay real negotiations while creating facts on the ground that signaled to Palestinians that they would always remain subjugated and defeated. Anger and frustration swelled. The straw that broke the Palestinians' back and triggered the new uprising in 2000 was more obvious than in 1987 and was provided by the visit of Ariel Sharon, surrounded by 1,000 armed Israelis, to the holy Muslim site of Al-Aqsa on September 28, 2000. Brutal Israeli suppression of the peaceful demonstration held the next day left six Palestinian civilians dead. In the first week of the Al-Aqsa intifada, 76 Palestinians were murdered, nearly half of them children.[19] No Israeli civilians were killed in the first few weeks of the uprising when Israeli brutality exceeded all bounds. An Israeli general told *Ha'aretz* that one million bullets were fired in the first two weeks. The Israeli army was apparently intent on ensuring the uprising would end quickly and effectively, unlike the uprising of 1988–93, so that it would bring an end, once and for all, to Palestinian aspiration for freedom and self-determination. Amnesty reported on patterns of deaths showing that the Israeli army mainly killed civilians.[20]

As the months after that fateful Al-Aqsa provocation wore on, Israel unleashed its army of destruction which demolished much of what had been built since Oslo. Nigel Parsons put it succinctly:

> Accelerated Zionist colonization and the concomitant failure to realize an acceptable national project collapsed the sociopolitical foundation of the PA rule; Oslo imploded as the new millennium broke forth. The colonizing power then visited massive destruction on the PA and collective punishment on Palestinian society, the former for failing to quell the revolt, the latter for lending support to it. Palestinian institutions were reduced to rubble, local leadership decapitated, communities isolated and impoverished.[21]

Tal Etlinger, a 'border guard' trained to quell demonstrations, stated that at Um Al Fahm, scores of unarmed Palestinian citizens of Israel were shot by snipers and many killed, but the demonstrations were much less violent than Jewish riots such as in Tiberias. The latter, he stated, were 'much worse ... but we handle Jewish riots differently ... to a demonstration like this we know in advance to come without weapons.. These are the orders from above, and we use only *gas*'.[22] Later, Human Rights Watch would issue a report on Israeli atrocities in Jenin, stating in part:

> civilians [in Jenin] were killed willfully or unlawfully [by the Israeli military] ... [which] used Palestinian civilians as 'human shields' and used indiscriminate and excessive force ... The abuses we documented in Jenin are extremely serious, and in some cases appear to be war crimes ...'[23]

Home Demolitions

'What pushed me beyond Zionism into a much more critical but contested and prickly political space was the demolition of Salim's house ... [for resisting the demolition] Salim was beaten, handcuffed, and thrown out of the house ... Arabiya, Salim's wife, managed to quickly slam the door shut and lock it with her and her six children inside. I arrived just after the soldiers had thrown canisters of tear gas through the windows of the house to flush Arabiya and the children out and had broken the door. I saw Arabiya being carried out unconscious ... I threw myself in front of [the bulldozer] to stop the demolition ... I watched Salim's face contort in pain and disbelief. 'But I didn't do anything wrong', he kept saying ... Wiping the perspiration from his pained face, trying to find words of awkward consolation, I promised him that the world would hear his story. On that day, lying on the ground at gunpoint with a Palestinian innocent of any wrongdoing witnessing one of the most wrenching experiences that can ever happen to a person, I found myself in another country I thought no longer existed, Palestine, among people who were supposed to be my enemies yet who shared their suffering with me at the hands of what could only be called Israeli state terrorism.' [24]

Jeff Halper founded The Israel Committee against Home Demolitions (ICAHD). Salim's house was rebuilt with the help of ICAHD and many donors and was torn down three more times. It was last rebuilt as a Peace Center. ICAHD states that over 18,000 homes were demolished in the areas occupied since 1967. In the areas occupied in 1948, over 500 villages and towns were completely depopulated and most of the villages were razed to the ground. ICAHD leads civil resistance against the demolitions.

On October 1, 2000, a nonviolent demonstration by Palestinian citizens of Israel was targeted with a barrage of live ammunition; twelve people died. The next few days brought massive demonstrations throughout Palestine on both sides of the Green Line. This action incensed and helped mobilize Palestinians who succeeded, again by acts of popular resistance, to push the government to open an investigation into the killing. The findings were never implemented.[25]

Students and teachers developed friendships and forged partnerships during the difficult months of the uprising. For example, teachers at St Joseph School, Bethlehem helped students deal with their trauma in creative educational ways: an oral history project beginning in October 2000 which challenged students to record their families' stories; and a diary writing project, beginning in November 2000.[26]

THE FOUNDING OF THE INTERNATIONAL SOLIDARITY MOVEMENT

The Palestinian Center for Rapprochement between People (PCR) was founded in April 1988 by a group from Beit Sahour during the first intifada. Their goal was to 'bridg[e] the gap between Palestinians and peoples from all around the world, informing the public about the reality in Palestine, and empowering the community with nonviolent direct actions for peace with justice'. The founders were involved in neighborhood committees which mobilized to cope with life under siege and to engage directly in popular resistance through community organizing efforts under Israeli occupation. PCR was instrumental in the tax revolt in Beit Sahour in 1989, especially in mobilizing international support and breaking the siege and curfew imposed during that episode.

It was the mobilization of internationals in December 1989 that convinced PCR activists and others to use more internationals in future actions. PCR took a leading role in the peaceful resistance and set up a peace camp to protest against the construction of Har Homa settlement in the Abu-Ghneim area in 1994–97. One peace camp, which housed Palestinians and internationals, remained on the hill for four months, 24 hours a day. PCR coordinated dozens of events, including solidarity visits and demonstrations, and pioneered attempts to stop the bulldozers physically with human bodies. These experiences, whether successes or failures in their immediate goals, proved to be valuable lessons when the Al-Aqsa intifada ignited in September 2000.

The report from the Rapprochement Center read in part:

Today, Thursday December 28th, hundreds of Palestinians, Israelis and internationals marched together demanding an immediate evacuation and dismantlement of this military base. The march was organized by the Municipality of Beit Sahour, Beit Sahour Emergency Committee and PCR. Israelis from Gush Shalom and Stop the Occupation, and Rapprochement Center – West Jerusalem Italians from the Women in Black and CGL Trade Union, Italian Peace association (Associazione per la pace),

French from France – Palestine Association, and many other internationals along with Palestinians from Beit Sahour marched together demanding from the Israeli Government that it dismantle the military base and evacuate it immediately, especially since it has no security justification to exist. The march started from the Shepherds' Field in the town and reached the military base. We entered the main gate of the base and asked the soldiers to leave the military base saying 'Go home'. The march was nonviolent and peaceful in which signs were raised in English, Arabic and Hebrew. We delivered a demand of evacuation to the officer of the base. The march ended by raising a Palestinian flag over the watchtower as the crowds cheered and clapped after which we visited the houses demolished by the Israeli bombardment from this military base.[27]

Inspired by the Beit Sahour tax revolt of 1989 when internationals were called in to break the siege, and by the success of this demonstration in December 2000, the PCR organized many other demonstrations in spring 2001 which involved internationals, and The International Solidarity Movement (ISM) was born. The key initiators were Ghassan Andoni, Neta Golan and Luisa Morgantini.[28] The ISM offices, then housed at the PCR in Beit Sahour, were raided on May 9, 2003 by the Israeli occupying forces and all computers, data disks and papers were seized, and two volunteers and one visitor taken into custody.[29]

ISM defined itself as 'a Palestinian-led movement committed to resisting the Israeli occupation of Palestinian land using nonviolent, direct-action methods and principles' and 'aims to support and strengthen the Palestinian popular resistance by providing the Palestinian people with two resources, international protection and a voice with which to nonviolently resist an overwhelming military occupation force'.[30] The ISM and the Grassroots International for the Protection of the Palestinian People performed outstanding deeds from 2001 onwards.[31]

Israel intensified its use of collective punishment against the civilian population for any acts of violent or nonviolent resistance. A rifle fired in Khan Younis was 'answered' by a barrage of shelling that left hundreds homeless on February 11, 2001. The very next day saw Israel lobbing an unidentified gas on the town of Khan Younis and the Gharbi refugee camp. The gas had a sweet odor, but 10–30 minutes later, victims were suffering stomach cramps, chest pains, vomiting, convulsions, and comas, etc. Israel used this gas for nearly six months while denying that it was banned or poisonous. Indicators are that it was a novel, non-lethal but internationally banned nerve gas.[32] Nonviolent resistance was also met with violence. For example, on April 18, 2001, a demonstration and popular resistance action in the village of Bidya to remove a road block was carried out. Here is what the Rapprochement Center had to say:

> About 300 people joined (Palestinians, Israelis and internationals) as we all did our best to dismantle the roadblock. At the beginning the soldiers did not interfere with our work, we managed to remove two big rocks from the blockade, however, as more soldiers and policemen arrived, and the closer we got to complete the work, they moved in forcing the participants back and arrested 16 of those who ignored them. We all waited for the arrested group until they were released and then hit our way back home. However, it was not easy for the group staying in Bethlehem area to reach home especially that Bethlehem, Beit Sahour, Al-Khader and Beit Jala were under shelling. The bus was not allowed to come into Zone 'A' because it has an Israeli License. So, we had to leave the bus somewhere to find a taxi to Bethlehem. We found two vans and the drivers were ready to take us to Bethlehem. However, they could not. So, they dropped us two hundred meters before the checkpoint at Bethlehem. The moment we stepped out of the car, a tank shell was fired at Beit Jala from Gilo colony. Then we had to walk from the checkpoint in the fields to avoid passing through the checkpoint until we reached the main road. We arrived to Beit Sahour at 1:30 am.[33]

On August 13, 2001 there was a protest attended by Palestinians and internationals outside Orient House, Jerusalem, which Israel had closed in violation of the Oslo commitments. Arrests were made. The Orient House functioned inside East Jerusalem as a coordination center and, essentially, a PLO governmental facility. But even when this was closed, Jerusalemites continued to resist:

> The Palestinians in East Jerusalem have managed to develop a sociopolitical network with which to counter Israel's negligence to address their daily needs and, at the same time, to resist the annexationist policies that sought to dilute their national rights. This ran the gamut from political forums and conflict resolution mechanisms, to a sort of shadow municipality, to social services

and institutional networking. All of these efforts led to some form of independence of East Jerusalem from Israel.[34]

Forty internationals managed to get into the besieged compound in Ramallah with Arafat at the end of March and early April 2002. As Israeli tanks and infantry bombarded and fired on the compound, they risked their lives and perhaps managed to help bring pressure on their governments which, in turn, put pressure on Israel not to kill or capture those who were inside, including Arafat. More internationals arrived in late April, in some cases, using diversionary tactics; for example, on April 21, 2002 one team approached from the front while a second team entered during the ensuing commotion from the rear.[35] When the siege was lifted the activists took credit for facilitating it.[36]

ISM members helped end the siege and violent attack on the Church of the Nativity. In one report, they wrote:

> At 17:40 this afternoon [May 2, 2002] a group of international peace activists of the International Solidarity Movement (ISM) successfully evaded Israeli military patrols and entered the Church of the Nativity in Bethlehem. This was the second time in four days that the ISM attempted to breach the Israeli military siege of the church to bring sorely needed food supplies to the 100+ people taking refuge in this holiest of Christian shrines ... On this second penetration of the military cordon around the church, a primary purpose was to put international peace activists in the structure to underscore to the international community the severity of the conditions there and the illegality of the Israeli military occupation of the city of Bethlehem.[37]

It would be hard to know how much more killing and damage in Bethlehem would have occurred had these Palestinians and internationals not engaged in such brave actions.

Defying curfews became a staple of civil disobedience from earlier uprisings such as in 1936 and 1987. It was developed into a systematic method with the help of internationals under the umbrella of the ISM in the Al-Aqsa intifada. A report on defying the curfew in Nablus read in part:

> Yesterday [June 28, 2002] was incredible. We had a great demonstration of about 100 people – 30 internationals and 70 Palestinians. We walked through the old city of Nablus on the

main street, and in the main square in defiance of the curfew. It was covered on CNN [International], BBC, and Al-Jazeera and by local paper and TV. Everyone here was so pleased ... it was completely nonviolent ... it was a complete victory for breaking curfew. Later in the day we went to an apartment building that has been taken over by Israeli soldiers. They have evicted the residents of the roof flat ... and are holding six families with 25 children and 18 adults in house arrest ... we are trying to help them negotiate basic things with the soldiers, but their main concern is to get the soldiers out ... The warmth and hospitality of people here is beyond anything I have experienced. It will be difficult to leave here in a few days. People here are very appreciative of our efforts and say that our involvement is helping to boost their spirits and solidarity with one another.[38]

In September 2002, thousands of Ramallah residents 'beat drums, honked horns, and made a general ruckus protesting the week-long Israeli-imposed curfew on the town'.[39] Susan Barclay similarly reported on October 2, 2002:

Today marks 104 days of curfew, 104 days in which 200,000 people have been imprisoned in their homes – over three months, over 2,020 hours inside (curfew has been lifted for about 70 hours in total). The inhabitants of Nablus have been breaking the curfew en masse, especially since the beginning of the school year, refusing to abide by this truly inhuman Israeli Army practice that punishes and oppresses the entire civilian population. In response, the army has been using more violence (physical and psychological) to impose the curfew, attempting to keep the population caged in their homes like animals through the use of terror and excessive military force ... In spite of the ever present tanks, tear-gas, injuries, bullets, tank shells, humiliation, jeeps and checkpoints, Nablus residents are determined to continue to live.[40]

Gila Svirsky described a joint Palestinian/Israeli event on April 15, 2001:[41]

The event was initiated and sponsored by the Center for Rapprochement, a Palestinian peace organization based in the town of Beit Sahour, not far from Bethlehem. On the Israeli side, the sponsors were the

▶

Coalition of Women for a Just Peace, Gush Shalom, Rapprochement and the Committee against House Demolitions. The internationals – split between both sides – included people from Italy, Germany, the US, England, France, and probably many other countries. We were about 200 on each side. As agreed, the Palestinians started out from the Paradise in Bethlehem, which has suffered so much severe shelling in recent weeks. Israelis started from the Mar Elias Monastery on the Israeli side. At the prearranged time, both groups walked simultaneously towards the checkpoint separating Bethlehem from Jerusalem ... Soldiers prevented the Palestinians from continuing along the main road, but they took side streets and were finally brought to a halt about 100 meters from the checkpoint. The Israelis took the main road and walked right up to the checkpoint, where the soldiers formed a cordon to block us from going through. They presented an order that the area was a 'closed military zone'. After some negotiation, they agreed to allow in a 'small delegation'. Our 'small delegation' turned into thirty, as more and more people slipped through the soldiers and became delegates. The delegation walked down the road and we could see the Palestinians at the other end waiting for us, and we began to chant, 'Peace – Yes! Occupation – No!' When we reached the Palestinians, we fell into each other's arms and embraced, even though most of us barely knew each other.

Moved by the moment, the group spontaneously turned to walk together to the checkpoint, even though the soldiers now formed a solid wall of armed men to block us. We interlocked arms and walked right up to them and began to push through. They fortunately did not draw their weapons, but locked their arms against us. But how could they possibly win, with no moral strength on their side? And we were infused with a burning sense of doing the right thing. We pushed and they pushed back, and there seemed to be a standoff, and the soldier pushing me said, 'You don't have a chance against us,' and I heard myself say, 'You have no idea how powerful a moral purpose can be,' and one of us was apparently right, because soon I felt them giving way, and our group was pushing them backwards, and we were moving forward. They dropped back and regrouped, and again we had our pushing game, and this went on for nearly half an hour, until they could not contain this powerful group, and we pushed through their entire cordon and broke through to the group of Israelis cheering us on and waiting at the checkpoint.

▶

> The meeting of both groups was as inspired a moment as can be. People were clapping and whistling and hugging and shaking each other's hands and slapping backs. There were meetings of old friends, and making of new friends. The moment felt so sweet. There were speeches, but nobody could hear us, and who cares what we said. The very fact of our presence together, united in our yearning for peace, for justice, for a state of Palestine side by side with a state of Israel, was all that really mattered.

RESISTING THE APARTHEID WALL

The Israeli government decided in 2002 to add to its violations of international law by building a wall round Palestinian communities, isolating people from their lands, schools, workplaces, hospitals and families. The Israeli government called it *Geder Ha Hafrada* (the barrier or fence of segregation; in Afrikaans the word for segregation is apartheid). Palestinians call it the wall of racial segregation. The nearly 700 km long barrier isolates tens of thousands of Palestinians between the wall and the Green Line. It allows Israel to lay claims to a significant portion of the West Bank (itself with Gaza a mere 22 percent of historic Palestine).

For years, Palestinians have protested at land confiscations for settlement activities. For example, in September 2002, internationals, including Israeli members like Jonathan Pollack, joined Palestinians of the village of Jayyous to protest against the vast amount of village lands taken over for the settlement enterprise.[42] But this abominable structure was far too big a crime against humanity to be challenged quietly. The resistance to it started strongly and continued strongly. The struggle took an organizational leap forward when the Palestinian NGO Network (PNGO) initiated a program to resist the wall, which evolved into the Grassroots Palestinian Anti-Apartheid Wall Campaign (Stop the Wall) on October 2, 2002. Local resistance committees formed in their areas. On November 9, 2002, women from Salfit, the region where Az Zawiya is located, set up 'Women against the Wall' to coordinate women's efforts. The Salfit region is heavily scarred by Israeli settlements. The wall is being built to surround these settlements and to take over much of

Salfit's agricultural land. In Az Zawiya, it is cutting off 80 percent of the village's agricultural land.[43]

Between 2005 and 2009, at least 1,566 Palestinians were injured in weekly protest demonstrations in four villages (Bil'in, Ni'lin, Al-Ma'sara and Jayyous).[44] The Grassroots Campaign, which coordinated these activities, called for designating November 9–13, 2003 a week of anti-apartheid activities. In September 2003, the International Coordination Network on Palestine (ICNP) adopted the week during the annual civil society conference of the UN Committee for the implementation of Palestinian inalienable rights, held in New York. Demonstrations were held during that week in many Palestinian cities and about 30 cities around the world.

A nonviolent demonstration on Easter Monday in Beit Jala was met with live ammunition. The injured included three British citizens (Lilian Pizzichini, Kunle Ibidun and Chris Dunham), a Japanese woman, an Australian woman and an elderly American.[45]

Israeli authorities, taking advantage of the accommodating international political climate, had begun a process of constructing a wall deep inside the West Bank in mid-2002, beginning in the north of the West Bank where it was closer to the Green Line. As the months progressed and it became clearer that the wall in the west would cut far deeper into the West Bank, protest and complaints about its impact began to escalate. During the US attack on Iraq in March 2003, Israeli forces accelerated the construction of the wall. The protests were harshly suppressed and, being ad hoc and unorganized, were not very successful in attracting attention. The focus on Iraq by Israeli and Western media minimized news coverage. Budrus, with a population of 1,400, became the first village to organize a weekly protest beginning on November 9, 2003. Other villages followed. One of the people involved, Ayed Murrar, was approached by Jonathan Pollack, an Israeli peace activist, and from that encounter, there was a significant increase in Israeli participation in these demonstrations.

In the village of Masha, local activists Nazeeh Shalabi, Tayseer Ezzedeen, Ra'ad Amer and Rizk Abu Nasser organized a camp against the wall which lasted four months, with Palestinians, Israelis and internationals maintaining a 24-hour presence seven days a week. Among the Israeli participants were Jonathan Pollack, Oren Medics (Gush Shalom), Dorothy Naor and Tanya Reinhart.[46]

But the protests along the route of the wall continued. In January 2004, the focus moved to Budrus, and this time, unlike in Masha, Fatah joined the other factions. Nevertheless, one of the key

Kindness amid Tragedy

It is always instructive to examine acts of kindness in situations of injustice. We are always amazed that internationals and locals put themselves in danger à la Rachel Corrie to do unimaginable acts of kindness among increasing brutality. It takes significant courage to break curfew to help needy people or to ride in ambulances to protect Palestinian drivers and medics from the attacks, harassment and delays that prevented them from serving patients, including mothers in labor.[47]

And this story is one of several that touch our hearts:

One of the most moving stories coming out of the struggle to end occupation took place during the current intifada, when a thirty-three-year-old Palestinian pharmacist from Shufat named Mazen Joulani was shot in the head and killed while sitting at a café in East Jerusalem. According to AP wire service reports, it was suspected that the drive-by shooting was carried out by an Israeli settler. The family, dedicated to the peace process, wanted to do something to make a difference. This was not the first time tragedy had struck the family. In 1998, when a cousin from Aida refugee camp in Bethlehem was killed by bullets from IDF troops, the family donated three of his organs to Israelis. Now, even though violence had escalated between Israelis and Palestinians, they again announced that they would offer his organs for transplant. As Muslims, that was a difficult decision. Yet five organs, including his heart, were donated to save the lives of others, no matter who they were. 'Islam does not forbid donating organs to save another's life,' said the aged father, Lufti Joulani. 'So, I donated organs to save the lives of others, no matter if they were Jews, Christians or Muslims.' It turned out that four went to Israelis and one to a Palestinian. Today five people have better lives because of this gift.

A young Israeli father of two, Yigal Cohen, would have died had he not received a heart transplant from Joulani. 'This is a noble act that really, really touched us. We were very surprised yesterday to find out the identity of the donor,' Cohen's father David told Israel Radio ... This Muslim family followed the path of nonviolence. The witness they gave cannot but help to awaken the conscience of the Israeli people and all people throughout the world.'[48]

organizers, Ayed Murrar, was bitter about the lack of participation or even moral support from the PA.[49] That month also witnessed the formation of the Popular Committee against the Wall, which had representatives from nine villages north of Jerusalem affected by the wall. From Budrus, the struggle spread to Biddu to the south. Biddu also took a legal course of action and the pressure of the demonstrations by the villagers forced Israel's Supreme Court to rule on June 30, 2004 that 30 km of the wall in this area should be rerouted. In anticipation of a ruling by the International Court of Justice, which was delivered in early July, Israel's Supreme Court was trying to give legitimacy to the wall by saying it could be adjusted to take into consideration people's suffering while affording security to Israelis (settlers).

On July 9, 2004 the ICJ issued its advisory opinion. The ruling reads in summary:

> THE HAGUE, July 9, 2004. The International Court of Justice (ICJ), principal judicial organ of the United Nations, has today rendered its Advisory Opinion in the case concerning the Legal Consequences of the Construction of a Wall in the Occupied Palestinian Territory (request for advisory opinion).
>
> In its opinion, the Court finds unanimously that it has jurisdiction to give the advisory opinion requested by the United Nations General Assembly and decides by fourteen votes to one to comply with that request.
>
> The Court responds to the question as follows:
>
> A. By fourteen votes to one,
> The construction of the wall being built by Israel, the occupying Power, in the Occupied Palestinian Territory, including in and around East Jerusalem, and its associated régime, are contrary to international law;
>
> B. By fourteen votes to one,
> Israel is under an obligation to terminate its breaches of international law; it is under an obligation to cease forthwith the works of construction of the wall being built in the Occupied Palestinian Territory, including in and around East Jerusalem, to dismantle forthwith the structure therein situated, and to repeal or render ineffective forthwith all legislative and

regulatory acts relating thereto, in accordance with paragraph 151 of this Opinion;

C. By fourteen votes to one,
Israel is under an obligation to make reparation for all damage caused by the construction of the wall in the Occupied Palestinian Territory, including in and around East Jerusalem;

D. By thirteen votes to two,
All States are under an obligation not to recognize the illegal situation resulting from the construction of the wall and not to render aid or assistance in maintaining the situation created by such construction; all States parties to the Fourth Geneva Convention relative to the Protection of Civilian Persons in Time of War of August 12, 1949 have in addition the obligation, while respecting the United Nations Charter and international law, to ensure compliance by Israel with international humanitarian law as embodied in that Convention;

E. By fourteen votes to one,
The United Nations, and especially the General Assembly and the Security Council, should consider what further action is required to bring to an end the illegal situation resulting from the construction of the wall and the associated régime, taking due account of the present Advisory Opinion.[50]

The ruling not only declared the wall illegal in international law, but also that settlement activities in the occupied areas are also illegal and must be stopped and reversed, and that Israeli authorities must compensate Palestinians for damages.[51]

The PA failed to mobilize or follow up on this critical ruling by demanding sanctions. It was left to civil society in Palestine to begin organizing for a campaign of boycotts, divestments and sanctions (see Chapter 13). Demonstrations in support of the ruling were held before, during and after it was handed down.[52] About a week later, on July 17, 2004, villagers of Izbat At-Tabib near Qalqilia and PCAW organized a march and rally against their classification as area C, against the wall and for freedom.[53]

In September 2004, two months after the ICJ ruling, hundreds of Palestinian children held a demonstration at the wall in Al-Ram (a suburb of Jerusalem) with the theme 'Let us learn'. The nonviolent demonstration was dispersed by police and border guards.[54]

ISRAELI ESCALATION IN 2003

The spring of 2003 saw a dramatic increase in violence directed against Palestinian and international civilians in the occupied territories because Israel calculated that the international media were focusing on the preparations for and invasion of Iraq. On March 16, 2003, Rachel Corrie, a 23-year-old student from Evergreen College, Olympia, Washington, was killed by an Israeli soldier driving an armored bulldozer while she was trying to prevent the home of a pharmacist from being demolished. She had come to Palestine, like thousands of internationals before her, knowing there was an injustice but not knowing how deep the injustice was or the level of brutality that Israel was engaged in. Rachel was wearing a fluorescent orange jacket and addressing through a loudspeaker the 60-ton bulldozer driver who could see her clearly, but he decided it was more important to demolish the house, one of a row knocked down to extend a buffer zone near the border with Egypt.

Rachel and other internationals were camping in houses slated for demolition in violation of international law. Israel demolishes homes of resistance fighters who were killed as collective punishment on the entire family, but this comprises only a tiny fraction of the home demolitions. Most were simply to remove Palestinians from areas needed for the Zionist scheme of 'maximum geography with minimum demography'. ISM members successfully prevented, and in some cases delayed by months, the demolition of many homes.[55] Rachel's misfortune was to become involved at a time when the Israeli authorities were on a murderous rampage, which included committing massacres in Rafah, Nablus and Jenin.

In a letter to her mother dated February 27, 2003, Rachel had written:

> When I come back from Palestine, I probably will have nightmares and constantly feel guilty for not being here, but I can channel that into more work. Coming here is one of the better things I've ever done. So when I sound crazy, or if the Israeli military should break with their racist tendency not to injure white people, please pin the reason squarely on the fact that I am in the midst of a genocide which I am also indirectly supporting, and for which my government is largely responsible.[56]

The killings continued in March and April 2003 during which over 200 Palestinians were murdered and other internationals killed or injured. On April 6, 2003, Brian Avery from North Carolina was shot in the face in Jenin. A British citizen, Tom Hurndall, was shot in the head six days later in Rafah; he lapsed into a coma and died nine months later on January 14, 2004. Iain Hook, a British UN volunteer, was killed in Jenin. Caoimhe Butterly was injured. Palestinians will never forget Rachel, Tristan Anderson, or the other activists injured or killed trying to achieve something positive by civil resistance. On the fourth anniversary of her death, the children of Rafah erected a permanent memorial to their 'American with Palestinian blood':

Children from the Mini Palestinian Parliament commemorated the fourth anniversary of the loss of the American solidarity activist Rachel Corrie by enacting a permanent exhibit for her that includes pictures and personal belongings at the parliament site in the center of Rafah governorate. The exhibit, which was attended by a large number of children and others concerned, included pictures of Rachel and statements and other documents released upon her loss, as well as some personal belongings and a symbolic coffin covered by the Palestinian flag. The exhibit was opened by reading commemorative poems two girls wrote in English: Nadeem Al-Mahaydeh (11 years old) and Islam Abu Sharkh (12 years old). The two girls spoke about Rachel's heroic stand in front of an Israeli bulldozer in an attempt to stop the demolition of a Palestinian home, a stand that cost her life. The two girls emphasized in their poems that the children of Rafah in particular and all children of Palestine will never forget Rachel and she will be in their memories as long as they live. The children then hung placards with slogans that commemorate Corrie and wish that she was with them, among the signs: 'Rachel we will not forget you', 'Rachel we need you', 'Rachel Corrie died as a Palestinian', 'We welcome her in the highest esteem and honor'. Children then put wreaths and olive branches on her symbolic coffin. They sent their wishes and respect to Rachel's parents who live in the US and who joined the children in the third anniversary commemorations last year.

After posting a large picture of Rachel on the wall of the exhibit, the child Ameer Barakeh (14 years) took a few steps to Rachel's symbolic coffin, placed some flowers and then looked for a long time at her picture and his eyes got misty and tears rolled down his cheeks. Barakeh said, 'Even though a long time has passed, she is still in my mind and every day I remember her wide smile when she used to come to this parliament, sit with us, talk to us, and give us gifts of toys and clothes.'[57]

Israel was intent on breaking all resistance to its colonization schemes. Locals and internationals responded to the pressure not by backing down but by accelerating and expanding their actions. Locals and international activists became a fixture wherever and whenever Palestinian lives and livelihoods were threatened. The Palestinian call for international support also started to echo deeper even in Israeli society. For example, a meeting was held in the Gush Shalom offices in Tel Aviv on March 12, 2003 to discuss the Palestinian call for support. More discussion ensued at computer listserves such as those of the Coalition of Women for a Just Peace. Those discussions resulted in a significant international (including Israeli) presence at the village of Masha, which had lost a lot of land to colonial Jewish settlements.[58]

In addition to protests, other forms of civil disobedience and resistance were enacted. Locals and internationals helped take down barriers placed to block access to villages by the Israeli army, which was intent on making life in the countryside impossible. This happened in Barqin in the spring of 2003.[59]

A non-violent demonstration was held at Masha on December 26, 2003 and an Israeli activist, Gil Na'amati (aged 22), was shot in both legs and badly injured, as was an American citizen.[60] On December 29, 2003, Jonathan Pollack, an Israeli peace activist, sent an urgent plea for help from the villagers of Budrus, and internationals and Israelis flocked to their aid. A follow-up protest was held on December 31, 2003. It included the Israeli group Anarchists against the Wall.[61]

BUT THE STRUGGLE CONTINUES

In late June and early July 2004, Israeli attempts to build the wall, of land theft and annexation accelerated. An anticipated ruling by the ICJ assured significant participation in the demonstrations, vigils and protests. For example, Azmi Bishara, then a member of the Israeli Knesset, organized a camp to protest against the wall in Al-Ram near Jerusalem. He started a hunger strike with Archimandrite Atallah Hanna (a leader and later bishop of the Greek Orthodox Church), Sheikh Tayseer Tamimi (chief judge of the Islamic court), Michael Warshawsky (an Israeli peace activist) and leading Palestinians representing the different political factions.[62]

On March 22, 2004 Israeli forces killed the quadriplegic spiritual leader of Hamas, Sheikh Ahmed Yassin, by aerial bombardment. They later killed the Hamas leader Abdel Aziz al-Rantissi, on April 17. Israel also intensified its destruction of civilian infrastructure and stepped up its attempts to isolate and fragment Palestinian communities by erecting walls and hundreds of barriers and checkpoints, and destroying roads. A poll conducted by Birzeit University in late 2004 found increased economic desperation and anger, but there was still support for continued negotiations among the majority of Palestinians in the West Bank and Gaza.[63]

Many demonstrations were held in the second half of 2004 and most were dispersed with lethal weapons, ranging from regular ammunition to rubber bullets. But even the gas that Israel used was destructive. For example, on June 10, 2004, the two local clinics in Az-Zawiya treated 130 patients for acute symptoms (seizures, convulsions, shock, etc.) of gas inhalation.[64]

On August 26, 2004, Arun Gandhi, the grandson of Mahatma Gandhi, addressed rallies in Ramallah, Abu Dis and Bethlehem.[65] He was head of the M. K. Gandhi Institute for Nonviolence in the United States until he was expelled by a Zionist lobby for speaking the truth about what he had seen.

The Freedom March

Palestinians, internationals and Israelis marched along the path of the apartheid wall being constructed in what was dubbed the 'Freedom March'. The march began July 30, 2004 from the village of Zububa in the Jenin district, through cities, towns and villages affected by the wall all the way to Jerusalem. They arrived in Jerusalem nearly three weeks later. They had a number of adventures along the way. Here is part of their march blog entries:[66]

Day 6: August 4
Impact of Wall on Jbarra
The Freedom March was joined by 30–40 Palestinian women from the Tulkarem area who accompanied the march for part of the route.

Traveling south from Tulkarem, the Freedom March arrived at Jbarra village. Jbarra is a small village that has been completely surrounded by the apartheid wall and cut off from the rest of the West Bank. There are

▶

only two gates to enter and exit the village; one in the north and one in the south. However, only residents of Jbarra can exit or enter through the gate and only with a permit obtained from the Israeli military. Palestinians in the areas surrounding Jbarra may not enter the village and cannot obtain permits. Children as young as one year old, who are residents of Jbarra village, must obtain a permit to exit or re-enter the village. In addition, any vehicle traveling to and from the village must have a permit to do so.

www.palsolidarity.org/pictures/PHOTOS_3Aug04_13_40_31Tulkare mHuwaida.htm.

Day 8: August 6
Freedom March Protest Policy of Barring Israelis
Friday, late afternoon, the Freedom March was stopped by the Israeli army as they approached Qalqilya. The army demanded that each marcher hand in their identity cards and passports in order to identify any person with Israeli citizenship. Israelis are prohibited from entering area A of the West Bank.

The freedom marchers decided to protest the policy of not allowing Israelis into Area A of the West Bank and refused to hand over their passports and identity cards. This policy has several consequences. Israelis are unable to witness the conditions Palestinians live in under military occupation and the suffering imposed as a result of the construction of the apartheid wall. In addition, Palestinians living within the 48 borders are separated from families and friends and unable to visit loved ones, and goods and services are unable to move between areas.

www.palsolidarity.org/pictures/PHOTOS_8Aug04_05_39_04Qalqili aSimon.htm.
www.palsolidarity.org/pictures/PHOTOS_7Aug04_02_57_31Qalqilia Mahmoud.htm.

Day 10: August 8
Protest of Detained Palestinians; Activist Arrested
The Freedom March left Qalqiliya around 10:00 am. Palestinians and internationals were joined by approximately thirty additional internationals after spending Saturday in Qalqiliya and surrounding villages.

▶

At around 6:00 pm as the freedom march arrived at a gate in the fence section of the apartheid wall, which also serves as a checkpoint, between the village of Azzun Atmah and Beit Amin, they witnessed 15–20 young Palestinian men being detained by the Israeli army.

The freedom marchers demanded that the men be released and refused to leave until they were set free. They then sat down in the road and chanted. They were surrounded by eight army jeeps and humvees. After five minutes the Israeli soldiers attempted to physically drag internationals away. Although the freedom marchers tried to protect each other non-violently, the soldiers managed to detain Karl, a 23-year-old peace activist from New York.

The marchers believe they targeted him for detention because he had led the negotiations with the soldiers, as well as the chants during their protest of those already detained.

Karl was taken to Ariel police station where he is at the time of this report, 10:00 pm local time.

All but four of the young Palestinians detained at the checkpoint were released after the Freedom March protested their being held by the army. The last two Palestinians were released by 9:30 pm and told the freedom marchers that they had been detained at the checkpoint for over 24 hours.

Update on Karl. Released August 10, 2004:

Karl was released Monday night on condition that he not go near the wall or participate in demonstrations for the next five days. According to Karl, he was beaten upon his arrest and he was told he would be deported for holding a megaphone.

The number of freedom marchers peaked at 1,000 on Tuesday, August 10, 2004 when residents of Deir Balut, Az Awiya, Qiri and Rafat marched from Masha to the land around Az Awiya that was taken for the construction of the apartheid wall. The number of protesters overwhelmed the Israeli army and border police; the demonstrators held their ground.[67]

About 500 Palestinian residents of Bethlehem protested on Sunday afternoon, March 5, 2006 near the Church of the Nativity condemning the attack carried out by an extremist Israeli family against the Church of the Basilica in Nazareth. On May 19, 2006, Palestinians from Shufat refugee camp tried to enter Jerusalem for

Friday prayers. They were violently attacked, but the situation could have been far worse had it not been for international support. Two Palestinians, one Israeli and an English journalist were beaten and detained. The English journalist reported later:

> The demonstration was completely peaceful until the soldiers attacked us without provocation. A couple of children who were not part of the demonstration threw stones back at them. The Israeli soldiers then rushed forward after a few moments to grab the kids. The kids had made good their escape by then, so instead the soldiers grabbed a Palestinian who had gone over from the demonstration to get the kids to stop throwing stones. As they handcuffed him they were brutally beating him on the head. I went over to film this and to tell them to stop. They did not like someone witnessing their brutality so they beat me up too and shoved me in the van with the other three.[68]

The hilly area south of Hebron was the location of repeated settler and army attacks on Palestinian residents because the land was coveted by the Zionist state. Colonial settlements activity intensified after 2001 and it became common to see the demolition of homes, attacks on shepherds, denial of access to land or schools, and much more. On January 11, 2002, a protest was organized that involved over 50 cars carrying more than 250 activists of various backgrounds. They delivered blankets and stood in defense of cave dwellers in the hills.[69]

In Tel Rumeida and other areas in Hebron, Palestinians try to survive against incredible odds and attempts to remove them. They were and currently are helped by internationals, including Christian Peace Maker teams.[70]

BIL'IN

In Bil'in (population 1,300) near Ramallah, residents have engaged in weekly nonviolent demonstrations and other creative nonviolent direct actions for years. The demonstrations that take place after Friday prayers attract people from around the world.

Writing in the *International Herald Tribune* in 2005, Mohammad Khatib explained:

> We have held more than 50 peaceful demonstrations since February [now hundreds]. We learned from the experience and

advice of villages like Budrus and Biddu, which resisted the wall nonviolently. Palestinians from other areas now call people from Bil'in 'Palestinian Gandhis'. In the face of our peaceful resistance, Israeli soldiers attack our peaceful protests with teargas, clubs, rubber-coated steel bullets and live ammunition, and have injured over 100 villagers. They invade the village at night, entering homes, pulling families out and arresting people. Our demonstrations aim to stop the bulldozers destroying our land, and to send a message about the wall's impact. We've chained ourselves to olive trees that were being bulldozed for the wall to show that taking trees' lives takes the village's life. We've distributed letters asking the soldiers to think before they shoot at us, explaining that we are not against the Israeli people, but against the building of the wall on our land. We refuse to be strangled by the wall in silence. In a famous Palestinian short story, 'Men in the Sun', Palestinian workers suffocate inside a tanker truck. Upon discovering them, the driver screams, 'Why didn't you bang on the sides of the tank?' We are banging – we are screaming ...'[71]

Villagers have held weekly demonstrations against the wall since 2005. Their wonderful, rebellious and inventive spirit inspired demonstrations of varying themes which became contagious, spreading to other towns. The Israeli army continues to try different methods of extreme violence to crush the spirit of the resistance. Here are just a few examples:

- September 9, 2005: The town placed under curfew as a closed military zone.
- March 3, 2006: Palestinians and Israelis chained themselves to the annexation barrier. Israeli soldiers beat the demonstrators with batons and rifle butts and wounded two of them. Mohammad Khatib from the Bil'in popular committee and Yossi Bartal from Israeli Anarchists against the Wall both sustained injuries.
- April 7, 2006: Commemoration of Eyad Taha Salame Taha, a 28-year-old man from Beit Annan, drowned in a flood caused by the construction of the wall in Bil'in on April 2, 2006.
- April 14, 2006: Troops installed barbed wire across the streets and closed the main iron gate of the wall preventing villagers from crossing. Four Israeli peace activists, one Palestinian of the ISM, and one American were arrested.
- April 23, 2006: Israeli products burnt.

- May 5, 2006: Israeli and international activists with pictures of Western leaders taped to their chests carried a barbed wire cage in which a Palestinian, dressed in Palestinian flags, was symbolically trapped to signify the fact that Palestine is being made into a prison by the Israeli state and its Western financiers.[72]
- May 12, 2006: Israeli forces fired rubber bullets, injuring seven Palestinians and two internationals (one Danish, the other Australian who were both hit in the head).[73]
- May 19, 2006: 23 nonviolent protesters injured and seven arrested during an anti-wall protest in Bil'in.
- June 2, 2006: Politicians invited from both the Israeli Knesset and the Palestinian Legislative Council to join to commemorate the start of the occupation.[74]
- June 24, 2006: Demonstrators draped in flags of the countries participating in the World Cup carried a huge balloon representing a football and a big wooden box symbolizing a coffin.
- June 30, 2006: Protestors wore orange clothes, resembling the clothes prisoners sentenced to death wear before execution.
- August 18, 2006: the Israeli army sprayed demonstrators with a blue liquid chemical.[75]
- September 1, 2006: soldiers used (experimental) bean-bag bullets, injuring several demonstrators.[76]
- September 15, 2006: A sit-down protest in face of baton- and shield-wielding Israeli forces.[77]
- August 2006: Mordechai Vanunu joined the demonstration (Vanunu was the whistleblower who exposed Israel's military nuclear program and spent 18 years in jail for it, much of it in solitary confinement.)
- April 20, 2007: Nobel Peace Prize winner Mairead Corrigan shot in the leg during a demonstration.[78]
- June 6, 2008: European Parliament Vice-President Luisa Morgantini injured.
- December 19, 2008: Protesters carried pictures of President Bush having shoes thrown at him. They also carried their own shoes as a symbolic rejection of the Israeli occupation. Dozens suffered gas inhalation and eight demonstrators were shot by rubber bullets as well as two journalists, one of them an Israeli.

- April 17, 2009: A new tear gas canister in the form of a high-velocity projectile was fired by the army, killing a peace activist, Basim Ibrahim Abu Rahmah.
- August 7, 2009: Israeli forces sprayed water contaminated with manure and fecal matter at protesting villagers.
- August 21, 2009: Children from Bil'in marched to protest against the night raids. Many boys were arrested. They carried banners and chanted 'We want to sleep', 'No more night raids', 'Let us live', 'We want peace', and so on. The children led the demonstration towards the wall with villagers and Palestinian and international activists following them.
- October 16, 2009: Giant scales were carried representing the need for justice and accountability following the UN Human Rights Council vote to endorse the report on war crimes committed during Israel's attack on Gaza.
- December 2009: Abdallah Abu Rahmah, a coordinator of the local PCAW, was arrested and charged with 'possession of weapons' because he had displayed to international and other visitors spent army shells, rubber bullets, empty concussion grenades and gas canisters used by the army to quell civil resistance.

Media and international attention clearly had an impact as, on September 4, 2007, the Israeli Supreme Court asked the state to reroute the wall because the current route was 'highly prejudicial' to villagers. In fact, the very next day the same court ruled to legalize the Israeli settlement of Mattiyahu East built on Bil'in's land.[79] The village vowed to continue the weekly protests. Eithan Bronner recognized that:

It is one of the longest-running and best organized protest operations in the history of the Israeli-Palestinian conflict, and it has turned this once anonymous farming village into a symbol of Palestinian civil disobedience, a model that many supporters of the Palestinian cause would like to see spread and prosper. For that reason, a group of famous left-leaning elder statesmen, including former President Jimmy Carter ... came to Bil'in.[80]

THE VILLAGE UPRISING SPREADS

The number of villages participating in popular resistance increased dramatically in 2006. Besides Jayyous and Bil'in, we saw, in the second half of 2006, a number of demonstrations and events in at least a dozen other locations. Here are some examples:

- On June 4, 2006, students and their supporters held a demonstration at Atara checkpoint on the road to Birzeit University to protest against the Israeli forces, who were preventing them from attending classes. Palestinian and Israeli students, including Palestinian Israelis, were joined by international solidarity activists.[81]
- Mohammad Mansour, a father of five from the village of Biddu, was arrested on June 26, 2004 during a nonviolent demonstration against the wall in Al Ram area. He refused to pay a fine and desist from participating in demonstrations. His case dragged on for two years.[82]
- Six people were injured as they tried to stop bulldozers, protected by the military, from destroying trees to clear land near their village of Umm Salamona on December 26, 2006.[83]
- Awad Abu Sway and other villagers of Artas near Bethlehem appealed to Palestinians and internationals to join them to prevent the confiscation of their lands. Tents were erected and activists slept on the threatened lands. After two nights in the camp, on May 20, 2007 at 5:30 am, heavily armed Israeli soldiers invaded the site, removed the tents, pushed the people back and even threw them over a wall into an adjacent field. They then uprooted all the old olive trees, as Awad kept repeating to the soldiers: 'I promise you, we will replant these trees.'[84]
- The people of Al-Khader near Bethlehem were losing over 20,000 dunums of prime agricultural lands to the wall. Their protests started on June 12, 2009, each with about 300 residents participating, and demonstrations continued every week and went on for months.[85]
- In Al-Walaja, a small village isolated in the seam zone between the wall and the Green Line, there were actions involving locals and internationals. Joshua Mitnick reported:

> Ten shouting Palestinians were pushing against one boulder, but the primitive Israeli roadblock cutting off the tiny Palestinian village from Bethlehem was not budging. Then, with the help of two giant crowbars, an Israel protester, and a Japanese backpacker, the group heaved the stone aside, opening the road for the first time in three years. 'Tomorrow

they'll bring a bulldozer and move it back,' sighed Sheerin Alaraj, a village resident and a demonstration organizer. 'Then next week we'll come back again to protest.'[86]

These regular demonstrations against the wall were pre-planned and always involved an international (including Israeli) presence. Sometimes villagers had to demonstrate against other, unanticipated atrocities. For example, after Israeli navy shells killed eight members of a family picnicking on a beach in Gaza, Palestinian anti-wall activists organized a demonstration two days later (June 11, 2006), in which hundreds participated, some wearing white shirts with red lettering to signify blood.[87] On November 19, 2006, Palestinians and international supporters held a nonviolent demonstration at the Qalandia checkpoint near Ramallah against Israeli attacks in Gaza and the Beit Hannoun massacre. The activists held a 'die-in', with protesters donning white T-shirts splattered with fake blood.[88]

Internationals also helped locals harvest olives, a form of nonviolent resistance under a colonial occupation that tries to destroy all life and livelihood for local Palestinians. Olives are the mainstay of the Palestinian agricultural economy. Hundreds of thousands of olive trees have been uprooted or damaged to advance colonial settler activities. Tens of thousands of trees are in areas near colonial settlements, areas slated for expansion of these settlements. Some are in the area between the wall and the Green Line. Harvesting the trees means risking one's life as soldiers and, more often, settlers protected by soldiers attack the farmers. On November 4, 2002, Adam Keller (an Israeli in his late forties), Tom Dale (a British 18 year old), Emily Winkelstein (American, aged 27), Heidi Niggeman (German, aged 29) and Dan O'Reilly-Rowe (Australian/US, aged 25) were attacked by settlers and private contractors while trying to prevent trees from being cut down.[89] On March 27, 2003, several internationals providing protection for farmers in Yanoun village near Nablus were brutally attacked. The injured included James Delapin (American, aged 74), Nary Hughes-Thompson (American/ British, aged 68), Robin Kelly (Irish, aged 33) and Omer Alon (Israeli, aged 24). Money and the passports of the internationals were stolen.[90]

Ghassan Andoni wrote about the importance of the olive harvest:[91]

Despite brutality, intimidation, physical attacks, and continued provocations; Palestinian villagers and ISM international and local activists are proceeding with harvesting olives. Many of the olive groves that were out of reach for villagers for years and years are being harvested. This year no one could expropriate the olive harvesting season.

For the first time in years the occupation army and Israeli settlers were forced to accommodate to the determination and strong will of Palestinian villagers and international activists. For the first time those peaceful, empty-handed, decent people proved that power, aggressiveness and intimidation have limits, that the occupier cannot always dictate the rules of the game. This is the time in which people discovered the strength in being peaceful and determined at the same time; that people could step out of their fears and exert their natural rights against the will of the occupier; it is the time in which the empty hands and proud souls won against guns and occupation violence. It is the time in which peace and justice stepped forward and greed and aggression retreated.

The first days of the campaign were hard. Settlers and soldiers used all the oppressive tools available to crack the will of the people. Settlers burned olive groves (Mazraa Alsharqia); they moved into Palestinian olive groves with foreign workers and harvested and stole the olives (Jayous); they physically attacked olive harvesters by shooting at them and throwing stones (almost in all places); the army prevented harvesters from going to their fields; they forced harvesters out of the fields; tear gas, sound bombs and machine guns were fired at the peaceful harvesters; many were arrested; and a few were injured. All of this did not stop the harvesters from coming back again and again. As an army officer in Yassuf said, 'Today we failed and you won.'

Today we won because we were full of determination, because we were peaceful, because we were active and they were reactive. [We won] because we controlled anger and did not respond to their intimidation, when they lost control. We won because we struggled for life and they stood against it. We waged peace with more determination than their desire for war. Today we won because no one, regardless of how cunning and smart he is, could disguise the occupation or could turn the issue into an existential war or a war against terrorism. We won because we fought for life to continue.

We won because hundreds of Palestinian villagers became proactive in defending their rights. We won because of the great local community leaders who showed a great level of leadership and demonstrated an outstanding ability in leading the campaign.

We won because what was a dream is on its way to coming true. The civil-based resistance is spreading wide and is becoming an important and integral part of the Palestinian efforts to end the Israeli occupation. We won because we fought out of hope and not out of desperation. This is the glory of Palestine; seeds of hope can still be planted in the midst of the overwhelming despair.

We are winning a campaign but we know that it is only a step in the road to end the occupation. Huge work is still ahead of us all. We need to stand against the concrete monster, we need to dismantle the inhuman network of road blocks and checkpoints; we need to protect the land from settlers' greed. We need to deprive the occupation of its oppressive tools of control. We need to cut the occupation's claws. We need to force the occupiers to adjust to the needs of an active, civil-based resistance.

With this campaign we took the first steps on a long road. With more determination and with more massive and regular work we will be able to move steadily towards peace and justice.

Ghassan Andoni and Jeff Halper of the Israeli Committee against Home Demolitions were nominated for the Nobel Peace Prize in 2006.[92]

POLITICAL PRISONERS

Peaceful demonstrators during the 1987–91 uprising were fined 500–1,000 shekels (about US$200–400, a significant sum to impoverished Palestinians) and jailed for 8–12 months.[93] The ranks of prisoners in Israeli jails swelled to over 20,000 at one point. In September 1988, the Israeli army stated that the number of detainees it held was 23,600 and Peter Kandela reported cases of the use of torture on detainees.[94] After the Oslo Accords many thousands of Palestinians were released. But many thousands more were imprisoned in the uprising that started in 2000. In total, over 700,000 Palestinians spent time in Israeli jails. On occasion, nearly 20 percent of the political prisoners were minors.[95]

Political prisoners in Israeli jails also participated in nonviolent resistance. Israeli radio reported on a hunger strike by prisoners in the camps of Jenin, Ramallah and Nablus, who demanded improvement in their deplorable conditions in 1987.[96] Al-Ansar prison in southern Lebanon, where thousands of Palestinians and Lebanese political prisoners were held by Israeli occupation forces, showed incredible acts of resistance and resilience, ranging from hunger strikes to refusal to obey orders to writing.[97]

Thousands of Palestinian prisoners went on a hunger strike from August 15 to September 2, 2004. During this time, the Israeli authorities tried various methods from persuasion to threats to beatings to break the strike; 13 UN agencies operating in the occupied areas expressed their concern.[98]

Outside the prisons, Palestinians and internationals protested and worked diligently to spread the word about the prisoners' demands and their plight. It started with the prisoners' families, many of whom joined the hunger strike. Crowds assembled on August 16, 2004 outside local offices of the Red Cross and marched to the Gaza headquarters of the United Nations where they delivered a letter addressed to Secretary General Kofi Annan, calling for him to apply pressure on Israel and improve the prisoners' conditions. They demonstrated again in the thousands two days later.[99] The PA, Palestinians inside the Green Line and the ISM called for hunger strikes to be staged outside the prisons to support the prisoners' demands.[100] The strike slowly gained momentum despite repressive measures.[101] Israel's Public Security Minister Tzahi Hanegbi stated: 'Israel will not give in to their demands. They can starve for a day, a month, even starve to death, as far as I am concerned.'[102] Eventually, the prison authorities conceded that the prisoners were entitled to some basic humanitarian rights.

Palestinian female political prisoners in Telmud Prison were mistreated and, on November 28, 2004, their spokeswoman who complained about this was beaten and punished. When others complained, they too were punished. They too went on hunger strike.[103]

Prisoners continued to use hunger strikes to protest against ill treatment and draw attention to their plight. For example, on February 16, 2006, Jamal Al-Sarahin died in prison. He was a 37-year-old 'administrative detainee' (held without charge or trial) who had been detained for eight months and badly mistreated. Prisoners called a one-day hunger strike.[104]

On March 11, 2006, a sit-down strike in front of the ICRC in Hebron was held to demand better treatment of prisoners. On June 27, 2006, 1,200 Palestinian political prisoners in the Negev desert started a hunger strike to protest against the arbitrary and oppressive practices of the prison administration. In total, over 700,000 Palestinians have spent time in Israeli jails and the latest data show that 11,000 are still being held according to the Palestinian Prisoners Society.[105]

By 2009, Palestinians in Israeli prisons had achieved a number of successes by nonviolent struggle and civil disobedience, including wearing civilian clothes (no orange uniforms), access to news, reasonable visiting rights and better access to healthcare. But the Prison Administration continues to chip away at those rights.[106] Unfortunately, the PA and families are forced to subsidize the cost to Israel of maintaining Palestinian prisoners.

Because so many people are jailed for their resistance activities, Palestinian society has a profound respect and appreciation for the sacrifices of the prisoners. Time spent in prison is considered a badge of honor. Prisons also shape character. One former prisoner stated:

> Like any human community, there are contradictions, but there is a common thread in the experience in prison that gives us strength, a common goal, a common purpose. We are joined together in struggle, so our shared experiences only make us stronger.[107]

MANY FORMS OF RESISTANCE

Palestinians succeeded in stopping Israeli attacks on targeted homes by forming human shields. According to an electronic intifada article about an incident in Beit Lahia on November 19, 2006:

> Israeli warplanes have already destroyed more than 60 houses belonging to activists from Palestinian factions across the Gaza Strip, using the same method of ordering the residents, through a telephone call at short notice, to evacuate their home prior to bombardment. This new phenomenon [of human shields] began when Muhammad Baroud, 29, a leader in the Popular Resistance Committees [PRC], received a warning phone call at 8 pm from the Israeli intelligence service ordering him to evacuate his house within 10 minutes because the Israeli air force was going to destroy the house. But he ignored this threat and said, 'We are not leaving our house'. Once again his mobile rang, and Muhammad again ignored the warning. After that, Muhammad and I went on the rooftop of our house and started chanting slogans 'Death to Israel! Death to America!', and we started shooting in the air. A few minutes later an Israeli F-16 was hovering in the sky above our heads, Wael Baroud, Muhammad's brother, explained. And Yousef Al-Helou writing from Beit Lahiya the day after stated

that 'The whole world and the international community turned a blind eye and failed to protect us from the continuous Israeli attacks. We have to do something, so we are facing the threats of the Israeli F-16 fighter jets. We are ready to be killed and martyred for the sake of God and freedom. We don't fear the Israelis. We are no better than the children of Beit Hanoun, who were slaughtered while they were sleeping in the latest Israeli massacre in Beit Hanoun.'[108]

A Story of Beautiful, Non-violent Resistance
Abdelfattah Abusrour

Every nation in this world looks forward to living in freedom and safety, to multiplying and presenting a brilliant image of its culture, traditions and civilization, in order to be honored and respected by other nations. It is clear in the Middle East, and more specifically in Palestine which has been suffering from the Israeli occupation since 1948, and from the tireless propaganda which is widely disseminated by the international media portraying the oppressed, uprooted and occupied Palestinian people as the aggressor, the criminal, the barbarian and the terrorist.

Mahatma Gandhi says: 'If we are to teach real peace in this world, and if we are to carry on a real war against war, we shall have to begin with the children.'

I started from here, volunteering in Aida refugee camp where I was born, and in which about 5,000 people live who come from 41 different villages, destroyed by Israeli occupation in 1948. About 66 percent of this population are under 18 years old.

Aida, located to the north of Bethlehem, is surrounded by Israeli military posts and colonies, and suffers frequent incursions and curfews. At the same time, the camp does not have green spaces or playgrounds for children and, since 2005, is shut off by the 9 metre-high illegal apartheid wall along its northern side. By 2006, the eastern side was also caging the camp with the separation wall. With the frequent military incursions, the children are in almost daily confrontation with Israeli soldiers.

We do not want our children to feature on the lists of martyrs, or be handicapped for the rest of their lives, or perish in prisons, or reproduce the same images we see endlessly in the media. Alrowwad uses theater, arts, cultural heritage and education as a way to reclaim,

▶

defend and keep intact our humanity and beauty. We are human beings and we are equal partners in creating a positive and long-lasting change. Everybody is a change-maker and everybody has a responsibility to make a positive change and be a role model for the children and the generations to come.

Alrowwad creates normality in situations of conflict through beautiful, non-violent resistance, to break stereotypes disseminated in the media and show another image of Palestinian people and children, their humanity and beauty and their nonviolent resistance to the ugliness of occupation and its violence. This is done through creative artistic activities and allows them to express themselves in a positive and constructive way via theater, arts, education and sports, to find the peace within themselves in order to make peace with the world.

With a group of friends, I founded Alrowwad [Pioneers] Cultural and Theater Training Center, in 1998, and initiated 'The beautiful nonviolent resistance'. Arts in general, and theater more specifically, are very powerful means of expression and effective methods of change at individual and community levels. The children are the actors and artists.

Alrowwad, the initiator of beautiful, nonviolent resistance through arts, devised supportive education programs and psycho-social follow-up for children with difficulties, set up the first professional photo and video training program in a refugee camp, created the first fitness program for women in a refugee camp, established the first outdoor film festival in Palestine and partnered with others to create the first Palestinian folktale festival in Palestine.

Alrowwad works in a spirit of social entrepreneurship and independence. Alrowwad has toured Europe and the USA to promote beautiful, nonviolent resistance and build bridges of exchange as equal partners at the human level.

Alrowwad creates hope in a world of despair. As Palestinians, as human beings, we cannot afford the luxury of despair. Alrowwad works with children, but involves parents and schools to make the impact and change durable. Alrowwad works to restore the values that make humanity what it is – when we speak about human rights, international law, democracy, freedom, peace, justice, these values don't mean anything nowadays because they are violated by those who pretend they are defending them. But for us, these values make humanity what it is and they should be respected and their values

▶

should be restored. We build faith and belief in these values and protect children and human rights.

Alrowwad performances in Europe, the United States, Egypt and Palestine have made a great impact: on one side, the audiences have seen an image of Palestinian humanity and beauty and culture, and many of them have said: 'When we watch the news now, we will watch with different ears and eyes.' At another level, these tours have allowed our children to meet other people and visit other countries, and to experience what it is like to live in a free country without checkpoints or tear gas or occupation soldiers, and without a segregation wall. These tours were also an opportunity for them to meet others and to break stereotypes whatever their origin. We are all human beings, and we are equal partners for building a better future for ourselves and the generations to come. We all work so that the future will be more beautiful than the present that envelops our lives.

aabusrour.blogspot.com
alrowwad.virtualactivism.net
www.imagesforlifeonline.com

Palestinian farmers defied the Israeli authorities and regularly brought their produce to sell in the streets of occupied Jerusalem despite the wall, the checkpoints and other restrictions.[109] In one act of civil disobedience, farmers, with the aid of internationals, hoped to dump crates of grapes on Route 60, which cuts through the West Bank. Their grapes, which used to be marketed throughout Palestine and neighboring countries, were unsaleable due to checkpoints, barriers and other restrictions. The demonstrators were brutally attacked and six arrested, including Israelis, even before they reached the checkpoint near Al-Khader leading to Route 60. Six people were arrested: two Palestinian males, one international female and two Israeli males.[110]

On May 8, 2008, Israeli forces violently dispersed a nonviolent demonstration held in commemoration of the *nakba* in the demolished Palestinian village of Saffuriya.[111] On May 15, 2008, to commemorate the *nakba*, Palestinians turned the skies over Jerusalem black by releasing 21,915 balloons – one to mark each day of Palestinian dispossession.[112]

In the weekly nonviolent demonstration in Ni'lin (population 4,600), the Israeli occupying army killed many civilians, among them Yousef Akil Srour (36), Mohammed Khawaje (20), Arafat Rateb Khawaje (22), Yousef Amira (17) and Ahmed Mousa (10).[113] This same village organized a Holocaust Memorial Day on January 27, 2009 which coincided with the UN World Holocaust Remembrance Day with photographs purchased with help from the Nazareth-based Arab Institute for Holocaust Research and Education.[114] In June 2009, an unarmed demonstrator, Aqel Srour, was killed with .22 caliber live ammunition in Ni'lin.[115] On the twentieth anniversary of the fall of the Berlin Wall (November 6, 2009), 300 Ni'lin residents and internationals toppled a section of the wall that separates the village from part of its lands.

In 2010, the Israeli army and settlers were trying to take over the hill in Beit Sahour called Ush Ghrab (Crow's Nest) (the army had vacated it in 2006). For the past few years, the struggle here has involved popular resistance and the municipality building a peace park with a children's playground on part of the abandoned military camp area.

GAZA AND BEYOND

Israel attacked the besieged Gaza Strip with heavy bombardment from land, sea and air for three weeks in late December 2008 and January 2009: 1,400 Palestinians, most of them civilians (including 400 children), died. Here is part of a testimony by a Catholic priest in Gaza, Father Manuel Musallam, during the first two weeks of the attack:

My brothers and sisters in Christ Jesus, what you see and hear on your television screens is not the complete painful truth about what our people in Gaza are going through. Their suffering is so widespread over our land that no television or radio could report the whole truth about it. The brutal siege on Gaza is a storm that escalates by the hour; it is not only a war crime but a crime against humanity. Today, the suffering people of Gaza are appealing to the conscience of every human being with goodwill, but it will soon be our just God who decides the case ... I would like to tell you a short story about something that happened in a hospital to the Abdul-Latif family. One of the children disappeared during the first attack, and his parents spent the first two days of the war looking for him but did not find him. On the third day, as the family was walking around a hospital, they found some people from the Jarada family gathered around a disfigured and injured boy whose leg had been amputated. His face was distorted not because of the F-16 attacks he had suffered but because of the glass that had fallen onto his face when part of the hospital was attacked. The Adul-Latifs approached the Jaradas to console them. When they reached the injured boy, Mr Abdul-Latif realized that it was his son and not the Jaradas'. The families argued with each other over the issue and waited for the boy to wake up and tell them who he was so that he could be taken by the Abdul-Latifs.[116]

Demonstrations and other civil resistance actions were held around the world. In the Bethlehem area there were six demonstrations and a nightly vigil in Beit Sahour which lasted for 22 nights. Palestinian police arrested eleven youths who participated in one demonstration but released them after a few hours. In Ramallah, a demonstration was met with beatings. On December 29, 2008, 90 people were arrested in Jerusalem by the Israeli police for demonstrating their solidarity with the people of Gaza.[117]

The situation in Jerusalem has been grave since Israel illegally annexed east Jerusalem following the occupation of 1967 and intensified in 2009; both Israeli attempts to colonize Palestinian neighborhoods like Sheikh Jarrah and Silwan and the Palestinian resistance to those schemes grew.[118]

The Gaza Strip is home to 1.5 million Palestinians, of whom two-thirds are refugees or displaced people packed into a tiny area with no resources; they are virtually cut off from the rest of the world. The Gaza Strip was subjected to Israeli policies of de-development and strangulation which impoverished the population. The four million Palestinian residents of the West Bank and Gaza represent less than 40 percent of the worldwide Palestinian population. Those eligible and allowed to vote in those areas preferred Hamas (the Islamic Resistance movement) to Fatah in 2006 elections. Hamas had entered the elections reluctantly as its moderate wing and many others pushed it to suspend armed resistance and enter the elections. Had the result of the election been accepted and negotiations on a peace agreement ensued with Hamas, many analysts believe there would have had a far better outcome. Instead, Israel and many Western countries engaged in a total boycott and applied sanctions that made life extremely difficult.

When this isolation failed to break the will of Hamas and its supporters, the US put pressure on Fatah to take steps to regain control. This erupted into violence in the Gaza Strip culminating in

Hamas taking *de facto* control in 2007. Israel imposed a total siege on the area. In January 2008, the people of the southern Gaza Strip, especially in Rafah, broke through the wall at many points and tens of thousands rushed across the border to get medicines, buy food and meet relatives on the Egyptian side.[119] But the barriers were re-erected. Egyptian security was stepped up along the border and the siege was tightened. The people of Gaza increasingly relied on smuggling food, medicines and other necessities through tunnels. Having failed to subdue the population, the Israeli army launched operation 'Cast Lead' in late December 2008. In three weeks, 1,400 Palestinians, most of them civilians and 400 children, were killed and thousands injured. Thousands of homes were destroyed and billions in damage to infrastructure, the economy and livelihoods were sustained.

The Free Gaza Movement attempted over the three years, and on few occasions succeeded, to break the siege. The movement is composed of Palestinians, Israelis and internationals challenging the siege from the sea. On August 23, 2008, two ships (SS *Free Gaza* and SS *Liberty*) set sail and arrived carrying dozens of people and relief aid. On October 29, the SS *Dignity* again managed to reach Gaza with such prominent passengers as Mairead Maguire, the winner of the 1976 Nobel Peace Prize.

The UN called the situation in Gaza a humanitarian disaster, but the inhumanity went on largely unchallenged. More than 255 sick people have died as a result of this medieval siege imposed on 1.5 million civilians. The Free Gaza Movement's fifth shipment attempted to reach Gaza with medicines and supplies (donated by Qatar) on December 19, 2008, but was attacked and had to abort its mission.[120] Yet, both when they succeeded and when they were forcibly prevented and detained by the Israeli navy, the Free Gaza Movement scored notable successes. As one member explained:

On June 30, 2009 Israeli occupation forces forcibly boarded one of our boats, the *Spirit of Humanity*, and kidnapped 21 human rights workers and journalists who were on their way to deliver much needed humanitarian and reconstruction supplies to besieged Gaza, including Nobel Peace Prize laureate Mairead Maguire and former US Congresswoman Cynthia McKinney. They were held in jail for a week before being deported. Though we were stopped on this particular voyage, it was not a 'failure'. In the month after our boat was hijacked, over 100,000 news stories, essays, blog entries, action alerts, and radio and television segments were made on Israel's violent response to our mission. It's true that the ordeal of our 21 volunteers pales in comparison to the 11,000 Palestinian political prisoners held in Israeli prisons. The seizure of our small cargo of 3 tons of medical aid and reconstruction kits is insignificant in light of the US$4 billion of aid promised to Gaza – aid that has not and will not be delivered because of the Israeli blockade. But that too misses the point. By choosing to violently confront and kidnap unarmed human rights workers on a mission of mercy, Israel publicly demonstrated both the illegality and the absurdity of the Gaza siege. The siege is abjectly not about 'security'. No one could possibly have believed that our small boat was a physical threat to Israel. This public demonstration of the siege's illegality resulted in record action at the governmental level as well. Both the Irish and Greek governments formally intervened to protect their citizens and property.[121]

International members of the Free Gaza Movement accompanied Gaza fishermen into Gaza waters. While international treaties support the right of fishermen to fish off their coasts, Israeli naval boats harass and fire at them. When internationals are on board, water cannons are sometimes used.[122] The Israeli navy acted like pirates by hijacking a ship of the Free Gaza Movement in international waters.[123] The fifth trip by the Free Gaza movement, *The Dignity*, arrived on December 20, 2008 and included two envoys from Eid, a Qatar charity, who assessed the tragedy and went back with proposals on what they could do to help alleviate Israel's collective punishment.

On December 31, 2008, 90 people were arrested in East Jerusalem as Israeli police tried to prevent protests of solidarity with Gaza through intimidation. On the anniversary of 'Operation Cast Lead', 400 internationals and Palestinians attempted to cross into Gaza from Egypt. They were prevented by the Egyptian authorities, who allowed a token 90 people in.[124] Simultaneously, the 'Viva Palestina' convoy of vehicles and supplies managed, after much struggle with Egyptian authorities, to enter Gaza on January 6, 2010.[125] Egypt expelled the Scottish politician George Galloway who led the convoy and announced no convoys or international aid would be allowed through Egyptian territory to Gaza. Egypt is also building an underground barrier to block the tunnels that smuggle food and medicine into Gaza.

The Palestinian Campaign to Free Gaza (www.end-gaza-siege.ps), the Free Gaza Movement (www.freegaza.org), Viva Palestina and other organizations have promised to continue their efforts to break the siege. The struggle against the wall, occupation and colonization in the West Bank continues. Palestinians' struggle inside the Green Line and in exile also continues. Ultimately, surrender is not an option and the Palestinians' will can never be broken.

13
Boycotts, Divestments and Sanctions

BDS action is a life-saving antidote to violence. It is an action of solidarity, partnership and joint progress. BDS action serves to preempt, in a nonviolent manner, justified violent resistance aimed at attaining the same goals of justice, peace and equality.

Udi Aloni, filmmaker and artist[1]

We explained in Chapter 2 what Palestinians envisaged as a future of justice and peace despite incredible challenges. Israeli authors described how we face politicide,[2] ethnic cleansing programs,[3] ethnocracy[4] and apartheid.[5] Such a system of colonization, apartheid and oppression requires resources: financial, physical, public relations, propaganda and diplomatic. Money comes from direct aid in the form of billions in US aid, from Israeli exports mostly of security-related products and armaments, tourism and from foreign direct investment. From its inception, Zionism was also maintained by direct political and diplomatic support beyond material resources. Whether emanating from Arab or Western governments or the United Nations, this has been a history of cowardice, collusion and cooptation. Amira Hass, writing in *Ha'aretz*, suggested:

> Every few weeks some international body issues a report directly linking the policy of restricted movement imposed by Israel on the occupied territories and the state of economic deterioration there ... The countries issuing the warnings continue to purchase Israeli manufactured arms and other security-related products. They host military officers who are directly responsible for the killing of hundreds of Palestinian citizens and fervently implement the siege policy. They invite Israeli ministers who are responsible for the economic and social de-development of a whole people.[6]

At the height of the atrocities, Nehemia Stessler in *Ha'aretz* similarly wrote that Israel was deliberately committing murders, fracturing limbs, etc., during the largely nonviolent uprising of 1987–91 and:

Israel's dependence on the United States is far greater than suggested by the sum of $3 billion. Israel's physical existence depends on the Americans in both military and political terms. Without the US, we would not be equipped with the latest fighter planes and other advanced weapons. Without the American veto, we would have long since been expelled from every international organization, not to speak of the UN, which would have imposed sanctions on us that would have totally paralyzed Israel's international trade, since we cannot exist without importing raw material.[7]

In South Africa under apartheid, similar Western complicity was only undermined by the growth, in South Africa and the rest of the world, of a boycotts, divestments and sanctions (BDS) movement. A boycott is the refusal to buy products or to interact with entities or individuals that support oppression or are part of a system of oppression. Divestment requires withdrawing financial support that props up the oppressive system. Sanctions prevent dealing with oppressive governments or other entities. These three elements work in tandem. The struggle against South African apartheid was successful for many reasons and BDS campaigns played a significant role in that. When elite white South Africans realized that they could not continue with the apartheid system in the face of world anger, the final nail went into the coffin of apartheid. The same will happen with apartheid in the form of Palestinian 'Bantustans'. The same forces must be deployed.

In earlier chapters we alluded to many examples of BDS. These included the 1880s and 1890s when Palestinians, whose lands were taken, called for no economic cooperation with Zionist colonies. We explained that Palestinian representatives in the Ottoman parliament protested against ongoing colonization and asked for sanctions and sometimes succeeded in stemming the onward drive of Zionism. We further elaborated the much more widespread BDS campaigns of the 1930s, which included strikes and boycotts directed at both British and Zionist interests. After the creation of the state of Israel and Palestinian *nakba*, the Arab world imposed sanctions on Israel and companies doing business in Israel. However, the Israeli lobby in the US ensured that the might of the US could prevent any pressure on Israel to comply with international law and supported Israel diplomatically and economically to oppress the Palestinians. The peak of the impact was achieved when oil-producing countries sympathetic to the plight of the Palestinians applied a blanket ban in 1973–74 on exports to the US and other countries that financed and supported the Israeli occupation. Since then, there has been a steady decline in the impact and effectiveness of sanctions undermined by poor enforcement due to structural shortcomings in decision-making and implementation by authoritarian regimes, many of which covertly depended on Western support and intelligence agencies to stay in power.[8] There are problems with the Arab League boycott as compared with grassroots boycotts that are now in place:

> Coercion and economic force shared little of the moral or ethical arguments that typically characterize solidarity work, and opened the boycott up to greater vulnerability to attacks from the pro-Israel lobby. Moreover, this problem was exacerbated as the proponents of the boycott represented increasingly authoritarian governments and regimes and in which cases of corruption emerged. Within these dynamics the boycott failed to resonate with many groups and movements who have extended solidarity to Palestinians.[9]

Thus, Palestinians had repeatedly to return to the tried-and-tested methods of depending on themselves to effect change by popular resistance, among which is the BDS movement. The intifada of 1987–91 especially included highly successful BDS actions which are detailed in Chapter 11. The third declaration of the United Leadership of the Resistance issued on January 18, 1988 called for a boycott of all Israeli products for which local alternatives could be sourced and suggested a tax strike and other methods of popular resistance.[10] That intifada had a significant negative impact on the Israeli economy in the areas of agriculture, tourism, construction and military expenditure.[11] Since we have already covered those areas, we shall highlight here the more logarithmic growth of the grassroots movements related to BDS in the last ten years and especially how the international community has responded positively to the Palestinian call for BDS.

While Palestinians have called for boycotts for decades and have enforced them, a boost came when a tentative step was taken by Gush Shalom by placing paid advertisements in *Ha'aretz* on September 26 and October 4, 1997 which called for a boycott of settlement products[12] and published a list of these products.[13] This step was significant because it allowed the European Commission to recommend on May 13, 1998 a boycott of all products imported from Jewish settlements. In response, the Israeli Ministry of Agriculture threatened to cancel all trade privileges given to Palestinian agricultural produce marketed inside Israel and, a week later, Netanyahu threatened 'to fire Palestinian laborers and exclude Europe from the peace efforts if the EU takes any action to boycott Jewish settlements produce'.[14]

In April 2001, 35 Israelis called on the world community to organize and boycott Israeli industrial and agricultural exports and goods, as well as leisure tourism, in the hope that it will have the same positive result that the boycott of South Africa had on Apartheid organized by the pressure group Matzpun (Hebrew for conscience) and subsequently signed by nearly 1,000 individuals.[15]

In September 2001, the NGO Forum of the UN World Conference Against Racism, Racial Discrimination and Related Intolerances was held in Durban, South Africa following brutal Israeli attacks on Palestinian civilians. The conference gave overwhelming support to the Palestinian calls for BDS by articulating clearly the nature and goals of the Zionist colonial project as a system of racism and apartheid.[16]

In April 2002, and at the height of Israeli attacks on civilians in the West Bank, we started collecting signatures in support of an academic boycott of Israel centered in the US. By July, we had collected over 500 signatures (a figure later doubled) and created both a webpage and a listserve for 'Academics for Justice'. While the webpage has not been updated, the listserve continues to function as a forum for the signatories to organize campaigns for academic boycotts and support academics threatened by it. In one case, the list proved critical in protecting academics at Central Connecticut State University who organized an educational program on Islam and the Middle East.[17]

A campaign for total academic boycott was also launched in the UK led by Stephen and Hilary Rosen. It began by publishing a letter signed by 115 prominent intellectuals in the *Guardian* on April 6, 2002. The letter stated:

Despite widespread international condemnation for its policy of violent repression against the Palestinian people in the occupied territories, the Israeli government appears impervious to moral appeals from world leaders (Fear of wider conflict as army pushes on, April 5). The major potential source of effective criticism, the US, seems reluctant to act. However, there are ways of exerting pressure from within Europe. Odd though it may appear, many national and European cultural and research institutions, including especially those funded from the EU and the European Science Foundation, regard Israel as a European state for the purposes of awarding grants and contracts. Would it not therefore be timely if at both national and European level a moratorium was called upon any further such support unless and until Israel abides by UN resolutions and opens serious peace negotiations with the Palestinians along the lines proposed in many peace plans, including most recently that sponsored by the Saudis and the Arab League?[18]

We started a boycott campaign of Israeli goods and services in the US after a workshop at Yale on February 23, 2002 attended by local activists and Zvika Havkin from Matzpun. The first alert (February 28, 2002) we issued stated in part:

Boycotts and divestments constitute effective nonviolent resistance to the ongoing occupation and oppression perpetuated by Israel. The educational aspects of these campaigns can be the most powerful tool to activists to reach out to consumers and the economic sector. The precedent of the success of this campaign is found in the major part it played in the abolition of Apartheid in South Africa. This call to boycott Israeli goods and leisure tourism is herby launched with a specific and first step: a call to action on one product for the month of March (Israeli tomatoes on-the-vine).

The Boycott Israeli Goods listserve, with hundreds of activists participating since February 2002, is now a main forum in the US to post BDS-related news and calls for action.[19]

In March 2004, nearly 300 academics published an open letter calling on Israeli academic leaders to take a stance against the Israeli government's criminal policies or face the academic boycott.[20]

THE PALESTINIAN CAMPAIGN FOR THE ACADEMIC AND CULTURAL BOYCOTT OF ISRAEL (PACBI)

PACBI was launched in April 2004 following a statement issued by Palestinian academics and intellectuals in October 2003.[21] PACBI articulated the vision and direction of the movement in a public statement of July 7, 2004:[22]

Israel's colonial oppression of the Palestinian people, which is based on Zionist ideology, comprises the following:

- Denial of its responsibility for the *nakba* – in particular the waves of ethnic cleansing and dispossession that created the Palestinian refugee problem – and therefore refusal to accept the inalienable rights of the refugees and displaced stipulated in and protected by international law.
- Military occupation and colonization of the West Bank, including East Jerusalem, and Gaza since 1967, in violation of international law and UN resolutions.
- The entrenched system of racial discrimination and segregation against the Palestinian citizens of Israel, which resembles the defunct apartheid system in South Africa.

Suggested Guiding Principles
- Since Israeli academic institutions, mainly state-controlled, and the vast majority of Israeli intellectuals and academics have either contributed directly to maintaining, defending or otherwise justifying forms of oppression, or have been complicit in them through their silence;
- given that all forms of international intervention have so far failed to force Israel to comply with international law or to end its repression of the Palestinians, which has manifested itself in many forms, including siege, indiscriminate killing, wanton destruction and the racist colonial wall;
- in view of the fact that people of conscience in the international community of scholars and intellectuals have historically shouldered the moral responsibility to fight injustice, as exemplified in their struggle to abolish apartheid in South Africa through diverse forms of boycott;
- recognizing that the growing international boycott movement against Israel has expressed the need for a Palestinian frame of reference outlining guiding principles;
- in the spirit of international solidarity, moral consistency and resistance to injustice and oppression;

We, Palestinian academics and intellectuals, call upon our colleagues in the international community to comprehensively and consistently boycott all Israeli academic and cultural institutions as a contribution to the struggle to end Israel's occupation, colonization and system of apartheid, by applying the following:

1. Refrain from participation in any form of academic and cultural cooperation, collaboration or joint projects with Israeli institutions.
2. Advocate a comprehensive boycott of Israeli institutions at the national and international levels, including suspension of all forms of funding and subsidies to these institutions.
3. Promote divestment and disinvestment from Israel by international academic institutions.
4. Exclude from the above actions against Israeli institutions any conscientious Israeli academics and intellectuals opposed to their state's colonial and racist policies. [*subsequently deleted*]
5. Work towards the condemnation of Israeli policies by pressing for resolutions to be adopted by academic, professional and cultural associations and organizations.
6. Support Palestinian academic and cultural institutions directly without requiring them to partner with Israeli counterparts as an explicit or implicit condition for such support.

THE PIVOTAL INTERNATIONAL COURT OF JUSTICE RULING AND GROWTH OF BDS CAMPAIGNS

BDS efforts received a significant advance from the ICJ ruling on the illegality of the Israeli apartheid wall in 2004. The Palestinian Civil Society's call to action on the anniversary of that ruling in 2005 (see Chapter 2, box, p. 17) revolutionized the BDS movement. The latter was an initiative of what became known as the Palestinian National Committee for BDS (BDS National Committee, BNC). The members of the BNC include:[23]

- Palestinian Non-Governmental Organizations Network (PNGO)
- Occupied Palestine and Golan Heights Advocacy Initiative (OPGAI)
- Grassroots Palestinian Anti-Apartheid Wall Campaign (Stop the Wall)
- Palestinian Campaign for the Academic and Cultural Boycott of Israel (PACBI)
- Council of National and Islamic Forces in Palestine
- Palestinian General Federation of Trade Unions (PGFTU)
- General Union of Palestinian Workers

- Global Palestine Right of Return Coalition
- Federation of Unions of Palestinian Universities Professors and Employees
- General Union of Palestinian Women (GUPW)
- Charitable Organizations Union
- Independent Federation of Unions – Palestine (IFU)
- Palestinian Farmers Union (PFU)
- National Committee for the Commemoration of the *Nakba*
- Civil Coalition for Defending the Palestinians Rights in Jerusalem
- Coalition for Jerusalem
- Union of Palestinian Charitable Organizations
- Palestinian Economic Monitor
- Union of Youth Activity Centers – Palestinian Refugee Camps (UYAC)

August 2002 Call: Boycott Israel to Enforce Respect and Implementation of International Law, Human Rights, and UN Resolutions[24]

In September 2001, one year after all international efforts at halting Israel's violent military repression of the second Palestinian uprising had failed, some 3,000 civil society organizations from around the world met at the third World Conference Against Racism in Durban, South Africa and approved their NGO Declaration and Program of Action. These NGO documents address racism and racial discrimination related to the root causes of the Israeli-Palestinian conflict, including military occupation and the denial of the right of return of Palestinian refugees and internally displaced persons to their homes and properties.

Already in Durban, representatives of 3,000 civil society organizations from around the world were united in their call for global boycott and sanctions against Israel. Among others, the NGO Program of Action:

- Calls for the launch of an international anti-Israeli apartheid movement as implemented against the South African apartheid through a global solidarity network of international civil society, UN bodies and agencies, business and communities to end the conspiracy of silence among states, particularly the European Union and the United States (article 424).

▶

- Calls upon the international community to impose a policy of complete and total isolation of Israel as an apartheid state as in the case of South Africa, which means the imposition of mandatory and comprehensive sanctions and embargoes, the full cessation of all links (diplomatic, economic, social, aid, military cooperation and training) between all states and Israel (article 425).

One year after Durban, Israel was engaged in the destruction of Palestinian civil society and its political leadership and the re-establishment of direct military occupation in the West Bank and the Gaza Strip. More than ever, Israel, protected by the United States and tolerated by the European Union, violates international law, human rights, and UN resolutions.

Therefore, we as members of Palestinian civil society welcome all recent initiatives to boycott Israel, which have been launched in many parts of the world. For the sake of freedom and justice in Palestine and the world, we call upon the solidarity movement, NGOs, academic and cultural institutions, business companies, political parties and unions, as well as concerned individuals to strengthen and broaden the global Israel boycott campaign.

Israel Boycotts International Law and Human Rights – We Boycott Israel!

With greetings of solidarity,

Applied Research Institute Jerusalem (ARIJ)
Arab Center for Agricultural Development (ACAD)
BADIL Resource Center for Palestinian Residency and Refugee Rights
General Federation of Trade Unions in Palestine (GFTUP)
High Coordination Committee of the Local Committees for the Rehabilitation of the Disabled – West Bank
LAW – The Palestinian Society for the Protection of Human Rights and the Environment
Palestinian Center for Peace and Democracy (PCPD)
Palestinian Federation of Women Action Committees (PFWAC), Nablus
PNGO – Palestinian NGO Network
Palestinian Prisoners Society

▶

Popular Committees of the Palestinian Refugees – West Bank and Gaza Strip
Residents of Destroyed Palestinian Cities and Villages in 1948 Palestine, Ramallah
Union of Agricultural Work Committees (UAWC)
Union of Health Care Committees
Union of Palestinian Medical Relief Committees (UPMRC)
Union of Youth Activity Centers – Palestine Refugee Camps (UYAC)

The support of academics and activists like Naomi Klein, Rachel Giora, Tanya Reinhardt and Ilan Pappé was and continues to be important.[25] A recent group started what is called BOYCOTT! inside Israel to support the Palestinian BDS call of 2005. It affirms that:

We, Palestinians, Jews, citizens of Israel, join the Palestinian call for a BDS campaign against Israel, inspired by the struggle of South Africans against apartheid. We also call on others to do the same. As people devoted to the promotion of just peace and true democracy in this region, we are especially opposed to the international community's decision to boycott the Palestinians in the Occupied Palestinian Territories. This is particularly outrageous given the international community's prolonged support of Israel's apartheid and other daily violations of international law.[26]

The BDS movement received stalwart support from South African leaders like Ronni Kasrils and Archbishop Desmond Tutu and others who articulated why the system is an apartheid system.[27] The international community took up Palestinian calls for BDS. In the last ten years, hundreds of examples can be cited. Below is just a few dozen.[28]

August 26, 1999: After months of pressure, Burger King orders its subsidiaries in Israel to close the franchise opened in the settlement of Ma'ale Adumim.
April 2001: Israel socialist group Matzpun issues call for boycotts.
April 2001: Concordia University students calls for BDS.
May 2001: United Methodist Council of Bishops calls for sanctions.

July 4, 2001: Palestine Solidarity Campaign launched Campaign in the House of Commons.

August 2001: Lutheran Church called on the US government to withhold all economic and military aid to Israel until it improves conditions for Palestinians.

April 2002: Campaigns for academic boycott initiated in North America, Britain, France and Australia.

2002: Inner Bookshop, Oxford, announces a ban on Israeli publishers and refuses to stock their books.

2002: Danish trade unions call for boycotts.

2002: A professor at UMIST (UK) removes two Israeli scholars from the editorial boards of journals she edits and owns.

2002: Derry-based Gaslight Productions refuses to participate in the Haifa International Film Festival.

November 2002: Columbia University divestment campaign launched.

January 27, 2003: The administrative council of Marie Curie University – Paris VI calls for ending association and collaboration on December 16, 2002 and, after pressure mounts, reaffirms its decision.

2003: Caterpillar Campaign Launched.

2003: Jewish Voice for Peace supports selective BDS.

May 2003: Interfaith Council for Peace and Justice, Ann Arbor, USA.

July 2003: An Oxford University professor dismisses an application from an Israeli student on the grounds that he had served in the Israeli military.

April 2004: Student Council of Wayne State University passed the US's first university divestment resolution.

April 2004: Palestinian Campaign for Academic and Cultural Boycott of Israel (PACBI) launched. By July 2005, 170 organizations back the call.

April 2004: 'Labor for Palestine' founded in New York to organize BDS and other support among labor unions.

July 2004: US Presbyterian Church to start divestment procedure.

2004: Italian, French and Norwegian BDS campaigns launched.

July 2004: The Presbyterian Church USA (PCUSA) general assembly adopted a resolution that called for initiating 'a process of phased selective divestment in multinational corporations operating in Israel, in accordance to General Assembly policy on social investing'.

October 2004: National Lawyers' Guild supports BDS.

October 2004: Congress of South African Trade Unions (COSATU) supports BDS.

October 2004: The Episcopalian Church in the US considers divestment.

November 2004: Jews against The Occupation, New York.

November 2004: Presbyterian Church USA (PCUSA) targets Caterpillar, Motorolla, Citigroup and ITT.

December 2004: University of Wisconsin divestment campaign launched.

January 2005: ICAHD (Israeli Committee against House Demolitions) calls for sanctions.

January 2005: Not in My Name (NIMN).

February 2005: New Profile (Israeli group).

February 2005: Activists disrupt a basketball match in Barcelona against the Maccabi Tel Aviv team.

March 2005: Corrie Family Lawsuit vs. Caterpillar, Inc.

April 2005: York and Hull District Methodist Synod, England.

April 2005: Association of University Teachers (AUT), UK supports BDS.

April 2005: The Association of University of Wisconsin Professionals (TAUWP) passed a resolution by 24 to 2 to divest from companies supporting Israel.

April 2005: The Communist Party of India (CPI) and the CPI-M (Marxist), voted to impose sanctions and end military agreements and ties with Israel.

2005: European Jews for a Just Peace (EJJP).

May 2005: South African Council of Churches (SACC).

2005: US Campaign to End the Israeli Occupation takes up BDS as a priority.

Spring 2005: Friends of Sabeel, North America issues 'A Call for Morally Responsible Investing: A Nonviolent Response to the Occupation'.

June 2005: New England Methodists approve a resolution of divestment.

June 2005: United Methodist Church, Virginia, USA.

June 2005: Irish activists mobilize against a football match involving an Israeli team.

2005: The World Council of Churches urged its 340 member churches to consider nonviolent economic measures, such as divestment from international corporations like Caterpillar, and from Israeli companies that support the occupation and human rights violations.

2005: The regional council of the Sør-Trøndelag, Norway calls for a boycott of Israeli goods to be followed up with an awareness raising campaign across the region.

June 2005: Vlaams Palestina Komitee, Flanders.

July 2005: Palestinian Civil Society Call to Action.

July 2005: UN International Civil Society conference.

July 2005: Anglican Church of Kenya decides to divest from companies engaged with supplying goods to the Israeli occupation.

July 2005: United Church of Christ, US adopts an 'economic leverage' resolution against Israel, calling on Israel to 'tear down' the wall.

August 2005: Veterans for Peace.

August 2005: Global Exchange.

August 2005: The Evangelical Lutheran Church in America adopts a policy of divestment from Israel.

September 2005: UK lawyers obtain an arrest warrant for Israeli Commander Almog who cancels his trip.

October 2005: Episcopalian Executive Council (US).

November 2005: Green Party, US.

November 2005: Anglican Church of Canada.

November 2005: Arbizu, Basque Country, passes a motion banning complicity and support for the Israeli occupation.

December 2005: Coalition for Justice and Peace in Palestine, Quebec.

December 2005: The Norwegian Provincial Parliament of the Sør-Trondeleim district.

December 2005: Women's International League for Peace and Freedom (WILPF), Canadian section.

February 2006: Church of England 'to disinvest from companies profiting from the illegal occupation'.

February 2006: [British] Architects and Planners for Justice in Palestine announce plans to boycott construction companies involved in building Israel's apartheid wall.

February 2006: The Interfaith Group for Morally Responsible Investment (IMRI)-UK.

February 2006: OISM Italy boycott actions at Olympic Games in Milan.

February 2006: PSM Washington.

March 2006: Collectif Urgence Palestine (CUP) (Swiss).

April 2006: Rachel Corrie Foundation for Peace and Justice.

April 2006: Roger Waters of Pink Floyd cancels appearance in Tel Aviv.

May 2006: Canadian Union of Public Employees (CUPE).

May 2006: Presbyterian Church of Scotland.

May 2006: National Association of Teachers in Further and Higher Education (NATFHE), UK. Shortly afterwards, NATFHE merges with the AUT to form a new union, the University and College Lecturers' Union (UCU).

June 2006: The Ontario branch of the Canadian Union of Public Employees (CUPE) passes motion to support BDS.

June 2006: UNISON (UK labor union).

June 2006: Presbyterian Church, USA, 2006 General Assembly.

June 19, 2006: Collectifs Urgence Palestine and the European Coordination for Palestine (ECCP) in Geneva support the BDS call.

June 2006: Central Única dos Trabalhadores (CUT) Brazil and other trade unions in South America join the mobilization that blocks the signing of the Free Trade Agreement between the Mercosur countries and Israel.

July 2006: The Services, Industrial, Professional and Technical Union of Ireland calls for sanctions against Israel and immediate suspension of the Euro-Mediterranean Association Agreement with Israel until such time as that country ends its violations of international law.

July 2006: Pax Christi Catholic International Peace Movement.

July 2006: Organizers of the Locarno International Film Festival in Switzerland drop the Israeli Ministry of Foreign Affairs as a festival sponsor after a call for action from Palestinian filmmakers.

July 2006: Eighty-six MPs of various parties ask the government to immediately suspend arms purchases from Israel and seek global sanctions against it.

July 2006: Gaza University Teachers' Association calls for academic and cultural boycott of Israel.

August 2006: Religious Society of Friends (Quakers).

August 2006: The United Church of Canada (Presbyterian, Methodist, United Church of Christ).

Autumn 2006: Stanford University.

August 2006: Jews for a Just Peace – Vancouver, Canada.

August 2006: Dublin Tram System.

August 2006: Palestinian Filmmakers, Artists and Cultural Workers Call for a Cultural Boycott.

August 2006: Edinburgh International Film Festival boycotts Israeli films.

August 2006: Venezuela withdraws its ambassador in protest at escalating Israeli war crimes in Gaza and Lebanon.

August 2006: The Greek Cinematography Center (GCC) withdraws all Greek films from the Haifa Film Festival.

September 2006: U2U, Belgian Hi-Tech Company refuses to use material made in Israel.

September 2006: United Nations International Conference of Civil Society in Support of Middle East Peace.

September 2006: The largest South African trade union COSATU unanimously passes a resolution submitted by the National Union of Metalworkers (NUMSA) that calls for sanctions.

October 2006: Church of England. Virginia Water Parish, Guildford Diocese takes steps on its own.

November 2006: Palestine Solidarity Campaign – Ireland calls for boycott of Israeli diamonds.

November 2006: ASN Bank, Holland.

November 2006: Ireland-Palestine Solidarity Campaign (IPSC) succeeds in getting Israeli products off shelves.

2006 and 2007: The Somerville, MA divestment campaign works diligently to educate town people on divestment and succeeds on getting the subject on the ballot.

January 2007: FAWU – Food and Allied Workers Union, South Africa.

January 2007: Sanctions Against Israel Coalition – South Africa branch.

January 2007: Global Palestine Solidarity (GPS) campaign includes conflict diamonds (Israel-processed diamonds).

February 2007: Women in Black Boycotts Israel Philharmonic in Los Angeles.

2007: British Jews call for boycotting Israel.

2007: Israeli citizens launch an organized campaign to support the BDS, see boycott-occupation.mahost.org.

May 2007: 130 British doctors call for a boycott of the Israeli Medical Association and its expulsion from the World Medical Association.

May 2007: National Union of Journalists – UK.

2007: Northern Ireland's biggest trade union NIPSA.

June 2007: People's Food Co-op – Ann Arbor, USA.

June 2007: New England Conference of the United Methodist Church issues recommendations for divestment.

July 2007: British Transport and General Workers Union (TGWU).

July 2007: Irish Congress of Trade Unions (ICTU).

August 2007: The Jewish Voice – Germany.

August 2007: Evangelical Lutheran Church of America (ELCA).

2007: University and College Union (UCU), England reaffirms BDS support. Church of England divested from £3.3 million worth of Caterpillar stock.

2009: Launch of Coalition of Women for Peace's website 'Who profits' (www.whoprofits.org).

January 2009: The Canadian Union of Postal Workers (CUPW) call on the Canadian government 'to adopt a program of boycott, divestment and sanctions until Israel recognizes the right of the Palestinian people to self-determination and complies with international law, including the rights of Palestinian refugees to return to their homes as stipulated in UN resolution 194'.

February 2009: Church of England announces it has divested from Caterpillar.

February 2009: Hampshire College becomes the first American college to divest from companies that profit from the Israeli occupation.

March 2009: Many universities in North America and Europe and over 40 cities host Israeli Apartheid Week.

March 2009: Boycott Motorola Campaign launched in New York.

April 2009: The Scottish Trade Union Congress, representing all Scottish trade unions, supports BDS.

May 2009: University College Union (UCU), representing over 100,000 academics and related staff in UK colleges and universities, passes resolutions on applying effective pressure on Israel and holding it accountable for its colonial and apartheid policies.

June 2009: The United Methodist Church.

July 2009: Andy Bichlbaum and Mike Bonanno, co-directors of the film *Yes Men*, withdraw from the Jerusalem Film Festival.

July 2009: New York Campaign for the Boycott of Israel engaged in a highly visible campaign against Motorola.

July 2009: The British group Stop Arming Israel (www.stoparmingisrael.org) partly successful in revoking the sale of some of the military components sent from Britain to arm Israel. Coalition of 300 peace organizations approves boycott of Israel – a turning point for the US solidarity movement. See electronicintifada.net/v2/article10778.shtml.

September 2009: Norwegian government divests from the Israeli firm Elbit System.

September 2009: US retirement giant (academics) TIAA-CREF divests from Africa Israel Investments.

September 2009: Brazilian parliament calls for freeze of the Israel–Mercosur Free Trade Agreement.

September 2009: The British Trades Union Congress (TUC), representing over six million workers, adopts BDS.

November 2009: Students for Justice in Palestine at Hampshire College host a National BDS student conference.

November 2009: The second largest Dutch pension fund (PZFW) divests from Africa-Israel.

November 2009: Norwegian academics in Trondheim commit to an academic boycott.

December 2009 Turkish BDS campaign launched.

December 11, 2009: Christian Palestinians release the Palestine Kairos document titled 'A Moment of Truth'. See kairospalestine.ps.

As we can see, the number of actions over the years, 2009 in particular, shows significant and concrete results. Let us now consider briefly some interesting cases for the lessons learned.

Intel's president and chief executive Craig Barrett said, on June 18, 2001 while visiting Israel, that Intel was reconsidering a $3 billion expansion of the company's Kiryat Gat plant built on the lands of Iraq Al Manshiya due to 'the current economic climate and industry slowdown' (*Jerusalem Post*, June 19, 2002). This followed Salman Abu Sitta's call for activists to contact Intel to protest the company's investments in Israel. Over 2,000 letters were sent. After the announcement that the expansion would be delayed, Intel worked with the Jordanian government to facilitate the introduction of computers into schools and invested in a computer laboratory in Gaza via the American Near East Refugee Aid. The campaign continued; articles and opinion pieces were also published in newspapers in the Arab world including: *Al-Dustour* (Jordan), *Al-Watan* (Qatar), *Al-Hayat*, *Al-Safeer* (Lebanon), *Al-Quds*, *Al-Ayyam* (Palestine), *Al-Ahram* (Cairo), *Al-Watan* (Kuwait) and *Al-Khaleej* (United Arab Emirates). The media coverage caused other companies to pay attention, as we learned from private conversations with competitors.

When students organized a divestment conference in the US in 2002, the first actual divestment carried out at a university in the USA, the *Financial Times* wrote:

When student activists from 70 US universities descend on the University of Michigan for a conference tomorrow, companies and investors will be watching closely ... the campaigners have been successful in raising the profile of the Palestinian cause.[30]

Other highly successful conferences were held and the Zionist movement attempted in vain to shut each one of them down through threats and intimidation.[31] The divestment campaign on campuses continued to grow. In February 2006, 17-year-old Israeli citizen Matan Cohen was shot in the eye with a rubber bullet during a nonviolent demonstration in the village of Beit Sira. He later enrolled in Hampshire College and became a prominent organizer of a BDS campaign which was successful in getting his college to divest from six companies doing business in the occupied territories.[32]

Many churches began the process of examining investments they held in companies that profit from the Israeli occupation and oppression of the Palestinian people. Some moved faster than others in practical moves, and not merely in statements they issued. The Presbyterian Church in particular seemed to have moved significantly in a positive direction despite pressure applied to it.[33] In February 2005, the World Council of Churches urged its 340 member churches to consider selective divestment from international corporations like Caterpillar, and from Israeli companies that profit from and perpetuate the occupation and human rights violations. Some churches acted with the Church of England by divesting from Caterpillar.[34] But the success was not uniform

The Evangelical Lutheran Church in America rejected a pro-divestment resolution in 2005, and the House of Bishops of the Episcopal Church in the US, at its July 17, 2009 meeting in Anaheim, CA, rejected several resolutions, not only one calling for divestment, but also ones calling for dismantling the wall, ending the confiscation of Palestinian land, and the creation of a Palestinian state – all on the grounds that they were not 'balanced'. As far as Catholics are concerned, while some religious orders and local parishes have been very active in the BDS movement, both the Vatican and U.S. bishops have avoided the divestment question.[35]

Currently, the publication of the Palestine Kairos document in December 2009, like the document of the same name issued by South African Christians, is expected to galvanize and mobilize churches worldwide to act.[36]

The campaign against Veolia Transports and Alstom is another success story. The campaign started because the companies were participating in the construction of infrastructure for Jewish settlements in occupied Palestine. In November 2006, ASN, a Dutch bank, broke off financial relations with Veolia because of its Jerusalem contract. After a lot of hard work, pressure built on the company. The campaign gained steam when, on January 20, 2009, the Stockholm Community Council announced that it would not renew its contract with Veolia to operate the subways (worth US$4 billion). Others followed suit. In April 2009, the Greater Bordeaux local government announced that it would not award a $1 billion contract to Veolia and Sligo County Council called on the county manager 'not to sign or renew any contracts with Veolia'. On June 2, 2009, the Victoria State Government, Australia announced, after four months of campaigning and the distribution of over 100,000 pamphlets, that it had dropped Veolia (operating under the name of Cannex) as Melbourne's train system operator. *Le Monde* reported on June 5, 2009 that Veolia was losing a lot of money because of its involvement in Israel. Israeli media reported on June 8, 2009 that Veolia was abandoning its Jerusalem rail project. However, the company later advertised a job vacancy for the project and the campaign continued. In late July, Veolia lost a $3.5 billion contact for an Australian desalination project.[37] There was also a similar success against the Israeli cosmetics company Ahava in 2009.[38]

British labor unions took the lead in support of the BDS movement. It was noted by summer 2009:

> Public sector union PCS, the UCU and the Fire Brigades Union have all passed strong motions explicitly calling for a general policy of boycott of Israeli goods, divestment from Israeli companies and government sanctions against the state. Unions such as public sector union UNISON, the National Union of Teachers, USDAW and the Communication Workers Union (CWU) have this summer passed softer motions calling for elements of BDS. These are usually calls for a boycott of settlement goods, or for the government to suspend arms sales to Israel.[39]

With the founding of groups like American Labor for Palestine (www.laborforpalestine.org) and US Labor against the War (uslaboragainstwar.org), the labor movement in the US is catching up its European and South African partners.[40]

Palestinian NGOs have brought cases against Israelis for war crimes, as when the Israeli army dropped a one-ton bomb on a building killing many children because they wanted to execute extrajudicially one man who was living there with his family. Whether legal action is successful in specific court cases or not, it has certainly put the Israeli war criminals and the whole Zionist establishment on the defensive and curtailed travel by Israeli leaders outside the country.[41]

In summer 2009, several Canadian filmmakers, later supported by hundreds of artists, withdrew their films from the Toronto International Film Festival because the festival spotlighted Tel Aviv.[42] That same summer, the Israeli firm Elbit was dropped from the Norwegian government pension fund.[43]

The International Israel Apartheid Week, with BDS at its core, is now in its sixth year and has been growing every year, with more cities and towns around the world participating.[44] The BDS movement's most critical advantage is to prevent normalization of an apartheid colonial system, thus putting the system under stress and on the defensive.[45] Ultimately, that, combined with other pressures on the racist system, adds to the cost of maintaining the oppression to the point where rational calculation would lead to abandoning the system. This is what happened in South Africa. BDS is deemed threatening to the system of oppression as seen by the alarm and level of mobilization by the Israeli government and its supporters to challenge and thwart BDS actions.[46]

One personal example: I wrote several articles dealing with BDS over the years, even published in a Jewish magazine *Tikkun*, but none received as much attention and publicity as when my article titled 'Boycott Israel' appeared in the official magazine of The World Economic Forum (WEF) in January 2006. The WEF brings thousands of world political and business leaders to Davos to exchange information. Condoleezza Rice addressed the conference that day, via a satellite link. After complaints from some who did not believe in free speech, Klaus Schwab, founder and executive chairman of the WEF, apologized for publishing my article in *Global Agenda Magazine* (the official magazine of the WEF), which was distributed to all attendees. The article was also originally posted on their website, but subsequently, they pulled it.[47] The full article can be read on my website. Having received complaints from Israelis and Zionists in attendance, Schwab held a press conference to 'apologize' and asked attendees to return the magazines, though few did. Later it was decided to cancel the magazine altogether (it is still no longer published). The editors were not happy with this. However, the buzz around the attack, the dictatorial censorship of it by Schwab and the withdrawal all resulted in dozens of media stories (from *Ha'aretz* to the *New York Times*) reaching hundreds of thousands. Among the 5,000 world leaders who attended and were given the original article, many would not have read it had it not been for the controversy and media frenzy. I received hundreds of letters of support, including from key government officials. I also received an invitation for a speaking tour in Italy.

It is important not to overemphasize the role of BDS, but to 'note that it forms just one factor in inducing political and social change ... BDS has an important role to play but should not diminish the contribution of internal struggle, or of global forces and events that also play a role in determining history.'[48] In the previous chapters we cited more than 100 methods of challenging and resisting Israeli colonization – actions of civil disobedience, civil resistance, etc.

In addition, activists for BDS have moved in parallel to encourage purchases of the few remaining Palestinian products. Israel has systematically destroyed the Palestinian economy and left very few options for exportable products. Even here, there have been remarkable successes and great civil rights efforts. Local groups like Badil, PACBI, Stop the Wall and others engage in regular campaigns to encourage buying local products. The most recent campaign, 'Intajuna', is educational and is sponsored by a number of local groups (Paltrade, ARIJ, Sharek, Business Women Forum, Palestine Federation of Industries, UAWC and PARC, with major funding by the Swiss Agency for Development and execution by Solutions for Development Consulting Inc.). And of course, this extends to exports of Palestinian products through cooperatives and fair trade associations. In one instance, a Palestinian who returned from the US helped build a fair trade organization that now earns tens of millions of dollars. Here are some of the fair trade and other groups of Palestinian products sold over the internet:

www.palestinefairtrade.org
www.canaanfairtrade.com
www.zatoun.com
www.palestineonlinestore.com

14
Conclusions and Outlook for the Future

Only if we respect ourselves as Arabs and understand the true dignity and justice of our struggle, only then can we appreciate why, almost despite ourselves, so many people all over the world, including Rachel Corrie and the two young people wounded with her from ISM, Tom Hurndall and Brian Avery, have felt it possible to express their solidarity with us ... Isn't it time we caught up with our own status and made certain that our representatives here and elsewhere realize, as a first step, that they are fighting for a just and noble cause, and that they have nothing to apologize for or anything to be embarrassed about? On the contrary, they should be proud of what their people have done and proud also to represent them.

Edward Said [1]

It is important to learn from the successful experiences of Mahatma Gandhi and Martin Luther King, Jr. in nonviolent resistance. However, each situation has a set of social, political and cultural differences and we must develop appropriate and new responses to each situation.[2] For each stage of the injustice, we have documented inspiring and innovative acts of Palestinian popular resistance. This includes the period of Ottoman rule, the dispossessions of the early 1920s under the Zionist rule of Herbert Samuel, the great revolt of 1936–39, the period following the ethnic cleansing of 530 Palestinian villages and towns between 1947 and 1949, the 1987–91 uprising and, most recently, the Al-Aqsa intifada. The injustice took on new brutal forms in different periods; from the destruction of homes and livelihoods in 1936–39 period, to Jewish terrorism in the 1940s, to massacres and parades of victims during the establishment of Israel, to mass looting, to shooting anyone returning to ethnically cleansed areas, to breaking the bones of demonstrators in the late 1980s, and to attacking civilians with napalm in the 1980s and most recently white phosphorus. The colonization of Palestine was baptized in blood and tears; it continues to be maintained by Israeli military forces unchallenged by supine Western governments.

The colonial violence was accompanied by propaganda in Zionist-influenced mainstream media until the dawn of the internet. This *hasbara* campaign depicted the Palestinians as uncivilized savages and the resistance as inexplicable, barbaric terrorism. In parallel, the perpetrators of ethnic cleansing were depicted as innocent victims. We can cite similar propaganda about Native Americans in the first 200 years of European colonization, the French resistance to German occupation, the Algerian resistance to French occupation or the South African resistance to apartheid. The first thing to know about Palestinian resistance is that it is a symptom of the etiology of colonization and ethnic cleansing. There are legitimate forms resistance to oppression and colonization, approved and encouraged in the UN Charter and in international law, which may be armed or unarmed.

A SUMMARY OF POPULAR RESISTANCE

Over two-thirds of the eleven million Palestinians worldwide are refugees or displaced persons. This, like similar situations such as in Algeria and South Africa, could not have come about without massive resistance to the violence of colonialism. The brutal removal of villagers during Ottoman and later the British and, finally, Israeli rule over the past 13 decades would have proceeded much faster and certainly would have resulted in a far more homogeneous Jewish state had it not been for Palestinian resistance.

We reviewed resistance under Ottoman rule in Chapter 5 – a nonviolent resistance that was successful in terms of limiting land acquisitions by the Zionist movement. The Ottoman weaknesses in the nineteenth century, with conflicts at the periphery of the empire, enforced deals that enabled the Western powers to make inroads into Palestine. The intellectual Palestinians who supplied political leadership then provided inspiring examples for generations to come. However, effective resistance was hampered by isolation of the Palestinian elites from the masses, by Turkish-Arab rivalry and by feudal structures that tried to face up to a well-organized and well-financed international Zionist movement. The inroads Zionism made into Palestine before 1917 were small and inconsequential thanks to Palestinian civil resistance in a sympathetic Islamic Ottoman system.

This changed dramatically during the British rule in Palestine (1917–48). Palestinian society under British rule was beset with problems, but responded remarkably well to the onslaught of Zionist and British efforts to dismantle it and establish a Jewish homeland in its place. Becoming accustomed to the end of four centuries of Ottoman rule while adjusting with a British rule was traumatic in itself. Added to that, British-Zionist collaboration to transform the country into a Jewish homeland piled even more stress on a fragmented and weak society. The appointment of the Zionist Herbert Samuel was emblematic of this era and a key to advancing the Zionist project while keeping the British society in the dark about the reality on the ground in Palestine. The darkness was only penetrated in brief periods thanks to Palestinian popular resistance. The British elite responded by divide-and-rule policies, some of which worked, especially when a number of Palestinians cooperated with the authorities against the national cause. Most notably, the struggle for freedom was hampered by quarrels between the Husseini and Nashashibi factions and the elites' isolation from the interest of most Palestinians.

Systemic and unyielding support for the Zionist project faced a significant obstacle when Palestinians engaged in massive armed and civil resistance which disrupted life between 1936 and 1939. As in other uprisings, a grassroots movement pushed hard and the entrenched elite political leaders later joined to ride the wave of the uprising. The occupying authorities imposed collective punishment on the Palestinians and gave preferential treatment to armed Jewish settlers, assigned land deeds to them and changed the status of and access to holy sites such as the Western Wall. With the refusal to respect basic human rights of the locals, including the right to self-determination, these policies engendered resentment and resistance. The British policies at the time reflected those implemented elsewhere in the British colonies: they were brutal, calculating and divisive. Thousands were arrested for nothing more than voicing opposition or establishing political parties that challenged colonial rule. Those who resisted violently were hunted down and killed. Hangings were common. The lines between the colonial Zionist settlers, the British occupation and even local Jews continued to blur.

There were three flare-ups in the resistance under British rule – in 1921, 1929 and 1936–39 – each with its own peculiarities and challenges. Each showed opportunities taken and opportunities missed. The evolution of the Palestinian resistance in these periods was shaped by the British response, by the intensification of Zionist activities and by Palestinian society's evolution in terms of education and sophistication. The 1930s saw some Palestinian-organized guerrilla fighters who resisted systematically with arms. But, the great Palestinian revolt of 1936–39 also elevated the forms of popular resistance from petitions and protests to outright popular disobedience. The more aggressive measures of popular resistance, together with some violence, caught the British and Zionists unprepared. They quickly adapted and managed to take advantage of opportunistic squabbling Palestinian political leaders. The defeat of the 1936–39 revolt was due to a coincidence of interests and actions of three groups according to Ghassan Kanafani: 'the local reactionary leadership; the regimes in the Arab states surrounding Palestine; and the imperialist-Zionist enemy'.[3] Indeed, we have noted in Chapter 7 how such factors played a role in undermining perhaps the longest strike in Palestinian history – a strike that lasted 183 days. The Palestinians emerged politically weakened after most of their leaders had been imprisoned or deported. The local Palestinian economy, social cohesion and organizational abilities were dealt a very heavy blow. The void was filled by other forces after World War II, including the newly independent Arab states. It took another generation to find a truly independent Palestinian voice.

Palestinians mobilized essentially in complete isolation inside the Green Line from 1949 to 1966. Not only were they isolated from the Arab and Islamic hinterland, but they also faced a brutal military rule that attempted to crush them and at many times even to finish the job of 1948 by separating them from their remaining lands. Palestinians outside the Green Line (in Gaza, West Bank and exiled in other countries) had the reverse problem. They did not have direct contact with their oppressors, but they did have lots of contact and work in the Arab Islamic world. They had to develop ways of coping that were unimagined before 1948.

The 1967 war changed the landscape in both positive and negative ways. Israel's military superiority enabled it to occupy and control vast new Arab areas, but this time a mass exodus failed to materialize. The war shocked people into realizing that the Arab leaders were impotent to bring about change. Palestinians began to build their own representative institutions so that slowly the influence of King Hussein in the West Bank weakened, despite both Israeli and Jordanian policies. By 1974, nationalist trends dominated, with a very small minority representing Islamic and royalist support among Palestinians. Support for the PLO and the growth of civil institutions in the occupied territories mushroomed. PLO institutions established in the late 1960s included many branches working in popular resistance methods both outside and inside Palestine (e.g., the General Unions of Palestinian Students and Palestinian Women). These grew in parallel with the armed resistance. Israel tried all the tactics at its disposal to crush nationalist sentiment, as well as all forms of resistance, but to no avail. The harsher its repression, the stronger the resistance grew in different forms. Israel's adventure and massacres in Lebanon from 1975–87 were attempts to crush the resistance by killing its outside symbols and institutions (including bombing cultural centers and hospitals in the refugee camps).

The uprising of 1987 came as a shock to the Israeli system and to a compliant world community. Even the PLO's traditional leadership was caught off-guard and had to work hard to connect with (and often co-opt) the new generation of activists on the inside. Since Fatah was the largest faction, the actions of its members were critical in shaping the evolution of the 1987–91 intifada. But it was becoming clear that they were divided, especially along a generational and 'official' line. Those who represented the organization in an official capacity tended to be older and had close connections and adherences. The younger frontline activists mostly disliked the authority of the 'Tunis group' and favored innovative and rebellious actions. It was a schism between conservatives and progressives in many ways. Later, that schism would widen as the old guard became increasingly worried about their irrelevance as events on the ground created new leadership. Some became obsessed with the importance of the PLO and this led to the Oslo Accords.

Like the uprising of 1935–39, the 1987–91 uprising came to an end due to external circumstances, such as the encroachment of a war nearby, societal stress, factionalism imposed by a distant leadership (physically and metaphysically) and treachery by collaborative Arab leaders both near and far. In 1939, a British White Paper and Arab government interference played a role, as did the start of the war. The 'Uprising of the Stones' ended after:

- the first Gulf War commenced, bringing world attention to another part of the Middle East and dividing the Arab world between those who backed the US and Kuwaiti rulers and those who backed the Iraqi government;
- meetings between the US administration and the PLO leadership; and
- the launch of the Madrid peace process, which the PLO joined unofficially, which led to the Oslo Accords.

HOW OSLO CHANGED THINGS

PLO leaders who recognized Israel and renounced violence were put in charge of the population in the occupied territories. The

PLO harvested the fruits of labor and blood with some limited achievements that benefited a significant number of Palestinians, especially those who came from the diaspora, with the nascent Palestinian Authority. This fostered resentment between the newcomers and the locals who lived under occupation. But other negative trends ensued with Oslo, including a strengthening of the bourgeois trends and weakening of the revolutionary spirit. Said Aburish summarized it thus:

> Years ago, when all the PLO did was field militias to skirmish with Israeli border patrols and deal with the problems of creating a Palestinian national awareness, the PLO, like revolutionary movements elsewhere, needed fighters and intellectuals more than anything else. For the most part, the fighters and intellectuals belonged to the refugee camps and villages, although others came from the open atmosphere of Beirut and the universities of the West. But the moment the PLO turned conservative in order to deal with conservative Arab regimes who belatedly accepted it, it completely lost its revolutionary élan. The conservative oil sheikhs wanted to work with fellow-Palestinian conservatives and made it plain that they resented the PLO's revolutionary corps. So the PLO turned to the Palestinian bourgeoisie for new recruits, people to deal with the Arab establishment. Suddenly the old Palestinian names resurfaced, those who had been discredited for their failure to provide a Palestinian homeland in the thirties, forties and fifties. They are not fighters and have no stomach for suffering, but they are the money men who liaise with sheikhs and emirs, act as ambassadors to European capitals and assume positions as consultants and advisers to Yasser Arafat. To the people of the West Bank, the consequences of this transformation were an unforgivable crime. They bitterly point out that these people were nowhere to be seen during the difficult years of the PLO's struggle for recognition, and make accusations that the establishment will always take care of its own. Old Palestinian names such as Husseini, Nusseibeh, Masri and others took over important PLO positions – if not the whole organization – and the credentials of many of them have nothing to do with the Palestinians; rather, they are the darlings of Arab kings and presidents.[4]

I would go further and say that the collective work and sense of nationalism and self-sacrifice developed between 1987 and 1991 was also slowly snuffed out, to be replaced by cronyism, self-interest and indifference to the collective future. This was not an accidental by-product of Oslo. It was a direct and predictable development that Israeli planners would have foreseen and encouraged. Corruption in the PA, which had its roots before Oslo, was promoted and advanced to become systematic.

The Oslo process is now recognized universally, including by many who were initially supportive of it, as disastrous as it led to:

- the fragmentation of the Palestinian people and cause;
- normalization of Israel as a Jewish state in over 60 countries and significant expansion of Israel's economic power;
- weakening and marginalization of the PLO institutions to be replaced by the Ramallah-based Palestinian authority; and
- freeing up Israel to do what it wants in area C (over 60 percent of the West Bank and Gaza), doubling the number of settlers there in seven years and entrenching the system of apartheid.

Meanwhile the 'peace process' became an end in itself and a tool used by Israel to gain time to enforce more colonization. The system was bound to collapse and did with the 2000 intifada.

The Al-Aqsa intifada started nonviolently, but violence crept in as a response to Israeli brutality. The engagement of international solidarity activists, including many Israelis, was a notable quantitative and qualitative shift in that direction. The founding of the International Solidarity Movement (ISM) in Beit Sahour and its subsequent spread was critical to counteract the violent Israeli responses. The most recent manifestations have been the attempts to break the siege of Gaza. The second uprising also saw the use of the internet not only to mobilize and educate, but also to hack into Israeli and Palestinian websites. Palestinian computer experts used their knowledge to overwhelm Israeli sites, including the Knesset and army websites.[5]

An examination of the history of Palestinian resistance shows that armed resistance came late to the game, after 40 years of Zionist colonization. For the first few decades (1880s–1920s), all resistance was popular and unarmed. Later, all uprisings started as popular resistance, but some was marked by armed resistance in response to the brutality of the occupiers and colonizers. As such, armed resistance was limited, considering the injustice compared to places like South Africa, Algeria and Vietnam. The number of Israelis killed by Palestinians was minuscule compared to other colonial situations. As we have seen, popular resistance was extensive, lasted longer and employed innovative and indigenous forms unique to the Palestinian experience. It is indeed remarkable to note the depth and strength of the unarmed resistance when considering the depravity and violence Palestinians faced over decades.

WHAT WE DID NOT COVER

In this book we have listed hundreds of examples, out of millions, of Palestinian popular resistance, ranging from petitions, to strikes, to demonstrations, to civil disobedience, to non-cooperation, to boycotts and many more ways. How many in the West have heard of the women's movement of the 1920s against the British occupation and its support of colonial Zionism? How many have heard of Christian and Muslim religious leaders imprisoned in 1936 for saying that Palestine should remain a multi-ethnic/multi-religious society and not be transformed into a Jewish state? How many know about the struggle of Palestinians inside the state of Israel where many of their villages that remain are 'unrecognized'? How many know about Land Day, which started in 1976 – a key date for popular resistance for Palestinians at home and exiled around the world? How many know about the tax revolt in 1989? How many know about the incredibly innovative resistance in villages like Jayyus, Bil'in, Ni'lin and Al-Ma'sara today? And if the people in the West are allowed to hear of these things, would they not put pressure on their governments to stop supporting the Israeli apartheid regime as they did with apartheid South Africa?

As we explained in the introduction, the topic of popular resistance is broad and we obviously cannot provide here a survey of all forms of resistance. We have chosen and focused on a few examples from different periods in the history of popular resistance in Palestine. We have not covered actions by Palestinians in exile (*shatat* in Arabic)[6] and by the global community in support of the Palestinian struggle, except in Chapter 13, where we listed a few of the thousands of campaigns in support of the Palestinian calls for BDS. Some of those have worked closely with Palestinians over decades locally in the form of support and development that constitute popular resistance such as the Mennonite Central Committee and the American Friends Service Committee.[7] We also have not mentioned Palestinians in exile who remain outside but continue to support their families and charitable causes inside Palestine or in refugee camps around the Arab world. These are all forms of civil resistance. There are also

Palestinians who leave a life of comfort in the diaspora and return to live and struggle in Palestine (when and if they are allowed to).[8]

We gave very few examples of resistance by art, including all forms of cultural expression from folkloric *dabkes* to traditional dress.[9] The symbolism and strength of the *hatta* or *kufiya* headdress in Palestinian culture resulted in a significant attack on its use, as well as its subversive use by Israeli undercover agents.[10] We have not discussed acts of resistance by writing poetry about exile, resistance, perseverance, love and more.[11] We have given a few examples of resistance by writing and speaking, such as the authors cited in the notes and a whole genre of Palestinian resistance literature.[12] Palestinians perform acts of civil resistance when they take their sheep to pastures like those in the South Hebron Hills where settlers regularly attack and harass them.[13]

Even in what we have covered, we have been selective. Books could be written on subsets of the information presented. In selecting our examples from different eras, we have tried to give some insight into the energy and vitality of that era but we did not want to reduce a popular resistance to the actions of one or a few people. Popular resistance by definition involves social movements not necessarily led by charismatic or effective leaders. The most effective forms are those carried out by teamwork. We mentioned by name some people of importance, giving brief biographies, but did not have space to do them justice. Other books relating their stories and thinking are needed.[14] I think good books can also be written about popular resistance by Palestinian women (see box, p. 117), Palestinian students and faith-based popular resistance – all areas touched on only briefly here due to space limitations. We could write volumes about resistance by simply living, eating, breathing in a land that is coveted. We resist by going to school, by cultivating what remains of our lands, by working under harsh conditions and by falling in love, getting married and having children. Resistance includes hanging on to what remains and doing all the mundane tasks of trying to live (survive) in what remains of Palestine when it has been made crystal-clear in words and deeds that we are not welcome on our lands. That is what is called *sumud* in Arabic (the closest translation is steadfastness, but in Arabic it also implies more positive action).

Clearly, all these forms of resistance will continue as long as the underlying etiology remains. Resistance (both violent and nonviolent) in South Africa ended the day apartheid came to an end. While it is not the ideal outcome, at least it opened the door for reconciliation and for joint struggles in other areas of justice (e.g., economic equality). People in the West are encouraged to learn more about what is going on because it is moral and right, but also because it has an impact on their lives too; for in many of these countries, the government supports the oppression in their name and with their taxes. Palestinians in civil society organizations issued a specific call in 2005 for boycotts, divestments and sanctions. We urge all to read and heed that call if they are interested in a peaceful resolution to this conflict (see bdsmovement.net). Such a resolution would not only have direct and positive impact on the people living here (Jews, Christians, Muslims, etc.) but on all of humanity. With help from friends of peace and justice, we could indeed become a light unto the nations.

CHALLENGES AND OPPORTUNITIES

Zionism created an entrenched and well-funded local form of settler colonialism whose interests were maximum geography for the Jewish state with minimum demography of natives. Crucial factors in the success of Zionism included Western backing, a vast network of support from committed Jewish Zionists and local Zionist 'toughness' with the natives. Zionists could draw on their political skills, experience of political mobilization, diplomatic expertise, education, scientific knowledge, financial resources, understanding of modern bureaucratic systems and other elements of a civilization which, in the nineteenth century, dominated the world. To express the same point another way, they could utilize the experience of 300 years of political revolution and reform, industrialization and the rise to global hegemony of Western capitalism.

The natives had few resources or allies to challenge it and also had internal weaknesses among Palestinians and even more so among the Arab countries that were to be the strategic depth of the resistance. The Palestinian Arabs, like other people in Asia, Africa, Australia and the Americas in earlier eras, had a society which functioned well enough when left alone, but was ill-adapted to withstand a determined assault from Europe. Palestinians after 1948 were separated into refugees around the world and a portion inside who now were divided among three sovereign entities: Egypt, Israel and Jordan. This division is unusual and different from struggles of other people against colonial rule. In other situations (e.g., in Algeria), while natives were dispossessed and suffering, they remained within the same sociopolitical unified environment.

Many Palestinians living outside their homeland feel that they have been abandoned by the leadership which they supported, often with their blood, for a quarter of a century. Those in the West Bank and Gaza Strip are appalled at the state of division and confusion that reigns now. Many Palestinians are becoming more individualistic, concentrating on the interests of those dearest to them and putting to the back of their minds the dreams they once had for Palestine. This is directly related to the divisions created after Oslo.

Today, Palestinians are more divided and fragmented than ever. Within the Green Line 1.5 million live as nominal citizens, but without basic equality or rights of citizenship. Many are increasingly squeezed into concentrated areas and more and more villages are targeted for destruction. A further 250,000 Palestinians live in illegally annexed East Jerusalem. Millions live as refugees in neighboring countries (Jordan, Lebanon, Syria, Egypt, etc.) and experience varying degrees of mistreatment. Jewish settlements in areas occupied in 1967 house 450,000 colonists on land belonging to the native Palestinian people. Israel wanted the land but not the people. They proceeded to confiscate farms, hills and valleys to build settlements, military bases and other points of control. Israel has literally fenced in 1.5 million people in a massive prison called Gaza; 70 percent of them are Palestinian refugees in a place now with the highest rate of poverty in the Middle East. Israel is currently building walls to 'fence off' the towns of the West Bank in an analogous fashion.[15]

The Palestinian social fabric developed resilience and resistance under extremely difficult circumstances, from the old rule by Empire to subjugation during British occupation, to expanded Zionist colonization.[16] But they also faced internal challenges. We noted that Palestinian political fragmentation and squabbling restricted the achievements of the uprisings of 1921, 1929, 1936, 1970s, 1980 and 2000; these came from a tradition not free from the negative influences of clan structures and patronage.[17]

The problems between Fatah and Hamas escalated in 2007 and 2008. The two 'authorities' in Gaza and the West Bank behave like leaders of gangs in prison; strong on each other and weak in dealing with the prison guards. The divisions were unfortunate by-products of the strategies and tactics of Oslo, as well as ideological differences between the groups. When Hamas decided to enter elections and won a majority of the legislative council in 2006, the Western and collaborative Arab regimes laid siege to the occupied population, despite signs of moderation from Hamas.[18]

Unfortunately, the Palestinian Left is far too fragmented and did not articulate a program of resistance to achieve Palestinian liberation. It also failed to take serious steps to end the Hamas/Fatah divisions. As such, it has failed to provide a credible third alternative.[19] It also became clear that, in many cases, different political factions put their own interests ahead of national interests. The divisions were sometimes useful to them in that sense. Hamas can articulate grievances against Fatah for 'collaborating' with Israel and the US, thus bolstering Hamas's credentials. Fatah uses Hamas's 'outlaw' status to win concessions from Israel and support from Western countries. Each can vilify the other to gather and strengthen support for their narrow agendas. Overall, they all recognize that these tactics and divisions harm the common goals of all Palestinians: return, freedom and self-determination. But I also think many exaggerate the divisions (which obviously serve Israel's interests) and overestimate the significance of these sorry developments and entrenched positions of protagonists fighting for leadership of an occupied and colonized people. Focusing on this also ignores the positives. As Walid Salem argued, we can look at the political performance in Palestine as a glass half full or half empty. It is difficult to call it empty or full.[20]

Palestine had and continues to have a vibrant and rebellious society unafraid of change. No faction or organization is permanent in Palestinian politics. We can simply look at the succession of organizations in our history dating back to the 1920s: the Muslim Christian Societies, the Executive Committee of the Arab Congress, *Hizb Al-Istiqlal* and *Hizb Al-Difa'*, *Al-Kutla*, *Al-Islah*, *Arab Higher Committee*, *Al-Kaf Al-Aswad*, *Al-Hizb Al-Arabi*, *Hizb Asha'ab*, *'Isbat Al-Tahrrur Al-Watani*, *Jaish Al-Inkaath* and *Al-Jihad Al-Muqaddas*. There was even a short-lived Palestine government in October 1948. The only constant through the ups and downs of the political structures, and through the ebbs and flows of the armed resistance, was popular resistance. The latter emanates from a reservoir of deep cultural, linguistic, and social roots that can be boiled down to love of Palestine. It will be hard for any divisions and any oppression to extinguish the flame.

The most dramatic positive change in the factionalism of our struggle came during the uprising of 1987 when Palestine itself was put above every other consideration.[21] In the last ten years, we have seen more examples of teamwork, individual sacrifice, heroic resistance, kindness and solidarity that made life very difficult for the colonizers. I personally believe that the changes in our society during those years are irreversible, especially in respect of self-reliance and distrusting charismatic leaders. I would venture to say that those who supported the move towards partial justice in 1988 in Madrid, and later in Oslo, were most afraid of erosion in the public's trust. The actions taken did not restore that trust because that had already been superseded by a can-do attitude – a genuine popular empowerment.

While the Zionist movement has financial and military might thanks to the great powers, it has significant weaknesses in facing up to empowered native Palestinians. First, most Zionists for the first eight decades (i.e., 1880–1960s) were Europeans who had used a religious connection to Palestine to acquire a base but had otherwise mixed agendas and no clear picture of the future. Their attitude towards non-Jews was simply that native Palestinians do not belong in Eretz Yisrael. Transfer was the leitmotif and the program unfolded after the British appointed a Zionist to rule Palestine.

To convince Jews that they are not safe unless they have their own state, the Zionist program went to extremes and thus spawned local resistance. Zionists became convinced that the land must be 'redeemed' as Jewish and that natives are 'vermin' that had infested this land that consequently had to be cleansed (*nichsayon* in Hebrew). This left no doubt in the minds of colonial Zionists and the native Palestinians that it is an 'existential struggle': them or us. After Israel was established, many Israeli Jews came to realize the system is not sustainable; Palestinians cannot be expected to disappear and Ben-Gurion's statement that 'the old [Palestinians] will die and the young will forget' was only half-true. The growth of the Israeli anti-Zionist and post-Zionist movements among Jews was directly related to the inherent weakness of Zionism as an ideology.

We cannot deny that the Zionist movement grew rapidly, first as fortified *Yishuv* communities and later as a heavily armed 'live-by-the-sword' fortress of Israel. But this also created heavy dependency on warfare to achieve the goal of subjugating any resistance and maintaining the colonial apartheid system. The nature of warfare evolved and Israel was not facing armies, but increasingly mobile resistance fighters in addition to the longstanding popular resistance. The strategies Israeli politicians adopted were complex and beyond the scope of this book. Our focus is popular resistance which faced Israel's increasingly barbaric, sometimes erratic, sometimes sophisticated forms of oppression. The deployment of excessive violence on occasion as a means of reining in Palestinian resistance continues to backfire and Palestinians find new forms of resistance.[22]

We have shown clear evidence to support what Jamal Juma stated: 'a choice that will be sufficient to upset all the formulas is the Palestinian people'.[23]

Today, even with the fifth strongest army in the world, Israel as a colonial settler state is vulnerable. Demographics continue to shift against the racist Zionist idea of maintaining a 70 percent Jewish Israel. In a globalized world, Israel's economy is susceptible to pressure from outside and within by the nature of its mutant structure.[24]

The Palestinian BDS movement stated:

What Israel does have in common with apartheid South Africa's economy is the dependence upon export markets, constant sources of foreign investment and financing. Israel also maintains core identifiable trades that may be targeted. Moreover, it relies on support from countries whose public has the potential to sympathize with the Palestinian cause and recognize the BDS call … With Israel it is clear that with capital investment sanctions, a drop in foreign direct investment, or a climate in which investor confidence is lowered, that the structures which sustain growth and production will weaken. Whereas Israel was previously characterized by its isolation during the 1960s and 1970s, and relied upon German reparation and US aid to manage deficits, it has today a highly globalized economy susceptible to similar challenges that South Africa faced in the mid 1980s from a global mass movement promoting the BDS call.[25]

Unfortunately, the 'normalization' forces in the Arab world and abroad are strong and have been boosted by the Camp David Accords of 1978–79 and the Oslo Accords of 1993–94, which normalized the occupation and left Israel with little cost to its continued occupation and colonization of our lands. In fact, Israeli governments developed a system whereby they profited from the occupation and from denying other basic rights, including the right of return.

There are reasons to be optimistic. Israeli arrogance and over-reach has resulted in increased resistance. Palestinian popular resistance hastens the inevitable demise of an unsustainable colonial settler project. The growth of the movement is staggering. There are now insufficient places in training sessions for nonviolence held in Palestinian institutions.[26] It is also notable that more emphasis is now on collective leadership and less reliance is placed on charismatic leaders. Leadership in a civil rights or popular resistance movement is best not vested in charismatic individuals but in the collective.[27] Israel's attempts to crush popular resistance increased in 2009[28] because in that year there was no other organized form of resistance; Palestinian factions had suspended armed resistance for three years after Hamas decided to enter the political elections of 2006. Yet, the local popular resistance is rising to the challenge.

The lessons of the past show that when popular resistance increased the cost of the occupation, divisions were created within the Israeli society that worked to advance Palestinians' quest for peace with justice. This happened most effectively in the uprising of 1987–91. The Oslo Accords undermined these tactics and worked to reverse the accomplishments and strengthen Israeli society in regards to their potential for getting away with 'deals' that deny Palestinian rights and maintain Israel's control and expansionism.

Another factor is that this conflict is more internationalized than any other in history and shaped not just by the natives and the Jewish communities that came from abroad but by powerful actors beyond. Those included Britain and France in the early part of the twentieth century and the US and the USSR after 1948, and of course the Arab countries. Most of these outside actors caused significant damage. Internationalization is a double-edged sword; on the one hand it gave the Balfour Declaration and US sponsorship of Israel, but on the other, it resulted in international law and the International Solidarity Movement.

SUMMARY OF LESSONS LEARNED

We can reach some generalizations from studying the history of popular resistance in Palestine and elsewhere:

a) Colonial situations, especially those that strip people of their lands and homes, by nature involve the use of violence against the population. Such colonial situations generate resistances that are recognized as legitimate in international law. That resistance is a bell-shaped curve. A small portion is collaborative, most of it nonviolent, some of it violent and some of it extremely violent. As any statistician can tell you, eliminating a portion of the curve causes it to renormalize in short order, whether what you eliminate is those who engage in violence or nonviolence.

b) The violence of the colonizers always kills many times more natives than colonial settler populations. For example the ratio of civilians killed is 10:1 (Palestinian: Israeli) to >100:1 (European settlers: Native Americans).

c) Having a political strategy ahead of engaging in nonviolent resistance may seem important, but all the Palestinian uprisings (1920–21, 1929, 1936, 1987 and 2000) were spontaneous and without an overall strategy or direction. Political leadership came later and in many cases was counterproductive as politicians either tried to end the uprising or use it for narrow interests.

d) Popular resistance can succeed locally with strategy and direction as we saw in Bil'in. Without it, it fails. An example of this is when Hanna Seniora asked residents of Arab East Jerusalem to participate in municipal elections when most of them were convinced that participation would legitimize the illegal annexation.[29]

e) The struggle for freedom, whether armed or unarmed, requires clear communication both within and without the oppressed group. Our goals must be clear and reasonable. In the case of Palestine, the right to return to our homes and lands, the right to live in equality and the right to self-determination are all reasonable and rational and can be explained to friend or foe. How we get there is integral. The ends do not justify any means, and the means are critically linked to an outcome that we can all live with as human beings. In 2005, Palestinian civil society came up with a call to action that articulated Palestinians just demands and requested the solidarity and support of the international community along the same lines extended to people in South Africa who struggled under another apartheid regime. The growth of the movement since then is a direct testament to the clarity of the goals and the methods that it called for.

f) While few ideologues tried to portray Palestinians as either falling into the camp that supports violent resistance and those that support nonviolence, the polls indicate that the majority support both.[30] In the decades of the struggle against Zionism, a classic evolution of violent and nonviolent resistance has emerged that is no different from those seen in Algeria and South Africa. Perhaps we have witnessed far more diversity among groups and tactics than those other countries (see, for example, the description of the dozens of Palestinian groups and organizations formed to resist the Zionist colonization).[31] It is meaningless to lecture people about tactics and strategies.

It is far better to get engaged and work with the growing popular resistance movement to help accelerate changes already taking place.

g) Popular resistance was very effective in extracting recognition of Palestinian rights even though this was partial in some periods (e.g., after the 1936 and 1987 uprisings).

h) Palestinians resist by simply living in their homes, going to school, eating and living because the occupation wants all Palestinians to leave the country to give Israel maximum geography with minimum native demography. When the Palestinian shepherds in Atwani village continued to go to their pastures despite repeated attacks by settlers, even attempts to poison their sheep, that was nonviolent resistance. When Palestinians walk to school while being spat on, kicked and beaten by settlers and soldiers, that is nonviolent resistance. When Palestinians stand in line for hours at checkpoints to reach hospitals, farms, work, schools or to visit their friends, that is nonviolent resistance. Palestinians have resisted by countless other ways as detailed in this book.

i) The vast majority of the popular resistance detailed in this book originated from the bottom up. Political parties and leadership are usually caught off-guard by the start of new uprisings and the new resistance methods. Some leaders try to ride the wave and others try to stop it. Movements may also evolve into political initiatives.

j) From the beginning, there were struggles between camps that favored cooperation with the occupiers in the hope of getting something and those who favor confrontation and non-cooperation. The camps at one time reflected family lines (e.g., the Nashashibis, Dajanis and Husseinis in the 1920s) or along broader political lines (e.g., the political parties of the early twenty-first century). This is a natural phenomenon of resistance to colonial rule, and ending colonial rule has never happened exclusively by cooperation or non-cooperation. Thus: Palestinians may need to [actually did] act simultaneously within distinct loci of power (currently existing or yet to be formed) both to check the power of their own political leadership and to sustain the momentum of the struggle.[32]

k) There was always popular resistance in Palestine, but the intensity sometimes increased and sometimes weakened due to external and internal factors; an ebb and flow that occurred every 9–15 years on average. It has succeeded in thwarting many

244 POPULAR RESISTANCE IN PALESTINE

Zionist programs that aimed to turn the country into a Jewish state at the expense of the native people.

l) Increasingly, the Palestinian popular resistance has come to involve internationals, including Israelis, to positive and energizing effect.[33]

m) The boycott, divestment, and sanctions campaign has grown logarithmically over the past few years and holds great promise for the future (Chapter 13).

n) Individuals can change and adopt a nonviolent lifestyle even after spending years in armed struggle.[34]

o) Societies are evolving in a direction that make military confrontation less acceptable and military might increasingly irrelevant. The cost of war has become unacceptable in an era of 2-ton bombs, nuclear, biological and chemical weapons. Having military superiority has become less likely to produce the results political leaders desire: take the quagmire of the US in Iraq and Afghanistan or the failure of Israel's massive attack on Lebanon in summer 2006 and Gaza in December 2008–January 2009.

LOOKING AHEAD

The history cited above, and links and resources appended to each chapter, show that popular resistance continues to evolve and adapt despite decades of violent suppression and ethnic cleansing and decades of being ignored or vilified in the Western media. Following the adage 'think globally, act locally' we must remember that actions start with ourselves and in our local communities. Looking forward, we note certain criteria that characterize effective local actions:

- Activist preparation: Basic background information should be provided to all key participants. Reading the history of popular resistance provides inspiring examples that give activists a more optimistic outlook. In the age of the internet, acquiring information (and hence power) has become far easier.
- Careful, clear and achievable objectives: Not understanding what we aim for or having conflicting objectives within the group of activists can frustrate action. Much of this can be avoided by early preparation and discussion. Sometimes trial and error and learning on the job are unavoidable. Knowing the specific objectives permits a measure of proximal success, as well as fine-tuning and productive work to improve in the next event.

- Defining whom the action is directed towards: Activists should discuss what their goals are in relation to the audience. A demonstration's audience can be passers-by, the 'authorities', the media, the public at large, the event participants, the soldiers and police confronting it, or a combination of these.
- Maintenance of open-minded, peaceful and yet direct perspectives: Our goal is to convince those who oppress us, those who oppress others, those who support the oppression and those who are indifferent that there is another way. This is not a zero-sum game where our gains are someone else's losses. No matter how disinterested or how deeply involved in unjust and violent systems people are, our goal is to succeed in our resistance in positive ways.[35]
- Willingness to sacrifice is critical, as Mubarak Awad put it: 'The greatest enemy to the people and the most powerful weapon in the hands of the authorities is fear. Palestinians who can liberate themselves from fear and who will boldly accept suffering and persecution without fear or bitterness or striking back have managed to achieve the greatest victory of all. They have conquered themselves, and all the rest will be much easier to accomplish.'[36]

The words of George Antonius written over 70 years ago remain true about the way forward:

No lasting solution of the Palestine problem is to be hoped for until the injustice is removed. Violence, whether physical or moral, cannot provide a solution. It is not only reprehensible in itself: it also renders an understanding between Arabs, British and Jews increasingly difficult of attainment. By resorting to it, the Arabs have certainly attracted an earnest attention to their grievances, which all their peaceful representations in Jerusalem, in London and in Geneva had for twenty years failed to do. But violence defeats its own ends; and such immediate gains as it may score are invariably discounted by the harm which is inseparable from it. Nothing but harm can come of the terror raging in Palestine; but the wise way to put an end to it is to remove the causes which have brought it about. The fact must be faced that the violence of the Arabs is the inevitable corollary of the moral violence done to them, and that it is not likely to cease, whatever the brutality of the repression, unless the moral violence itself were to cease. *To those who look ahead, beyond the smoke-screen of legend*

*and propaganda, the way to a solution is clear: it lies along the
path of ordinary common sense and justice. There is no room
for a second nation in a country which is already inhabited,
and inhabited by a people whose national consciousness is fully
awakened and whose affection for their homes and countryside
is obviously unconquerable.* (emphasis added)[37]

Activists continue to work diligently for a peaceful and just
future behind the scenes and 'beyond the smokescreen of legend
and propaganda'. I have had the privilege in the past two years to
participate with hundreds of these unsung heroes on the ground
and have observed at first hand their sacrifices, humility and above
all their amazing persistence despite the odds and challenges. Eyad
Bornat and colleagues of Bil'in still go out every week demonstrating
against the apartheid wall. Having been injured and arrested many
times, Bornat does not speak about himself. When we ask how
we can help, he mentions the last people injured or jailed whose
families may need help. Awad Abu-Swai of the Popular Committees
in the Bethlehem district works with the Ministry of Agriculture
to help landowners reclaim their land and protect threatened land
by rehabilitation and tree planting. He spends more than half his
income on travel, but there is no activity that he is invited to which
he does not attend. I saw him on numerous occasions speaking to
soldiers and officers in a calm but assertive voice about what is going
on and why we will do the action with or without their approval.
George Nimr Rishmawi of Beit Sahour works hard in a group that
on principle and, in my presence, rejected a direct offer of $20,000
in US aid even when the funders told him he would not have to
sign the paper that others have signed that prevents dealings with
groups the US government does not like. In meetings, he is busy
typing reports about nonviolent resistance to disseminate to the
world through IMEMC.net while still engaged in productive multi-
tasking. When I asked him if he had spent time in jail, he replied
that it was 'nothing'. Later, I learnt he spent a total of four months
in jail on two convictions as a teenager.

Lubna Masarwa spends her time shuttling between communities
in distress, whether in East Jerusalem, Gaza or Bil'in. With no
resources she spends what little money she has and all the time
needed to help in any way she can. Sami Awad of the Holy Land
Trust was roughed up in front of me and detained as we were
protesting nonviolently at settler attempts to take over yet another
hill (Ush Ghrab in the Bethlehem area). After his release and with

a broad smile on his face he simply talked about the future plans of the Holy Land Trust and popular resistance. Saed Abuhijleh works day and night for Palestine, using many tactics of popular resistance despite the pain of having lost his mother who was gunned down by Israeli soldiers in her home in Nablus. He himself was arrested, beaten, injured and humiliated by the colonial occupiers. When asked how he keeps his sanity he laughs and answers you in jocular spirit: 'Who said we are sane?' Marwa Al-Sharif spoke honestly and without bitterness to a Jewish foreign reporter, telling him that Palestinians simply want freedom and peace – this after a bullet fired by an Israeli was removed from her brain when she was an eleven year old.

And as I was arrested with villagers of Al-Walaja and together we suffered tear gas in Al-Ma'sara and Wad Rahhal and Beit Jala, I cannot help but admire the common folks who sacrificed so much in those places and many others. One can write many books to include some of the thousands of these stories of unsung heroes of Palestine, each working in his or her own way. But the beauty of the transformation over the past few decades, solidified in the uprising of 1987 and made irreversible in the popular uprising underway in villages and towns around Palestine, is that no single or even small group of heroes are leading us. Palestinians as a people who refuse to die give us millions of heroes.

Of course, as Desmond Tutu stated:

> I know that truth-telling is hard. It has grave consequences for one's life and reputation. It stretches one's faith, tests one's capacity to love, and pushes hope to the limit ... No one takes up this work on a do-gooder's whim. It is not a choice. One feels compelled into it. Neither is it work for a little while, but rather for a lifetime – and for more than a lifetime. It is a project bigger than any one life. This long view is a source of encouragement and perseverance. The knowledge that the work preceded us and will go on after us is a fountain of deep gladness that no circumstances can alter.[38]

While this book is a history of popular resistance, it is but a brief glimpse into a complex subject. Ultimately, to get a sense of popular resistance in Palestine, experience trumps knowledge. Tens of thousands of internationals have indeed had a taste (and a sense and a smell and bruises) of what millions of Palestinians have engaged in over decades. Those who cannot join us here can certainly use their knowledge to act for peace and justice. This is happening all over the world.

If we believe that we must wait for others to do something for us, we are doomed to fail, not as 'Palestinians', 'Israelis' or 'Americans', but as humans. We can find some useful guidance in our varied backgrounds, whether philosophical, religious or cultural. In the Arab-Islamic traditions we say '*Wala Yughayiur Allah Ma Biqaumen 3atta Yughaiyuru ma biAnfusihim*' (Verily, God does not change [the condition of] people until they change what is within themselves). We can draw inspiration from what millions of Palestinians have done over the past 130 years to successfully challenge and hinder the Zionist project. That project, of transforming Palestine from multi-ethnic and multi-religious society into a 'Jewish state', is destined to fail not only because of this resistance but because of its internal contradictions and increasingly apparent racism. History will not be kind to any of us if we do not do all we can to accelerate the inevitable arrival of justice which carries with it the sweet fruits of peace.

> You give but little when you give of your possessions; it is when you give of yourself that you truly give. For what are your possessions but things you keep and guard for fear you may need them tomorrow? And what is fear of need but need itself.
>
> Khalil Gibran, *The Prophet*

Appendix
Local Civil Resistance Nonviolent
Struggle Groups

Directory of some of the thousands of groups and organizations that support Palestine from abroad are listed at www.palestinefreedom.org/organizations?country=af. Here we list some 80 groups among more than 200 engaged in popular resistance in Palestine.

Adalah: www.adalah.org
The Adam Institute: www.adaminstitute.org.il
Addameer Human Rights and Prisoner's Support Association: www.addameer.org
Al-Haq: www.alhaq.org
Al-Mezan Center for Human Rights: www.mezan.org
Al-Rowwad Cultural and Theater Training Center: www.alrowwad.
 virtualactivism.net
Alternative Information Center: www.alternativenews.org
Alternative Tourism Group www.atg.ps
Anarchists Against the Wall: www.awalls.org
Arab Association for Human Rights, The: www.arabhra.org
Association for Civil Rights in Israel, The: www.acri.org.il
Association of Forty, The: www.assoc40.org
Aswat: www.aswat-palestiniangaywomen.org
BADIL Resource Center for Palestinian Residency and Refugee Rights:
 www.badil.org
Bil'in Village Popular Resistance Committee@ www.bilin-village.org;
 www.bilin-ffj.org
Birzeit University Right to Education Campaign: right2edu.birzeit.edu
BOYCOTT!: boycottisrael.info
Breaking the Silence: www.shovrimshtika.org
B'tselem: www.btselem.org
Civil Coalition for Defending the Palestinians' Rights in Jerusalem: www.ccdprj.ps
Coalition for Jerusalem: coalitionforjerusalem.blogspot.com
Coalition of Women for Peace: www.coalitionforpeace.org
Combatants for Peace: www.combatantsforpeace.org/
Dar Annadwa: www.annadwa.org
Defense for Children International-Palestine: www.dci pal.org
Global Palestine Right of Return Coalition: www.rorcoalition.org; www.badil.org
Grassroots Palestinian Anti-Apartheid Wall Campaign (Stop the Wall):
 www.stopthewall.org
Gush Shalom www.gushshalom.org
Hebron Rehabilitation Committee: www.hebronrc.org
Holy Land Trust: www.holylandtrust.org
Independent Commission for Human Rights (ICHR): www.ichr.ps

International Solidarity Movement: www.palsolidarity.org
Ir Amim: www.ir-amim.org.il/Eng
Israeli Citizens in Support of BDS: boycott-occupation.mahost.org
Israel Committee against Home Demolitions: www.icahd.org/eng
Ittijah:The Union of Arab Community Based Organizations: www.ittijah.org
Jerusalem Legal Aid & Human Rights Center: www.mosaada.org
Joint Advocacy Initiative between the YMCA and YWCA: www.jai-pal.org
Library on Wheels for Nonviolence and Peace Association: www.lownp.com
Maaber: www.maaber.org
Machsom Watch machsomwatch.org
Mandela Institute for Human Rights: www.mandela-palestine.org
Matzpun, Israel Campaign: www.matzpun.com/
Neve Shalom/Wahet Asalam: nswas.org
Nilin Village Popular Resistance Committee: www.nilin-palestine.org
Nonviolence International: www.nonviolenceinternational.net
Occupation Magazine: www.kibush.co.il
Occupied Palestine and Golan Heights Advocacy Initiative: www.opgai.net
Open Bethlehem: www.openbethlehem.org
Open Shuhada Street Campaign: openshuhadastreet.org
Palestinian Boycotts, Divestments and Sanctions Movement: bdsmovement.net
Palestine Center for Human Rights: www.pchrgaza.org
Palestinian Campaign for Academic and Cultural Boycott of Israel: www.pacbi.org
Palestinian Center for Rapprochement between People: www.rapprochement.org;
    www.PCR.PS
Palestine Heritage Center: www.palestineheritagecenter.com
Palestinian Human Rights Monitoring Group: www.phrmg.org
Palestinians and Israelis for Nonviolence: pinv.org
Palestinian Non-Governmental Organizations Network: www.pngo.net
Palestinian Prisoners' Society: www.ppsmo.org
Parents' Circle/Families Forum, The: www.theparentscircle.com
Popular Struggle Coordinating Committee: popularstruggle.org
Rabbis for Human Rights: www.rhr.israel.net
Rebuilding Alliance, The: www.rebuildingalliance.org
Regional Association of the Unrecognized Villages: rcuv.wordpress.com/about-
    the-rcuv
Right to Education Campaign: right2edu.birzeit.edu
Right to Enter Campaign www.righttoenter.ps
Sabeel Ecumenical Liberation Theology Center: www.sabeel.org
Sawt Al-Amel (The Laborer's Voice): www.laborers-voice.org
Shabakat Al-Muqata'a Al-Sha'biya: www.whyusa.net
Ta 'ayush: www.taayush.org
Tent of Nations: www.tentofnations.org
Union of Palestinian Medical Relief Committees: www.upmrc.org
Union of Palestinian Women's Committees: www.upwc.org/E_Home.htm
Yesh Din: www.yesh-din.org
Yesh-Gvul: www.yesh-gvul.org
Wi'am: Palestinian Conflict Resolution Center: www.alaslah.org
Women's Center for Legal Aid and Counseling: www.wclac.org
Zochrot: www.zochrot.org

Notes

CHAPTER 1

1. Martin Luther King, Jr., 'A proper sense of priorities', speech, Washington, DC, February 6, 1968.
2. Jesse L. Jackson, Sr., open letter to Yasser Arafat, National Council of Churches, May 19, 2002, www.ncccusa.org/news/02news50.html. Accessed September 19, 2009.
3. www.whitehouse.gov/the_press_office/Remarks-by-the-President-at-Cairo-University, June 4, 2009. Accessed December 23, 2009.
4. See Uri Dan, *To the Promised Land: The birth of Israel*, New York: Doubleday, 1988; Benjamin Netanyahu, *A Place Among the Nations: Israel and the world*, New York: Bantam Books, 1993; Yaacov Lozowick, *Right to Exist: A moral defense of Israel's wars*, New York: Doubleday, 2003; Howard M. Sachar, *A History of Israel: From the rise of Zionism to our time*. New York: Alfred A. Knopf, 2007.
5. See Philip Khuri Hitti, *History of Syria: Including Lebanon and Palestine*, Piscataway, NJ: Georgias Press, 2002; Albert Habib Hourani, *A History of the Arab Peoples*, Cambridge, MA: Belknap Press of Harvard University Press, 2003; Edward Said, *The Question of Palestine*, London: Vintage Press, 1992; Mustafa Murad Al-Dabbagh, *Biladuna Falastin [Our Country Palestine]*, part 1, Beirut: Dar Al-Tali'a, 1965 (first published 1947); Agustin Velloso de Santistiban, 'One hundred years of conflict: a bibliographical view', *Palestine-Israel Journal*, 4(3/4), 1997.
6. Johan Galtung, *Nonviolence and Israel/Palestine*. Honolulu: Institute for Peace, University of Hawaii, 1989.
7. Phil Ackerman and James Duvall, *A Force More Powerful: A century of nonviolent conflict*, New York: St. Martin's Press, 2000.
8. Mary Elizabeth King, *A Quiet Revolution: The first Palestinian intifada and nonviolent resistance*, New York: Nation Books, 2007.
9. Joost Hiltermann, 'Limitations of ideology: review of *A Quiet Revolution: The first Palestinian intifada and nonviolent resistance*', *Journal of Palestine Studies*, 37(2), January 2008, pp. 108–9.
10. Adam Heribert and Kogila Moodley, *Seeking Mandela: Peacemaking between Israelis and Palestinians*, London: UCL Press, 2005.
11. See, for an example of this genre of work, Ruth Margolies Beitler, *The Path to Mass Rebellion: An analysis of two intifadas*, Lanham, MD: Lexington Books, 2004.
12. Aimee Ginsburg, 'Gandhi's olive country', *Outlook India*, March 17, 2008: 22–8. www.outlookindia.com/article.aspx?236980. Accessed September 20, 2009.
13. Abdul Jawad Saleh, 'The Palestinian nonviolent resistance movement', in Nancy Stohlman and Laurieann Aladin (eds), *Live from Palestine: International and Palestinian direct action against the Israeli occupation*, Cambridge, MA: South End Press, 2003, pp. 49–52.

14. Mohammed Omar Hamadeh, *A'lam Falastine: Min Al-Qarn Al-Sabe' Hatta Al-Qarn Al-Ishreen* [*Notables of Palestine: From the seventh to the twentieth century AD*], Damascus: Dar Qutaibah, 1985.
15. Ackerman and Duvall, *A Force More Powerful*.
16. Howard Zinn, *A People's History of the United States*, New York: Harper Collins, 1980.
17. Idelbar Avelar, *The Letter of Violence: Essays on narrative, ethics, and politics*, New York: Palgrave Macmillan, 2004.
18. Dale Peterson and Richard Wrangham, *Demonic Males: Apes and the origins of human violence*, New York: Mariner Books and Houghton Mifflin Harcourt, 1997. And compare Frans de Waal and Brian Ferguson, in William L. Ury (ed.), *Must We Fight? From the battlefield to the schoolyard – a new perspective on violent conflict and its prevention.* New York: John Wiley & Sons, 2001.
19. Avelar, *The Letter of Violence*, p. 10.
20. Ran HaCohen, 'The Palestinian Gandhi', *Global Research*, May 4, 2005, www.globalresearch.ca/index.php?context=va&aid=164. Accessed December 23, 2009.
21. Jean-Marie Muller, 'Stratégie de l'action nonviolente', transl. Mary Touq, *Harakat Huqook Alnas*, Beirut: Aljmiza, 1999, p. 21.
22. Stanford Prison experiment: www.prisonexp.org.
23. William J. Thomson, 'The case of the Palestinian nonviolent direct action', July 26, 2002. qumsiyeh.org/thomsononnonviolence. Accessed September 19, 2009.
24. Paul Virilio, *Pure War: Interviews with Sylvère Lotinger*, New York: Semiotext, 1997, p. 28.
25. Robert A. Pape, *Dying to Win: The strategic logic of suicide terrorism*, New York: Random House, 2005; Nadia Taysir Dabbagh, *Suicide in Palestine*, New York: Olive Branch Press, 2005.
26. Khalid Al-Kashtini, *Nahwa Al-Launf: Al-Mukawama Al-Madaniya 'Abr Al-Tareekh* [*Towards Nonviolence: Civil resistance across history*], Amman: Dar Al-Karmel, 1984, p. 336.
27. Al-Kashtini, *Nahwa Al-Launf*, p. 23.
28. Munib Younan, *Witnessing for Peace: In Jerusalem and the world*. Minneapolis, MN: Fortress Press, 2003, p. 42.
29. Khalid Kishtainy, 'Nonviolence and "civilian jihad"', *Common Ground News*, www.commongroundnews.org/article.php?id=21078&lan=en&sid=0&sp=1. Accessed September 20, 2009.

CHAPTER 2

1. Martin Luther King, Jr., Acceptance speech for the Nobel Peace Prize, nobelprize.org/nobel_prizes/peace/laureates/1964/king-acceptance.html.
2. Hendrik Verwoerd, the architect of apartheid in South Africa, stated that 'Israel, like South Africa, is an apartheid state', *Rand Daily Mail*, November 23, 1961; Uri Davis, *Israel: An apartheid state*, London: Zed Books, 1987; Marwan Bisharah, *Palestine/Israel: Peace or apartheid: Occupation, terrorism and the future*, London: Zed Books, 2002; Desmond Tutu, 'Apartheid in the Holy Land', *Guardian*, April 29, 2002, www.guardian.co.uk/world/2002/apr/29/comment. Accessed September 20, 2009.

3. Martin Luther King, Jr., letter to Jimmy Bishai, January 7, 1957, qumsiyeh. org/martinlutherking. Accessed December 20, 2009.

4. Mohandas (Mahatma) Gandhi, 'The Jews', *Harijan*, July 21, 1946; and 'Palestine', *Harijan*, July 21, 1946, www.gandhiserve.org/information/ writings_online/articles/gandhi_jews_palestine.html. Accessed September 20, 2009.

5. David K. Shipler, *Arab and Jew: Wounded spirits in a promised land*, New York: Penguin Books, 2002, p. 216; 'Former Israeli army chief drowns', *BBC News*, November 23, 2004, news.bbc.co.uk/1/hi/world/middle_east/4034765. stm. Accessed December 22, 2009.

6. Amnesty International, 'Developing a human rights agenda for peace', March 26, 2001, www.amnestyusa.org/document.php?id=F631E2C3C616E1FB80 256A1C003D4C41&lang=e. Accessed September 20, 2009.

7. 'The Freedom Charter', Adopted at the Congress of the People, Kliptown, June 26, 1955, www.anc.org.za/ancdocs/history/charter.html. Accessed September 20, 2009.

8. Mazin Qumsiyeh, *Sharing the Land of Canaan: Human rights and the Israeli-Palestinian struggle*. London: Pluto Press, 2004.

9. Mazin Qumsiyeh, 'True peace based on human rights versus the endless "peace process" based on lies', in Moises Salinas and Hazza Abu Rabia (eds), *Resolving the Israeli-Palestinian Conflict: Perspectives on the peace process*, New York: Cambria Press, 2009; Karma Nabulsi, 'Justice as the way forward', in Jamil Hilal (ed.), *Where Now For Palestine?* London and New York: Zed Books, 2007.

CHAPTER 3

1. www.un.org/en/documents/udhr.

2. Francis Anthony Boyle, *Palestine, Palestinians and International Law*, Atlanta, GA: Clarity Press, 2003; Izz Al-Din Foudi, *Al-Ihtilal Al-Israeli wa Al-Moqawama fi Du' Al-Qanoon Al-Duwaly Al-'Am* [*Israeli Occupation and Palestinian Resistance in General International Law*], Beirut: PLO Research Center, 1969.

3. Foudi, *Al-Ihtilal Al-Israeli*, p. 125.

4. Hans Lebrecht, *Ha Palestinaim – Avar veHoveh* [*The Palestinians – Past and present*], Israel: Tel-Aviv University Publishers, 1987, in Hebrew, p. 219, translated by Lebrecht and shared over the internet on a listserve of Israelis, April 3, 2002, peacepalestine.blogspot.com/2006/06/hans-lebrecht-right-to-resistance.html. Accessed December 22, 2009.

5. Young India, *Collected Works of Mahatma Gandhi*, November 8, 1920, vol. 21, New Delhi: Ministry of Information and Broadcasting, Government of India, pp. 133–4, cited in Mary Elizabeth King, *A Quiet Revolution: The first Palestinian intifada and nonviolent resistance*, New York: Nation Books, 2007, p. 21.

6. King, *A Quiet Revolution*, p. 280.

7. www.combatantsforpeace.org; www.refusersolidarity.net; www.yeshgvul. org. Accessed December 3, 2009.

8. Henry David Thoreau, 'On the duty of civil disobedience' (original title: 'Resistance to civil government', 1849), publicliterature.org/books/civil_disobedience/xaa.php. Accessed December 3, 2009.

9. The Papers of Martin Luther King, Jr., Vol. II: 'Rediscovering Precious Values', July 1951–November 1955, mlkpp01.stanford.edu/index.php/kingpapers/article/volume_ii_rediscovering_precious_values_july_1951_november_1955. Accessed December 22, 2009.

10. Gene Sharp, 'The role of power in nonviolent resistance', in Saad Eddin Ibrahim (ed.), *Al-Mukawema Al-Madaniya Fi Al-Nidhal Al-Siyasee* [*Civil Resistance in the Political Struggle*], Amman: Muntada Al-Fikr Al-Arabi, 1988, pp. 9–23.

11. Jonathan Kuttab and Mubarak Awad, 'Nonviolent resistance in Palestine: pursuing alternative strategies', Information briefing 29, Washington, DC: The Jerusalem Fund, 2002.

12. Khaled Al-Qashtini *Nahwa Alla Unf: Almukawama almadiniya abr altarikh* [*Towards Nonviolence: Civil resistance through history*], Amman: Dar al Karmel Publishing, 1984, p. 39.

13. Basil H. Liddel Hart, *Defense of the West*, London: Greenwood Publishing, 1950, p. 55, cited in Khaled Alqashtini, *Nahwa Alla Unf*, p. 27.

14. Ran Hacohen, 'The Palestinian Gandhi', *Global Research*, May 4, 2005, www.globalresearch.ca/index.php?context=va&aid=164. Accessed December 22, 2009.

15. www.qumsiyeh.org/honorlist. Accessed December 3, 2009.

16. Howard Zinn, *A People's History of the United States: 1492–Present*, New York: HarperPerennial, 2003.

17. 'Analysis: Palestinian suicide attacks', BBC News, January 29, 2007. news.bbc.co.uk/2/hi/middle_east/3256858.stm. Accessed December 3, 2009.

18. pinv.org/article2.html. Accessed December 3, 2009.

CHAPTER 4

1. Cited in Thomas Baylis, *How Israel Was Won: A concise history of the Arab-Israeli conflict*, Lanham, MD: Lexington Books, 1999, p. 3.

2. Suad Dajani, 'Al-Muqawama Al-Madaniya Fi Al-Dhiffa Al-Gharbiya' [Civil resistance in the West Bank], in Saad Eddin Ibrahim (ed.), *Al-Muqawema Al-Madaniya Fi Al-Nidhal Al-Siyasee* [*Civil Resistance in the Political Struggle*], Amman: Muntada Al-Fikr Al-Arabi, 1988, p. 89.

3. Munib Younan, *Witnessing for Peace: In Jerusalem and the world*, Minneapolis, MN: Fortress Press, 2003, pp. 77–8.

4. Muhammad Abu-Nimer, *Allaunf wa Sun' Al-Salam Fi Al-Islam*, Amman: Al-Ahliya Linnashr, 2007, p. 40.

5. Abu-Nimr, *Allaunf*, p. 70.

6. Sahih Muslim, *Kitab Al-Iman* [*The Book of Faith*], Dar Alwatan, 1997, Book 001, Hadith 0079.

7. Mubarak Awad and Abdul Aziz Said, 'The power of nonviolence', *Nonviolent Change Journal*, XVII(2), Winter 2003.

8. Abu-Nimr, *Allaunf*, p. 47.

9. Abu-Nimr, *Allaunf*, p. 52.

10. Mohammed Abu-Nimer, 'Nonviolence in the Islamic context', *Common Ground*, January 1, 2000, www.commongroundnews.org/article.php?id=2095. Accessed December 22, 2009.

11. Eknath Easwaran, *A Man to Match His Mountains: Badshah Khan, nonviolent soldiers of Islam*. Petaluma, CA: Nilgiri Press, 1984.

12. Abu-Nimer, *Allaunf*, pp. 48–50.
13. Abu-Nimer, *Allaunf*, pp. 50–1.
14. Abu-Nimer, *Allaunf*, pp. 234–5.
15. Abu-Nimer, *Allaunf*, p. 236.

CHAPTER 5

1. *Falastin*, April 29, 1914; also cited in Abdel Wahhab Al-Kayyali, *Tarikh Falastin Al-Hadith* [*Modern History of Palestine*], Beirut: Almu'assasa Al-Arabiyya Liddirasat Wa Alnashr, 1990, pp. 66–7.
2. Baruch Kimmerling and Joel S. Migdal, *The Palestinian People: A history*, Cambridge, MA: Harvard University Press, 2003, pp. 8–14.
3. Martin Sicker, *Reshaping Palestine: From Muhammad Ali to the British Mandate, 1831–1922*, Westport, CT: Praeger, 1999, pp. 20–1.
4. Abd Al-Wahhab Kayyali (transl.), *Palestine: A modern history*. London: Croom Helm, 1978, p. 11.
5. Al-Kayyali. *Tareekk Falasteen*, p. 39.
6. Mazin Qumsiyeh, *Sharing the Land of Canaan: Human rights and the Israeli Palestinian struggle*, London: Pluto Press, 2004, p. 69.
7. Awni Farsakh, *Juthoopr Al-Tahaddi wa Al-Istijaba fi Alsira' Al-Arabi Al-Sahyouni: Al-Sira' wa Qawaninu Aldhabita* [*The Roots of the Challenge and Response in the Arab Zionist Struggle and its Guiding Laws, 1799–1949*], Beirut: Markiz Dirasat Al-Wihda Al-Arabiyya, 1995, pp. 86–8.
8. Farsakh, *Juthoopr Al-Tahaddi*, pp. 91–4.
9. Salwa Alamad, *Malameh Alwade' Alektsadi wa Alejtma'e fi Falastine Hata Nehayet Alharb Ala'lamia Alola* [*Glimpses of the Economic and Social Situation in Palestine until the End of the First World War*], Sho'on Falstenia, 1981, pp. 114–16.
10. Farsakh, *Juthoopr Al-Tahaddi*, pp. 203–4.
11. Sicker, *Reshaping Palestine*, p. 29.
12. Beshara Doumani, 'Rediscovering Ottoman Palestine: writing Palestinians into history', in Ilan Pappé (ed.), *The Israel/Palestine Question*, London: Routledge, 1999, p. 19.
13. Rashid Khalidi, *Palestinian Identity: The construction of modern national consciousness*, New York: Columbia University Press, 1997, pp. 112–13 and references therein.
14. Mustafa Murad Al-Dabagh, *Biladna Falastine*, Beirut: Dar Altalia, 1965 (first published 1947), pp. 51–2.
15. Abdullah S. Schleifer, 'The life and thought of 'Izz-id-Din al-Qassam: preacher and mujahid', *Islamic Quarterly*, 22(2), 1979, p. 70.
16. Kayyali, *Palestine*, p. 16; Neville J. Mandel, *The Arabs and Zionism before World War I*, Berkeley, CA: University of California Press, 1976, pp. 35–7.
17. Kayyali, *Palestine*, p. 17.
18. Khalidi, *Palestinian Identity*.
19. Kayyali, *Palestine*, p. 18.
20. Elias Shufani, *Al-Mowjaz fi Tareekh Falastine Al-Seyasi – Month fajer Altarekh Hata Sanet 1949* [*A Concise Political History of Palestine – From the dawn of history to the year 1949*], Beirut: Institute of Palestine Studies, 1996, p. 301.

21. Henry Lamans, *Al-Yahoud fi Falastine wa Mosta`mratehem* [*Jews in Palestine and Their Colonies*], Beirut: Al-Mashreq, 1899, pp. 1088–94.
22. Rashid Khalidi, 'Palestinian peasant resistance to Zionism before WWI', in Edward W. Said and Christopher Hitchens (eds), *Blaming the Victims: Spurious scholarship and the Palestinian question*, London: Verso, 2001 (first published 1988), p. 217; and www.palestinemonitor.org/spip/spip.php?article49. Accessed December 27, 2009.
23. Neguib Azoury, *Le reveil de la nation arabe dans l'Asie turque en presence des interêts et des rivalités de puissances étrangères, de la curie romaine et du patriarcat oecumenique, parties asiatique de la question d'Orient et program de La Ligue de la partie Arabe*, Paris: Plon-Nourrit et cie. Cited in Awni Farsakh, *Juthoopr*, p. 27; see also Shufani, *Al-Mowjaz fi Tareekh Falstine Al-Seyasi*, p. 301.
24. Nasri Saliba, 'Bandali Aljozi', *Falastine Althawra*, January 11, 1984. Republished in *Al-Ettehad*, February 3, 1984.
25. Izzat Tannous, *The Palestinians: Eyewitness history of Palestine under British Mandate*, New York: I.G.T. Co., 1988, pp. 21–3.
26. Neville Barbour, *Nisi Dominus: A survey of the Palestine controversy*, Beirut: Institute of Palestine Studies, 1969, pp 41–52; cited in Mary Elizabeth King, *A Quiet Revolution: The first Palestinian intifada and nonviolent resistance*, New York: Nation Books, 2007, p. 27.
27. Adnan A. Musallam, 'From wars to *nakbeh*: Developments in Bethlehem, Palestine, 1917–1949', *Al-Liqa' Journal* (Bethlehem and Jerusalem), July 30, 2008. admusallam.bethlehem.edu/publications/From_Wars_to_Nakbeh.htm. Accessed December 27, 2009.
28. Kayyali, *Tareekk Falasteen*, pp. 46–7.
29. Ibrahim Nijem, Ameen Aql and Omar Abu Al-Nasr, *Jihad Falastin Al-Arabiya* [*The Struggle of Arab Palestine*], Beirut and Ramallah: Institute of Palestine Studies, 2009, p. 161.
30. Gershon Shafir, *Land, Labor and the Origins of the Israeli-Palestinian Conflict, 1882–1914*, Berkeley, CA: University of California Press, 1996, p. 205.
31. Kayyali, *Palestine*, p. 22.
32. Shafir, *Land, Labor and the Origins of the Israeli-Palestinian Conflict*, p. 207.
33. Shufani, *Almowjaz fi Tareekh Falstine Alseyasi*, p. 302.
34. Qustandi Shomali, *Jareedat Filastine 1911–1967: Deraseh Nakdyeh wa Fahras Tareekhi* [*Filastin Newspaper 1911: A critical study and an historical index*], Jerusalem: Jerusalem Research Center, 1992.
35. Qustandi Shomali, *Jareedat Al-Karmel 1908–1941: Deraseh Nakdyeh wa Fahras Tareekhi* [*Al-Karmel Newspaper 1908–1941: A critical study and an historical index*], Jerusalem: Aliqa Center for Religious and Cultural Studies, pp. 11–13.
36. Shomali, *Jareedat Al-Karmel*, p. 40.
37. Kayyali, *Palestine*, p. 24.
38. Kayyali, *Tareekk Falasteen*, pp. 66–8.
39. Khalidi, 'Palestinian peasant resistance', pp. 220–2.
40. Khalidi, 'Palestinian peasant resistance', p. 235.
41. Farsakh, *Juthoopr Al-Tahaddi*, p. 218.
42. Akram Zueiter, *Diaries of Akram Zueiter (1935–1939)*, Beirut: Institute of Palestine Studies, 1980, pp. 38–40.
43. Farsakh, *Juthoopr Al-Tahaddi*, p. 219.

44. Mandel, *Arabs and Zionism*, p. 220.
45. Khalidi, 'Palestinian peasant resistance', p. 155.
46. Sarah Graham Brown, *Education, Repression, Liberation: The Palestinians*, WVS (UK), 1984, p. 14.
47. Abdel Majid Hamdan, *Itlalah Ala Al-Qadiya Al-Falastiniya [An Overview of the Palestinian Cause]*, Ramallah: Palestinian Center for Issues of Peace and Democracy, 2009, p. 118.

CHAPTER 6

1. Edward Said, *The Question of Palestine*, New York: Vintage Books, 1992, p. 16.
2. Donald Neff, 'It happened in November: Britain issues the Balfour Declaration', *Washington Report on Middle East Affairs*, October/November 1995, pp. 81–2; Ronald Sanders, *The High Walls of Jerusalem: A history of the Balfour Declaration and the birth of the British Mandate for Palestine*. New York: Holt, Rinehart & Winston, 1983; Samuel Landman, a noted British Zionist, also carefully articulated in 1936 the machination of the leading Zionists on this front: desip.igc.org/1939sLandman.htm. Accessed December 12–27, 2009.
3. Mazin Qumsiyeh, *Sharing the Land of Canaan: Human rights and the Israeli-Palestinian Struggle*, London: Pluto Press, 2004, p. 146.
4. Faisal Horani, *Juthoor Al-Rafdh Al-Falastini [Roots of Palestinian Rejection]*, Muwatin: Palestinian Institution for the Study of Democracy, 1983, p. 38. For the disgraceful texts of those agreements, see Abd Alwahab Kayyali, *Watha'iq Al-Muqawama Al-Falastiniya Dhid Al-Ihtilal Al-Biritani Wa Al-Sahyuniya 1918–1939 [Documents of the Palestinian Resistance against the British Occupation and Zionism 1918–1939]*, Beirut: Institute of Palestine Studies, 1968, pp. 5–7.
5. Izzat Tannous, *The Palestinians: Eyewitness history of Palestine under British Mandate*. New York: I.G.T. Co., 1988, pp. 88–93; see also Mary Christina Wilson, *King Abdullah, Britain and the Making of Jordan*, Cambridge: Cambridge University Press, 1987.
6. For a good discussion of the role of these societies, see Bayan Nuweihid Al-Hoot, *Al-Qiyadat Wal-Muassasat Al-Siyasiya Fi Falastin 1917–1948 [Political Leaders and Institutions in Palestine 1917–1948]*, Beirut: Institute of Palestine Studies, 1983.
7. Awni Farsakh, *Juthoopr Al-Tahaddi wa Al-Istijaba fi Al-Sira' Al-Arabi Al-Sahyouni: Al-Sira' wa Qawaninu Al-Dhabita 1799–1949 [The Roots of the Challenge and Response in the Arab Zionist Struggle and its Guiding Laws]*, Beirut: Markiz Dirasat Al-Wihda Al-Arabiyya, 2008, p. 301.
8. Al Hoot, *Al Qiyadat Wal Muassasat*, pp. 86–7.
9. Weizmann's report, cited in Kayyali, *Watha'iq Al-Muqawama*, p. 305.
10. Al-Hoot, *Al-Qiyadat Wal-Muassasat*, pp. 80–1.
11. Kayyali, *Watha'iq Al-Muqawama*, pp. 3–4.
12. Roselle Tekiner, Samir Abed-Rabbo and Norton Mezvinsky (eds), *Anti-Zionism: Analytical Reflections*, New York: Amana Books, 1988.
13. President Wilson speech on Independence Day, July 4, 1918, text in Tannous, *The Palestinians*, p. 72.

14. Abdel Wahhab Al-Kayyali, *Tarikh Falastin Al-Hadith* [*Modern History of Palestine*], Beirut: Almu'assasa Al-Arabiyya Liddirasat Wa Alnashr, 1990, p. 110.
15. Adnan Musallam, 'Turbulent times in the life of the Palestinian Arab press: the British era, 1917–1948', *Al-Liqa' Journal*, December 31, 2008, admusallam. bethlehem.edu/publications/Turbulent_Times.htm. Accessed December 27, 2009.
16. Tannous, *The Palestinians*, pp. 84–5.
17. Abd Al-Wahhab Kayyali, *Palestine: A Modern History*, London: Croom Helm, 1978, pp. 75–6, 84; Yeheshua Porath, *The Emergence of the Palestinian-Arab National Movement*, vol. 1, *1918–29*, London: Frank Cass, 1974, p. 86, cited in Mary Elizabeth King, *A Quiet Revolution: The First Palestinian Intifada And Nonviolent Resistance*, New York: Nation Books, 2007, p. 31.
18. Al-Hoot, *Al-Qiyadat Wal-Muassasat*, pp. 119–20.
19. Al-Hoot, *Al-Qiyadat Wal-Muassasat*, pp. 119–20; Akram Zueiter, *Diaries of Akram Zueiter (1935–1939)*. Beirut: Institute of Palestine Studies, 1980, p. 65.
20. For a summary of these events of 1920, see Farsakh, *Juthoopr Al-Tahaddi*, pp. 314–18.
21. Herbert Samuel, *Memoirs*, London: Crescent Press, 1945, p. 168; Cited in Farsakh, *Juthoopr Al-Tahaddi*, p. 325.
22. See Farsakh, *Juthoopr Al-Tahaddi*, p. 322.
23. Al-Kayyali, *Tarikh Falastin*, p. 86; Farsakh, *Juthoopr Al-Tahaddi*, p. 325; Ellen Fleischmann, *Jerusalem Women's Organizations during the British Mandate: 1920s–1930s*, Jerusalem: Palestinian Academic Society for the Study of International Affairs, 1995, p. 21.
24. Farsakh, *Juthoopr Al-Tahaddi*, p. 326.
25. Farsakh, *Juthoopr Al-Tahaddi*, pp. 335–6.
26. King, *A Quiet Revolution*, p. 33.
27. Farsakh, *Juthoopr Al-Tahaddi*, p. 33.
28. Ibrahim Nijem, Ameen Aql and Omar Abu Al-Nasr, *Jihad Falastin Al-Arabiya* [*The Struggle of Arab Palestine*], Beirut and Ramallah: Institute of Palestine Studies, 2009 (first published 1936), p. 169; May Seikaly, *Haifa: Transformation of a Palestinian Arab society, 1918–1939*, London: I. B. Taurus, 1995, pp. 163–4.
29. Baruch Kimmerling and Joel S. Migdal, The *Palestinian People: A history*, Cambridge, MA: Harvard University Press, 2003, pp. 84–5.
30. David Hirst, *The Gun and the Olive Branch: Roots of violence in the Middle East*, London: Futura, 1979 (in Arabic Riyad: Al-Rayyis For Publishing, 2003, pp. 144–5).
31. Saleh Masoud Bouyasbir, *Jihad Falastin Khilal Nisf Qarn* [*The Struggle of Palestine over Half a Century*], Palestinian Ministry of Culture, 1987, p. 120; *Al-Karmel Newspaper*, 704, April 5, 1921, p. 1.
32. *Al-Karmel Newspaper*, 704, April 5, 1921, p. 2.
33. Al-Kayyali, *Tarikh Falastin*, p. 143.
34. Bouyasbir, *Jihad Falastin*, p 121.
35. *Al-Karmel Newspaper*, 712, May 4, 1921, p. 2.
36. Tannous, *The Palestinians*, p. 117.
37. *Al-Karmel Newspaper*, 716, May 18, 1921, p. 3.
38. Bouyasbir, *Jihad Falastin*, p. 125; Tannous, *The Palestinians*, p. 120.
39. *Al-Karmel Newspaper*, 721, June 11, 1921, p. 2.

40. *Al-Karmel Newspaper,* 733, July 23, 1921, p. 3.
41. Al-Hoot, *Al-Qiyadat Wal-Muassasat,* p. 148.
42. Farsakh, *Juthoopr Al-Tahaddi,* pp. 385–6; Nijem et al., *Jihad Falastin Al-Arabiya,* p. 79.
43. Haroon Hashem Rashid, *Abu Jildeh Wa Al-Armit, Yama Kassaroo Baraneet,* Amman: Majdalawi Publishing, 2006.
44. Farsakh, *Juthoopr Al-Tahaddi,* p. 348.
45. Chaim Weizmann, *Trial and Error: The autobiography of Chaim Weizmann,* New York: Harper, 1949. p. 360.
46. For details on the Mandate resolution, see Farsakh, *Juthoopr Al-Tahaddi,* pp. 353–68.
47. Al-Kayyali, *Tarikh Falastin,* p. 166.
48. Elias Shufani, *Al-Mowjaz fi Tareekh Falstine Al-Seyasi – Munth fajer Al-Tarekh Hata Sanet 1949* [*A Concise Political History of Palestine – From the dawn of history to the year 1949*], Ramallah: Institute of Palestine Studies,1996, pp. 425–7; Neil Caplan, 'The Yishuv, Sir Herbert Samuel, and the Arab question in Palestine 1921–25', in Elie Kedourie and Sylvia Kedourie (eds), *Zionism and Arabism in Palestine and Israel,* London: Frank Cass, 1982, p. 37.
49. Shufani, *Al-Mowjaz fi Tareekh,* p. 427.
50. Farsakh, *Juthoopr Al-Tahaddi,* p. 371.
51. See, for example, Shafiq Al-Hoot's interview (in Arabic) with the Institute for Palestine Studies, www.palestine-studies.org/files/pdf/mdf/6338.pdf.in. Accessed December 27, 2009.
52. Farsakh, *Juthoopr Al-Tahaddi,* pp. 380–4.
53. 'Arabic-Jewish joint struggles prior to the partition of Palestine', www. marxist.com/MiddleEast/arab_jewish_struggles1.html. Accessed December 27, 2009; www.zen12064.zen.co.uk/books.htm. Accessed December 27, 2009.
54. Musa Budeiri, *The Palestine Communist Party 1919–1948,* London: Ithaca Press, 1979; 'The Communist movement in Palestine 1919–1949', written January 2003, modified April 2007, 321ignition.free.fr/imp/en/ana/pag_003/pag.htm. Accessed December 27, 2009.
55. Farsakh, *Juthoopr Al-Tahaddi,* p. 427; Shufani, *Al-Mowjaz fi Tareekh,* p. 427.
56. Peel Report, July 1937, p. 79, www.jewishvirtuallibrary.org/jsource/History/peel1.html. Accessed December 27, 2009.
57. Philip Mattar, *The Mufti of Jerusalem: Al-Haj Amin al-Hussaini and the Palestinian national movement,* New York: Columbia University Press, 1988, p. 17.
58. P. H. H. Massy, *Eastern Mediterranean Lands: Twenty years of life, sport, and travel,* London,: George Routledge & Son, 1928, p. 70, cited in King, *A Quiet Revolution,* p. 36; Shufani, *Al-Mowjaz fi Tareekh,* p. 430.
59. Al-Hoot, *Al-Qiyadat Wal-Muassasat,* p. 211.
60. Farsakh, *Juthoopr Al-Tahaddi,* pp. 377–8.
61. Bouyasbir, *Jihad Falastin,* pp. 149–51; Ali Mahaftha, *Al-Fikr Al-Siyasi fi Falastin: Min Nihayet Al-Hukmm Al-Othmani Ila Nihayet Al-Intidab Al-Biratani 1918–1948* [*Political Thought in Palestine: From the end of Ottoman rule to the end of the British Mandate 1918–1948*], Beirut: Arab Institute for Studies and Publishing, 2000.
62. Al-Kayyali, *Watha'iq Al-Muqawama,* pp. 67–8.

63. Faisal Horani, *Qira'a Naqdiya Li-Tareikh Al-Muqawama Al-Falastiniya* [*A Critical Reading of the History of Palestinian Resistance*], Ramallah: Bada'el: Palestinian Center for Communication, Research, and Studies, 2008.
64. Freud's letter to Chaim Koffler Keren Ha-Yassod, Vienna, February 26, 1930; www.freud.org.uk./arab-israeli.html.
65. Al-Kayyali, *Tarikh Falastin Al-Hadith*, p. 206.
66. Vincent Shean, *Personal History*, Garden City, NY: Doubleday, Doran, and Coman, 1935; Tannous, *The Palestinians*, p. 120.
67. Farsakh, *Juthoopr Al-Tahaddi*, p. 407.
68. Al-Kayyali, *Tarikh Falastin*, p. 206.
69. *Falastin*, August 9, 1930, 122–1502, p. 3.
70. *Falastin*, August 27, 1930, 137–1517, p. 3.
71. Julie M. Peteet, *Gender in Crisis: Women and the Palestinian resistance movement*, New York: Columbia University Press, 1992, pp. 42–6.
72. Matiel E. T. Mogannam, *The Arab Women and the Palestine Problem*, London: Herbert Joseph, 1937.
73. King, *A Quiet Revolution*, p. 89.
74. Nijem et al., *Jihad Falastin*, pp. 174–5.
75. Mogannam, *The Arab Women and the Palestine Problem*, p. 76.
76. King, *A Quiet Revolution*, p. 91.
77. Mogannam, *The Arab Women and the Palestine Problem*, pp. 79, 83.
78. Shabtai Teveth, *Ben-Gurion and the Arabs of Palestine*, London: Oxford University Press, 1985 (Arabic transl. Ghazi Al-Saadi, Amman: Dar Al-Jalil, 1987).
79. Farsakh, *Juthoopr Al-Tahaddi*, p. 497.
80. Al-Kayyali, *Tarikh Falastin*, pp. 224–5; Sir John Hope Simpson, 'Palestine: report on immigration, land settlement and development', *Parliament Publication*, Vol. 3686 of Cmd Palestine, the British Mandate, London: HMSO, 1930.
81. Horani, *Qira'a Naqdiya*, p. 176; Tannous, *The Palestinians*, p. 166.
82. *Falastin*, June 29, 1930, 87–1467, p. 20.
83. Horani, *Qira'a Naqdiya LiTareikh Al-Muqawama Al-Falastiniya*, pp. 113–14.
84. Farsakh, *Juthoopr Al-Tahaddi*, p. 428; Saleh Masoud Bouyasbir, *Jihad Falastin Khilal Nisf Qarn*, p. 177.
85. Abdel Wahhab Al-Kayyali, *Tarikh Falastin Al-Hadith* [*Modern History of Palestine*], Almu'assasa Al-Arabiyya Liddirasat wa Alnashr, Beirut, 1990, pp. 234–5.
86. Mahaftha, *Al-fikr Al-Siyasi*, p. 60.
87. Peel Report, July 1937, p. 79; www.jewishvirtuallibrary.org/jsource/History/peel1.html.
88. Mahaftha, *Al-fikr Al-Siyasi*, p. 109.
89. Tannous, *The Palestinians*, p. 170.
90. Al-Hoot, *Al-Qiyadat Wal-Muassasat*, p. 283.
91. Farsakh, *Juthoopr Al-Tahaddi*, p. 454.
92. Farsakh, *Juthoopr Al-Tahaddi*, p. 455.
93. Al-Kayyali, *Watha'iq Al-Muqawama*, pp. 259–61.
94. Mahaftha, *Al-fikr Al-Siyasi*, p. 67.
95. Farsakh, *Juthoopr Al-Tahaddi*, pp. 445–6.
96. Tannous, *The Palestinians*, pp. 172–3.
97. Farsakh, *Juthoopr Al-Tahaddi*, pp. 457–63.
98. Horani, *Qira'a Naqdiya*, p. 182.

CHAPTER 7

1. John F. Kennedy, White House speech, 1962.
2. Nathan Weinstock, *Le Sionisme – Contre Israël*, Paris: Maspéro, 1969, cited in Ghassan Kanafani, *The 1936–39 Revolt in Palestine*, New York: Committee for a Democratic Palestine, 1972/London: Tricontinental Society, 1980. Kanafani's book is perhaps the best on the conditions that led to the 1936–39 revolt.
3. Awda Al-Ashhab, *Safahat Min Al-Dhakira Al-Falastiniya* [*Pages from Palestinian Memory*], Ramallah: Birzeit University Publication, 1999, p. 12.
4. Saleh Masoud Bouyasbir, *Jihad Falastin Khilal Nisf Qarn* [*The Struggle of Palestine over Half a Century*], Ramallah: Palestinian Ministry of Culture, 1987, p. 198.
5. Akram Zueiter, *Diaries of Akram Zueiter (1935–1939)*, Beirut: Institute of Palestine Studies, 1980, p. 109.
6. *Falastin*, 68–1444, July 23, 1930, p. 3.
7. Susan Boyle, The *Betrayal of Palestine: The story of George Antonius*, Boulder, CO: Westview Press, 2001.
8. George Antonius, *The Arab Awakening: The story of the Arab national movement*, London: International Book Center, 1985, p. 406 (first published 1938).
9. Awni Farsakh, *Juthoopr Al-Tahaddi wa Al-Istijaba fi Al-Sira' Al-Arabi Al-Sahyouni: Al-Sira' wa Qawaninu Al-Dhabita, 1799–1949*, Beirut: Markiz Dirasat Al-Wihda Al-Arabiyya, 2008, pp. 530–1.
10. Farsakh, *Juthoopr Al-Tahaddi*, p. 531.
11. Kalkas, *Revolt of 1936*, p. 248, cited in Mary Elizabeth King, *A Quiet Revolution: The first Palestinian intifada and nonviolent resistance*, New York: Nation Books, 2007, p. 50.
12. Ibrahim Nijem, Ameen Aql and Omar Abu Al-Nasr, *Jihad Falastin Al-Arabiya* [*The Struggle of Arab Palestine*], Beirut and Ramallah: Institute of Palestine Studies, 2009, p. 189; Farsakh, *Juthoopr Al-Tahaddi*, p. 533.
13. Nijem et al., *Jihad Falastin Al-Arabiya*, p. 186.
14. Bayan Huweihid Al-Hoot, *Al-Qiyadat Wal-Muassasat Al-Siyasiya Fi Falastin 1917–1948* [*Political Leaders and Institutions in Palestine 1917–1948*]. Beirut: Institute of Palestine Studies, 1983, pp. 341–2.
15. Nijem et al., *Jihad Falastin*, p. 189.
16. Edwin Black, *The Transfer Agreement: The untold story of the secret pact between the Third Reich and Jewish Palestine*, New York: Macmillan, 1984; Lenni Brenner, *51 Documents: History of the Nazi-Zionist Collaboration*, New York: Barricade Books, 2002.
17. Taysir Jbara, *Palestinian Leader, Hajj Amin al-Husayni, Mufti of Jerusalem*. Princeton, NJ: Kingston, 1985.
18. Zueiter, *Diaries*, p. 101.
19. Nijem et al., *Jihad Falastin Al-Arabiya*, p. 190.
20. Nijem et al., *Jihad Falastin Al-Arabiya*, p. 197.
21. Nijem et al., *Jihad Falastin Al-Arabiya*, p. 179; Farsakh, *Juthoopr Al-Tahaddi*, p. 378.
22. Ted Swedenburg, *Memories of Revolt: The 1936–1939 Rebellion and the Palestinian National Past*, Little Rock, AR: University of Arkansas Press, 2003, p. 18; Faisal Horani, *Qira'a Naqdiya Li-Tareikh Al-Muqawama Al-Falastiniya* [*A Critical Reading of the History of Palestinian Resistance*]

Ramallah: Bada'el Palestinian Center for Communication, Research and Studies, , 2008, pp. 315–17; Samih Hamoudeh, *Al-Wa'i wa Al-Thawra: Dirasa Fi Hayat Wa Jihad Al-Sheikh Izz El Din Al-Qassam* [*Awareness and Revolution: A study of the life and jihad of Sheikh Izz Eddin Al-Qassam*], Jerusalem: Institute of Arab Studies, 1986.

23. Emil Tuma, *Sittoon 'Aman 'An Al-Haraka Al-Qawmiyya Al-Arabiya Al-Falastinya* [*Sixty Years of the National Arab Palestinian Movement*], np: Ibn Rushd Press, 1978, pp. 120–1.

24. Horani, *Qira'a Naqdiya*, p. 335.

25. Horani, *Qira'a Naqdiya*, pp. 339–40.

26. Farsakh, *Juthoopr Al-Tahaddi*, p. 629.

27. Farsakh, *Juthoopr Al-Tahaddi*, p. 634.

28. 'France-Palestine 70 years of resistance', azls.over-blog.com. Accessed December 27, 2009; Izzat Tannous, *The Palestinians: Eyewitness history of Palestine under British Mandate*. New York: I.G.T. Co., 1988, p. 191.

29. Farsakh, *Juthoopr Al-Tahaddi*, pp. 555–6.

30. Tannous, *The Palestinians*, p. 186.

31. Ann Mosely Lesch, 'Zionism and its impact', August 1, 2001, www.palestineremembered.com/Acre/Palestine-Remembered/Story452.html. Accessed December 27, 2009.

32. Ann Mosely Lesch, *Arab Politics in Palestine, 1917–1939: The frustration of a nationalist movement*. Ithaca, NY and London: Cornell University Press, 1979, pp. 217–21; Tannous, *The Palestinians*, p. 233.

33. Nidal Mohammed Al-Hindi, *Adwa' 'Ala Nidhal Al-Mar'a Al-Falastinyya* [*Lights upon the Struggle of the Palestinian Woman*], Amman: Dar Al-Karmel, 1995, p. 24.

34. Rashid Khalidi, 'The Palestinians and 1948: the underlying causes of failure', in E. L. Rogan and A. Schlaim (eds), *The War for Palestine: Rewriting the history of 1948*, Cambridge: Cambridge University Press. 2001.

35. Hiba Lama, 'Nonviolence is not a synonym for negotiation', October 2, 2008, PNN, english.pnn.ps/index.php?option=com_content&task=view&id=3660&Itemid=27. Accessed August 13, 2009.

36. Farsakh, *Juthoopr Al-Tahaddi*, pp. 564–5.

37. Abdel Majid Hamdan, *Itlalah Ala Alqadiya al-Falastiniya* [*An Overview of the Palestinian Cause*], Ramallah: Palestinian Center for Issues of Peace and Democracy, 2009, p. 122.

38. For reasons that are discussed in Horani, *Qira'a Naqdiya*, pp. 369–72.

39. Jonathan Dimbleby, *The Palestinians*, photographs by Donald McCullin, London: Quartet Books, 1979, p. 82.

40. Mohammed Fadhel Jamali (former Prime Minister of Iraq), 'Experiences in Arab Affairs 1943–1958', physics.harvard.edu/~wilson/Fadhel.html. Accessed July 27, 2009.

41. King, *A Quiet Revolution*, p. 57.

42. Ilan Pappé, *A History of Modern Palestine: One land, two peoples*, Cambridge: Cambridge University Press, 2006, p. 88.

43. Swedenburg, *Memories of Revolt*, p. 33.

CHAPTER 8

1. Izzat Tannous, *The Palestinians: Eyewitness history of Palestine under British Mandate*. New York: I.G.T. Co., 1988, p. 396.

2. Bayan Nuweihid Al-Hoot, *Al-Qiyadat Wal-Muassasat Al-Siyasiya Fi Falastin 1917–1948* [*Political Leaders and Institutions in Palestine 1917–1948*], Beirut: Institute of Palestine Studies, 1983, p. 469.

3. Awni Farsakh, *Juthoopr Al Tahaddi wa Al-Istijaba fi Alsira' Al-Arabi Al-Sahyouni: Al-Sira' wa Qawaninu Aldhabita* [*The Roots of the Challenge and Response in the Arab Zionist Struggle and its Guiding Laws, 1799–1949*], Beirut: Markiz Dirasat Al-Wihda Al-Arabiyya, 1905, p. 704.

4. Faisal Horani, *Juthoor Al-Rafdh Al-Falastini* [*Roots of Palestinian Rejection*], Ramallah: Muwatin, Palestinian Institution for the Study of Democracy, pp. 394–5.

5. Abdel Majid Hamdan, *Itlalah Ala Al-Qadiya Al-Falastiniya* [*An Overview of the Palestinian Cause*], Ramallah: Palestinian Center for Issues of Peace and Democracy, 2009, p. 90.

6. Tannous, *The Palestinians*, p. 386.

7. PASSIA Palestinian Personalities, www.passia.org/palestine_facts/personalities/alpha_a.htm. Accessed December 1, 2009.

8. Imad Ghayyatheh, *Al-Harakah Al-Tulabiya Al-Falastiniya: Al-Mumarasa Wa Al-Fa'ilya* [*Palestinian Student Movement: Practice and efficacy*], Ramallah: Muwatin, Palestinian Institute for the Study of Democracy, 2000; Muhammad Mustafa, *Al-Harakah Al-Tulabiya Al-'Arabiya Al-Falastiniya*, Markiz Al-Dirasat Al-Mu'asera, Um Al-Fahm, 2002.

9. Baruch Kimmerling and Joel S. Migdal, *The Palestinian People: A history*, Cambridge, MA: Harvard University Press, 2003, p. 35.

10. Odeh Al-Ashhab, *Safahat min Al-Thakera Al-Fastenia* [*Pages from the Palestinian Memory*], Ramallah: Bir Zeit University, 1999, p. 118.

11. Mousa Al-Budeiri, *Tatawer Al-Haraka Al-Omalia Fi Falastin* [*Evolution of the Labor Movement in Palestine*], Dar Ibn Khaldoun, Gaza, 1981; Adnan Al-Sabbah, 'On what can be learned', *Alwatan Voice*, May 19, 2008, pulpit. alwatanvoice.com/content-133912.html.

12. Al-Hoot, *Al-Qiyadat Wal-Muassasat*, p. 480.

13. Farsakh, *Juthoopr Al-Tahaddi*, pp. 783–4.

14. Ali Mahaftha, *Al-fikr Al-Siyasi fi Falastin: Min Nihayet Al-Hukmm Al-Othmani Ila Nihayet Al-Intidab Al-Biratani 1918–1948* [*Political Thought in Palestine: From the end of Ottoman rule to the end of the British Mandate 1918–1948*], Beirut: Arab Institute for Studies and Publishing, 2000, pp. 92–9.

15. Tannous, *The Palestinians*, pp. 387–8.

16. Abdullah Al-Tal, *Karithat Filastin: Muthakirat Abdula Al-Tal, Qaid Ma'rakat Al-Quds* [*The Calamity of Palestine: Memoirs of Abdullah Al-Tall, commander of the battle of Jerusalem*], Cairo: Dar Al-Huda, 1959.

17. Tannous, *The Palestinians*, p. 431; see also John Snetsinger, *Truman, the Jewish Vote, and the Creation of Israel*, Stanford, CA: Hoover Institute Studies, 39, 1974.

18. Mohammed Fadhel Jamali (former Prime Minister of Iraq), *Experiences in Arab Affairs 1943–1958*, physics.harvard.edu/~wilson/Fadhel.html. Accessed July 27, 2009.

19. Bahjat Abu Gharbyeh, *Mothakarat Al-Monadel Bahjat Abu Gharbyeh: Min Al-Nakbeh Ela Al-Intifada (1949–2000)*, Beirut: Arab Institution for Studies and Publishing, 2005, p. 145.

20. For details, see Ilan Pappé, *The Ethnic Cleansing of Palestine*, London: Oneworld Publications. 2006.

21. Tannous, *The Palestinians*, p. 464.
22. The declaration is reproduced in Tannous, *The Palestinians*, p. 487.
23. Nidal Mohammed Al-Hindi, *Adwa 'Ala Nidal Al-Mara'a Al-Falastinia 1903–1992 (Lights on the Struggle of Palestinian Women, 1903–1992)*, Amman: Dar Al-Karmel, 1995, pp. 34–5.
24. Joshua Landis, 'Syria in the 1948 Palestine war: fighting King Abdullah's Greater Syria plan', in Eugene Rogan and Avi Shlaim (eds), *Rewriting the Palestine War: 1948 and the history of the Arab-Israeli conflict*, Cambridge: Cambridge University Press, 2001, pp. 178–205.
25. Avi Shlaim, *Collusion across the Jordan: King Abdullah, the Zionist movement and the partition of Palestine*, New York: Columbia University Press, 1988; Tannous, *The Palestinians*; Abdullah Al-Tal, *Karithat Filastin [The Calamity of Palestine]*, Cairo: Dar Al-Qalam, 1959; Mary Christina Wilson, *King Abdullah, Britain and the Making of Jordan*, Cambridge: Cambridge University Press, 1987.
26. www.palestineremembered.com.
27. Orayb Aref Najjar, *Portraits of Palestinian Women*, Salt Lake City, UT: np, 1992, p. 30, cited in Maria Holt, *Half the People: Women, history of the Palestinian intifada*, Jerusalem: PASSIA, 1992, p. 26.
28. Shlaim, *Collusion across the Jordan*; Abdullah Al-Tal, *Karithat Filastin [The Calamity of Palestine]*, Cairo: Dar Al-Qalam, 1959.

CHAPTER 9

1. Nur Masalha, *Expulsion of the Palestinians: The concept of 'transfer' in Zionist political thought, 1882–1948*, Washington, DC: Institute for Palestine Studies, 1992; Ilan Pappé, *The Ethnic Cleansing of Palestine*, Oxford: Oneworld, 2006.
2. Public Record Office, FO 371/104778, Lt-Gen. Glubb, 'Note on Refugee Vagrancy', cited in Benny Morris, *Israel's Border Wars 1949–1956: Arab infiltration, Israeli retaliation, and the countdown to the Suez War*, London: Oxford University Press, 1997, p. 37.
3. See orders issued by Israel's southern command, cited in Morris, *Israel's Border Wars 1949–1956*, pp. 125, 129, 132.
4. David McDowall, *The Palestinians: The road to nationhood*, London: Minority Rights Group, 1995.
5. Aref Al-Aref, *Al-Nakbeh: Nakbet Beit Al-Maqdes wa Al-Ferdawas Al-Mafkod 1947–1955 [Nakba: The plight of Jerusalem and the lost paradise 1947–1955]*, Beirut: Al-Maktaba Al-Asriya, 1956.
6. Elia Zureik, *The Palestinians in Israel: A study in internal colonialism*, London: Routledge & Kegan Paul, 1979.
7. Jabril Mohammed and Wasef Nazal, *Falastiniyo 48: Nidal Mostamer 1948–1988 [Palestinians of 48: Continuous Struggle 1948–1988]*, Jerusalem: Al-Zahra Center for Studies and Research, 1990, p. 23.
8. Sabri Jiries, *Al-Arab fi Isreal [The Arabs in Israel]*, Palestine Liberation Organization Research Center, *Palestine Studies*, 14, 1967, pp. 143–5.
9. Jiries, *Al-Arab fi Isreal*, p. 139.
10. Jiries, *Al-Arab fi Isreal*, p. 95.
11. Sami Khalil Mar'i, *Arab Education in Israel*, New York: Syracuse University Press, 1978.

12. Lawrence Louër, *To be an Arab in Israel*, London: C. Hurst, 2007, p. 48.
13. Mohammed and Nazal, *Falastiniyo 48*, p. 46.
14. Qustanti Shomali, *Madkhal ela Al-Adab Al-Falastini fi Al-Mothalath wa Al-Jalil* [*Introduction to Palestinian Literature in the Triangle and the Galilee*], Bethlehem: Department of Arabic Language, Bethlehem University, 2007, p. 14.
15. Zureik, *The Palestinians in Israel*, p. 172.
16. Mohammed and Nazal, *Falastiniyo 48*, p. 45.
17. Mohammed and Nazal, *Falastiniyo 48*, p. 50.
18. Sabri Jiryis, *Al-Arab fi Israel*.
19. Mohammed and Nazal, *Falastiniyo 48*, pp. 52–3.
20. Mohammed and Nazal, *Falastiniyo 48*, pp. 54–6.
21. Ostesky-Lazar, 'Crystallization of mutual relations between Arabs and Jews in the State of Israel in the first decade 1948–1958'. PhD thesis, University of Haifa, 1996 (in Hebrew), cited in As'ad Ghanem and Mohammad Mustafa, *Al-Falatiniyon fi Isreal: Siyasat Al-Aqalliya Al-Asliya Fi Al-Dawla Al-Ithniya* [*Palestinian in Israel: The politics of the indigenous minority in the ethnic state*], Ramallah: Madar, the Palestinian Forum for Israeli Studies. 2009, p. 32.
22. Jiryis, *Al-Arab fi Israel*, p. 188.
23. Zureik, *The Palestinians in Israel*, p. 172.
24. Ghanem and Mustafa, *Al-Falatinyon fi Isreal*, p. 155; Mohammed and Nazal, *Falastiniyo 48*, p. 6.
25. Odeh Al-Ashhab, *Safahat min Al-Thakera Al-Fastenia* [*Pages from the Palestinian Memory*], Ramallah: Bir Zeit University, 1999, pp. 265–6.
26. Jiryis, *Al-Arab fi Israel*, pp. 74–5.
27. Mohammed and Nazal *Falastiniyo 48*, p. 43.
28. Ian Lustik, *Arabs in the Jewish State*, Austin, TX: University of Texas Press, 1982, pp. 127–8; see also Muhammad Mostafa, *Al-Haraka Al-Tullabiya Al-Arabiya Al-Falastiniya* [*The Arab Palestinian Student Movement*], Um Al-Fahm: Markiz Al-Dirasat Al-Mu'asara, 2002.
29. Mustafa, *Al-Haraka Al-Tullabiya*.
30. David McDowall, *Palestine and Israel: The uprising and beyond*, London: IB Tauris, 1989, p. 127.
31. Zureik, *The Palestinians in Israel*, p. 123.
32. Laurie A. Brand, *Palestinians in the Arab World: Institution building and the search for state*, New York: Columbia University Press, 1988 (in Arabic, Beirut: Institute of Palestine Studies, 1991, pp. 71–2).
33. Shahada Mousa, 'Hawl Tajribat Al-Ittihad Al-'Am Li-Talabet Falastine' [On the experience of the General Union of Palestinian Students], *Sho'on Fastenia*, 5, November 1971, p. 181.
34. Mousa, *Hawl Tajribat Al-Ittihad*, p. 182.
35. Avi Shlaim, *Collusion across the Jordan, King Abdullah, the Zionist Movement, and the Partition of Palestine*, New York: Columbia University Press, 1988, p. 139.
36. Avi Plascov, 'The Palestinians of Jordan's border', in Roger Owen (ed.), *Studies in the Economic and Social History of Palestine in the Nineteenth and Twentieth Centuries*, Carbondale and Edwardsville, IL: The Southern Illinois University Press, 1982. pp. 203–42, 208–10.

37. Ahmed Shuqeiri, *Arb'oon 'Aman Fi Al-Haya Al-Arabia wa Al-'Alamia* [*Forty Years of Arab and International Life*], Beirut: Dar Al-Nahar, 1969; and www. ahmad-alshukairy.org. Accessed December 27, 2009.

CHAPTER 10

1. Mubarak E. Awad, 'Nonviolent resistance: a strategy for the occupied territories', *Journal of Palestine Studies*, 13(4), Summer 1984, pp. 22–36.
2. Bob Hepburn, 'Wiped off the map: park funded by Canadian Jews hides ruins of Arab villages', *Toronto Star*, October 6, 1991.
3. Stuart A. Cohen and Efraim Inbar, 'A taxonomy of Israel's use of force', *Comparative Strategy*, 10, 1991, p. 129.
4. David Dean Shulman, *Dark Hope: Working for peace in Israel and Palestine*, Chicago: University of Chicago Press, 2007, p. 2.
5. Rashid Khalidi, *Palestinian Identity: The construction of common national consciousness*, New York: Columbia University Press, 1998; Ramzi Suleiman, 'On marginal people: the case of Palestinians in Israel', in John Bunzi and Benjamin Beit-Halahmi (eds), *Psychoanalysis, Identity and Ideology*. Norwell, MA: Kluwer Academic Publishers, 2002, pp. 71–84.
6. Jabril Mohammed and Wassif Nazzal, *Falastiniyo 48: Nidal Mostamer 1948–1988* [*Palestinians of 48: Continuous struggle 1948–1988*], Jerusalem: Al-Zahra Center for Studies and Research, 1990, pp. 128–31.
7. Mohammed and Nazzal, *Falastiniyo 48*, p. 82.
8. As'ad Ghanem and Mohammad Mustafa, *Al-Falatiniyon fi Israel: Siyasat Al-Aqalliya Al-Asliya Fi Al-Dawla Al-Ithniya* [*Palestinian in Israel: The politics of the indigenous minority in the ethnic state*], Ramallah: Madar, the Palestinian Forum for Israeli Studies, 2009, pp. 158–9.
9. Ghanem and Mustafa, *Al-Falatiniyon fi Israel*, pp. 172–3; Mohammed and Nazal, *Falastiniyo 48*, pp. 133–4.
10. Ghanem and Mustafa, *Al-Falatiniyon fi Israel*, pp. 166–8.
11. Said Jawad, *Al-Nohod Al-Watani Al-Falastini fi Al-Diffa wa Ghaza wa Al-Jalil 1974–1978* [*National Advancement for Palestinian in the West Bank and Gaza and the Galilee 1974–1978*], Beirut: Dar Ibn Khaldon, 1982, p. 310; Emil Tuma, *Sittoon Aman An Al-Haraka Alqawmiyya Al-Arabia Al-Falastinya* [*Sixty Years of the National Arab Palestinian Movement*], Beirut: Ibn Rush Press, 1978, p. 310.
12. Ahmad H. Sa'di, 'The Koenig Report and Israeli policy towards the Palestinian minority, 1965–1976: old wine in new bottles', *Arab Studies Quarterly*, Summer 2003.
13. Mohammed and Nazzal, *Falastiniyo 48*, pp. 86–7, 108–9.
14. Mohammed and Nazzal, *Falastiniyo 48*, pp. 83–4.
15. Mohammed and Nazzal, *Falastiniyo 48*, p. 89.
16. Mohammed and Nazzal, *Falastiniyo 48*, pp. 94–5, 158–9.
17. Mohammed and Nazal, *Falastiniyo 48*, pp. 96–7.
18. David McDowall, *Palestine and Israel: The uprising and beyond*, London: IB Tauris, 1989, p. 149.
19. Lawrence Louër, *To be an Arab in Israel*, London: C. Hurst, 2007, p. 60.
20. Louër, *To be an Arab in Israel*, p. 62.
21. Baruch Kimmerling and Joel S. Migdal, *The Palestinian People: A history*, Cambridge, MA: Harvard University Press, 2003, p. 203.

NOTES 267

22. www.palestineonly.net/vb/archive/index.php/t-2786.html. Accessed December 31, 2009.
23. Hatim Kanaaneh, *A Doctor in Galilee: The life and struggle of a Palestinian in Israel*, London: Pluto Press, 2008, p. xiii.
24. Susan Nathan, *The Other Side of Israel: My journey across the Jewish/Arab divide*, New York: Random House, 2005.
25. Amir S. Cheshin, Bill Hutman and Avi Melamed, *Separate and Unequal: The inside story of Israeli rule in East Jerusalem*, Cambridge, MA: Harvard University Press, 1999, p. 62; Meron Benvenisti, *Jerusalem: The torn city*, Jerusalem: Books on Demand, 1976, pp. 216–17; Anne Latendresse, *Jerusalem: Palestinian dynamics, resistance, and urban change*, Palestinian Academic Society for the Study of International Affairs, 1995, pp. 27–8; Meir Margalit, *Discrimination in the Heart of the Holy City*, International Peace and Cooperation Center, 2006, ipcc-jerusalem.org.
26. Latendresse, *Jerusalem*, p. 30.
27. Benvenisti, *Jerusalem*, p. 166.
28. Michael Dumper, 'Jerusalem's infrastructure: is annexation irreversible?' *Journal of Palestine Studies*, 22(3), 1993: pp. 78–95.
29. Ibrahim Dakkak, 'Vivre à Jerusalem', *Revue d'Études Palestiniennes*, 1983, pp. 87–122, cited in Latendresse, *Jerusalem*, p. 34.
30. Jihad Ahmad Dakkor, *Al-Mar'a Al-Fastenia Qabl Al-Nakba* [*The Palestinian Woman before the Nakba*], Beirut: New Press, 2009.
31. Nidal Mohammed Al-Hindi, *Adwa' 'Ala Nidhal Al-Mar'a Al-Falastinyya* [*Lights on the Struggle of the Palestinian Woman*], Amman: Dar Al-Karmel, 1995, p. 44.
32. Geoffrey Aronson, *Israel, Palestinians, and the Intifada: Creating facts on the West Bank*, Washington, DC: Institute for Palestine Studies, 1991 (from the Arabic, Beirut, p. 60).
33. Eileen Kuttab and Nida Abu Awwad, 'Developments in the Palestinian women's movement', in Yasser Akawi, Gabriel Angelone and Lisa Nessan (eds), *From Communal Strife to Global Struggle: Justice for the Palestinian people*, Jerusalem: Alternative Information Center Publication, 2004.
34. Al-Hindi, *Adwa' 'Ala Nidhal Al-Mar'a Al-Falastiniya*, p. 32.
35. Aronson, *Israel, Palestinians, and the Intifada*, p. 63.
36. Zahira Kamal, 'Institution building in the West Bank', in Suha Sabbagh, *Survey of the Literature of Palestinian Women*, Washington, DC: West Bank and Gaza Technical Support Project, 1994; Orayb Najjar and Kitty Warnock, *Portraits of Palestinian Women*, Salt Lake City, UT: Salt Lake City University Press, 1992; Indiana University Press, 1995.
37. Suha Sabbagh, *Palestinian Women of Gaza and the West Bank*, Bloomington, IN: Indiana University Press, 1998; Juliet M. Peteet, *Gender in Crisis: Women and the Palestinian resistance*, New York: Columbia University Press, 1991; Cheryl Rubenberg, *Palestinian Women: Patriarchy and resistance in the West Bank*, Boulder, CO: Lynn Rienner, 2001; Suha Sabbagh and Ghada Talhami, *Image and Reality: Palestinian women under occupation and in the diaspora*, Washington, DC: Institute of Arab Women's Studies, 1990; Joost Hiltermann, *Behind the Intifada: Labor and women's movement in the occupied territories*, Princeton, NJ: Princeton University Press, 1990; Jihad Ahmed Dakkor, *Al-Mar'a Al-Falastiniya Qabl Al-Nakba* [*The Arab Woman Before the Nakba*], Beirut, New Press Publishers, 2009.

38. *Jerusalem Post*, August 30, 1967, cited in Lesch, *Israel's Occupation*, p. 50; Thomas Simmerling, 'Imkaniyat Qiyam Haraka La 'Unfiya Fi Al-Dhiffa Al-Gharbiya' [The possibility of the initiation of a nonviolent movement in the West Bank], in Saad Eddin Ibrahim (ed.), *Al-Mukawema Al-Madaniya Fi Al-Nidhal Al-Siyasee [Civil Resistance in the Political Struggle]*, Amman: Muntada Al-Fikr Al-Arabi, 1988, p. 115.

39. Geoffrey Aronson, *Israel, Palestinians, and the Intifada: Creating facts on the West Bank*, Washington: Institute for Palestine Studies, 1991 (in Arabic, Beirut: IPS, 1999, p. 60).

40. *Journal of Palestine Studies*, 9, Autumn 1973, pp. 187–9.

41. Ghassan Kanafani, *Men in the Sun and Other Palestinian Stories*, London: Heinemann Educational, 1978.

42. Olga Kapeliouk, 'The Palestinian universities under occupation', *Arab Studies Quarterly*, 7, 1985, pp. 88–91; Emile F. Sahliyeh, *In Search of Leadership: West Bank politics since 1967*, Washington, DC: The Brookings Institution, 1988, pp. 133–5.

43. Salim Tamari, 'What the uprising means', in Zachary Lockman and Joel Beinin (eds), *Intifada: The Palestinian uprising against the Israeli occupation*, Boston, MA: South End Press, 1989, p. 131.

44. Yusif A. Sayigh, 'The Palestinian economy under occupation: dependency and pauperization', *The Journal of Palestine Studies*, 15(4), 1988, pp. 52–8; Said Jawad, *Al-Nohod Al-Watani Al-Falastini fi Al-Diffa wa Ghaza wa Al-Jalil 1974–1978 [National Advancement for Palestinians in the West Bank and Gaza and the Galilee 1974–1978]*, Beirut: Dar Ibn Khaldon, 1982, pp. 90–1.

45. Sayigh, 'The Palestinian economy under occupation'; Jawad, *Al-Nohod Al-Watani Al-Falastini*, p. 120.

46. Muhammad Abu-Nimer, *Allaunf wa Sun' Al-Salam Fi Al-Islam [Nonviolence and Peace Making in Islam]*, Amman: Al-Ahliya Linnashr, 2007, p. 186.

47. Jawad, *Al-Nohod Al-Watani*, pp. 158–65.

48. Seán MacBride, 'International commission to enquire into reported violations of international law by Israel during its invasion of the Lebanon 1983', in Robert Fisk, *Pity the Nation: The Abduction of Lebanon*, New York: Nation Books, 2002.

49. McDowall, *Palestine and Israel*, p. 103.

50. Aronson, *Israel, Palestinians, and the Intifada* (in Arabic, Beirut: IPS, 1999, p. 204).

51. Aronson, *Israel, Palestinians, and the Intifada*, p. 207.

52. Simmerling, 'Imkaniyat Qiyam Haraka La 'Unfiya Fi Al-Dhiffa Al-Gharbiya', p. 115.

53. Yaqoub Al-Atrash, *75 Aman Fi Qitar Al-'Umor [75 Years in the Train of Life]*, Al-Beit Sahour: Andalus Press, 2008, pp. 98–105.

54. Al-Atrash, *75 Aman Fi Qitar Al-'Umor*, pp. 114–22.

55. Mustapha Barghouti, 'Popular/mass movement in the community', *Journal of Palestine Studies*, 2(1), 1989 p 126; see also www.pmrs.ps. Accessed December 28, 2009.

56. Sari Nusseibeh (with Anthony David), *Once Upon a Country: A Palestinian life*, New York: Farrar, Straus & Giroux, 2007, pp. 189–96.

57. Gabi Baramki, 'Palestinian university education under occupation', *Palestine-Israel Journal*, 3(1), 1996.

58. Aronson, *Israel, Palestinians, and the Intifada*, p. 210.

59. As'ad Abd Al-Rahman and Nawwaf Al-Zaru, *Al-Intifada: Muqadimat, Waqa'e, Tafa'ulat, aw Afaq* [*The Uprising: Beginnings, happenings, interactions, and outlooks*], Beirut: Institute of Arab Research, 1989, p. 43.
60. David McDowall, *Palestine and Israel: The uprising and beyond*, London: IB Tauris, 1989, p. 101.
61. Nusseibeh, *Once upon a Country*, pp. 197–9.
62. Said K. Aburish, *Cry Palestine: Inside the West Bank*, Boulder, CO and Oxford: Westview Press, 1993.
63. Martha Diaz, 'Profiles of Israelis and Palestinians concerned for peace', in Elizabeth Warnock Fernea and Mary Evelyn Hocking (eds), *Israelis & Palestinians: The struggle for peace*, Austin, TX: University of Texas Press, 1992, p. 210.
64. Mary Elizabeth King, *A Quiet Revolution: The first Palestinian intifada and nonviolent resistance*, New York: Nation Books, 2007, pp. 78–9.
65. Anon., *Al-Intifada Mubadara Sha'biya: Dirasa Li-Adwar Al-Qiwa Al-Sha'biya* [*The Intifada is a Popular Initiative: A study on the role of civilian forces*]. Available at Bethlehem University Library, 1990, p. 413.
66. Madiha Rashid Al-Madfai, *Jordan, the United States, and the Middle East Peace Process, 1974–1991*, Cambridge: Cambridge University Press, 1993, p. 123.
67. Mohammed Khalid Al-Az'ar, *Al-Muqawama Al-Falastiniya Bayn Ghazw Lubnan wa Al-Intifada* [*Palestinian Resistance between the Invasion of Lebanon and Al-Intifada*], Beirut: Center for the Study of Arab Unity, 1990, p. 52.
68. 'Israel: complaints about treatment of detainees', *The Lancet*, October 29, 1988, p. 1012–13.
69. Hillel Schenker, 'Dialogue: Israelis and Palestinians in Jerusalem', *New Outlook*, 27, May 1984.
70. Simmerling, 'Imkaniyat Qiyam Haraka La 'Unfiya Fi Al-Dhiffa Al-Gharbiya', p. 115.
71. Shaul Ephraim Cohen, *The Politics of Planting: Israeli Palestinian Competition for Control of the Land in the Jerusalem Periphery*, Chicago: University of Chicago Press, 1993, pp. 133–48.
72. Mubarak E. Awad, 'Nonviolent resistance: a strategy for the occupied territories', *Journal of Palestine Studies*, 13(4), Summer 1984, pp. 22–36.
73. King, *A Quiet Revolution*, p. 140.
74. King, *A Quiet Revolution*, p. 137.
75. King, *A Quiet Revolution*, pp. 142–3.
76. King, *A Quiet Revolution*, pp. 146–7; Robert Hirschfield, 'Practicing nonviolence on the West Bank', *Christian Century*, October 8, 1986, p. 853.
77. Virginia Tilley, 'Israel authority breaks a promise: uproots new saplings', *Al-Fajr*, January 31, 1986.
78. Victor Shoenfeld and Jennifer Millstone (dirs), *Shattered Dreams*, British Cinema and ITV, 1986, cited in King, *A Quiet Revolution*, pp. 151–2.
79. Saida Hamad, 'Families demand reunion', *Al-Fajr*, June 21, 1987.
80. King, *A Quiet Revolution*, pp. 145, 156–7.
81. Andy Court, 'Landmark high court ruling: Awad deportation is legal', *Jerusalem Post*, June 6, 1988.
82. Robert Holmes, 'Nonviolence and the intifada', in Laurence F. Bove and Laura Duhan Kaplan (eds), *From the Eye of the Storm: Regional conflicts and the philosophy of peace*, New York: Rodopi, 1995, pp. 209–48.

83. King, *A Quiet Revolution*, pp. 160–1; see also Jonathan Kuttab and Mubarak Awad, 'Nonviolent resistance in Palestine: Pursuing alternative strategies', Information Brief 29, of the Jerusalem Fund.

84. Simmerling, Imkaniyat Qiyam Haraka La 'Unfiya Fi Al-Dhiffa Al-Gharbiya', p. 114.

85. Mohammed Khalid Al-Az'ar, *Al-Muqawama Al-Falastiniya Bayn Ghazw Lubnan wa Al-Intifada* [*Palestinian Resistance between the Invasion of Lebanon and Al-Intifada*], Beirut: Center for the Study of Arab Unity, 1990, pp. 55–6.

86. *Al Quds*, 6238, January 8, 1987, p. 3.

87. *Al Quds*, 6231, January 1, 1987, p. 4.

88. *Al Quds*, 6310, March 22, 1987, p. 4.

89. R. Scott Kennedy, 'The Druze of the Golan: a case of nonviolent resistance', *Journal of Palestine Studies*, 13(2), 1984, pp. 48–64.

90. *Al Quds*, 6314, March 31, 1987, p. 7.

CHAPTER 11

1. Edward Said, 'Intifada and independence', in Zachary Lockman and Joel Beinin (eds), *Intifada: The Palestinian uprising against Israeli occupation*, Washington, DC: Middle East Research and Information Project, 1989, p. 20.

2. Ghassan Andoni, 'A comparative study of Intifada 1987 and Intifada 2000', in Roane Carey (ed.), *The New Intifada: Resisting Israel's apartheid*, London and New York: Verso, 2001, p. 209; Helena Cobban, *The Palestinian Liberation Organization: People, power, and politics*, New York: Cambridge University Press, 1984, p. 257.

3. Report on the Commission of Inquiry into the Methods of Interrogation of the Special Security Service in Regard to Hostile Terrorist Activity; October 1987, para. 4.7.

4. Lisa Taraki, 'Mass mobilization in the West Bank', in Naseer Aruri (ed.), *Occupation: Israel over Palestine*, Association of Arab-American University Graduates, 1989; Souad Dajani, *The Intifada*, Amman: Center for Hebraic Studies, 1990, p. 124; Ralph E. Crow, Philip Grant and Saad Eddin Ibrahim, *Arab Nonviolent Political Struggle in the Middle East*, Boulder, CO: Lynne Rienner Publishers, 1990; Michael Hudson, *The Palestinians: New directions*. Washington, DC: Georgetown University, Center for Contemporary Arab Studies, 1990, p. 268; and references cited below.

5. Saad Ed-Din Ibrahim, *A'mal Mu'tamar Amman (November 15–18, 1986) 'Al-Muqawama Al-Madaniyya Fi Al-Nidhal Al-Siyasi'* [*Proceedings of the Amman Conference (November 15–18, 1986), 'Civil Resistance in the Political Struggle'*], Amman: Muntada Al-Fikr Al-Arabi, 1988.

6. Souad Dajani, 'Civilian resistance under the Israel occupation: The West Bank', Paper presented at the conference on nonviolent political struggle, November 15–17, 1986, Amman, Jordan; Abdel-Fattah Al-Jayyusi, *Falastin Al-Muhtala 1985–1987: Al-Sumood wa Al-Tahaddi* [*Occupied Palestine 1985–1987: Steadfastness and challenge*], Amman: Dar Al-Karmel, 1988, p. 13.

7. *Al-Quds*, 6502, October 4, 1987, p. 1.

8. *Al-Quds*, 6507, October 9, 1987, p. 1.

9. *Al-Quds*, 6509, October 11, 1987, p. 1.

10. *Al-Quds*, 6511, October 13, 1987, p. 1.
11. *Al-Quds*, 6513, October 15, 1987, p. 1.
12. *Al-Quds*, 6516, October 18, 1987, p. 1.
13. *Al Quds*, 6527, October 29, 1987, p. 1.
14. *Al-Quds*, 6528, October 30, 1987, p. 1.
15. *Al-Quds*, 6559, November 30, 1987, p. 1.
16. *Al-Quds*, 6561, December 2, 1987, p. 1.
17. *Al-Quds*, 6569, December 10, 1987, p. 1; Glenn Frankel, *Beyond the Promised Land: Jews and Arabs on a hard road to a New Israel*, New York: Touchstone Press, 1996, pp. 42–4.
18. Patrick White, *Children of Bethlehem: Witnessing the intifada*, Leominster: Gracewing Publishing, 1989, pp. 45–7.
19. Chris Wood, 'Where will the revolt end?', *Maclean's*, April 18, 1988, p. 23, in Mary Elizabeth King, *A Quiet Revolution: The first Palestinian intifada and nonviolent resistance*, New York: Nation Books, 2007, p. 7.
20. Al-Haq (Law in the Service of Man), *Punishing a Nation: Human rights violations during the Palestinian uprising, December 1987–December 1988*. Boston, MA: South End Press, 1990.
21. *Al-Quds*, 6575, December 17, 1987, p. 1.
22. *Al-Quds*, 6591, January 1, 1988, p. 1.
23. Maarive, December 22, 1987, cited in *Al-Quds*, 6582, December 23, 1987, p. 4.
24. *Al-Quds*, 6581, December 22, 1987, p. 1.
25. Jibril Mohammed and Wasif Nazzal, *Falastiniyo 48: Nidal Mustamir* [*Palestinians 48: Constant Struggle*], Jerusalem: Al-Zahra Center for Studies and Research, 1990, pp. 179–80.
26. Anon., *Al-Intifada Mubadara Sha'biya: Dirasa Li-Adwar Al-Qiwa Al-Sha'biya* [*The Intifada is a Popular Initiative: A study on the role of civilian forces*], available in Bethlehem University Library, 1990, pp. 430–1.
27. Abdel-Jabbar Adwan, *Al-Intifada 'Ala Tareeq Al-Istiqlal Al-Falastini: Anyab Al-Kharoof* [*The Uprising on the Road to Palestinian Independence: Canines of the Sheep*], London: np, 1988, p. 11; Rub'i Al-Madhoon, *Al-Intifada Al-Falastiniya: Al-Haykal Al-Tantheemi wa Asaleeb Al-'amal*, Akka: Palestine Cultural Institute, 1989.
28. Helena Cobban, 'The PLO and the intifada', in Robert Owen Freedman (ed.), *The Intifada: Its impact on Israel, the Arab world, and the superpowers*, Gainesville, FL: Florida International University Press, 1991, pp. 70–106; Sari Nusseibeh, 'A true people's revolution', *Middle East International*, December 15, 1989, p. 15; my interviews with Jad Isaac, Sari Nusseibeh and others conducted in 2009.
29. Shaul Mishal and Reuben Aharoni, *Speaking Stones: Communiqués from the intifada underground*, Syracuse, NY: Syracuse University Press, 1994, p. 340.
30. King, *A Quiet Revolution*, p. 214; my 2009 interviews with Hanan Ashrawi, Fuad Kokaly, Jad Isaac, Hazem Qumsiyeh and others.
31. King, *A Quiet Revolution*, p. 216.
32. King, *A Quiet Revolution*, p. 211.
33. Mohammed Khalid Al-Az'ar, *Al-Muqawama Al-Falastiniya Bayn Ghazw Lubnan wa Al-Intifada* [*Palestinian Resistance between the Invasion of Lebanon and Al-Intifada*], Beirut: Center for the Study of Arab Unity, 1990, p. 340.

34. White, *Children of Bethlehem*, p. 112.
35. Amal Jamal, *The Palestinian National Movement: Politics of Contention: 1967–2005*, Bloomington, IN: Indiana University Press, 2005, p. 75; Lonnie R. Sherrod, *Youth Activism: An international encyclopedia*, Vol. 2, Westport, CT: Greenwood Press, 2006, pp. 449–53.
36. King, *A Quiet Revolution*, pp. 116–19.
37. King, *A Quiet Revolution*, p. 118.
38. Eric Goldstein, 'Prison conditions in Israel and the occupied territories', *Human Rights Watch*, 1991.
39. Anthony Lewis, 'When silence comes', *New York Times*, September 4, 1988.
40. Baruch Kimmerling and Joel S. Migdal, *The Palestinian People: A history*, Cambridge, MA: Harvard University Press, 2003, p. 366.
41. *Al-Quds*, 6595, January 5, 1988, p. 1.
42. 'The Palestinians' fourteen demands', *Journal of Palestine Studies*, 17(3), Spring 1988, pp. 63–5.
43. Geoffrey Aronson, *Israel, Palestinians, and the Intifada: Creating facts on the West Bank*, Washington, DC: Institute for Palestine Studies, 1991(in Arabic, Beirut, 1999, p. 344).
44. Adwan, *Al-Intifada 'Ala Tareeq Al-Istiqlal Al-Falastini*, p. 97. The price of mules and donkeys went up (supply and demand) in the area of Bethlehem from my recollections.
45. Patrick White, *Children of Bethlehem: Witnessing the intifada*, Leominster: Gracewing Publishing, 1989, p. 89.
46. Yossi Melman and Dan Raviv, *Behind the Uprising: Israelis, Jordanians, and Palestinians*, New York: Greenwood Press, 1989. p. 238.
47. Frankel, *Beyond the Promised Land*, pp. 52–3.
48. Ghassan H. Andoni, 'Nonviolent tax resistance in Beit Sahour', Palestinian Center for Rapprochement between People, August 1993, p. 28; and my interviews with the key people in the tax revolt, including Fuad Kokaly, Elias Rishmawi, Ghassan Andoni, Jad Isaac and others.
49. White, *Children of Bethlehem*, p. 66.
50. The Palestinian Center for Rapprochement between People archives, 1989.
51. Rapprochement mass activities, August 1993, The Palestinian Center for Rapprochement between People.
52. Andoni, 'Nonviolent tax resistance in Beit Sahour'.
53. 'Israeli bailiffs enlisted to crush Palestinian tax revolt: refusal to pay rates turns "Christian triangle" into symbol of resistance', *Guardian*, October 20, 1989.
54. 'Envoys turned back on road to Beit Sahour', *The Globe and Mail*, October 7, 1989, p. A9; 'Israeli troops bar Western envoys', *Los Angeles Times*, October 6, 1989, p. 1.
55. The events of that day were confirmed by a two-hour interview with Yaqoub Al-Atrash, retired school principal, November 19, 2008, interviews with Jad Isaac and Elias Rishmawi, August 2009, and references such as the detailed account in Izzat Daraghma, *Al-Thawra Al-Bayda' Fi Al-Masdina Al-Mutamirrada Haql Alru'a* [*The White Revolution in the Rebellious City Shepherds Field*], 1990.
56. *Al-Sha'b* and *Al-Quds*, October 15, 1989.
57. 'U.S. vetoes UN resolution that Israel return property seized in tax revolt', *The [Montreal] Gazette*, November 8, 1989, p. A14.
58. Daraghma, *Al-Thawra Al-Bayda*.

NOTES 273

59. Elias Rishmawi, speech at fifth International Conference on War Tax Resistance and Peace Tax Campaigns – Hondaribia, Spain 1994, www.cpti.ws/conf/94/94pg/fri_aft.html. Accessed November 15, 2008.
60. White, *Children of Bethlehem*, pp. 64–6.
61. Martha Diase, 'Profiles of Israelis and Palestinians', in Elizabeth Warnock Fernea and Mary Evelyn Hocking (eds), *Israelis & Palestinians: The struggle for peace*, Austin, TX: University of Texas Press, 1992, pp. 210–11.
62. George Martin and James Manney, 'Tax strike for justice: Report from Beit Sahour: building autonomy', *Commonwealth*, 117(2), January 1990, p. 38.
63. Anne Grace, 'The tax resistance at Bayt Sahur', *Journal of Palestine Studies*, 19(2), Winter 1990, pp. 99–107.
64. Said K. Aburish, *Cry Palestine: Inside the West Bank*, Boulder, CO and Oxford: Westview Press, 1993, p. 100.
65. Said K. Aburish, 'A licence to visit Mr. Jesus', *The Forgotten Faithful: The Christians of the Holy Land*, London: Quartet Books, 1993, p. 31.
66. Sami Khalil Mar'l, *Arab Education in Israel*, New York: Syracuse University Press, 1978, p. 10.
67. World Universal Service, JMCC, 1989, 'Palestinians: education denied', in Sami Khalil Mar'l (ed.), *Arab Education in Israel*, New York: Syracuse University Press, 1978, p. 9.
68. Ian Black, 'Confusion spreads as West Bank leaders squabble over strike', *Guardian*, May 26, 1988, p. 9.
69. John B. Quigley, *Palestine and Israel: A challenge to justice*, Chapel Hill, NC: Duke University Press, 1990, p. 203.
70. Kenneth Kaplan, 'Intifada could go on indefinitely', *Jerusalem Post*, July 8, 1988, cited in Al-Madhoon, *Al-Intifada Al-Falastiniya*, p. 51.
71. Frankel, *Beyond the Promised Land*, p. 120.
72. Nada Abdel-Samad, *Ayyam Alhijara*, a book of transcripts of Sawt Alshaab radio interviews, including with 50 Palestinian grassroots leaders, Beirut, Lebanon; Dar Al-Faraby, 1989, p. 118.
73. Aburish, *Cry Palestine*, p. 125.
74. Dan Izenberg, 'Israel outlaws Arab committees', *The Commercial Appeal*, August 19, 1988.
75. *Jerusalem Post*, January 26, 1988.
76. Frankel, *Beyond the Promised Land*, p. 75.
77. 'Two years of the uprising in Palestinian and Israeli statistics', *Dirasat Falastiniya*, Winter 1990, pp. 173–7.
78. Brian K. Barber. 'Palestinian children and adolescents during and after the intifada', *Palestine-Israel Journal*, 4(1), 1997, pp. 23–33.
79. John T. Duelge, 'Seeing the light: unhealthy occupation', *The Washington Report on Middle East Affairs*, July 1988, p. 28.
80. King, *A Quiet Revolution*, p. 258.
81. As'ad Abd Al-Rahman and Nawwaf Al-Zaru, *Al-Intifada: Muqadimat, Waqa'e, Tafa'ulat, aw Afaq [The Uprising: Beginnings, happenings, interactions, and outlooks]*, Beirut: Institute of Arab Research, 1989, pp. 165–6.
82. Gila Svirsky, *Standing for Peace: A history of women in black in Israel*, 1996. Chapter 4 available at www.gilasvirsky.com/wib4.html.
83. *Faisal Husseini Foundation*, www.fhfpal.org/Faisal/fcul1_e.htm; King, *A Quiet Revolution*, pp. 165–75; Father Raed Awad Abusahlia, 'Faysal

el-Husseini: The Palestinian Gandhi', *Maaber*, 7, www.maaber.org/eighth_ issue/el_huseyni_en.htm.

84. Levi Morai, 'The intifada: the true cost', *Al Hamishmar*, quoted in Al-Madhoon, *Al-Intifada Al-Falastiniya*, pp. 83–4.

85. King, *A Quiet Revolution*, p. 268.

86. King, *A Quiet Revolution*, p. 269.

87. Salah Khalaf (Abu Iyad), 'Lowering the sword', *Foreign Policy*, 78, 1990, p. 104.

88. Hanan Ashrawi, *This Side of Peace*, New York: Touchstone, 1996, pp. 64–8.

89. Timothy Phelps, 'Betrayal in their hunger for peace', *Newsday*, June 3, 1990, p. 3.

90. Frankel, *Beyond the Promised Land*, p. 304.

CHAPTER 12

(All web links accessed January 22, 2010.)

1. Ghassan Andoni, 'A comparative study of Intifada 1987 and Intifada 2000', in Roane Carey (ed.), *The New Intifada: Resisting Israel's apartheid*, London and New York: Verso, 2001, pp. 209–18.

2. Edward Said, *The End of the Peace Process: Oslo and after*, New York: Pantheon Books, 2001; Hanan Ashrawi, *This Side of Peace: A personal story*, New York: Touchstone, 1996.

3. Azmi Bishara, 'Palestine in the new order', *Middle East Report*, 22(2), 1992, p. 4; Edward Said, *Peace and its Discontenders: Gaza-Jericho 1993–1995*, New York: Vintage Books, 1995; Cheryl Rubenberg, *The Palestinians: In search of a just peace*, Boulder, CO: Lynn Rienner Publishers, 2003.

4. Baruch Kimmerling and Joel S. Migdal, *The Palestinian People: A history*, Cambridge, MA: Harvard University Press, 2003, p. 391.

5. Tanya Reinhart, *The Road Map to Nowhere: Israel/Palestine since 2003*, New York: Verso, 2006, p. 147.

6. Alexander Bligh, 'The intifada and the new political role of the Israeli Arab leadership', *Middle East Studies* 34(1), 1999, pp. 134–66; Alexander Bligh, *The Israeli Palestinians: An Arab minority in the Jewish state*, London: Frank Cass, 2003.

7. Helena Cobban, *The Palestinian Liberation Organization: People, power, and politics*, Cambridge: Cambridge University Press, 1984.

8. Amal Kawar, *Daughters of Palestine: Leading women of the Palestinian national movement*, New York: SUNY Press, 1996.

9. Nigel Craig Parsons, *The Politics of the Palestinian Authority: From Oslo to al-Aqsa*, New York: Routledge, 2005, pp. 199–200; Said, *Peace and its Discontenders*.

10. Parsons, *Politics of the Palestinian Authority*, p. 185.

11. Ghada Hashem Talhami, *Palestinian Refugees: Pawns to political actors*, New York: Nova Science Publishers, 2001, pp. 211–12.

12. '2,000 Palestinian prisoners on hunger strike as Clinton visits', *The Independent*, December 7, 1998.

13. As'ad Ghanem and Mohammad Mustafa, *Al-Falatiniyon fi Israel: Siyasat Al-Aqalliya Al-Asliya Fi Al-Dawla Al-Ithniya* [*Palestinians in Israel: The politics of the indigenous minority in the ethnic state*], Ramallah: Madar, the Palestinian Forum for Israeli Studies, 2009, pp. 299–300.

14. Ghanem and Mustafa, *Al-Falatiniyon fi Israel*, p. 209.
15. Ghanem and Mustafa, *Al-Falatiniyon fi Israel*, pp. 217, 226.
16. Ghanem and Mustafa, *Al-Falatiniyon fi Israel*, pp. 176–7.
17. Ghanem and Mustafa, *Al-Falatiniyon fi Israel*, pp. 166–70.
18. Ahmed Qurei', *Al-Riwaya Al-Falastinya Al-Kamila Lil Mufawadhat min Oslo Ila Mufawadhat Camp David (Taba wa Stockholm) [The Palestinian Complete Narrative for Negotiations from Oslo to Camp David (Taba and Stockholm)]*, Beirut: Palestine Studies Institute, 2005.
19. Haroon Hashem Rashid, *Intifadhet Al-Aqsa: 'Am Min Al-Butula wa Al-Istishhad [Al-Aqsa Intifada: A year of heroism and martyrdom]*, Al-Dar Al-Misriya Al-Lubnaniya, 2002.
20. Donald Macintyre, 'Most Palestinians killed in Israeli raids were civilians, Amnesty says', *The Independent*, May 24, 2007, news.independent.co.uk/world/middle_east/article2578484.ece; see also Richard Falk, *Human Rights Situation in Palestine and Other Occupied Arab Territories*, Report of the Special Rapporteur on the situation of human rights in the Palestinian territories occupied since 1967, UN Human Rights Council, March 17, 2009. www.reliefweb.int/rw/RWFiles2009.nsf/FilesByRWDocUnidFilename/SNAA-7QF9WC-full_report.pdf/$File/full_report.pdf.
21. Parsons, *Politics of the Palestinian Authority*, p. 282.
22. *Yediot Aharonot*, Hebrew edition, November 17, 2000.
23. Human Rights Watch, 'Jenin', May 2, 2002, www.hrw.org/en/reports/2002/05/02/jenin-0.
24. Jeff Halper, *An Israeli in Palestine: Resisting dispossession, redeeming Israel*, London: Pluto Press, 2008, pp. 18–20.
25. Kimmerling and Migdal, *Palestinian People*, p. 209; Adalah's initial response to the Ministerial Committee's report regarding the implementation of the Or Commission conclusions, June 3, 2004. www.adalah.org/eng/pressreleases/pr.php?file=04_06_03–1.
26. Susan Atallah, 'The power to have an impact', in Toine van Teefelen (ed.), *Challenging the Wall: Towards a pedagogy of hope*, Bethlehem: Arab Educational Institute, 2007, pp. 97–104.
27. The Palestinian Center for Rapprochement between People documents.
28. Josie Sandercock et al. (eds), *Peace under Fire: Israel/Palestine and the international solidarity movement*, London and New York: Verso, 2004; PCR archives; interview with Ghassan Andoni, December 19, 2008.
29. ISM press release, www.theexperiment.org/?p=232.
30. International Solidarity Movement, www.palsolidarity.org.
31. GIPP, www.nonviolentpeaceforce.org.
32. James Brooks, 'The Israeli poison gas attacks: a preliminary investigation', June 27, 2004, www.vtjp.org/report/The_Israeli_Poison_Gas_Attacks_Project.htm.
33. The Palestinian Center for Rapprochement between People documents.
34. Nazım Ju'bah, 'East Jerusalem: 40 years of occupation', *Palestine Israel Journal of Politics, Economics, and Culture*, 14(1), 2007, pp. 16–17.
35. Joel Greenberg, 'Peace advocates in Arafat compound hope to deter Israeli troops', *New York Times*, April 3, 2002; Sandercock et al., *Peace under Fire*, pp. 60–1.
36. Doug Struck, 'For activists with Arafat, a whiff of relief: deal to end siege is hailed as success for their tactics', *Washington Post*, May 1, 2002; in Sandercock et al., *Peace under Fire*, pp. 62–4.

37. Dennis B. Warner, 'International peacemakers enter Bethlehem Church of the Nativity', in Sandercock et al., *Peace under Fire*, pp. 78–80.
38. Rae Levine, 'Defying curfew in Nablus', in Sandercock et al., *Peace under Fire*, p. 106.
39. See 'A timeline of Palestinian nonviolent resistance', Holy Land Trust, www.holylandtrust.org/index.php?option=com_content&task=view&id=122&Itemid=96.
40. Susan Barclay, 'Report, October 2, 2002', in Sandercock et al., *Peace under Fire*, pp. 112–15.
41. Gila Svirsky, 'The Israeli peace movement since the Al-Aqsa intifada', in Carey, *The New Intifada*, pp. 324–30.
42. Reinhart, *Road Map to Nowhere*, p. 177.
43. 'Salfit women resist the wall', www.iwps-pal.org/en/articles/article.php?id=227; Fatima Khaldi, 'Women against the wall', *Electronic Intifada*, July 16, 2004, electronicintifada.net/v2/article2923.shtml.
44. 'Repression allowed, resistance denied: Israel's suppression of the popular movement against the apartheid annexation wall', Palestinian Grassroots Anti-Apartheid Wall Campaign, July 9, 2009, www.stopthewall.org/downloads/pdf/repress.pdf.
45. Nicholas Blinco, 'Under fire in Bethlehem', *Guardian*, April 3, 2002; Jeremy Hardy, 'Four days in hell', *Guardian*, April 15, 2002.
46. Reinhart, *Road Map to Nowhere*, pp. 184–5.
47. See, for example, Tamara's letters of July 15, 2002: 'Births in Jenin' and 'Jenin fever', and Eric Levine's 'No foreseeable end to this tour of duty', July 9, 2002, in Sandercock et al., *Peace under Fire*, pp. 152–5 and pp. 156–7.
48. Munib Younan, *Witnessing for Peace: In Jerusalem and the world*, Minneapolis, MN: Fortress Press, 2003, pp. 88–9.
49. Mitch Potter, *Toronto Star*, March 6, 2004, cited in Reinhardt, *Road Map to Nowhere*, p. 200.
50. International Court of Justice, Legal Consequences of the Construction of a Wall in the Occupied Palestinian Territory, Advisory Opinion, July 9, 2004, www.icj-cij.org/docket/index.php?pr=71&code=mwp&p1=3&p2=4&p3=6&case=131&k=5a.
51. Applied Research Institution – Jerusalem, 'The International Court of Justice (ICJ) advisory opinion on the legal consequences of the construction of a wall in the occupied Palestinian territory: where we are 5 years later', July 8, 2009, www.poica.org/editor/case_studies/view.php?recordID=2017.
52. See, for example, stopthewall.org/worldwideactivism/650.shtml.
53. PENGON, 'The people of Izbat At-Tabib's call for support against occupation's attempts to expel them', July 14, 2004, stopthewall.org/latestnews/661.shtml.
54. 'Palestinian children's fence protest ends in clashes', *Ha'aretz*, September 13, 2004, www.haaretz.com/hasen/pages/ShArt.jhtml?itemNo=477405&contrassID=1&subContrassID=5&sbSubContrassID=0&listSrc=Y.
55. Sandercock et al., *Peace under Fire*, pp. 159–73.
56. Rachel's emails to her family were published by the *Guardian*, www.guardian.co.uk/world/2003/mar/18/usa.israel and on a memorial site www.rachelcorrie.org.
57. *Al-Ayyam*, March 16, 2006; www.rachelswords.org/2007/03/16/gaza-children-honor-rachel-corrie-on-fourth-anniversary-of-her-death.
58. Reinhart, *Road Map to Nowhere*, p. 179.

59. Lasse Schmidt, 'Locals and internationals remove crippling roadblock', message of March 2, 2003, in Sandercock, et al., *Peace under Fire*, pp. 140–1.
60. 'Continued nonviolent resistance to land confiscation is met with violence', *ISM* press release, December 31, 2003.
61. Ida Audeh, 'A village mobilized: lessons from Budrus', *Electronic Intifada*, June 13, 2007, electronicintifada.net/v2/article7005.shtml; PENGON, 'The people in Budrus continue their struggle against the wall', Stop The Wall Campaign, January 4, 2004, stopthewall.org/latestnews/249.shtml.
62. Virginia Tilley, 'A line in the sand: Azmi Bishara's hunger strike', *Counterpunch*, July 4, 2004, www.counterpunch.org/tilley07072004.html.
63. Development Studies Program, Poll 19, 'An opinion poll concerning living conditions, emigration, the Palestinian government, security conditions and reform', Birzeit University, October 5, 2004, home.birzeit.edu/cds/opinionpolls/poll19.
64. James Brooks, 'Dispersing demonstrations – or chemical warfare?', *Electronic Intifada*, July 12, 2004, electronicintifada.net/v2/article2900.shtml.
65. Amira Hass, 'Gandhi's grandson to kick off unarmed Palestinian campaign', *Ha'aretz*, August 13, 2004, www.haaretz.com/hasen/pages/ShArt.jhtml?itemNo=464085&contrassID=1&subContrassID=1&sbSubContrassID=0&listSrc=Y.
66. 'Palestine freedom walk – July 30–August 19, 2004', *The Scoop*, www.scoop.co.nz/stories/WO0408/S00095.htm.
67. See 'Freedom march against the wall: hundreds march against the wall', August 10, 2004, bellaciao.org/en/article.php3?id_article=2577.
68. 'Israeli occupation forces violently suppress peaceful protest over right to worship', *ISM*, palsolidarity.org/2006/05/1131.
69. David Dean Shulman, *Dark Hope: Working for peace in Israel and Palestine*, Chicago: University of Chicago Press, 2007, pp. 14–20.
70. Gideon Levy, 'Mean streets of Tel Rumeida: in the twilight zone', *Counterpunch*, September 12, 2005, www.counterpunch.org/levy09122005.html.
71. Mohammed Khatib, 'Help us stop Israel's wall peacefully', *The New York Times*, July 12, 2005, www.iht.com/articles/2005/07/11/opinion/edkhatib.php.
72. 'Bil'in: un-cage Palestine!' *ISM Report*, May 5, 2006, palsolidarity.org/2006/05/1083.
73. 'Israeli soldiers shoot two international peace activists in the head at Bil'in', *ISM Report*, May 12, 2006, palsolidarity.org/2006/05/1101.
74. 'Large-scale unity demonstration in Bil'in on Friday', *ISM Report*, May 30, 2006, palsolidarity.org/2006/05/1196.
75. 'Bil'in demonstration against the wall turns blue', *ISM Report*, August 18, 2006, palsolidarity.org/2006/08/1480.
76. 'Nonviolent resistance in Bil'in works', *ISM Report*, September 15, 2006, www.palsolidarity.org/main/2006/09/15/bilin-15-09.
77. 'Bil'in demonstrators attacked by experimental weapons', *ISM Report*, September 1, 2006, palsolidarity.org/2006/09/1510.
78. 'Nobel peace laureate Corrigan injured in anti-fence protest', *Ynet News*, April 20, 2007, www.ynetnews.com/articles/0,7340,L-3390314,00.html.
79. 'High Court: controversial settlement neighborhood to remain in place', *Ha'aretz*, November 29, 2007; Ethan Bronner, 'Bil'in journal: in village,

Palestinians see model for their cause', *New York Times*, August 27, 2009, www.nytimes.com/2009/08/28/world/middleeast/28bilin.html?eta1.

80. 'Students unite against checkpoints', *ISM Report*, June 3, 2006, www.palsolidarity.org/main/2006/06/03/students-unite-against-checkpoints.

81. 'Nonviolence on trial', *ISM Report*, September 9, 2006, www.palsolidarity.org/main/2006/09/09/nonviolence-on-trail.

82. 'Palestinian villagers to hold nonviolent protest against Israeli ghettoization and annexation', November 15, 2006, www.palsolidarity.org/main/2006/11/15/azun-atme.

83. Anne Paq, 'We will replant these trees again: resisting the ongoing *nakba*: the story of Artas', *Al Majdal*, 9(34), 2007.

84. 'Al Khader unites in mounting protests against ghettoization', *Stop the Wall*, June 16, 2006, stopthewall.org/latestnews/1196.shtml.

85. 'Palestinians in Al Khader village nonviolently resist the Israeli wall, despite violent response', *Palestine News Network*, August 25, 2006, english.pnn.ps/index.php?option=com_content&task=view&id=393&Itemid=49.

86. Joshua Mitnick, 'Nonviolent protest gains in West Bank: A Supreme Court decision in favor of one protesting village has inspired others', *Christian Science Monitor*, September 24, 2007, www.csmonitor.com/2007/0924/p06s02-wome.html. Translated into Arabic, www.commongroundnews.org/article.php?id=21800&lan=ar&sid=0&sp=0.

87. 'Protests against Gaza beach killing', *Al-Jazeera Net*, June 11, 2006, palsolidarity.org/2006/06/1248.

88. 'Palestinians to hold nonviolent demonstration at Qalandia checkpoint against Israeli war crimes in Gaza', *ISM Report*, November 18, 2006, www.palsolidarity.org/main/2006/11/18/qalandia-beit-h.

89. ISM press release, pp. 184–5; Levine, 'No foreseeable end to this tour of duty', pp. 156–7.

90. ISM press release, pp. 181–2; Levine, 'No foreseeable end to this tour of duty'.

91. Ghassan Andoni, October 27, 2002, circulated electronically.

92. 'Jeff Halper and Ghassan Andoni: Nobel Peace Prize nominees', AFSC press release, February 9, 2006, electronicintifada.net/v2/article4474.shtml.

93. *Al-Quds*, 6319, March 31, 1987, p. 3.

94. 'Israel: complaints about treatment of detainees', *The Lancet*, October 29, 1988, pp. 1012–13.

95. Catherine Cook, Adam Hanieh and Adah Kay, *Stolen Youth: The politics of Israel's detention of Palestinian children*, London: Pluto Press, 2004.

96. *Al Quds*, 6314, March 26, 1987, p. 4. A similar hunger strike was declared by 90 prisoners in the Ansar 2 jail in Gaza, *Al Quds*, 6305, March 17, 1987, p. 1.

97. Karim Marwa, *Al-Muqawama: Afkar Lil-Niqash wa Al-Tajrioba wa Al-Afaq* [*Resistance: Ideas for discussion, experience, and outlook*], Beirut: Al-Fadi Publishing House, 1985, p. 46.

98. 'Prisons Service heads to discuss hunger strike by Palestinians', *Ha'aretz*, August 13, 2004, www.haaretz.com/hasen/pages/ShArt.jhtml?itemNo=464103; 'Prisoners' hunger strike 15 August 15, 2004–September 2, 2004', www.palestinehistory.com/issues/prisoners/prisoners.htm.

99. 'Thousands demonstrate in Gaza supporting Palestinian prisoners', *Xinhua*, August 18, 2004, news.xinhuanet.com/english/2004–08/18/content_1815128.htm.

100. 'PA, Israeli Arabs plan show of solidarity with hunger strikers', *Ha'aretz*, August 17, 2004, www.haaretz.com/hasen/pages/ShArt.jhtml?itemNo=465 531&contrassID=1&subContrassID=5&sbSubContrassID=0&listSrc=Y.
101. 'Palestinian strike gains strength', *BBC News*, August 18, 2004, news.bbc. co.uk/1/hi/world/middle_east/3575946.stm.
102. 'Hunger strike', *Al-Ahram*, August 19–25, 2004, weekly.ahram.org. eg/2004/704/re2.htm.
103. www.dci-pal.org/english/Display.cfm?DocId=315&CategoryId=1.
104. english.wafa.ps/?action=detail&id=8994.
105. Jon Elmer, 'Prison toughens Palestinian women', *IPS News*, August 7, 2009, www.ipsnews.net/news.asp?idnews=47998.
106. 'New Israeli committee undermines achievements made by Palestinians through protest in Israeli jails', *Palestine News Network*, July 25, 2009, english.pnn.ps/index.php?option=com_content&task=view&id=6269.
107. Jon Elmer, 'Prison toughens Palestinian women', *Electronic Intifada*, August 11, 2009, electronicintifada.net/v2/article10702.shtml.
108. Yousef Alhelou, 'Palestinian mass resistance blocks Israeli air strike', *Electronic Intifada*, November 20, 2006, electronicintifada.net/v2/article6074.shtml; see also 'Protests force Israel to halt air strikes', *Washington Post*, November 19, 2006, www.washingtonpost.com/wp-dyn/content/article/2006/11/19/AR2006111900210.html.
109. See, for example, 'Nonviolent resistance: I sell grapes', *Palestine News Network*, October 12, 2006, english.pnn.ps/index.php?option=com_conte nt&task=view&id=769&Itemid=1.
110. 'March of grapes brutally attacked: 6 arrested, many injured', October 8, 2006, www.palsolidarity.org/main/2006/10/08/khadrgrape.
111. See video, www.palestineremembered.com/GeoPoints/Nakba_Refugees_ and_R_O_R_5366/Article_9586.html.
112. '60 years of *nakba*: 21,915 black balloons over Jerusalem', *ISM Report*, May 7, 2008, palsolidarity.org/2008/05/3095.
113. 'Israeli forces kill resident of Ni'lin and leave another in critical condition during demonstration of solidarity with Gaza', *ISM Report*, December 28, 2008, palsolidarity.org/2008/12/3714; 'Israeli forces shoot 2 cameramen with live ammunition in the West Bank village of Ni'lin', *ISM Report*, September 4, 2009, palsolidarity.org/2009/09/8278; Tristan Anderson was shot in a nonviolent demonstration: 'American citizen critically injured after being shot in the head by Israeli forces in Ni'lin', *ISM Report*, March 13, 2009, palsolidarity.org/2009/03/5324; see also justicefortristan.org.
114. 'Hundreds of West Bank Palestinians commemorate Holocaust', *Maan News*, January 28, 2009, www.maannews.net/en/index. php?opr=ShowDetails&ID=35355.
115. Jonathan Pollak, 'The ongoing repression of Palestinian protesters', *Huffington Post*, December 18, 2009, www.huffingtonpost.com/jonathan-pollak/the-ongoing-repression-of_b_397132.html.
116. 'Parish priest recounts tragedy of Gaza: testimony of Father Manuel Musallam', January 19, 2009, www.zenit.org/article-24842?l=english.
117. 'Ninety people arrested in East Jerusalem as Israeli police look to prevent protests of solidarity with Gaza through intimidation', *ISM Report*, December 31, 2008, palsolidarity.org/2008/12/3737.
118. See palsolidarity.org/tag/jerusalem; 'IR AMIM: evictions and settlement plans in Sheikh Jarrah', Jerusalem, Australians for Palestine background

paper, August 8, 2009, australiansforpalestine.com/ir-amim-evictions-and-settlement-plans-in-sheikh-jarrah-july09-report.
119. 'Palestinians pour into Egypt after Rafah border wall destroyed', *Maan News*, January 23, 2008, www.maannews.net/eng/ViewDetails.aspx?ID=20078.
120. www.freegaza.org.
121. Ramzi Kysia, 'On the right of resistance', *Al-Jazeera*, July 31, 2007, www.aljazeera.com/news/newsfull.php?newid=255575.
122. 'One Italian was injured', video, www.youtube.com/watch?v=87NrkNV_owM.
123. www.youtube.com/watch?v=mpqnMrLv1bQ.
124. www.gazafreedommarch.com.
125. vivapalestina.org.

CHAPTER 13

(All web links accessed January 22, 2010)
1. Filmmaker and artist Udi Aloni, Ynet, January 5, 2010, www.ynetnews.com/articles/0,7340,L-3829694,00.html.
2. Baruch Kimmerling, *Politicide: Ariel Sharon's war against the Palestinians*, London: Verso, 2003.
3. Ilan Pappé, *The Ethnic Cleansing of Palestine*, London: Oneworld Publications. 2006.
4. Oren Yiftachel, *Ethnocracy: Land and identity politics in Israel/Palestine*, Philadelphia, PN: University of Pennsylvania Press, 2006.
5. Uri Davis, *Apartheid Israel: Possibilities for the struggle within*, London: Zed Books, 2003; Neve Gordon, 'Boycott Israel: An Israeli comes to the painful conclusion that it's the only way to save his country', *Los Angeles Times*, August 20, 2009, articles.latimes.com/2009/aug/20/opinion/oe-gordon20; Naomi Klein, 'Israel: boycott, divest, sanction', *The Nation*, January 7, 2009, www.thenation.com/doc/20090126/klein; also B'Tselem used the term apartheid in their report *Land Grab: Israel's settlement policy in the West Bank*, Jerusalem, May 2002.
6. Amira Hass, 'Words instead of actions', *Ha'aretz*, May 22, 2007, www.haaretz.com/hasen/spages/861119.html.
7. Nehemia Stessler, *Ha'aretz*, May 12, 1989.
8. Hossein Askari, *Economic Sanctions: Examining their philosophy and efficacy*, New York: Praeger, 2003, p. 59.
9. 'Towards a global movement: A framework for today's anti-apartheid activism', Grassroots Palestinian Anti-Apartheid Wall Campaign, June 2007, p. 34, bdsmovement.net/files/bds percent20report percent20small.pdf.
10. Geoffrey Aronson, *Israel, Palestinians, and the Intifada: Creating facts on the West Bank*, Washington, DC: Institute for Palestine Studies, 1991 (in Arabic, IPS, Beirut, 1999).
11. Azmi Bishara, 'The uprising's impact on Israel', in Zachary Lockman and Joel Beinin (eds), *Intifada: The Palestinian uprising against Israeli occupation*, Washington, DC: Middle East Research and Information Project, 1989, pp. 225–6; Howard Rosen, 'Economic consequences of the intifada on Israel and the administered territories', in Robert Owen Freedman (ed.), *The Intifada: Its impact on Israel, the Arab world, and the superpowers*, Miami, FL: Florida International University Press, 1991, p. 384; Avi Shlaim,

The Iron Wall: Israel and the Arab world, New York: Penguin Books, 2000, p. 455.

12. Paid advertisement, *Ha'aretz*, September 26 and October 4, 1997, israelipalestinianpeace.org/issues/81toi.htm#Consumers.

13. gush-shalom.org.toibillboard.info/boycott_eng.htm.

14. Najat Hirbawi, 'Chronology of events, April 1, 1998–October 1, 1998', *Palestine-Israel Journal*, 5(3 & 4) (1998).

15. www.matzpun.com/supporters.html.

16. The follow-up conference in Geneva was structured to avoid reaffirming the Durban decisions, but in essence let them stand. See Nora Barrows-Friedman, 'UN protects Israel from racism charges', *Electronic Intifada*, April 17, 2009, electronicintifada.net/v2/article10470.shtml.

17. To subscribe to the list and view archives, email the author or simply send a message to academicsforjustice-subscribe@yahoogroups.com.

18. Steven Rose and Hilary Rose, 'The choice is to do nothing or try to bring about change: why we launched the boycott of Israeli institutions', *Guardian*, July 15, 2002; Andy Becket and Ewin MacAskill, 'British academic boycott of Israel gathers pace', *Guardian*, December 12, 2002; 'More pressure for Mid-East peace', *Guardian*, April 6, 2002.

19. To subscribe, see BoycottIsraeliGoods-subscribe@yahoogroups.com.

20. Polly Curtis, 'Academic boycott of Israel gathers momentum', *Guardian*, March 24, 2004, phrconline.org/articles.php?ArtID=808.

21. www.pacbi.org/etemplate.php?id=868.

22. right2edu.birzeit.edu/news/article178; PACBI has since deleted item 4 listed here in a revision of January 28, 2006 because it 'has been misunderstood as a position condoning a boycott of individuals or supporting "blacklisting" or "political tests", both of which are entirely incompatible with PACBI's position', www.pacbi.org/etemplate.php?id=1051.

23. www.pngo.net/default.asp?i=190.

24. August 2002 press release from Badil and signing organizations, www.badil.org/en/press-releases/55-press-releases-2002/330-press268–02, in Arabic www.badil.org/ar/press-releases/117-press-releases-2002/1328-a-51–2002.

25. Tanya Reinhardt, 'Academic boycott: in support of Paris VI', *Electronic Intifada*, February 4, 2003, www.monabaker.com/pMachine/more.php?id=96_0_1_12_M5; Rachel Giora, 'Milestones in the history of the Israeli BDS movement: a brief chronology', January 18, 2010, www.bricup.org.uk/documents/history/IsraeliBDS.pdf; Ilan Pappé, 'To boldly go', *Guardian*, April 20, 2005, www.guardian.co.uk/education/2005/apr/20/highereducation.uk3; www.haaretz.com/hasen/pages/ShArt.jhtml?itemNo=569361; Naomi Klein, 'Israel: boycott, divest, sanction', *The Nation*, January 26, 2009.

26. boycottisrael.info.

27. Desmond Tutu and Ian Urbina, 'Against Israeli apartheid', *The Nation*, June 27, 2002, www.thenation.com/doc/20020715/tutu; Ronnie Kasrils, *Guardian*, May 25, 2005; Hazem Jamjoum, 'Not an analogy: Israel and the crime of apartheid', *Electronic Intifada*, April 3, 2009, electronicintifada.net/v2/article10440.shtml; Anthony Lowstedt, *Apartheid: Ancient, past, and present: Systematic and gross human rights violations in Graeco-Roman Egypt, South Africa, and Israel/Palestine*, Vienna: Gesellschaft für Phänomenologie und kritische Anthropologie, 2007, 3rd edition.

28. Information from several sources primarily: www.stopthewall.org/downloads/pdf/listBDS.pdf; 'Towards a global movement: a framework for today's

anti-apartheid activism', *Grassroots Palestinian Anti-Apartheid Wall Campaign*, June 2007, p. 22, bdsmovement.net/files/bds percent20report percent20small.pdf; www.pacbi.org/pdfs/PACBI percent20Newsletter1-BDS-2009-Highlights-3-Jan-2010.pdf; and 'Boycott, divestment, and sanctions: a survey of diverse approaches to ethical economic engagement adopted by groups and individuals worldwide', August 2007, a review by the Palestine-Israel Action Group (PIAG), a subcommittee of the Peace and Social Concerns Committee of Ann Arbor Friends Meeting.

29. See 'Is Intel supporting an apartheid regime?', *Media Monitors*, June 26, 2001, www.mediamonitors.net/mazin7.html; 'Intel chip plant located on disputed Israeli land: Intel could face political, legal problems with chip plant in Israel', *San Francisco Chronicle*, July 8, 2002, www.sfgate.com/cgi-bin/article.cgi?file=/chronicle/archive/2002/07/08/BU162036.DTL&type=business.

30. Victoria Griffith, 'Insults fly in hallowed halls as students oppose Israeli links: a national campaign by student activists aimed at academic institutions comes to a head tomorrow', *Financial Times*, October 11, 2002.

31. See www.divestmentconference.com.

32. Joel Beinin, 'Building a different Middle East', *The Nation*, January 15, 2010, www.thenation.com/doc/20100201/beinin.

33. See Chris McGreal, 'Anglican group calls for Israel sanctions: campaigners inspired by boycott of apartheid South Africa', *Guardian*, September 24, 2004.

34. David Wildman, 'Why divestment and why now?', *The Link*, 39(3), August-September 2006 (published by Americans for Middle East Understanding), www.palestinecampaign.org/Index7b.asp?m_id=1&l1_id=4&l2_id=25&Content_ID=376.

35. John Mahoney, 'Ending Israel's occupation', *The Link*, 42(4), September-October 2009.

36. kairospalestine.ps.

37. Mahoney, 'Ending Israel's occupation'.

38. 'Boycott of Ahava Dead Sea products makes an impact', *Electronic Intifada*, December 2, 2009, electronicintifada.net/v2/article10925.shtml.

39. Asa Winstanley, 'Boycott movement takes hold in British unions', *Electronic Intifada*, August 14, 2009, electronicintifada.net/v2/article10711.shtml; see also www.tuc.org.uk/congress/tuc-16887-f4.cfm#tuc-16887-4.

40. Paul Abowd, 'Growing labor support for Palestine faces stiff opposition in the US', January 22, 2010, www.labornotes.org/2010/01/growing-labor-support-palestine-faces-stiff-opposition-us.

41. Anne Herzberg, 'Lawfare against Israel', *Wall Street Journal*, Europe, November 5, 2008.

42. Tahel Frosh, 'Filmmakers protest uncritical view of Tel Aviv at Toronto film festival', *Ha'aretz*, August 28, 2009, haaretz.com/hasen/spages/1110750.html; see also www.bdsmovement.net/?q=node/535.

43. www.norwatch.no/200909031329/english/fund/elbit-excluded-by-norwegian-goverment-pension-fund.html.

44. See apartheidweek.org.

45. For more on this subject, see Mohsen Awad, Mamduh Salem and Ahmed Obeid, *Muqawamat Al-Ta'bi': Thalathoon 'Aman min Ml-Muwajeha [Resisting Normalization: Thirty years of confrontation]*, Beirut: Center for the Study of Arab Unity, 2007.

46. Art Young, 'Pro-Israel lobby alarmed by growth of boycott, divestment movement', *Zmagazine*, www.zmag.org/znet/viewArticle/21807.
47. qumsiyeh.org/boycottisraell see also www.qumsiyeh.org/theworldeconomicsforumcontroversy.
48. 'Towards a global movement: a framework for today's anti-apartheid activism', Grassroots Palestinian Anti-Apartheid Wall Campaign, June 2007, p. 12, bdsmovement.net/files/bds percent20report percent20small.pdf.

CHAPTER 14

(All web links accessed January 22, 2010)
1. Edward Said, 'Arabs have nothing to apologize for: of dignity and solidarity', *The Dawn*, August 7, 2003, www.dawn.com/2003/08/07/op.htm.
2. Jean-Marie Muller, *Stratégie de l'action nonviolente*, transl. Mary Touq, *Harakat Huqook Alnas*, Beirut: Aljmiza, 1999, p. 12.
3. Ghassan Kanafani, *The 1936–39 Revolt in Palestine*, New York: Committee for a Democratic Palestine, 1972/London: Tricontinental Society, 1980.
4. Said K. Aburish, *Cry Palestine: Inside the West Bank*, Boulder, CO and Oxford: Westview Press, 1993, p. 185.
5. Ahron Bregman, *Israel's Wars: A history since 1947*, London: Routledge, 2002, pp. 217–18.
6. See Juliane Hammer, *Palestinians Born in Exile: Diaspora and the search for a homeland*, Austin, TX: University of Texas Press, 2005.
7. Alain Epp Weaver and Sonia K. Weaver, *Salt & Sign: Mennonite Central Committee in Palestine, 1949–1999*, Akron, PA: Mennonite Central Committee, 1999; Nancy Gallagher, *Quakers in the Israeli-Palestinian Conflict: The dilemmas of NGO humanitarian activism*, Cairo: The American University in Cairo Press, 2007.
8. Staughton Lynd, Sam Bahour and Alice Lynd, *Homeland: Oral history of Palestine and Palestinians*, New York: Olive Branch Press, 1994; Hammer, *Palestinians Born in Exile*.
9. See Mohammed Daraghmeh, 'Al-Fan wa Al-La'unf: Haya Tas'ud Min Kharab' [Art and nonviolence: life emerges from destruction], *Al-Hayah*, July 27, 2003; Samih K. Farsoun, *Culture and Customs of the Palestinians*, Westport, CT: Greenwood Press, 2004.
10. Ted Swedenburg, *Memories of Revolt: The 1936 rebellion and the Palestinian national past*, Minneapolis, MN and London: University of Minnesota Press, 1995, pp. 208–9.
11. See, for example, Muhammad Abdullah Atwat, *Al-Ittihjahat Al-Wataniya Fi Al-Shi'r Al-Falastini Al-Mu'aser* [*Nationalist Directions in Modern Palestinian Poetry*], Beirut: Dar Al-Afaq Al-Jadida, 1998; Salma Khadra Jayyusi, *Modern Arabic Poetry: An anthology*, New York: Columbia University Press, 1987; Izzat Ghazzawi, *Modern Palestinian Poetry in Translation*, Ramallah: The Palestinian Writers' Union, 1997.
12. Barbara Harlow, *Resistance Literature*, New York: Methuen, 1987; Salma Khadra Jayyusi, *Anthology of Modern Palestinian Literature*, New York: Columbia University Press, 1992; *Palestine and Palestinians: Guidebook*, Beit Sahour: Alternative Tourism Group, 2005; see also Mazin Qumsiyeh, 'Review of Palestine guidebooks', *The Middle East Journal*, 59(4), Autumn

2005, pp. 699–700; Mariam Shahin, *Palestine: A guide*, photography by George Azar, Northampton, MA: Interlink Publishing, 2005.

13. Joy Ellison, 'Nonviolent resistance in the south Hebron Hills'. *Electronic Intifada*, June 22, 2009, palsolidarity.org/2009/06/7293.

14. One such book is Maxine Kaufman-Lacusta (ed.), *Refusing to Be Enemies*, Reading, MA: Ithaca Press, 2010. It quotes at length from selected activists giving personal impressions. Analysis with a look forward based on personal experiences are provided by Jeff Halper, Ghassan Andoni, Jonathan Kuttab and Starhawk. I believe those reflections complement the historical analysis given in this book.

15. See stopthewall.org.

16. Khalil Nakhleh and Elia Zureik (eds), *The Sociology of the Palestinians*, London: Croom Helm, 1980; Majdi Malki, *Towards a Sociology of Civil Resistance: Palestinian Society the Second Intifada*, Ramallah: Muwatin, 2004.

17. See also Salim Tamari, 'Factionalism and class formation in recent Palestinian history', in Roger Owen (ed.), *Studies in the Economic and Social History of Palestine in the Nineteenth and Twentieth Centuries*, Carbondale and Edwardsville, IL: The Southern Illinois University Press, 1982, pp. 208–10.

18. Are Knudson and Basem Ezbidi, 'Hamas and Palestinian statehood', in Jamil Hilal (ed.), *Where Now for Palestine?* London and New York: Zed Books, 2007. Many Palestinians called for unity, see 'Prominent Palestinian figures appeal for national unity', *Maan News*, January 28, 2009, www.maannews. net/en/index.php?opr=ShowDetails&ID=35356; and Mubadaret Nida' Al-Wihda Al-Falastinia, *Quds Net*, January 28, 2009, www.qudsnet.com/arabic/news.php?maa=View&id=92833.

19. Nassar Ibrahim, 'A global fight? Whatever happened to the Palestinian Left?', in Yasser Akawi, Gabriel Angelone and Lisa Nessan (eds), *From Communal Strife to Global Struggle, Selected Presentations and Articles from 'A Middle East without Wars and Oppression is Possible: An international seminar on the Palestinian struggle and globalization'*, Jerusalem: Alternative Information Center, 2004; Jamil Hilal, *Al-Yasar Al-Falastini: Where to?*, Ramallah: Rosa Luxemburg Institution, 2009; Nayef Hawatma, *Al-Yasar Al-Arabi: Ru'ya Al-Nuhoodh Al-Kabeer* [*The Arab Left: Vision for a great promotion*], Ramallah: Al-Masar Center, 2009.

20. Walid Salem, 'Palestinian contemporary political performance: a bitter harvest', *Palestine-Israel Journal*, 15(1 & 2), 2008, www.pij.org/details. php?id=1166.

21. Ali Jarbawi, 'Palestinian elites in the occupied territories: stability and change during the intifada', in Jamal R. Nassar and Roger Heacock (eds), *Intifada: Palestine at the Crossroads*, New York: Praeger, 1990.

22. Neve Gordon, *Israel's Occupation*, Berkeley and Los Angeles: University of California Press, 2008, pp. 54–5.

23. Jamal Juma, *Duroos Al-Muqawama: Bil'in Namuthajan* [*Lessons of Resistance: Bil'in as a model*], Ramallah: Bada'el: Palestinian Center for Communication, Research and Studies, 2007, p. 177.

24. Shir Hever, *The Economy of the Occupation. Part 6: The question of sanctions and a boycott against Israel*, Jerusalem: The Alternative Information Center, 2006, www.alternativenews.org:80/publications/econoccupation.html.

25. 'Towards a global movement: a framework for today's anti-apartheid activism', Grassroots Palestinian Anti-Apartheid Wall Campaign, June 2007, p. 154, bdsmovement.net/files/bds percent20report percent20small.pdf.

26. Aimee Ginsburg, 'Gandhis in olive country', *Outlook*, March 17, 2008, pp. 22–8.

27. Mousa Abu Maria and Bekah Wolf, 'The lost lesson of the civil rights movement', *Mondoweiss*, January 19, 2010, mondoweiss. net/2010/01/the-lost-lesson-of-the-civil-rights-movement.html?utm_ source=feedburner&utm_medium=email&utm_campaign=Feed percent3A+feedburner percent2FWDBc+ percent28Mondoweiss percent29&utm_content=Yahoo percent21+Mail.

28. Ben Hubbard, 'Israel arrests seen as effort to crush dissent', Associated Press, in *San Francisco Chronicle*, January 20, 2010, www.sfgate.com/cgi-bin/article. cgi?f=/c/a/2010/01/20/MN2P1BKASC.DTL.

29. Mary Elizabeth King, *A Quiet Revolution: The first Palestinian intifada and nonviolent resistance*, New York: Nation Books, 2007, p. 188.

30. For example, a survey taken in 2002, www.sfcg.org/Documents/SFCGpoll. pdf.

31. Ali Badwan, *Safhat Min Tareekh Al-Kifah Al-Falastini: Contemporary political and commando formulations*, Damascus: Dar Al-Nash'a, 2008.

32. Souad R. Dajani, *Eyes without Country: Searching for a Palestinian strategy of liberation*, Philadelphia, PN: Temple University Press, 1995, p. 125.

33. See Chapters 10–13; also Maxine Kaufman-Lacusta, 'The potential for joint struggle: an examination of present and future participation by Israelis in Palestinian nonviolent resistance to the occupation', *Palestine-Israel Journal*, 15–16(3), 2008.

34. The Seville Statement on Violence was adopted by UNESCO at the 25th session of the UN General Assembly on November 16, 1986. Drafted by eminent scientists, it lays out facts and debunks mythologies, including myths that the human species which invented war cannot eliminate war, www.unesco.org/ shs/human_rights/hrfv.htm. This document lays the foundations for a world without war and injustice. The few hundred examples of Palestinian popular resistance (among many more) inspire and mobilize us to work towards such a world.

35. See also Jonathan Kuttab and Mubarak Awad, *Nonviolent Resistance in Palestine: Pursuing alternative strategies*, Washington, DC: Jerusalem Fund, Information Brief 90, March 29, 2002.

36. Mubarak E. Awad, 'Nonviolent resistance: a strategy for the occupied territories', *Journal of Palestine Studies*, 13(40), Summer 1984, p. 35.

37. George Antonius, *The Arab Awakening: The story of the Arab national movement*, London: International Book Center, 1938/1985, p. 409.

38. Desmond Tutu, 'Realizing God's dream for the Holy Land', *Boston Globe*, October 26, 2007, www.boston.com/news/globe/editorial_opinion/oped/ articles/2007/10/26/realizing_gods_dream_for_the_holy_land.

Index